FINAL

MOTORING
IN AMERICA
THE EARLY YEARS

Edited by Frank Oppel

Castle

CONTENTS

THE A B C OF THE AUTOMOBILE

BY CARRIE FOOTE WEEKS

A at the start was an Automobile.
It answers to motor car, just as you feel.

B is the Brake that gives you control.
If the Bubble Breaks you, you're in a Big hole.

C stands for Cylinder, and your Chauffeur,
Who takes many Chances at sixty-five per.

D is the up-to-Date Dealer serene,
And the Dance that he leads you about the machine.

E is Experience for young and old;
We pay dearly for it, and often are sold.

F is the Factory where you will find
It is Foolish to Fuss, if they're four months behind.

G is Garage, and the God, Gasoline,
Who Guides all his subjects, yet never is seen.

H is H. P., your Heaven and Hell.
What pace are you making? The police can tell.

I is Ignition, Insurance and Ice.
These three you must have on an expert's advice.

J might stand now for a new Jeremiah,
Who foretells disasters by flame, speed, or tire.

K stands for all Kinds of cars on the mart.
To pick the Kingpin would take cleverest art.

L stands for License, and Lawyer, and Lie—
You're in touch with them all when an auto you buy.

M is the Model you choose with great care,
The Map that you follow for roads that aren't there.

N is the Number attached to your car,
And the Name (not a rose) that proclaims it a star.

O is the Oil used for food and for drink,
By this Ogre, half human, the real missing link.

P stands for "Plain Clothes Men" always about.
Police you can spot. For the others, watch out.

Q is the Quest for a feminine hat,
That will stay on the head, and have style, and all that.

R stands for Rules which must be obeyed,
And the Races we win,—in our dreams, I'm afraid.

S means the Songs that we sing late at night,
As the Search light weaves Shadows, now ghostly, now bright.

T is the Tonneau for five, three or two.
If a Tack finds your Tire, it's all up with you.

U is the Unruly, and also Uncertain.
On the manners of autos and maids drop the curtain.

V is Vibration—in sunshine, in gale,
It's with us like goggles, or long auto Veil.

W stands for Weight, and all kinds of Wheels.
(Not Wheels in your head, or Weight in your heels)

X is Xcess. Pray keep well in hand,
For motor-car maniacs people the land.

Y stands for Yearnings to go far and fast.
O bright Yellow Moon! we'll reach you at last.

Z is the Zany so puffed up with Zeal,
That he thinks he has mastered the automobile.

The Detroit Races
Races at Lake Erie
Rhode Island
Automobile Club Races
A Serviceable
Steam Tourist
(1901)

The Detroit Races

THE first meeting of the Detroit Automobile Racing Association was held at Grosse Pointe Track on October 10, and proved to be a decided success, there being at least 8,000 spectators present. To give some idea of the interest taken it may be mentioned that many of the business houses closed for the afternoon and the court adjourned for the day. "Justice suspended" in order to give the attorneys an opportunity to see the flyers.

At half past ten in the morning a parade formed and "did" the town. It was led by a squad of mounted police followed by two steam vehicles propelling a tally-ho coach in which was a band playing all the popular music of the day. There were 68 vehicles of various types in line and taking into consideration the inclemency of the weather it was a very creditable showing.

This was the first automobile meeting at which a book was made on the events, but from the bookmaker's point of view it was not a success. In the second event he took in $48 and paid out $44—and on all the events he quit a loser of $109. So it is easily seen that those present were not there to speculate, but simply to witness the progress of a new sport. It is pleasant to note that this was the case. Previous to the first event the weather cleared and brought out a beautiful afternoon for the sport. The track which is a mile long with easy turns was in excellent condition, being very free from dust and an ideal one for automobile racing.

The 5-mile race for steam machines was won by W. T. White, White Sewing Machine Company in 10 minutes $1\frac{3}{5}$ seconds, by about ½ mile. H. H. Lytle, Toledo, was second.

The 1-mile race for electric machines was simply a procession until the home stretch was reached, when W. C. Baker, on a Baker, came away and finished first in the slow time of 4 minutes 9 seconds. It was very evident that Baker could have done very much better had he been pushed.

The 1-mile open to all machines weighing less than 1,500 pounds was won by H. H. Lytle in 1 minute $51\frac{4}{5}$ seconds, others finishing in the following order: William Rand, Toledo ; Stephen Hartnell, Duryea ; Henry Ford, Ford Auto Car Company.

The 10-mile race for machines weighing less than 1,000 pounds was won by W. T. White in 19 minutes $5\frac{4}{5}$ seconds. He also made the fastest mile in 1 minute $49\frac{3}{5}$ seconds. J. P. Chapin, Oldsmobile, was second.

The 10-mile race for machines weighing less than 2,000 pounds was won by Edgar Apperson, Haynes-Apperson, in 17 minutes $47\frac{1}{5}$ seconds. W. T. White second. The latter made the fastest single mile in 1 minute $45\frac{1}{5}$ seconds.

The championship race of 10 miles for all machines produced a surprise. There were eight entries for this event, but only two started. William N. Murray, of Pittsburg, at the last moment discovered trouble in one of his cylinders and could not start, so instead of the

Henry Ford on 26 H. P. Gasoline Racer of His Own Make

race that had been expected it was simply a contest between Alexander Winton in his 40 horse-power racer and Henry Ford on a gasoline machine he built himself and which he says has 26 horse-power. For the first 7 miles, Winton led the way, gradually increasing his lead until he was about ½ a mile ahead, but on turning into the eighth mile it was noticed by the decreased speed he was in trouble. Ford passed him and won the race by about 1 mile in 13 minutes $23\frac{4}{5}$ seconds. Winton claimed that some of his brasses, which were new, got hot. It was the general belief that Ford had a very fast machine, but owing to his inexperience as a chauffeur was afraid to take the turns at full speed and went very wide, thus losing much time.   Otherwise, he would unquestionably have made a much better showing in the earlier part of the race.

The obstacle race proved a great source of amusement and brought out four contestants.   W. C. Baker was a little too good for the others, and carried off the prize.

Mr. Winton then gave a 3-mile exhibition race against time, making the entire distance in 3 minutes 42⅔ seconds. The second mile he went in 1 minute 12⅔ seconds, being 1⅜ seconds better than his previous record.

Mr. Ford would not give a description of his car for, as he said, he had patents pending, but the illustration gives a good view of it exteriorly.   J. R. P.

Races at Fort Erie

THIS event consisted of a three-days' meet September 26, 27 and 28, at Fort Erie, Ontario, Canada.   It was arranged by the Buffalo Automobile Club and owing to there being no track in the local city the club was forced to go across the border.   It had been planned to have this meet follow the week of automobile events scheduled to be held at the Pan-American Exposition between September 16 and 25.   It was thought that many automobilists who would then be at Buffalo on account of the finishing of the endurance test and the automobile week would stay a few days longer and lend aid in making the Fort Erie races a great success.   The promoters of the latter event were unfortunate, for the abandonment of the automobile week on account of President McKinley's death caused the great majority of automobile followers to leave for home and other parts.   The officials of the Buffalo Automobile Club, however, went ahead, making the best of a bad situation and brought about some good racing.

The attractions of the meet were Henri Fournier and Alexander Winton on their 60 H. P. Mors and 40 H. P. Winton machines respectively.   Both of these famous drivers gave a good exhibition of speed for a track.   On September 26, Mr. Fournier made new track records for each mile from 4 to 25 miles, he not altering on that day

the 1, 2 and 3 mile records made this year by Albert C. Bostwick at
Elkwood Park, Long Branch, N. J., July 5.   The 25 mile times were
as follows:

	Time for Miles.	Total Time.		Time for Miles.	Total Time.
1	1 27	1 27	14	1 15 2-5	18 05 1-5
2	1 18	2 45	15	1 16 1-5	19 21 2-5
3	1 15 4-5	4 00 4-5	16	1 15	20 36 2-5
4	1 15 2-5	5 16 1-5	17	1 16	21 52 2-5
5	1 16 1-5	6 32 2-5	18	1 16	23 08 2-5
6	1 17 2-5	7 49 4-5	19	1 15 3-5	24 24
7	1 17 2-5	9 07 1-5	20	1 14	25 38
8	1 17 1-5	10 24 2-5	21	1 16 1-5	26 54 1-5
9	1 17 4-5	11 42 1-5	22	1 15 4-5	28 10
10	1 17 4-5	13 00	23	1 16 3-5	29 26 3-5
11	1 17 4-5	14 17 4-5	24	1 16 2-5	30 43
12	1 16	15 33 4-5	25	1 15 2-5	31 58 2-5
13	1 16	16 49 4-5			

Alexander Winton's 40 H. P. Racer With Tonneau On

The tires showed great wear on account of the sliding of the
machine in rounding the turns; they were so badly used up that on
Friday Mr. Fournier's exhibition was for two miles only; the first
mile was covered in 1.13 1-5, the second in 1.13 2-5 both of these
figures constituting the fastest track records, they supplanting those
made by Mr. Bostwick last July.   On this trial Mr. Fournier also cap-
tured the quarter, half and three-quarter mile records, doing 20,

18 1-5, 17 4-5 and 17 1-5 seconds respectively. The previous ones were held by Mr. Bostwick and were as follows: quarter mile 17 3-4 seconds, half mile 37 seconds, three-quarter mile 56 seconds. Fournier made at his trial 17 1-5, 35 and 53 seconds respectively but he beat two of these on a trial at the Empire City track October 10.

On Thursday, September 26, Alexander Winton gave an exhibition ride of 10 miles with his 40 H. P. Winton racer; he was assisted by W. N. Murray; his best time for the 10 miles was 13 minutes 39 seconds. On Friday Mr. Winton gave another exhibition of 2 miles which he covered in 2 minutes 33 seconds, the miles being 1.15 3-4 and 1.17 1-4 respectively.

Empire City Track Records

ON Thursday, October 3, on this fine track which is near Yonkers, N. Y., Albert C. Bostwick established some automobile track records, and on the following Thursday, October 10, on the same track, Henri Fournier made world's figures for from 1 to 6 miles. On the first date Mr. Bostwick was the only performer,

First Turn of Empire City Track

but on the second occasion both of these celebrated drivers tried for speed figures. On October 3, Mr. Bostwick sent his 40 H. P. Winton 25 miles around the track in 32 minutes 20 4-5 seconds, his times being as follows :

	Time for Miles.	Total Time.			Time for Miles.	Total Time.
I	I 20	I 20	14		I 18 3-5	17 57 1-5
2	I 16 3-5	2 36 3-5	15		I 17 3-5	19 14 4-5
3	I 16 1-5	3 52 4-5	16		I 17 4-5	20 32 3-5
4	I 16	5 08 4-5	17		I 17 4-5	21 50 2-5
5	I 15 4-5	6 24 3-5	18		I 18 3-5	23 09
6	I 15 1-5	7 39 4-5	19		I 19	24 28
7	I 16 2-5	8 56 1-5	20		I 19 1-5	25 47 1-5
8	I 16 1-5	10 12 2-5	21		I 18 2-5	27 05 3-5
9	I 15 4-5	11 28 1-5	22		I 18 2-5	28 24
10	I 17 1-5	12 45 2-5	23		I 18 2-5	29 42 2-5
11	I 17 2-5	14 02 4-5	24		I 19 3-5	31 02
12	I 18 1-5	15 21	25		I 18 4-5	32 20 4-5
13	I 17 4-5	16 38 3-5				

Back Stretch of Empire City Track

It will be noticed that Mr. Bostwick's figures for from 1 to 18 miles are better than Henri Fournier's Fort Erie records. Mr. Bostwick's car held the turns well, the hind wheels skidding only about 6 inches at these parts. His front wheels were about 2 feet from the pole.

On the following Thursday, October 10, Mr. Bostwick tried making more records on the same track, and succeeded in doing the following for 4 miles: 1.13 2-5, 2.27 4-5, 3.44, 5 4-5, which figures are considerably under these he made at those distances at Elkwood Park last July. He stopped at 4½ miles for the engine grew hot from working so rapidly on account of the low sprocket being on. Mr. Bostwick had anticipated wind which accounts for the absence of the high-speed sprocket. The accompanying illustrations show his car and parts of the track.   He did not skid on this occasion any more than was the case the previous week.

Henri Fournier then made a trial in his 60 H. P. Mors with Wm. K. Vanderbilt, Jr., sitting on the floor.   The speed shown was marvellous, the accompanying table analyzing the performances speaking strongly and briefly.   The quarter mile was made in 17 1-5 seconds, half mile 34 seconds, three-quarter mile 50 3-5 seconds, all of which are now the best records.   The fastest mile, it will be seen, was made in 1 minute 6 4-5 seconds :

Miles.				Separate Miles. Min. Sec.	Total Time. Min. Sec.
1	.	.	.	1.07 3-5	1.07 3-5
2	.	.	.	1.08 1-5	2.15 4-5
3	.	.	.	1.06 4-5	3.22 3-5
4	.	.	..	1.07 4-5	4.30 2-5
5	.	.	..	1.08	5.38 2-5
6	.	.	..	1.08 3-5	6.47

Wheel Marks of Machines of Messrs. Bostwick and Fournier

The illustration showing the small ridges the wheels of the vehicle made gives a good idea of how steadily the driver held his machine to the pole while going at this great speed.   His hind wheels skidded about 1 foot, they being about 4 feet from the pole, while his front wheels were 3 feet away while taking the curves.   It was a most inspiring sight to see the most celebrated chauffeur in the world going around at that pace with his celebrated guest, also famous as a chauffeur.

There had been no announcement made of these trials except one of a previous week, when Mr. Bostwick said he would try later the following Thursday, but in spite of this vagueness a large crowd assembled and they had the double entertainment of seeing Messrs. Bostwick and Fournier. Many of the onlookers are well known in automobile circles. Bradford B. McGregor with A. W. S. Cochrane and several ladies drove into the grounds on Mr. Bostwick's racing car. Messrs. McGregor and Cochrane are both owners of Winton machines, the former having quite a fast one of 12 H. P., which figured conspicuously in the Endurance Test. Frank Eveland, Richard Esterbrook, Wm. Ross Proctor, Percy Owen and Mortimer Worthley were present, having come up in various machines, mostly Wintons. Mr. Vanderbilt, with J. Dunbar Wright as his guest, reached the grounds in a DeDion-Bouton New York type motorette. After the trials the tonneau was put back on Mr. Bostwick's car and with eight people aboard it was started back to Mamaroneck, the owner's country home, where it arrived safely and in good time with its great load.

Rhode Island Automobile Club Races

THE Rhode Island Automobile Club held its annual race meet at Narragansett Park, Providence, R. I., Thursday, October 17. What would have been the most successful meet of motor vehicles ever held in this country was spoiled by a short but heavy shower that transformed the clay track into a course of slippery mud and necessitated the postponement of the major portion of the programme until the next day. The attendance was tremendous, there being over 10,000 people present. Governor William Gregory, of Rhode Island, and his staff were in the front row of the grand stand.

Two races had been run off when clouds appeared and Albert C. Bostwick (Winton) began what was to have been a 15-mile record ride in a drizzle. At 10 miles he retired because of the spark failure in one of the cylinders of his machine, his time for the distance being 14 minutes 10¾ seconds against his own record of 12 minutes 45 2-5 seconds. His only fast mile had been the ninth, which was covered in 1 minute 15¾ seconds. Mr. Bostwick was followed by Henri Fournier (Mors) but the rain fell more heavily and at 3 miles the

French chauffeur was forced to withdraw because of the slippery condition of the track. The heavy machine skidded dangerously at the curves but notwithstanding this disadvantage he traveled each of the first 2 miles in 1 minute and 9 seconds and the third mile in 1 minute 9¾ seconds, giving a total of 3 minutes 27¾ seconds for the 3 miles.

Mr. Fournier tried again the next day when the track was dry and hard and did a good performance as will be seen from the subjoined summary. The high wind militated against making faster time than he did on the Empire City Track.

Albert C. Bostwick in His 40 H. P. Winton. Car Stripped for Racing.
Fournier at Left

Most of the races were postponed until the following day. Following is a summary of both days' contests:

Electric vehicles, five miles.—Won by H. H. Rice's Waverly; Albert I. Russell's Waverly, second; C. I. Campbell's Columbia, third. Time, 14m. 51s. Won by forty yards, with third a quarter of a mile back.

Steam vehicles, five miles.—Won by George C. Cannon's Special; H. G. Martin's Locomobile, second. Time, 9m. 40 3-5s. Won by seven-eighths of a mile; other three starters, John Shepard, Jr.,

Locomobile; Arthur Lee's Toledo; E. Blakeley, Locomobile; finished one and a half miles back.

Gasoline 12 H. P. and under; five miles—First heat won by Percy

Gov. William Gregory, of R. I. (in center), and His Staff
Viewing Races of R. I. A. C.

Owen, 12 H. P. (Winton), W. P. Norton, 9 H. P. (Gasmobile), second; Howard Burdick, 9 H. P. (Packard), third. Time, 9m. 3 1-4s. Won by 1 3-8 miles, with Mr. Burdick 2 miles behind. F. Walsh's 9 H. P. (Gasmobile) started, but picked up a nail in tire and withdrew. First two qualified for final heat.

Samuel Brock in 9 H. P. Gasmobile

Second heat won by Albert T. Otto, 9 H. P. (Gasmobile); Rudolph Meyer, 9 H. P. (Gasmobile), second; C. Prescott Knight, 12 H. P. (Packard), third.   Time, 9m. 8 3-4s.   Won by 100 yards, with third a fourth of a mile back.   John Shepard, Jr., also started, but withdrew.   First two qualified for final.

Final heat won by Percy Owen; Rudolph Meyers, second; W. P. Norton, third.   Time, 8m. 51s.   Won by one-fourth of a mile, with third three-quarters of a mile back.

Final for winners in all classes; distance ten miles:—Won by

Percy Owen in 12 H. P. Winton

Kenneth A. Skinner on a tricycle 4 1-2 H. P. (DeDion); Percy Owen, 12 H. P. (Winton), second.   Time, 13m. 37 1-2s.   G. C. Cannon's special steam carriage started and held second place for six miles.

Record trial by Henri Fournier in a 60 H. P. (Mors)—Time for five miles, 5m. 44s.; six miles, 6m. 57s.; seven miles, 8m. 8 1-2s.; eight miles, 9m. 22 1-2s.; nine miles, 10m. 43 1-2s.   Time for the last three miles are records for a circular course.   The fastest mile was the first in 1m. 7 1-2s.

Special class; for gasoline carriages under 6 H. P.; five miles.—Won by Kenneth A. Skinner, 4 1-2 H. P. (De Dion) motorette; T.

Shaw Safe, 4 1-2 H. P. (De Dion) motorette second; Mr. Ralph Lewis, 4 1-2 H. P. (De Dion) motorette third.   Time, 12m, 58 1-2s.   Won by 5-8 mile, with third 7-8 mile in rear.

Motor tricycles, five miles.—Won by Kenneth A. Skinner, on a 4 1-2 H. P. tricycle (De Dion); Peter J. Berlo, on a tricycle (De Dion) second; C. S. Henshaw, on a tricycle (Aster), third.   Time, 6m. 54 1-2s.   Won by 7-8 mile, with Mr. Henshaw one mile behind.

A Serviceable Steam Tourist

AN enterprising member of the Harvard Automobile Club sends us the accompanying illustration descriptive of an automobile which he had constructed recently after his own designs. The machine is a touring steam carriage, similar in some ways to the

George C. Cannon's Steam Touring Carriage, Embodying His Own Ideas

"Locomobile" touring wagon, only of even heavier build.   It is equipped with a Mason engine, specially constructed for heavy work, and having a ¾ inch feed pump.   All the feed-water piping is ¼ inch and that, as well as all the piping of the carriage, is securely fastened to the body by small iron braces, thus rendering it very stable and durable.

The boiler is 16 inches x 15½ inches with 360 tubes, and supplies ample steam for the engine. In addition to the usual equipment this wagon carries a steam air-pump, feed-water pump, injector and a complete tool outfit, with extra parts, etc., under the floor. The gasoline tank is situated forward and holds 11 gallons, while the water capacity is 35 gallons. This carriage has been run over 800 miles without mishap, and has proved itself a true "touring wagon."

WAYBACK JONES—"Great Scott! What's that?"
SUBURB–UNITE—"Don't be frightened, that's only Van Bostnier taking a practice spin in his auto 'Green Imp'!"

Eagle Rock
Hill Climbing Contest
(1901)

Eagle Rock Hill Climbing Contest

THE Automobile Club of New Jersey, headquarters of which are located in Newark, celebrated its first birthday by holding a clever event, it being the successful carrying out of the hill climbing contest, election day, at Eagle Rock, Orange. Eagle Rock has become famous through the numerous bicycle climbing contests

W. J. Stewart in His Winning Locomobile

held there in the past, and it will become more so in the future, undoubtedly, as an automobile place of climbing test, it being admirably adapted for such a purpose. The grade starts comparatively easy, but each of the four successive turns brings new difficulties and near the top or crucial point as shown by the picture, the slope is about 18 per cent. The winner of the steam class went so rapidly around this corner that his hind wheels slewed. The total distance is one mile and an eighth, according to the surveyor. Like the majority of New Jersey roads it is in excellent condition, and is not of the Nelson Hill variety.

Secretary W. J. Stewart, of the club, had worked hard to call attention to the affair and he was ably seconded by the cycling and

Charles E. Duryea and W. J. Morgan in Former's Winning Gasoline Vehicle

automobile veteran President Kirk Brown, who just a year ago made up his mind that there should be an automobile club in New Jersey. The official call for the laudable purpose was responded to by just three people, but, "as tall oaks from little acorns grow," the devoted little band of three has, as Samuel Weller would say, swelled "wisibly" to almost fifty in one year.

Secretary Stewart, with much astuteness, had prepared for the climb so far as making some preliminary canters up the grade and used a gradometer and knew just where and on what rise to put on steam, and he succeeded in making the marvelous time of 2 minutes and 43 seconds with his Locomobile, the distance being about one mile and an eighth. Mr. Stewart's company is the agent for the winning machine in the State and he was congratulated by many people on his win, which is said to be a record for that style of work.

Of course, Charles Duryea was there with his three-wheeler and right well did the little tricycle phaeton do its work, as it defeated two

Thomas McCorts in His Winton

big competitors quite easily, and the cup for the gasoline class will go to Reading, Berks County, Pa., which place seems to be destined to become quite a manufacturing center in an automobile way, just as it was in bicycle making a few years ago.

About twenty automobilists journeyed to Eagle Rock election day. Ten steamers had a trial for the prizes, but only three gasoline machines tried the task. Harlan W. Whipple, the popular Orange automobilist and general sportsman, was there, with also Winthrop

E. Scarritt, equally popular, who can never be found without his friend Mr. Whipple, as they have been fellow sympathizers in the joys and trials of early automobilism. President Kirk Brown, of the New Jersey Automobile Club, acted as starter, and right well did he perform that function. With watch and pistol in hand, he marshalled the starters to a broad white tape at the foot of the hill. After the word "Get Ready," he gave the competitors a minute before the pistol crack, and the rush up the hill commenced. The time made by the winner was something marvelous, and it is doubtful if W. J. Stewart's 2.43 will be beaten at an early date.

The sporting blood of B. L. Wright, who had a Grout carriage,

The Crucial Point of Eagle Rock Hill

showed itself when, with his companion, he immediately challenged Mr. Stewart to another trial, but as it was getting late and the latter had some work to do in connection with the banquet, the test of strength was postponed until a later date. The Grout carriage went up in 2.57, and the cause of Mr. Wright's not doing better was his over-anxiety at the bottom when he let her out at nearly top speed, and had to wait for steam near the top.

Out of the three gasoline machines, Charles E. Duryea, with his wonderful little three-wheeler, which went through the New York to Buffalo trial successfully, did the best work, although Mr. Duryea said that his machine was not in A No. 1 condition just before the start. The pictures given herewith were secured for the Newark, N. J., *Evening News*, and that paper supplied the AUTOMOBILE MAGAZINE with copies. Following are the summaries :

Name.	Type.	Time Started.	Time Finished.	Time Elapsed.
W. R. Royce . . .	Loco	2.44	2.50.25	6.25
B. L. Wright . . .	Grout	2.47	2.49.57	2.57
J. Leibhardt	Loco	2.50	2.58.55	8.55
W. H. Stebbins . .	Toledo	2.53	2.57.19-2-5	4.19-2-5
A. Schmarzenbach .	Reading	2.59	3.04.53-2-5	5.53-2-5
O. L. Simpson . . .	Loco	3.02	3.06.55-2-5	4.55-2-5
H. W. Whipple . .	Packard	3.21	3.29.37-3-5	8.37-3-5
C. E. Duryea . . .	Duryea	3.05	3.08.54-1-5	3.54-1-5
J. M. Schmidt . .	DeDion	3.24	3.29.45	5.45
Wm. Weller . . .	Loco	3.08	3.16.36-2-5	8.36-2-5
Thos. McCorts . .	Winton	3.14	3.21.53-1-5	7.53-1-5
W. J. Stewart . . .	Loco	2.56	2.58.43	2.43

The winners were: Steam—W. J. Stewart, first ; B. L. Wright, second. Gasoline—C. E. Duryea, first ; J. M. Schmidt, second.

The banquet in the evening, which was the first given by the now well-known club, passed off very successfully, and took place at L. Achtel Stetters', where a fine menu was discussed by about thirty members and their friends. A string band performed during the evening, and among the speakers were Kirk Brown, Harlan W. Whipple, Winthrop E. Scarritt, Dr. Power, John A. Hill, President of the American Machinist Press, Mr. Coburn and Secretary W. J. Stewart. Mr. Whipple, in his well-known humorous vein, spoke of his early trials as an automobilist and his initiation into the mysteries of automobiling. He said he could almost confidently lay claim to a knowledge of the difference between a steam and a gasoline vehicle.

Mr. Scarritt, who sat opposite Mr. Whipple, gave an account of his valiant battles with a steam carriage he bought in Massachusetts, and stated that he had the temerity to personally conduct it from Massachusetts to New Jersey. It balked when he was half a mile from the factory, and the boiler blew up at Providence, but by careful nursing he got it on the Plank Road on the Newark Meadows, and there he lay on his back, alternately gazing at the stars and the mechanism of his machine. These things did not interest him quite as much as the army of mosquitoes that attacked him from all sides and with a voracity of the highest order. He declared that they punctured his water gauge. He lived to reach home and to later unload his purchase on his dear friend Mr. Whipple. Mr. Scarritt then told of his first imported French machine, which he took uptown and placed in a repair shop for overhauling. He stated that he went down into the pit and gazed up at the machinery and saw the two-thousand-odd parts in its make-up ; he vowed he would unload his latest purchase, if some kind friend came along, in a hurry. Mr. Whipple turned up thirty minutes later, and within an hour Mr. Scarritt had Mr. Whipple's check.

Mr. Hill made an amusing speach in which he told several funny stories.

The new officers elected before the banquet commenced were as

Automobile Club of New Jersey Dinner

follows : Winthrop E. Scarritt, president ; W. J. Stewart, vice-president and secretary ; Harlan W. Whipple, treasurer ; governors, William Power, Kirk Brown, John A. Hill, John Blevney and R. G. Du Bois.

Among those at the banquet were the following : Kirk Brown, W. J. Stewart, Richard T. Newton, Harlan W. Whipple, Linden S. Weaton, John W. Schmidt, John A. Hill, Winthrop E. Scarritt, Angus Sinclair, Dr. Constantine, William Power, Dr. H. M. Power, Richard Coughan, Jacob Dawson, L. B. Frisbie, Richard Striet, O. L. Simpson, Lysander Wright, William R. Royce and W. J. Morgan.

One of a Famous Quartet

THE accompanying picture represents one of the certificates given by the Automobile Club of America to all vehicles which finished the run within controls between New York and Rochester. There were three grades of certificates, first, second and third class, given to those who averaged from 12 to 15,

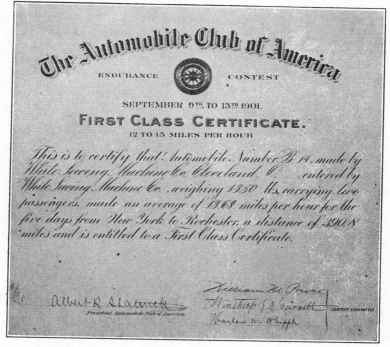

White Sewing Machine Co.'s First Class Certificate

10 to 12, and 8 to 10 miles per hour respectively. This particular certificate is a reproduction from one awarded to the White Sewing Machine Company. It will be remembered that four White vehicles were entered, all of which did a performance entitling each to a certificate like this one, all the diplomas awarded this company being "first class." The merit of the total performance can readily be appreciated.

The Manufacturer's Banquet
(1901)

The Manufacturers' Banquet

ON Thursday, November 7, the National Association of Automobile Manufacturers held its annual meeting and banquet. The first took place in the reception room of Madison Square Garden, the latter at the Hoffman House. About one hundred sat down to the dinner, the speakers' table having twelve. Samuel T. Davis, Jr., presided, and on his right were the following in the

Alexander Fischer in 35 H. P. Gasmobile
Most Imposing Looking Vehicle in the Show

order they are mentioned : General Nelson A. Miles, T. Cummerford Martin, editor of *Electrical World and Engineer ;* Winthrop E. Scarritt, of E. R. Chapman & Co., stock brokers ; J. Dunbar Wright, ex vice-president of the Automobile Club of America ; W. W. Niles, attorney for the Manufacturers' Association. On Mr. Davis' left, in the order mentioned, were : Albert R. Shattuck, president Automobile Club of America ; Amzi L. Barber, father-in-law of Mr. Davis and practical owner of the Locomobile Company ; Arthur J. Eddy, ex-president Chicago Automobile Club ; Louis R. Adams,

President Long Island Automobile Club ; Angus Sinclair, president of the Angus Sinclair Publishing Company and the Automobile Press.

Mr. Davis in his opening address spoke briefly and in his usual business-like way concerning the progress the association had made in advancing trade interests during the past year. He introduced Mr. Martin as the toastmaster. Those who are familiar with this gentleman's ability in gracefully introducing speakers knew that Mr. Martin would render just the service he did. He had prepared some verses styled after the much advertised placards of "Spotless Town"

Victor Sorchan in Albert T. Otto's 9 H. P. Gasmobile

in the lines of which appeared the characteristics of each speaker. The first to speak was Mr. Shattuck, who responded on behalf of the Automobile Club of America and who delivered ideas concerning the general subject of automobile embracing trade and legislation, that were thoroughly appreciated. Mr. Barber responded to Early Automobiling, and on account of his very influential position in the community at large his pointed, forceful and at times amusing remarks were listened to with unusual interest. It could readily be seen that although Mr. Barber seldom appears publicly in the subject of automobiling, he is thoroughly informed on it.

General Miles spoke on Good Roads and, although not exhausting the subject by any means, devoted the time he had allotted himself to generalizing on this important question in a way that would have made it difficult for one following him to say much on the same subject. Mr. Eddy spoke in the famous, brilliant way that always characterizes his public addresses. His subject was Automobile Touring. His remarks seemed all the more amusing because his predecessors in speaking had been allotted serious subjects and they had in the main handled them seriously. No one who has not heard Mr. Eddy on an occasion like this, can appreciate his ability. Mr.

W. A. Hatcher and A. L. McMurtry in Packard Model F

Scarritt, in speaking on Automobiling, gave a combined serious and amusing treatise which was warmly welcomed. Members of the various clubs he belongs to feel that whenever Mr. Scarritt rises to say anything, it will pay them to listen attentively. Mr. Niles was to have spoken on Legislation, but was suddenly taken ill.

Among those present were the following: A. Ward Leonard, president of the Ward-Leonard Electric Company, Bronxville, N. Y.; John Brisben Walker, editor of the *Cosmopolitan* and practical owner of the Mobile Company, Tarrytown, N. Y.; Emil Grossman, of the

Motor Review ; William Hazleton; E. B. Gallaher, of the Searchmont Motor Company, Philadelphia, Pa.; A. S. Winslow, of the Ohio Automobile Company ; George L. Weiss, of the Ohio Automobile Company ; George B. Adams and A. L. McMurtry, of Adams & McMurtry, agents for the Packard machine, Fifth Avenue, New York; Percy Owen, manager for New York Department of the Winton Motor Carriage Company ; Andrew L. Riker, vice-president Electric Vehicle Company ; Fred H. Colvin, manager of the AUTOMOBILE

James C. Church in 5 H. P. DeDion N. Y. Type Motorette with Victoria Body

MAGAZINE ; W. D. Gash, general sales manager of the Searchmont Motor Company ; Cornelius J. Field, vice-president and general manager of the De Dion-Bouton Motorette Company, Brooklyn, N. Y.; John T. Robinson, of the Robinson Motor Vehicle Company, Hyde Park, Mass.; A. H. Overman, of the Overman Automobile Company ; Samuel Brock, of the Automobile Company of America ; Homer W. Hedge, manager New York Department of Pettengill & Co.; S. M. Butler, secretary of the Automobile Club of America ; W.

P. Stevens, editor of the *Motor Review ;* E. E. Schwarzkopf, editor *Automobile Topics ;* Harry Fosdick, Mobile agent for Boston ; C. Harcourt Gunnett of the *Automobile Review.*

S. B. Starratt, of the John Simmons Co., dealers in automobile specialties ; M. C. Krarup, associate editor *Automobile Topics ;* W. S. Rogers, of the Steamobile Company, Keene, N. H. ; George J.

DeDion-Bouton 5 H. P. Coupé-Rockaway

Rockwood, Worcester, Mass.; Charles Cooke, Thornycroft Steam Wagon Company ; Charles Clifton, George N. Pierce Co., Buffalo, N. Y.; G. N. Bierce, of the Dayton Motor Vehicle Company, Dayton, Ohio ; Peter Forg, drop forgings, of Somerville, Mass.; James Artman, *Cycle and Automobile Trade Journal ;* L. H. Kittredge, of the Peerless Manufacturing Company ; John L. French, St. Louis

Motor Carriage Company ; Lucius T. Gibbs, Vehicle Equipment Company, Brooklyn N. Y.; D. E. Rianhard, secretary Overman Automobile Company ; C. A. Musselman, *Cycle and Automobile Trade Journal ;* W. C. Baker, Baker Motor Vehicle Company ; Charles E. Miller, dealer in automobile sundries, New York ; E. P. Ingersoll, editor *Horseless Age ;* William Van Wagoner, manager and engineer Century Motor Vehicle Company, Syracuse, N. Y.; E. P. Wells, President Steamobile Company, Keene, N. H.; J. A. Kingman,

C. J. Field in 5 H. P. Brooklyn Type DeDion

manager of advertising department Locomobile Company ; Charles H. Tucker, Chicago representative Locomobile Company ; George N. Barnes, vice-president Stearns Steam Carriage Company, Syracuse, N. Y.; Randolph Walker, of the Mobile Company ; James S. Holmes, secretary and general manager Remington Automobile and Motor Company ; E. L. Powers, editor *The Automobile ;* E. D. Knappen, secretary N. A. A. M.

An Early American Built Horseless Carriage (1901)

An Early American Built Horseless Carriage

THE AUTOMOBILE MAGAZINE exhibited at Madison Square Garden one of the earliest gasoline vehicles built in this country. Its constructors were Charles H. Nadig & Brother, of Allentown, Pa. It was supposed to have 2 H. P. Its large wheels, as shown in the illustration, are typical of nearly all early inceptions of automobiles. The subjoined account of some experiences furnish-

AUTOMOBILE MAGAZINE Exhibit—An 1893 Gasoline Machine
Built by Nadig Brothers

ed by its makers shows tribulations that are not surprising when it is remembered that they had no other vehicle to take pattern from.

Of their early experiences, the makers say the following :

" No doubt many of your readers will wonder where we got the idea of building a horseless carriage. We were not the first to have thought of that kind, but started out in February, 1893, to construct this automobile, which appeared at Madison Square Garden just as it did on our streets in the Summer of 1893, with the exception that we had steel tires (as you will see by the extra steel rimmed wheel sent along). It must be remembered that in those days we could not get what was most necessary to the automobile, rubber tires.   Our experience was some of the most trying until we finally had the automobile ready for the first trip.   In the month of May, 1893 (the date we do not recollect), we blocked up the carriage and gave it a trial before going on the street, which most naturally was after everybody was off the street.   While we were running that motor in the shop we came to the conclusion that there was not a hill around our country which we could not climb, so well did that little motor behave.   On the evening of the trial we started over the plank floor of our shop, where there was no unevenness of any kind to interfere with our first automobile ride, then we went on the street and did not go two blocks when we were stuck.   We started the motor again and lifted the rear

Searchmont—William Hazelton on Driver's Seat

wheels over a pebble which the steel tires could not press into the earth.   We saw at once that steel tires could not be used satisfactorily on an automobile, because the motor could not move the carriage over these pesky little stones, which we had never thought were in our way before that evening.   We were stuck several times on that account, so we started for home.

   " The next day we concluded to change the speed from fast to slow, which had been our mistake ; we wanted to run before we could walk. We soon had the pulleys changed and did not wait until dark for the second trial.   On this trial more troubles began.   It was a beautiful evening and every owner of a steed was out enjoying an evening ride until we came along.   We did not have to turn out, they gave us all the room we wanted.   People came running out of doors and wondered what had just passed ; they would stand in the streets and look after the threshing machine, as they called it.   Every teamster on the road had a few unpleasant and discouraging remarks to make before we could get out of hailing distance from them.   We have seen some bad accidents on the road and in every case the driver was not watching his horse.   We have often told drivers to watch their horses and not us.

"Our first country trip was as amusing to us as it was surprising to the farmers ; they would let their plows stand, and in some instances even forgot to stop the horses, and ran to the house and alarmed

The Autocar Exhibit

everybody into excitement.   At one place a woman stood at the pump near the house and when she saw us coming down the hill she yelled : "Great Heavens !   Here's a wagon running away without a horse !"   We must say that we heard remarks enough to fill volumes. We used the automobile up to September, 1895, before having it repainted and varnished.   The last Sunday in that month we started on a day's trip to the country and reached the outskirts of the city, when we heard a sudden crack in the gasoline tank.   The tank was in front and so we stopped to find the cause of that noise, and found that the tank had bulged somewhat.   To this tank was connected the inlet valve of the motor ; the motor was run at that time by what is called the vapor system, and the ignition was with a hot tube, and for some reason it fired back into the gasoline tank, although we had two check valves in the connection. This back firing had never happened before, so we concluded to go home. We went down a hill at a fair gait so as to get back before the motor would cough again. But alas ! we arrived only half way down when the motor coughed up a regular volcano. This time the top of the gasoline tank blew off (the

Mr. and Mrs. A. Ward Leonard in 3½ H. P. Knickerbocker

tank was square) and set the gasoline on fire. Being on the hill we could not stop, the burning oil preventing us from reaching the brake, so we let it run to the foot of the hill.

"We lost no time in getting off, and in less than ten minutes we had more than three hundred sympathizers, but nobody was willing to help extinguish the burning automobile. Finally the soldered joints melted and the gasoline ran out under the automobile. We lost no time in consulting anybody what to do and went into several houses to get two shovels. We scraped the dirt together and threw it on our freshly painted automobile, and after an hour's hard work we had it under control. Someone wanted to use water but we would not let them do that. This was another instance where we had to depend upon some of our enemies (the teamsters) to pull us to the nearest stable, and there we left the machine until the following day. We took a roundabout way in being towed home and were satisfied that not everybody knew whence we came. The lunch box was filled

Robinson Car—John T. Robinson, Jr. and Knight Neftel on Front Seat

yet, but soaked with mud. We washed off the mud, etc., and found that all that blaze had only burned the front part of the automobile, and ten dollars paid for all the damage.

"We repaired the automobile the same fall, and our next experience was a ride down a steep mountain, it being about two miles long. This ride will never be forgotten. We had gone several hundred yards when the brake broke and we could not hold the car at all. Fortunately we had a clear road, and stopped after a while with no damage done. Having always had more or less trouble with the electric batteries for the sparking, we in 1900 got a small sparking dynamo and it worked well for a while, but when we had used it for a few hundred miles it seemed as if the dynamo was done for. We soon found the cause : the platinum points were worn away. So we renewed the points quite often. The same year we built a steam carriage, and what a difference in riding ! A steam carriage is nice to use in a city, for they make very little noise and have no vibration. This is our experience in the automobile business.''

Peerless—Frederick Randall on Driver's Seat

One of the special features of the running gear made by the Reading Automobile and Gear Company is their compensating gear. This is of the spur gear type, is self-contained and does not permit the spreading of the rear truss, thus practically adding to the strength of this truss, which is sometimes a weak point in running gears. They are highly pleased over the performance of their running gears in actual service and are supplying large numbers to makers.

The Automobile Show
(1901)

THE AUTOMOBILE
MAGAZINE

VOL. III   DECEMBER, 1901   No. 12

The Automobile Show

THE second annual automobile show of the Automobile Club of America was commenced at the Madison Square Garden Saturday, November 2, and finished Saturday, November 9. As a whole it was an entirely successful affair, for it was given to encourage the industry of automobiling, and it enabled manufacturers to present their goods and meet intending customers under very favorable auspices. The total display was business-like, and perhaps for that reason was more satisfactory to the manufacturers than if there were spectacular features, which might have more or less disconcerted even though they interested onlookers. It is quite natural that those who hire booths and display their wares should desire a class of spectators who wish to buy. A manufacturer would rather have one of that kind parade the aisles than ten of the non-buying element.

There is, however, another side to this question. If future club shows are to consist merely of displays of motionless vehicles, just as would be seen in bazaars or emporiums, why is it necessary for a club composed mostly of an element not connected with the trade of automobiling to give them? It is not surprising that the manufacturers themselves, who, without doubt, know well what kind of a show they wish to hold, will soon co-operate in presenting their goods to the public. The only excuse a club organized on the lines of the Automobile Club of America can have for holding any display of this kind, is the thought of building up the recreation or sport side of the subject.   There was little of this kind at the show, it being an absolutely business affair in every sense of the word.

The only attempt made to give the show *éclat* or exclusiveness was the introduction of a loan exhibition, which consisted of an aggregation of unusually handsome and well-known machines owned by club members and others.   This was really a feature for, although a number of well-known names were not noticed on the individual signs affixed to these machines, still, there were enough celebrated owners to make this part of the exhibition thoroughly representative.   Among those who showed machines on this basis were the following :

Edward R. Thomas' 28 H. P. Daimler, formerly W. K. Vanderbilt, Jr.'s White Ghost

W. C. Greene, 40 H. P. Panhard-Levassor ; Foxhall P. Keene, 60 H. P. Mors ; Robert L. Niles, 5½ H. P. Steam Carriage of the Overman Automobile Co.; Percy Owen, 12 H. P. Winton ; Clarence A. Postley, 8 H. P. Panhard-Levassor ; Jules Peck, 6 H. P. Darracq ; Charles E. Duryea, 8 H. P. Duryea Power Co.; Sidney Chubb, 6 H. P. Automotor Co.; Cornelius J. Field, 5 H. P. DeDion-Bouton; S. R. Guggenheim, 16 H. P. Panhard-Levassor ; Smith & Mabley, 8 H. P. Renault ; Spencer Trask, 6 H. P. Searchmont ; Edward R. Thomas, 28 H. P. Daimler ; Rollin H. White, 6 H. P. White Sewing

Machine Co.; Albert R. Shattuck, 12 H. P. Panhard-Levassor; Jefferson Seligman, 5 H. P. DeDion-Bouton; Edward C. Stearns, 3½ H. P. Stearns Steam Carriage Co.; Charles M. Perry, 6 H. P. Steamobile; W. D. K. Wright, 5 H. P. Loomis Automobile Co.; William B. Oliver, 12 H. P. Panhard-Levassor; Albert C. Bostwick, 40 H. P. Winton; Park Densmore, 6 H. P. Foster Automobile Co.

Samuel T. Davis, Jr. loaned the first locomobile made by Stanley Bros., it being 3½ H. P. and weighing 400 pounds. Alexander Fischer sent the first gasomobile made by the Automobile Co. of America, it being 9 H. P. and weighing 1800 pounds. Thomas A.

Metallic Tires—Pulling on One in Attempt to Make It Slip on a Greased Block of Asphalt

Edison loaned a Cell of the new Edison iron-nickel storage battery. A sample of the sign-posts erected last summer by the club was among the exhibits, as was also one of the first gasoline carriages ever made in this country, it being loaned by the AUTOMOBILE MAGAZINE. This carriage was made in 1893 by Nadig Bros., Allentown, Pa., it being 2 H. P. and weighing 1,000 pounds.

There is no question that some of these exhibitors would not have loaned their cars had the show been held by any other organization than the Automobile Club of America, and just on this point alone the club stands in an enviable position to hold an exhibit consisting of something besides a trade show. Regarding this it may be asked what other motive besides a business one can there be for the club to hold a show? The ideas of Arthur J. Eddy, ex-president of the Chicago Automobile Club are interesting. Mr. Eddy last summer completed in a Winton machine the longest consecutive tour ever made in this country. He told the writer that in his opinion a club could not hold such a show as the recent one was, without giving the impression that it was connected too much with professionalism or the trade. Continuing, he said :

View From Front of Garden

"Fine as the show was, it was essentially a trade display, and in my opinion should not be given by an amateur organization. If the club wishes to encourage the subject of automobiling, let it hold contests at various times where its members and other amateurs can meet in friendly rivalry. There would be no question about the subject being advertised if such men as Messrs. Vanderbilt, Bostwick, Keene, Bishop and others should meet in a contest, but the affair at the

Garden was nothing but a business institution, and an amateur club should not hold it.''

Mr. Eddy was not prepared to say that there were really detrimental results in the club holding the show, but he was strongly of the opinion that if the custom became prevalent it would be an evil which would correct itself, for, as he said, '' you cannot mix amateurism with the trade, without the former suffering.'' It must be admitted that so far there are no detrimental indications caused by the

Exhibit of Automobile Co. of America

club having held two shows, although the first one had other features besides the mere showing and selling of vehicles.

The attendance was not so great as last year, owing to the fact that one examination of the display was enough for most people. Last year there were exhibitions and contests of various kinds on a track. These naturally interested many people who made several visits to the Garden, just to be amused. A careful canvass among the manufacturers revealed the fact that most of them were opposed to having a track on account of, as they claimed, its disconcerting people and thereby taking their minds off of perhaps a probable purchase. Among the manufacturers it was noticed that with those who make large, heavy gasoline vehicles the track was least in favor.   The steam men were about equally divided, while those representing electricity thought the track rather a good thing.   The philosophy of these various reasons is obvious, the gasoline manufacturers thinking that the public is influenced against their machines when hearing them on a small track. It is doubtful whether at this stage of enlightenment those who really intend to purchase an automobile would be influenced against a machine by seeing or hearing it in a small enclosure.

Concerning the attendance, the club secretary, S. M. Butler,

United States Long Distance

truthfully summarized as follows : "The club has not made as much money this year as it did last year.   The gate money is less, but the club is better satisfied.   It wants to promote the sport and industry. Last season we had a track and contests on it that attracted the public.   It was not a big exhibition, but there was something doing all the time.   The visitors came and watched the sport on the track and went away after a cursory glance at the machines.

"The exhibitors were not satisfied with the amount of business they did.   This year the show was a matter of interest to everyone. There were many more machines and many more improvements. Those who came to view them had nothing to distract their attention.

The exhibitors or manufacturers, whichever you choose to call them, have done more business. They are better satisfied and therefore the club is better satisfied.''

Some other features of the show are well brought out in the following review written by '' Senator '' Morgan :

'' The John Brisben Walker attack on the French machines at the Manufacturers' Association meeting at Madison Square Garden and his charge that the Automobile Club of America should not encourage importing them caused much comment. The consensus of opinion,

Dixon's Graphite

seems to be that there is little sympathy with Mr. Walker's ideas. Some of those spoken to and who had listened to the tirade, could not see where Mr. Walker was much interested as he does not build a gasoline machine and it is that type of automobile which our French cousins have taken the lead in, and truthfully have given the American manufacturers pointers on how to excel the French makes. One man declared that he would be pleased to see the 45 per cent. duty taken off from French machines so they could come in here free of duty and

stimulate American inventive genius and competitive power. **Mr.**
Walker did not give the French automobile manufacturer credit for
showing us the way in automobile making, just as they did in bicycle
manufacturing.   And the Frenchman is also leading England in automobile making just as he did in bicycle making.   I do not believe that
the French machine will have a long vogue in this country but that two
years will about see its finish here, judging from the marvelous
progress made by Americans in construction in one year.

" Speaking of the progress made, I may say that although not

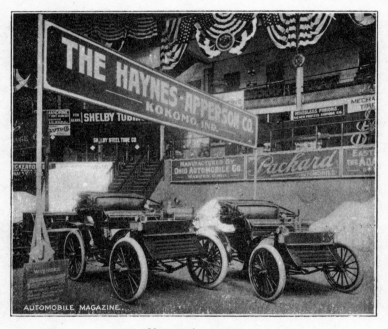

Haynes-Apperson

wishing to be called egotistical in a national way, I do not believe that
any country in the world could do as much in one year as have the
American automobile makers.   It is written in the stars that this nation
of ours is to excel in everything worth excelling in, and it is just as
well that we should have a pace-maker in France or any other country
that wishes to test Yankee mechanical speed power.   France, Germany
and England had about three years' start of us—possibly five, if we
count the earlier efforts, and the automobile can lay claim to being

born in France, just as the bicycle was, but the future will be marked by the best machines being built in America.

"Foreign governments are taking more interest in the automobile from an industrial progress standpoint than this country has. For instance Austria is delving into the transportation problem and believes that the automobile will supersede all other means of locomotion for short distances. It is even thought that it would become a competitor of the railway to connect terminals. The army is also ex-

American Bicycle Co.'s Exhibit

perimenting with the automobile, and the automobile car for baking and general feeding purposes is already an accomplished fact in some of the foreign armies. For baggage service, ammunition carrying, and in an ambulance way, the European armies will undoubtedly utilize the automobile in the next great war.

"A great scene escaped the notice of the descriptive New York writers Saturday night when the Madison Square Garden show closed. It was a scene never to be forgotten, and is undoubtedly the first of

the kind ever witnessed. I saw something like it in Rochester in the
great rink where the endurance test automobiles were stored the night
President McKinley died. The time was midnight and the death-
bells were tolling, and just previous to that the rink presented a rare
picture. Men worked noiselessly and energetically at their machines,
using lamps of electricity and oil to aid them in their getting ready
for the next day when the final run of the strenuous tour from New
York would be finished. Every bolt and nut was to be in position.
Every battery and boiler must be in good order, for the last dash. It
looked as if a great army was getting ready for an attack. When the
bells tolled and the whisper went around "He is dead!" tools were
dropped and the place was darkened as if by magic.

Electric Vehicle Co.

"On the closing night of the show at Madison square, when the
clock showed eleven, the band played Home Sweet Home and after
this was over, the clanging of bells and tooting of horns proved the
gladness with which the finish was hailed by the men who had stood
the strain of an arduous week. At 11:15, as if by magic, every machine
was wheeled to attention and the procession commenced toward the
Fourth Avenue exit, and in another fifteen minutes the building was
empty. The military precision and the entire novelty of the occasion
would have given Langden Smith and James Creelman a rare text for
descriptive writing.

"At first I questioned the policy of doing away with the track, which was an interesting feature of last year's show, but am now convinced that the good gained by not having the visitor's attention taken from exhibits more than made up for a seeming lack of life which the absence of the track caused.

"Some of the exhibitors and non-exhibitors played quite a game with their signs, several being offensively prominent, in the desire to dwarf their competitors. Some of the signs put one in mind of Lincoln's story about the Mississippi steamer which had a big whistle, so large that when it was blown, the steamer stopped for want of steam. The relative merits of some of the signs on the exhibits were in keeping with Lincoln's story.

"I am still of the opinion that a Spring show is the best for the

DeDion–Bouton

trade as there is too long an interval between November and say April, when the machines are usually delivered, and for that reason I believe that the Coliseum show in Chicago next March will again dwarf all others in the matter of sales, as it did last March. Manufacturers should be allowed to get their machines built at this time of the year and be in position to ship promptly and not hold their prospective customer's money for months as has been the case several times during the past year.

"Of course the pessimist is abroad, as usual. I met him in numbers in the Garden. One of them stood in the gallery and in an attitude of the devil tempting Christ, waved his hand over the exhibit and said 'Can you point out to me one of these concerns that has paid a dividend? notwithstanding all their tinsel and talk.' My reply was 'only several.' And why, pray, should any firm be expected to pay dividends in a short year or two years in a new business that requires so much outlay to start it successfully? The pessimist has always been on hand at all times. He has stood by good enterprises and by great commanders and croaked in their ear, 'Danger and defeat.' I prophesy that the future automobile will make more millionaires than any other individual business has done, and it is a rare field of promise, and I think will prove a manufacturing Eldorado.

"The shrewdest advertisers of the bunch will get the first money

The Mobile Co.'s Exhibit

and the halting ones who are inclined to the croaker's views, will be among the 'also rans.'"

———————————

L. B. Smyser, formerly with the Long Distance Automobile Co., and F. S. Barnnett have started for themselves at 136 Liberty St., N. Y., and have just completed plans of what looks like a very attractive gasoline vehicle. Mr. Smyser will be consulting engineer for a new concern which will start in New York for the purpose of buying and selling automobiles and giving advice to prsopective purchasers. Mr. Smyser has been in the business practically since it started, as he worked with Charles E. Duryea and is a mechanic of more than ordinary ability.

Motor Farm-Truck Deliveries (1902)

Motor Farm-Truck Deliveries

By George E. Walsh

FIGURE out the opportunities of simplifying the present unsatisfactory question of delivering farm products to city markets by means of auto-trucks built specially for the purpose and you will see that they are so great that it is quite natural that a number of experimental tests in that direction should already have been made. The Department of Agriculture in particular has had in view for some time tests of this nature, for in investigating the subject of truck farming the perplexing question of cheap and prompt transportation facilities always proved a stumbling block around which it seemed impossible to get.

Truck farming to-day near the large cities is limited in area so that our choicest perishable fruits and vegetables are raised on farming land valued at several hundred dollars per acre. So expensive is this land that farmers must be able to raise two and three, and even four, crops of produce from the land in one season.

The capital required to operate such a city truck garden is quite considerable, but in spite of the high prices obtained for the produce the farmers find less profit than before, and they are being pushed further and further from their markets. In the past these truck gardeners have kept within a distance from their market, which would enable them to drive in with their trucks over night and sell their goods the following morning. Where the perishable products must be intrusted to the care of the railroad companies loss through injury, delay and high cost of transportation have made the business largely unprofitable.

The most important question of the day in farming is to find some means of quick and efficient transportation for the perishable products of the truck farms to the city markets. In some New England localities the trolley lines have partly solved this problem. They have secured in their charter transportation privileges which enable them to run freight cars at certain hours of the day and night. By tapping rich agricultural regions they have in this way benefited the farmers by carrying their perishable goods promptly and cheaply directly to the city markets without change. But even in these cases there is always the necessity of double loading and unloading, which consumes time and expense.

The Department of Agriculture has recommended the use of independent auto-trucks which could load up at the farms and run direct to the city markets and unload without any intermediate handling of the goods. This would place the articles in the market in much better condition than when handled several times. These auto-trucks would have to be built of sufficient size to carry several tons of fruits and vegetables in each trip. They should be operated by individual farmers, or by several in one neighborhood co-operating together. The initial cost of such a truck would be from two to three thousand dollars, and this expense would deter most farmers from undertaking the enterprise until it had been demonstrated to be feasible.

The Department of Agriculture draws some of its data and conclusions from the experiments made by the Post Office Department in rural mail collecting and delivery by means of automobile wagons built for this purpose. These postal automobiles have demonstrated that in thickly populated sections of the country where the roads are good they will prove a paying investment. So far the experiments have been eminently satisfactory, and it is likely that in the near future a considerable number of these vehicles will be in operation by the Post Office Department to facilitate the delivery and collection of mail matter.

In both cases, however, the condition of the country and rural roads must be a somewhat deciding factor. Unless the roads are passable at all seasons of the year it would be impossible for either the postal or truck motor vehicles to prove a very profitable investment. But there are many parts of Long Island, New Jersey and Massachusetts where the country roads are good enough for such experimental work during most of the year.

It is estimated that under adequate auto-truck delivery methods our farm produce of a perishable nature could be brought daily from points fifty and sixty miles away, where to-day it must come from a distance no greater than ten and fifteen miles. The latter distance is almost as great, as it pays the truck farmers to drive into the city every day and back the next for another load. The truck gardeners who live much further out must depend upon boat or railroad transportation, and this has proved unsatisfactory because of the delays, injury to the goods and high cost of freight and handling. Where perishable goods have to be loaded on the farm wagons and carried to the nearest railroad station, where they are loaded on the cars and then unloaded in the city to other wagons and carted across town to unload at the market, there is always bound to be excessive charges for handling and great loss through breakage. The only satisfactory method of transporting such goods is to make one loading and unloading answer for the whole trip. This can be accomplished only through individual auto-trucks which could visit the different farms and take up daily the produce prepared for them.

The method generally recommended by those who have investigated the subject is either for the truck farmers of one place to co-operate in running one or two auto-trucks, dividing the initial cost among themselves and operating them for mutual benefit. A single large auto-truck carrying four or five tons could accommodate two or three truck gardeners, and the trip to the city and back again could be made without difficulty each day. The delivery of fresh goods in this way would place them far ahead of those handled through the several agencies mentioned. It would enable farmers distant forty and fifty miles from the city markets to compete openly and freely with those located within five or ten miles. The land of the farmers would be so much cheaper that it would more than pay them to enter into truck gardening for the purpose of sending fresh supplies of perishable goods direct to the city every day. There would be certain seasons of the year when the auto-trucks would not need to run oftener than once or twice a week, but the cost of keeping them would amount to nothing except for the small rate of interest on the first investment. This, compared with the cost of feeding and keeping truck horses, would be almost infinitesimal.

Under present conditions truck gardeners near the cities find that their land is so valuable, and the demand for fresh produce increasing so that many are covering their farms with glass so extra crops can be raised thereon. It costs more to cover an acre of land with glass-sash than two or three auto-trucks would amount to, and yet farmers are so sure of the profits in this business that they are gradually increasing their expenses in this way. The demand for fine, fresh truck produce is so steadily increasing that the supply will never be equal to it. Already all the available land within a radius of ten miles of our large city markets has been taken up by market gardeners, and some of it devoted to this work is even beyond the actual range of the so-called profitable zone. Some of this truck land near the cities pays the owners better than if houses and stores were erected thereon. One enterprising business truck gardener has even threatened to tear down some old houses on his land right near Brooklyn Bridge to erect in their place greenhouses and gardens in order to obtain better returns.

The possibilities in this direction are so remarkable that the question is being carefully studied from all sides, and within the next few years there will unquestionably be introduced new systems of transportation connecting the distant suburbs with the city markets by means of individual vehicles of some kind. Like the whaleback grain carriers of the lakes, the auto-trucks which can load up and deliver the goods directly to the market without breaking bulk will have an immeasurably superior advantage over all others. This system has been tried both in London and in this country on a small scale, and there is every reason to suppose that it will soon solve the problem which to-day is urgently pressing for a solution of some practical nature.

Military Motor Train in South Africa Crossing a Sprut.

A Preliminary
New York to Buffalo
Tour
(1901)

A Preliminary New York to Buffalo Tour

By. S. W. RUSHMORE

I RETURNED from my Buffalo trip September 21, and lay before you the log of my trip. Having taken a great interest in the widely advertised endurance run I decided to go over the route a day ahead of the crowd and enjoy the advantages of the sign posts and detailed information as to hotels and gasoline supply. I had planned to make the run in another machine that I had used previously, but a number of bad accidents on shorter runs made me change my mind, so a few days before I purchased a 12 horse-power Model "C" Packard machine taken from New York stock and without any special features. I found that there was ample space in the boot for all tools, including a full set of solid wrenches, hammers, chisels, hatchet, screws, rope, etc., and I therefore replaced the rear tool box with a 2½ gallon gasoline tank, a 1 gallon machine oil tank and a ¾ gallon cylinder oil tank.

Having strapped our baggage on the rear, Mrs. Rushmore and I climbed aboard at 10.30 Sunday morning, September 8, and started for Poughkeepsie via Hackensack, N. J., Suffern and Newburg to Highland Falls. Having run to Poughkeepsie several times by the east shore, we decided to try a new route and at the same time avoid the rough hilly roads north of Sing Sing. The roads to Newburg were mostly fine hard macadam, although part of the Swamp road after leaving Hackensack was deep sand and hard pulling, and we reached Newburg, 65¾ miles, at 2.45. Left Newburg 4.15 and ran 11¾ miles over the roughest sort of dusty, rocky road, reaching Milton 4.35. After calling on friends at Milton rode on 9 miles to Highland Falls over the rockiest roads we ever saw, reaching Poughkeepsie at 6.30. Here we filled tanks and found the run of 86½ miles had consumed 7½ gallons gasoline and 2 quarts of water.

Lighting our 9 inch mirror acetyline searchlight we left Poughkeepsie at 8.20 p. m, and made the run of 17½ miles to Rhinebeck in 1 hour and 10 minutes. The light showed up the road for nearly 1,000 feet, and much better time could have been made but for the uncomfortable shaking due to many crossings and unevenness of road; Mrs. Rushmore being quite tired out, we put up at the Rhinebeck House for the night.

73

After taking 1 gallon of gasoline to again fill tank, we left Rhine-beck at 8.35 the next (Monday) morning, September 9, and in a few minutes overtook Mr. W. L. Andrus, of Yonkers, in a 16 horse-power special Packard machine, with which we had an exciting race as far as Hudson. Our governor being set to a maximum of 23 miles per hour

Mr. and Mrs. S. W. Rushmore Ready for Their Tour

on the level, and Mr. Andrus having an intermediate maximum of but 20 miles and a top speed of 35 miles an hour, we would pull away from him at all times until a favorable stretch of road permitted him to use his high gear, then he would overtake us. I will never forget the spectacle of that machine rushing up upon us through deep light dust at a 35-mile clip. It seemed as though it had been shot from a cannon and was tearing up the whole road. We reached Hudson, 26 miles, in 1 hour and 45 minutes, much time being lost in passing frightened horses and pulling through ploughed up sections of road on hill gear.

From Hudson to Albany we saw almost none of the Buffalo signs, although we took the main road.   We lost the road at Kinderhook, and a mile further on the engine suddenly stopped.   Having had no previous experience with float feed carbureter or jump spark ignition, it took me two hours to locate the trouble which was due to a tiny lathe chip becoming wedged into the peculiar air valve used in the Packard carbureter and preventing its movement.   We reached Albany over narrow, sandy roads at 3.30, Monday, September 9, and found the excessive vibration due to rough roads had shaken the cyclometer to pieces.   At Albany we put in 4½ gallons gasoline and 3 quarts of water, replacing the amount used in the run from Rhinebeck, estimated at 36 miles.   The excessive consumption of gasoline on this run was no doubt due to the trouble with the carbureter. Leaving Albany at 5 o'clock p. m., we soon lost the road, being unable to find a single club sign.   None of the natives knew anything and we wandered over or through deep sand cross roads and potato patches until we found the so-called " State Road," which for 6 miles or more was simply a succession of holes about 10 feet apart, and this led us to Schenectady, the run of 25 miles taking nearly 2 hours. We stopped at Edison Hotel, a fine house, for the night.   There was only one place in town, a livery stable, which would take the machine for the night, 50 cents.

Leaving Schenectady at 9.45 a. m., Tuesday, September 10, we ran through without a single stop to Little Falls, 56.7 miles, through deep sand all the way, little traveled, in fact, an apparently abandoned road, arriving at 1.30 p. m.   Left Little Falls at 2 p. m., after seeing town but making no stops, reaching Herkimer 2.45 p. m. for lunch.   Left Herkimer at 3.30 p. m. and reached Utica, 15 miles, at 4 p. m.   Here we put in 6 gallons gasoline, the amount used on the run of 97 miles from Albany,. a very good showing considering that the roads all the way were hardly passable and the engine at all times working at its maximum, and for long stretche; through deep sand on the hill gear. We left Utica at 5 p. m., and reached Oneida, 23.4 miles, at 6.30, over uniformly wretched sandy or rutty roads.   Left Oneida Wednesday the 10th, at 8.45, and shortly after one of the rear wheels picked up a large nail, the first puncture since using the machine.

Soon after leaving Oneida a horse gave us battle with his fore feet, as follows : The road was narrow, and a farmer driving a pair of heavy horses to wagon ahead of us paid no attention to the horn. Farmers do not regard the horn, as they hear horns often, while town people have become so used to the trolley gongs that they often pay no attention to the bell. We crowded up to the farmer on the right-hand side and when he saw us he pulled his team out to let us pass. As we went slowly by, the horse nearest us struck out with his fore feet, the first blow striking a front wheel tire and doing no harm. The second hoof-stroke, however, tore away the front wheel mud guard. This is the first time I ever knew a horse to fight an automobile.

After putting a plug into our nail puncture and running some distance, the carbureter again acted badly, and the engine occasionally missed fire, but we reached Syracuse, about 27 miles, at 10.45 a. m., and at once called upon the Century Automobile Company, manufac-

Ditched

turers of a most elaborately finished chainless steam wagon, who placed their whole factory at our disposal and showed us every courtesy. It is a good shop, and every effort was made to give us needed assistance. Here it was found that a small brass ring that acted as a stop for the air valve of the carbureter had been pounded into a dozen pieces. This was replaced by a ring turned out of solid machine steel and the carbureter gave no further trouble. The punctured tire having lost some air was also replaced by the spare tire we carried along, and the entire repair work consumed three hours. We took on one gallon of machine oil, the first since leaving Jersey City, and three gallons of gasoline, the amount used in the thirty miles' hard pulling from Oneida with the engine missing fire most of the time.

We left Syracuse at 3.30 p. m. and were soon floundering at slow speed and full power through the miles of deep sand and mud, here called roads, but which were nothing but muddy ditches. This was the worst road yet for a long stretch, and very little traveled. Gladly would we have run across the open fields (except in the marshes) had the fences been out of the way. Such neglect of the highways is a disgrace, and a severe reflection upon the people of New York State. Any self-respecting man would spend his last cent, before allowing such a state of affairs to exist in his neighborhood. Reached Lyons for the night at 7.30, the last ten miles or so being fine macadam or good gravel road. Here we put on 4½ gallons gasoline consumed in the 48 miles from Syracuse.

At Lyons it rained all night and until noon, Thursday, September 12, when we started for Rochester. The roads were fairly level, but soft and very slippery, and when running at any speed without power the machine would simply try to waltz around and go rear end first, and then the only way to keep out of the ditch was to put on power and take chances of being able to slow down gradually without getting into other trouble. Ten miles from Lyons the roads again turned into deep sand and mud ditches, and in some places it took the full 12 horse-power on the hill gear to force through, the sand being almost up to the rear axle and fouling the chain badly.

We did the best running going up hills, as there the road was drained and we could run fast without slewing. Down grade, the defect of all American machines was shown by the persistence with which the heavier rear end would try to go to the front. This was shown unexpectedly when 16 miles from Rochester we went down a long dry hill at good speed, and at the foot came to a dry looking slippery spot not twenty feet long. Before I could put on power (the engine having been allowed to nearly stop while coasting) we slewed sideways fully ten feet and nearly upset in the ditch. The downward shock was so great that both front axles were badly bent outwardly at the bottom and we presented a queer sight as we limped into Rochester. No other damage was sustained and a blacksmith at Rochester straightened the axles in an hour.

The dry batteries gave out near Rochester and I bought a new set there. Will use storage battery and magneto in future. After running about Buffalo for a week I shipped machine home by rail.

Another thing not stated by the promoters of the run is that the alkali or other constituent of the mud about Rochester eats off the varnish over night and ruins the appearance of a new machine. At Rochester I was struck in face by a potato and blinded so that I nearly wrecked a machine following me. There were fully ten thousand spectators and not a single policeman.

We arrived at Rochester at 5.00 p. m., September 12. Put on 5 gallons gasoline, amount used in previous run of 39 miles, plus about 25 miles running about city, also one gallon machine oil, amount used from Syracuse.

Wait at Rochester all day Friday, the 13th, owing to rain and to meet machines coming in on endurance run. The bells were tolled for the death of the President about 2.30 in the night. Left Saturday morning, September 14, at 9.45 a. m., and ran without stop over poor and very slippery roads until near Buffalo, through the city without stop, through Tonawanda and arrived at Niagara Falls at 3.30 p. m. This run was remarkable, as for the entire distance of fully 95 miles, including distance lost trying to find better road than showed by signs, the engine ran continuously and I left my seat but once, to make sure the cylinder lubricator had enough oil and worked properly. I could have run 20 miles more without filling oilers.

The gasoline consumed in last 95 mile run was exactly 5 gallons. Two gallons filled up the water tank, that being the full amount used in the run from Albany.

Total gasoline consumed in run from Jersey City, 36¼ gals.

Total machine oil consumed in run from Jersey City, 2⅛ gals.

Total cylinder oil consumed in run from Jersey City, ⅝ gals.

Total jacket water evaporated on whole run, 3¼ gals.

Total miles run, about 530, including sight seeing and losing road.

Average miles per gallon gasoline, 14.72 gals.

Capacity gasoline tanks, 10½ gals.

Best record of machine on Hudson County Boulevard at 18 miles per hour nearly constant speed, 22½ miles per gallon.

Weight of wagon empty, 2,005 pounds. With all on, and myself and wife aboard, the weight must have been close on to 2,400 pounds.

Considering that the machine was new and quite strange to me and that I could not afford at any time to take chances, on account of my companion, I consider the above a good showing. No repairs were required other than described. I spent an average of one hour each night inspecting machine, tightening up bolts and oiling. The carbureter was removed twice as stated and at no other time.   I had taken the precaution to wrap it up completely in waste and thus kept out the dust and mud that gave so much trouble to the machines entered in the run.

The signs telling the road to Buffalo were of the greatest value, and without them much time would have been lost.   All the natives said that the route chosen was the poorest which could have been selected.   I had no idea that the roads could be so bad or would never have started.   Only our heavy construction carried us through, and it is marvelous that the little steamers and runabouts got through at all.   Having had a Mobile which I have run nearly 4,000 miles I feel competent to judge on this point.

In reference to water consumption, you will note that the consumption to Albany is much higher than for the longer run to Buffalo. This is no doubt due to the splashing over when the tank is full.   I also recall now that I filled the search light acetylene gas generator near Poughkeepsie from the water tank and this took about a quart. There was considerable loss from splashing or evaporation from the spare gasoline tank, although the same as the main tank and having a very small vent, and I think the loss from this cause was fully 10 per cent., which should be reckoned to the credit of the engine.

[In regard to Mr. Rushmore's decision to abandon primary batteries, Mr. Packard writes as follows : "I do not agree with Mr. Rushmore regarding dry batteries, and have already written him suggesting that his adjustments of sparking parts may have caused the unexpected depletion of his batteries.   On the six machines which we ran over the New York-Buffalo course, we had no battery troubles, and did not replace any batteries whatever.   Of course each of our machines is equipped with two sets of dry batteries." — Ed.]

The White Sewing Machine Company, builders of the White steam carriage, finds its automobile business so promising that it has been obliged to increase the capacity of its manufacturing department. It recently bought up the large building at the corner of Canal and Champlain Streets, Cleveland, O., adjoining its main factory, and as soon as necessary alterations can be made it will be used as a temporary plant.   Next spring the building will be torn down and replaced with a new seven-story brick structure which will have a floor space of 90,000 square feet.

The Growth of the Automobile Industry in America (1907)

THE GROWTH OF THE AUTOMO-
BILE INDUSTRY IN AMERICA

BY DAVID T. WELLS

ILLUSTRATED BY PHOTOGRAPHS

A T the Columbian Expo-
sition in 1893, there was
on exhibition a two-
seated buckboard. The
only differences between
it and the other carriages
of that time were that
on its common wooden wheels it had a
set of hard rubber tires, the "box" behind
the rear seat was covered over and, the
greatest difference of all, it had no shafts
in front. It excited some curiosity among
the persons who happened to visit the
building where Harold Sturges, its maker,
was exhibiting it, because it moved of its
own power, which was transmitted from
electric batteries in the inclosed box.

It did not move very swiftly, very surely,
or very comfortably, but it did move and
was "a horse-
less carriage."
It could hard-
ly be called an
automobile.
Except that
one other man
had experi-
mented slight-
ly with vehi-
cles propelled
by their own
power, this
queer carriage
of Sturges'
was the auto-
mobile indus-
try of Ameri-
ca, at the
time America
was showing
what progress

it had made since Columbus found it four
hundred years before.

Thirteen years later, in 1906, the cost of
the annual American output of automobiles was $65,000,000. There were 146
concerns in business, which represented a
capitalization of probably $25,000,000, and
were giving employment directly and indirectly to an army of men which reached
well up into the hundreds of thousands.

That, in brief, is the history of the automobile industry in America. The car
which Sturges built, battery, rubber tires
and all, could not have cost much more
than $500, and certainly would not have
sold for more than that. The gasoline car
which Charles Duryea was experimenting
on at the same time could not have cost
more than $500 more. So the increase in
the annual
output of
American
made motor
vehicles in
twelve years
was $64,999,-
000.

The increase
in the demand
has made men
who were en-
gaged in man-
ufacturing
everything
from railroad
locomotives
to clothes
wringers and
watches, go
from their
original field

The only American-built motor-car on exhibition at the Chicago
World's Fair, 1893.

Winton's first car, 1896. The first in the United States to combine vertical cylinders and shaft drive.

the progress, gradual but unbelievably swift, from one extreme to the other, is the history of the American automobile business. It is the history of struggles of men of brains, ingenuity, and perseverance, not only to solve the difficulties which confronted them, but to solve them better and more quickly than other men of brains, ingenuity, and perseverance, who were working along different lines toward the same solution. In the swiftness and sureness with which difficulties of construction and marketing have been overcome, the American automobile industry is typically American. In the time it takes a boy to develop from knickerbockers to shaving cup, the American automobile has de-

to take up the manufacture and improvement of this wagon without shafts. The process of making it has increased the population of one city alone, Detroit, some 75,000 souls, has added $5,200,-000 to the capital invested there, and has raised its annual output of manufactured goods $27,000,000.

That is the story of the commercial growth of the automobile industry in America. The synopsis of the other story of the automobile is contained in the difference between the slow, uncomfortable, and uncertain "horseless carriage" of 1893, with its difficulty of management, its straight-backed seats, its hard-tired, jouncing wheels, and the motor car of 1907, roomy, luxurious and capable of traveling sixty miles in as many minutes —not a wagon without a horse, but a parlor car without a track or a cinder. The story of

Henry Ford's first car, built in 1893.

veloped from a cart whose lack of a horse was sadly felt to a distance-annihilating

Plant of the Electric Vehicle Company, Hartford.

machine, which even our progressive older brothers who went to the Columbian Exposition while we stayed home to disturb the quiet of the swimming pool, would not have believed possible.

To the lay mind, the difficulties which had to be overcome to make the difference between 1893 and 1907 are so many and diverse as to be almost incomprehensible. The objects which had to be attained were comfort, ease of handling, speed,

Charles B. King, one of the first motor car builders in America.

and durability, and each object involved a maze of difficult interdependent problems which kept an army of experts in all lines of mechanical production busy, working, puzzling, and experimenting. How well their work succeeded is shown by the contrast between the little shaftless wagon of Sturges's, alone in one corner of one of large numbers of great buildings, and the long procession of powerful machines of all conceivable models and makes which made a solid line on the Jericho Turnpike from Mineola to Long Island City on the day of the last Vanderbilt cup race.

While Sturges was the first to publicly exhibit the results of his experiments in the building of a horseless vehicle, it is not fair to say that he was the first American in that field which afterward grew into the automobile industry. In 1888 Charles Duryea, in Massachusetts, had begun to experiment with motor vehicles, and in 1892, one year before Sturges's car was exhibited, Henry Ford had begun to experiment in Detroit, which was within ten years to become one of the great centers of the industry.

Duryea's car, like Sturges's, was simply a wagon built for a horse with an engine placed in it to give the driving power. This automobile, if it could be called an automobile, was probably the first gasoline car produced in America. It came into being in 1891. Ford's car was practically a remodeled bicycle. The engine which drove it was originally built from a bicycle, and the car itself was a sort of buggy mounted on bicycle wheels. It did not seem to enter the minds of the makers that the kind of a wagon suitable for a horse to draw was not the kind that could be best propelled by an engine, so new was the

The factory of the Packard Motor Car Company, in Detroit.

Moris and Salom "Electrobat"—first electric car commercially produced in the United States, 1894.

idea of self-propelled vehicles. The gradual evolution from the carriage to the car came when competition in the new industry began to get hot and the appearance of a car became a great factor in its salability.

And the original movers in the industry did not have long to wait for competition. As soon as the first cars came on to the market for sale and the public was found willing to spend money to experiment with them, men began to flock into the new industry to try their hands at making the horseless vehicle. The period from 1893 to 1906 contains the names of a dozen pioneers in the business, names that are still among the leaders of the industry as it has grown to its present great proportions. To these men in no small part is due the credit of the present perfected American automobile. Most of the men who were prominent figures in the industry at that time are still among the foremost figures in it. Charles Duryea was even earlier than that period. He built his first car in 1888. Henry Ford came into the industry in 1893; Col. Albert Pope in 1895, and in the following year Alexander Winton and Ransom Olds began the manufacture of automobiles. Haynes and Jonathan Maxwell also began to make gasoline cars during this period, and the air-cooled car introduced the Knox and Franklin into the automobile building industry during these years. The Whites and the Stanleys in the steam car field, and Andrew Ricker in the perfection of the electric

vehicle, were also members of the trade who came in during these years which covered the greatest progress of the automobile.

The first gasoline car which was put on the market, that of Duryea, had a single cylinder engine. Ford's, which came a year later, had two cylinders. That was one line of development. As the engines improved there was a tendency toward more cylinders to produce the power, until the makers of cars got to putting in two, four, and six cylinders, the numbers which are used in most of the cars of to-day. Duryea, in the second model which he built in 1893, also adopted the double cylinder engine and later was the first to apply a multiple cylinder engine to the commercial cars. Ford, however, is given the credit of producing the first engine with double cylinders opposed to each other instead of being placed horizontally.

It is hard to follow the improvement of each part of the car. New features came so fast in almost every part of the machines, which were put out from year to year, that they fairly overlapped each other. Very often on several models of the same year would be found almost identically the same improvements. It was not that one maker had stolen the plan of another, but that both had happened to hit on the same solution of a very apparent imperfection at the same time. Often, too, one model would solve several difficulties at the same time.

In 1894 George W. Lewis, of Chicago,

The Stanley Brothers, in the first locomobile car invented and built by them.

produced a car on which the power was transmitted by a series of friction discs. The cars which had been made before transmitted the power of the engine to the wheels either through belts as does a stationary engine to the machines of a factory, or through chains like that of a bicycle. The changes of speed were accomplished by the shifting of the belts in one case or different sized sprocket wheels in the other. The friction disc method of transmitting the power of the engine to the wheels was introduced in 1894. Two years later Alexander Winton, who had just entered the business, brought out a fourth method of transmitting the power. His system consisted of a propellor shaft from the engine and bevel gears on the rear axle of the car. Within three years after the first car was built four methods of solving the transmission difficulty, each of which claimed to be an improvement on its predecessor, had been produced. The perfection of the original solution of the transmission difficulty followed slowly. The secondary difficulty was to change the speed of the car by the transmission system, so that it could attain full speed on level ground; use a smaller gear on a grade, and be able with a low gear to climb the steepest hills. Winton's second model had three speeds forward and one reverse, and the other makers also improved their methods of managing the speed of their products. From the first car which had to

Photograph by
Marceau.

Col. A. A. Pope, whose bicycle business developed into automobile manufacturing.

maintain the same speed whether it was trying to climb Pike's Peak or running on a race course, the modern engine which can go forward at three different speeds and backward at two was evolved. While the difficulties with the two main parts of the car, the engine and the method of the transmission of power, and speed regulation were being solved, improvements were constantly being made on all the other parts of the car The clutch which is used to connect and disconnect the transmission was improved. In about 1895 Charles King invented an air clutch and a system of air brakes which proved successful. In 1898 J. W. Packard brought forward a spring clutch of original design, and in 1903 Jonathan Maxwell adopted a multiple spring clutch.

The other improvements and solutions of difficulties and inconveniences followed one another quickly as the competition grew and the field expanded. Almost every new model of almost every car brought out something which made the running and care of it more convenient and easy. There were improvements in the arrangement of the levers and treads which governed the engine. There were improvements in the valves which automatically admitted the gasoline to be vaporized and exploded. The nearer right the proportion of gasoline and air for the explosion, the greater efficiency and less odor and smoke as a result of the explo-

A Duryea Car of 1894; on the left Charles E. Duryea, pioneer motor manufacturer in the United States; with him his brother, J. F. Duryea. This is the model of car that won the first auto race in America—1895, and the only American car ever first in an international run, October, 1896.

the adoption and improvement of pneumatic tires the rubber industry, which the bicycle had somewhat helped, received a great boom. In 1896 Ransom Olds introduced a new spring frame construction which decreased the vibration on the engine. He used two long springs instead of reaches, and the engine was placed between the centers of the two springs. Later the engine which had been placed under the frame or beneath the seat began to appear in front, so that in case repairs had to be made the driver would not have to grovel in the earth beneath, but could stand up to do his repairing like a self-respecting mechanic. The arrangement of the chassis was also improved, so that the connecting rods and transmission could be reached with the least possible difficulty and still would be least likely to get into trouble from rough roads or other causes of breakdown.

sion. The material of the cars, too, had to be improved. It was a search for the alloy that would be the strongest and would best withstand the vibration, and yet be the lightest, and the experiments in this line opened a larger field for another industry, the making of steel.

Another trade was made larger by the attempt to stop the vibration and with

All these improvements came gradually but swiftly. Each year larger and larger corps of skilled men worked to overcome objections that might be made to the

Where the White Steam Cars are made in Cleveland.

model of the year before. It was competitive work, for as the field grew larger, there was a greater and greater prize for each puzzle solved. Each improvement, even the slightest, which caused a car to run swifter or surer, meant thousands of dollars in the pockets of the firm which perfected it.

Lack of improvement meant more than temporary stagnation. It meant failure. Firm after firm which went into the business and failed to improve on the models which then existed, had to stop work, while the companies which had men who could solve the problems which each new season presented, continued to expand with wonderful rapidity. Between the years of 1902 and 1907, two hundred and eighty-seven companies began the making of gasoline automobiles, and because of the lack of puzzle-solving brains or ability to please the public, failed of success and gave it up. In accordance with the law of the survival of the fittest others tried, succeeded and helped to add to the magnitude of the industry.

One problem which confronted the makers of gasoline cars and the solution of which made the greatest division in the gasoline machine was the problem of how to cool the engine. Its parts were bound to get hot from the constant explosions and friction, and the problem of how to keep them cool without adding greatly

The first car built by Haines and Apperson in 1894, containing Mr. Haines, the Apperson brothers, and Mr. J. D. Maxwell.

to the weight of the car and consequently decreasing its speed and durability was one which was constantly in the minds of the manufacturers. As early as 1894 George Lewis invented a system of water cooling which proved successful, but in the years which followed almost every maker of cars tried to make improvements in this regard.

Several of the men experimenting on the problem of how a cooling system could best be adapted to the needs of the industry, believed that the engines could be cooled without a water jacket by the air which the car stirred up as it moved. In other

The Studebaker plant in South Bend, where automobiles have been added to the carriage business.

words, they thought that instead of applying a cold water bottle a larger window would do the trick as well. The makers who finally solved the difficulty at almost the same time did it in entirely different ways. Henry Knox, in Springfield, Mass., kept his engine cool by substituting threaded pins for the flanges which had previously been used. In this way he got a broader surface of his engine exposed to the air or opened a wider window. The solution of John Wilkinson of the Franklin Company of Syracuse, was even simpler. He divided his engine into four small elements and gave it a larger radiating surface to keep it cool. He also invented an auxilliary escape valve and expelled a larger per cent. of the burned out gases which tended to heat the engine. All these improvements were made on cars driven by exploded gasoline.

At the same time men were bringing to perfection cars propelled by other means—steam and electricity. Up to 1901 or 1902, in fact, steam carriages were in the majority. Aside from the construction of the boilers and the use of fuel steam cars went through much the same evolution as did the gasoline wagons. Their special problems were how to make the boilers light but strong, and the method of using fuel to heat the steam.

After the first really modern steam carriage built by George S. Whitney, in Boston in 1895, almost every subsequent model showed lighter and stronger boilers, quicker methods of getting up steam and improved methods of burning fuel. Whitney discovered a vaporizing gas burner which afterward saw general adoption. In 1897 Francis Stanley, who was another pioneer, designed a boiler which, instead of being made of boiler plate, got its strength from three windings of piano wire, which successfully did away with weight and added strength. Soon after this Rollin White brought out a boiler which was so constructed that it could generate steam very quickly and produced a special water supply system and a number of automatic appliances which increased efficiency and safety. Another improvement came from Frederick Grout, of Orange, N. J., who perfected a condenser by which all the water which had been made into steam was condensed and returned to the boiler for use again.

The problem which confronted the makers of electric vehicles was to get a battery which would carry the car the greatest distance without being unwieldy and too heavy for use. This is a difficulty which has never been fully solved, but John T. Rainier successfully got around it. Because of the difficulty in the giving out of batteries the electric vehicle trade received a decided blow when, in 1900, two $25,000,000 companies went into liquidation, and another reduced its capital from $25,000,000 to $5,000,000. Ranier obviated the difficulty by organizing a chain of garages, especially in New York, so that a car could get prompt and skilled assistance whenever it was in trouble.

All this time while the automobile was growing from a horseless carriage to a machine which worked with such speed and certainty that almost the only use for a horse was in the computation of its comparative power, the business which it represented grew with a rapidity that gave it the power almost to make or unmake the prosperity of cities, and to such an extent that its sudden failure would materially affect the prosperity of the whole nation. At the Columbian Exposition the entire automobile output of the country, one car, was contained in one small obscure corner of one building. When the automobile manufacturers of 1907 wanted to exhibit in New York they had to rent not only Madison Square Garden to hold the exhibition cars of the makers who rest upon the Selden basic patent, but also one of the largest armories in town to hold the overflow of what are known as the independent makers. And the floor space of both great halls was crowded full of the different types of machines which the country had produced.

The manufacture of automobiles first began to assume the proportion of being one of the country's greatest industries in 1902. Figures compiled showing the great progress since that time make clear what a great place it has taken in America's industrial life.

Twenty-one concerns now in operation were doing business in 1902; 52 concerns were in the business that year, 18 of which discontinued before 1903.

In 1903 there were 71 new concerns in the business and 30 discontinued the same year. There were 106 in all doing business in that year.

In 1904 there were 54 new concerns in the business, and 40 discontinued the same year. There were 106 in all doing business in that year.

In 1905 there were 51 new concerns in the business, and 38 discontinued the same year. There were 141 in all doing business in that year.

In 1906 there were 43 new concerns in the business, and 29 discontinued the same year. There were 146 in all doing business in that year.

In 1907 there were 51 new concerns in the business, and about 168 concerns in all. There have been several discontinuances.

The following table illustrates the growth of the output of the American automobile industry since 1903 by the cost of the cars which were manufactured during those years :

In 1903 the output cost $16,000,000
In 1904 . . . . $24,500,000
In 1905 . . . . $40,000,000
In 1906 . . . . $65,000,000
In 1907 . . . . $89,000,000

Rollin H. White, who designed the White Steam Car.

To sum the figures up: Since 1902 America's output of automobiles of the gasoline type alone has cost $234,500,000. At least one-quarter more, $58,600,000, can be added for the vehicles propelled by other means of locomotion, making the total output for five years equal $293,-100,000. With a productive power like this no one can deny that the automobile trade in the short space of time in which it has existed has become one of America's greatest industries.

If there is nothing else to prove it, a list of the hard-headed business men who have either abandoned businesses which they have built up to begin the manufacture of automobiles or have become convinced that the making of motor cars would be a profitable addition to the industry which they were already carrying on, shows what a

The factory of the H. H. Franklin Mfg. Company, of Syracuse.

An assembling room in one of the great factories.

hold the automobile trade had taken on the business interests of the country. The Studebakers, who make wagons and built the prairie schooners that took the Mormons over the plains to Utah, added the making of automobiles to the building of shaft carrying vehicles. Rauch & Lang of Cleveland and the Columbus Buggy Company also added automobile building to carriage making.

The American Locomotive Company added the building of the road carriage to that of the rail carriage. Stevens went from the making of arms and tools to the building of automobiles. White added automobiles to sewing machines to make a

Another view of a great assembling department.

bigger concern. The Stanleys jumped from the making of dry plates to the building of cars, and the Peerless Company abandoned clothes wringers for motors. These are only a few who have heeded the call of the automobile and have helped to add to the greatness of the industry.

The description of a modern automobile factory alone would consume the space of a long article, for each is an army under a roof, where speed is a game for a great prize, and organization, machinery, and brains mean stacks of dollars that would dazzle Monte Cristo. There are executive officers, general officers, departments to make each part, annealing departments, assembling rooms for

One of the practical uses of the automobile. A Knox Truck.

An up-to-date rapid delivery of newspapers to the trains by Locomobile.

engine and chassis, painting departments, upholstering-departments, testing rooms, and inspection departments. A score of trades are welded into one in the making of a single machine. While the army is working the shop, the sales department is sending out scouts to pick the way. The publicity department is sending forth a covering fire of catalogues, advertisements and billboards, and arranging tests and races to show the durability, speed, and efficiency of the cars. When their preliminary campaign is over the output is ready to cover the country.

But by this time the minds of the general and the executive officers have evolved new plans and the army under the roof goes to work again to fill the demand of the season to come.

The growth of the business is shown by the success of some of the men who have gone into it. Henry Ford began the manufacture of automobiles in 1903. Now the concern which he started has to have a floor space of six acres for its manufacturing alone. Ransom Olds, who in 1896 built a car for his own use which was the "joke of Lansing, Michigan," has in ten years since that time organized two companies, each with a capital of

A 4-wheel driven electric wagon on a twenty-five per cent. grade, one of the most powerful trucks ever built.

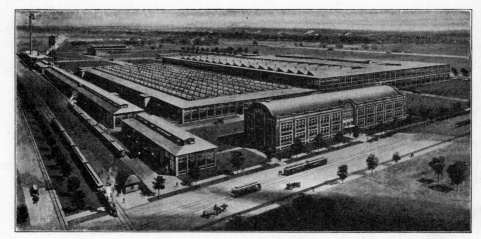

Factories of the George N. Pierce Company.

$1,000,000. The second of these has a six-acre factory to complete its output. The Maxwell-Briscoe Company, which was organized in 1903, has two factories, each of which employs 600 men, and one of which occupies 117,000 square feet of the town where it is built. George Pierce, who organized a company in 1901, has to have seven and one-half acres for his manufacturing plant, and the Thomas Company, which in 1905 produced 420 cars, in 1907 had almost tripled its production to 1,200 cars.

Col. Albert Pope, who came from bicycles to motor cars in 1895, now heads the company, which has six factories in as many different cities. The factory at Hartford, Conn., alone has a floor space of 400,000 square feet, and engines which have a total of 775-horse power.

A score of cities have become greater factors in the business world because of

The Pope Manufacturing Company plant in Toledo.

An American four-wheel driven gasoline truck, drawing thirteen tons in trailers.

automobiles. Cleveland, Syracuse, Hartford, Tarrytown, and Toledo are only a few. Ten important automobile companies have helped to make Detroit one of the great business centers of the West. They aggregate a capital of $5,200,000 and an annual output of more than $27,000,000. They furnish employment to 15,000 persons, which means an increase in population of at least 75,000, and the bringing to the city of other industries which have increased its population 25,000 more.

In hardly more than the space of ten years, from nothing but a desire to make speed, has grown an industry whose factories are measured by acres, whose output is reckoned in tens of millions, and whose employees and devotees make an army capable of carrying on several Spanish-American wars. Most of these dollars, acres, and men are used for the manufacture of a commodity which adds to the pleasure of the lives of its owners. The bicycle which rose in somewhat the same way had its fall because it could find no great place in the country's commercial life. The automobile, on the other hand, even if the time should ever come, which seems unlikely, when the demand for it as a pleasure vehicle is gone, still has a future before it greater than its past. The field of auto-

mobiles for commercial purposes has hardly been scratched. While many firms are manufacturing delivery wagons and trucks to the capacity of their plants, the possibilities for commercial vehicles have hardly begun to be exploited.

The horse, in spite of the romance that clings around "Black Beauty" and "Billy, the fire hero," is too slow and too expensive a means of locomotion to do the business of the world when one machine can do the work of "Billy," "Black Beauty," and several others better and quicker. "Black Beauty" very prettily noses into his master's pockets for sugar, but the sugar costs, so do the oats, and the groom, and the veterinary, and the horseshoer. A hard cold will reduce "Billy" to a simple figure in the profit and loss column. It is cheaper if less romantic to put in his place a car which does not eat, costs little for a physician and does ten times the work. The figures show that the demand for pleasure automobiles is increasing instead of diminishing, and to this industry which has been the mushroom among the industrial plants, is almost sure to be added a larger and even more healthy growth when the brains and energy are scattered over the fertile field which awaits the development of the commercial automobile.

A stretch of public highway near Michigan City, Ind. It would be wise to turn back if one could only turn around.

The Meaning of the Automobile
(1902)

THE MEANING OF THE AUTOMOBILE

By WILLIAM J. LAMPTON

"LIFE has not many better things than this," said Dr. Samuel Johnson a hundred and fifty years ago, as he took his ease riding along in an oldtime English postchaise. To those who did not live in the twentieth century and could not know the wonderful progress of the years since Johnson, a portly man of luxurious temperament, found such comfort in a postchaise, it might seem that the distinguished gentleman had reached the limit of vehicular development, yet in that same town of Lichfield lived Dr. Erasmus Darwin, a friend of Johnson's, who practised medicine, going about among his patients in a sulky, as many country physicians do to this day. Evidently, however, Dr. Darwin did not find his sulky such easy going as his friend Johnson found the postchaise, for his mind, between patients, was intent upon some better means of locomotion, and the dream of his life was a "fiery chariot" that might get about from place to place with speed and comfort under the propulsion of steam.

Newcomen and Watt and other engineers had made a practical application of steam power to stationary engines, but it had not yet ventured into the wider field waiting for it. Dr. Darwin, of Lichfield, Matthew Boulton, of Birmingham, and our own Benjamin Franklin, too busy then with the affairs of young America at the English capital to give the matter more than a passing notice, had discussed the subject of road carriages, but nothing definite came of it. A hundred years before, Sir Isaac Newton had included the mechanical propulsion of vehicles with his other fancies, but it had not extended beyond the great mind which had forged far ahead of its time. This was in England.

The first of all vehicles to go by its own power on land was invented in 1769 by Nicholas Joseph Cugnot, a French army officer, its primary object being for use as a gun carriage. At its first trial it developed a trait which has been transmitted to its descendants, if heredity may be considered in this connection, and ran away, butting into a stone fence and turning over. A second carriage was made, with some improvements, but it was not practicable, and it was retired, to become a curiosity, reposing at last in a Paris museum where it still attracts attention.

But the self-propelled carriage was a necessity to man's progress, and Cugnot was merely taking a little longer step in the great procession of those who never stand still. The world was developing fast through its rapidly growing population with their millions of needs and wants, and improved facilities for transportation were an insistent problem confronting every leader of mind and motion.

In all the earlier history of traction enginery England had first place, the urgent demand for more expeditious coal hauling from her great mines being the always unsatisfied complaint which permitted no rest to inventive minds. Her small area, bringing centres of population more closely together, broadened the demand, and passenger carriages were wanted as well as those for freight. Little advance was made, however, for two-thirds of a century after Cugnot's carriage had run its short course on the roads of France, but in 1830 Walter Hancock had manufactured a number of carriages and put them in operation, one, called the "Automaton"—another was called the "Autopsy"—having run for twenty weeks between Stratford, Paddington, and Islington, making a distance of 4,200 miles and carrying 12,761 passengers. There were other lines in contemplation, some even reaching out to cover the distances between continental capitals; but development was slow, for the vehicles were cumbersome, complicated, and expensive, and there was the ever-present prejudice which even twentieth century enterprise has not been wholly able to eradicate.

Roadways were, however, the most serious deterrent. Bad roads were the rule,

99

and each exception of a good one was held by every available legislation for the use of those who could afford to own horses and legislators. Under these circumstances the improvement of existing roads, or the building of roads for the especial use of mechanical carriages, became a co-study with the vehicles themselves, by those who were seeking a better way.

riages on the roads of that State. This, by the way, is the first automobile legislation in the Western Hemisphere. It may be added here that Oliver Evans, the first American automobilist, was born in Newport, a pretty Delaware town, near the Maryland line, and the automobilists of this country should make it one of the points of their tours, and in time a monu-

The Sort That May be Hired by Day or Month, with Man in Livery Included.

Wooden roads and stone roads were constructed, with more or less success, and at last the iron track of the present railway was evolved. This was the death blow to the road wagon as perfected by Hancock and others in England, and designed by Oliver Evans in America, who, as early as 1786, had secured from the Maryland legislature the right to operate his steam car-

ment should be erected there to his memory. But this is for the future.

The steam carriage had been brought to such a point of advancement that when a proper roadway was provided, it was short work to combine the two, and from the opening of the Baltimore and Ohio Railroad, on the 4th of July, 1828, the development of railroads in America and else-

A Popular Use of the Automobile; a Touring Stage of New York City.

was this true, her fine roads, free to all vehicles regardless of propulsion, being a powerful factor in the development of the machine. As early as 1888 the French manufacturers were turning out carriages for road service, but they lacked the proper tires until about 1890. They had taken advantage of all the modern improvements in machinery, and their carriages were free from most of the difficulties which handicapped their predecessors. We were somewhat slower in America, as we lacked the factor of good roads, and possessed such excellent railroad and trolley systems. We had very good horses, too, which we did not propose to surrender until we saw pretty clearly that we were going to have something considerably better in their stead.

where utterly overwhelmed the primal road locomotive, and it was scarcely heard of for half a century. The railways met all the requirements of the people, and the mud roads and turnpikes were given up to horse-propelled vehicles. But in time the railroads had reached most of the points to which they could be extended with profit, and the overflow of population and interests from these centres had created new demands for transportation beyond the ability of the horse to supply. Then came the trolley car, and about the same time the bicycle, with its pneumatic tire, that conqueror of rough roads and the real solution of the problem of self-propelled road wagons, and the long reposing ideas of Cugnot, and Boulton, and Darwin, and Evans were roused again into activity. Not fully awake in conservative England, but vigorously so in France and America, after sixty years of dormancy the automobile was to the fore again. Notably in France

But Yankee ingenuity and Yankee energy and enterprise do not wait on what others may do, and though they may pause to be sure they are right before they go ahead, it is not for long, and when they start they are not left in the ruck. About 1893 the first American machines made their appearance and the new movement in transportation began. It was an unknown business, however, with many possibilities of being no more than a "fad," and capital did not rush forward with the enthusiastic spirit of those who asked it to come. But it was moving in the right direction, and three or four years later the advance guard appeared. Not in force at first, but with the spirit of the pioneer that cannot be stopped by an obstacle. Six years of education were required, and in 1899 there were fifty automobiles—not generally called automobiles then, for it was difficult to decide upon a name for the newcomer, and the difficulty is not yet quite settled satisfactorily—in use in the United States. In 1902 the number had been increased to twelve thousand, an increase of over 4,000 per cent. in three years. France, which is the leading automobile country of the world at present, cannot make such a showing as this, and England is nowhere in sight. These twelve thousand machines, not all of American manufacture, may be said to represent a value of twelve millions of dollars, the present average price of an automobile being about one thousand dollars.

No official record of the number of manufacturers in America is made, but there are probably seventy-five establishments turning out machines for the trade, while there are many more small concerns which manufacture special machines on order. Forty-five firms are enrolled as members of the National Association of Automobile Manufacturers, the only organization of its kind in this country. The membership includes manufacturers in twelve States and four foreign makers. In addition to regular manufacturers there are numerous firms making parts of machines and supplies of all kinds. Millions of capital are invested and the annual output at present may be estimated at ten thousand machines valued at $10,000,000. This is largely guesswork, but it is known that up to March, 1902, one factory had turned out four thousand machines in all, and in June, one manufacturer refused to undertake the building of a machine for export because, although he was turning out twenty-three

The Plaything of the Wealthy; a Forty Horse-power French Motor Car.

One of the Lighter and Comparatively Inexpensive Road Type.

not be taken as any criterion of a business brought into being by a demand which will exist as long as man is capable of motion.

Six years ago there was no automobile literature in America, but at present a dozen publications thrive in the interests of the industry, while every newspaper of repute has its automobile department, hundreds of special articles are to be found in periodicals of general circulation, the advertisements of makers and dealers find places in almost every high class publication, and numerous books have come from the publishers.

machines a day, and had been doing so for some time, he was still six months behind with home orders. What is true of two may be assumed to be largely true of all, and from this some idea may be had of the enormous business that has grown up almost within a night. There is scarcely a firm that is not behind with orders, and very many state in their advertisements that they cannot accept orders for immediate delivery.

New companies are organizing every day, and although, except in St. Louis, there are no factories west of the Mississippi River, one is about ready to go into operation at Pueblo, Colorado, and one is under way at San Francisco. In every city of any size there is, at least, one automobile agency, and it is a poor town, indeed, to which the automobile is a stranger. The bulk of the manufacture is confined to the Eastern States, New York leading with about twenty factories at last reports, but Ohio, Michigan, and Wisconsin are producing machines which are doing record work in quality if not in quantity. Hundreds of companies have been formed, many of them mere stock jobbing schemes to catch the popular fancy, and a great deal of money has been lost to investors. But this is to be expected in a country as rich and reckless as ours, and can-

The phenomenal progress of the automobile as a perfected vehicle, after its rest of sixty years, is largely attributable to the great improvement in all kinds of mechanical appliances during those years, which made it possible to adapt machinery to the vehicles without the expenditure of time, labor, and money in constructing new devices and experimenting with them. Other forms of power had also arisen in the interval, and whereas the old makers found only steam available, the modern makers have been able to add to steam, which for certain purposes may always remain the best, electricity and gasoline, or similar by-products of petroleum. These three powers are now most in use and are about equally divided, each having its strength and its weakness, but the inventor, always on the alert, is combining alcohol with gasoline for something better than either, while all sorts of chemical combinations are receiving constant and careful study. In the opinion of the writer the final power, that which will secure the maximum of simplicity, safety, and strength with the minimum of cost, will be chemical—a combination whereby two component parts may be united, as water with calcium carbide, to produce the action when needed, without combustion.

Whatever the power, whatever the form of the road wagon to which it may be applied, it is a fact past all controversion that the automobile has made its final appearance as an experiment, and is now a demonstrated vehicle of transportation whose permanence is assured, and whose usefulness is practically limitless. As yet machines are too complicated and prices are too high for general adoption. The ratio of machines to population in the United

from $2,500 to $20,000—the record price, paid by a wealthy New Yorker, for a French machine—while the highest priced American machine is $5,000 and hundreds are in use which cost their owners from $650 to $800. A good horse and wagon may be had for $200, and the automobile must approximate this figure to become popular and give the horse some hope that at last he can quit hard work and live like a gentleman. That this may be done and still be profitable to makers is shown in the history of bicycle prices, and in the

Photograph by James Burton

As Seen on One Occasion at Newport ; Mrs. A. Ladenburg and John Jacob Astor in the Floral Parade.

States, 12,000 to 78,000,000, say, that is one to every 6,500 persons, does not at first glance appear promising, but when we consider that only three years ago the ratio was one to 1,500,000 persons, a very different aspect is presented; and it may be safely concluded that with such possibilities of demand, the automobile must, of necessity, grow to meet the measure of its greatness. American makers are quicker to see this opportunity than are their foreign rivals, as is proved by prices. Foreign machines are sold in this country at

further fact that one of the first American makers, with the popular idea in view, made machines to sell at from $400 to $600, and advanced his prices later because he could get whatever he asked, so enthusiastic were those who had caught the auto fever—and more people had it than could be relieved by manufacturers.

When Robert Dudgeon, fifty years ago, rode from his Long Island home to his New York office in his steam wagon, using two bushels of coal and a hogshead of water in transit, he probably imagined something

On the Track ; Mr. S. T. Davis in the Machine with Which He Made the World's Steam Record of 1 min. 12 sec.

of what may be seen on the streets of the big city to-day, for Robert was a pioneer with the great unexplored world rising on his sight. But he could scarcely have imagined the machine of to-day, or he would have improved his own sufficiently to have prevented the authorities from ruling it off the road as they did and turning it into the barn to rest and rust as an heirloom to his posterity. True the authorities are not yet all favorable, but it is not the machine to which they object so much as it is to the manner of the men who drive it. The insatiate thirst to go faster will not be quenched, and when the autoist gets out on the road he forgets himself as well as others, and the obedient but helpless machine is condemned for his offending. Time will in a measure prove the corrective to this, and as automobiles increase in number and use the novelty will wear off, and a saner speed will prevail, with only such occasional outbursts as are common to drivers of horses which thousands of years of use have not succeeded in suppressing. Accidents have happened and will continue to happen, as with locomotives, and steamboats, and horses, and

bicycles, and trolleys, and street cars, and to all forms of motion and rest—outside of the grave—but if we risk nothing we can have nothing, so the risk must remain as part of the price paid for possession.

But the automobile goes on. America leads the world in the number manufactured, France in the value. England is advancing, for the automobile is a liberalizer, and Germany is trying to repeal or modify her laws so that " Made in Germany " may appear on many automobiles as it now appears on many other articles of use and value. The distribution of the automobile is characterized by a universality never before known of any manufactured article at so early a stage of its existence, and there is scarcely a civilized country of the globe in which one or more automobiles may not be seen seeking the best roads and speeding along ahead of the horse. Every civilized ruler, King Edward, the Tsar, Emperor William, the Mikado, the president of France, sultans, ahkoonds, maharajahs, all, from Greenland's icy mountains to India's coral strand, have their automobiles, with one notable exception, the President of the

United States. Thus far it would seem that Mr. Roosevelt has reversed the established rule that two negatives make an affirmative, and, apparently believing that two affirmatives make a negative, has declined to combine his own strenuosity with that of the automobile lest dire disaster follow, to man and machine. The traveler may find an automobile to take him to the shadow of the Pyramids, a line of automobiles extends from Haifa to Jerusalem, they have crossed the Alps and the Cordilleras, they have tracked the sands of Sahara, they have rattled over the streets of three thousand years old Damascus, they have climbed the Chinese wall of obstruction, they have gone into regions of ice and sun, and they are following the equator and heading for the North Pole.

And what is the meaning of the automobile? Briefly it means that complete development of the entire country which without it could not be possible, for it will compel the building of good roads. No country can command its full strength until all its parts are easily accessible, and its people and their common interests are brought into the closest commercial and social union. We know what railroads have done in a general way for the ad-

vancement of nations, particularly this nation which has given right of way to more lines than all the rest of the world. What greater benefits may accrue from the automobile with good roads everywhere and speedy means of transportation within reach of each individual for himself and the products of his factory or farm, cannot thus early be estimated. The horse will not be entirely eliminated as a factor of industry, but his sphere will be circumscribed and the automobile will not only do what he attempted to do in the past, but it will do a millionfold more to meet the ever-increasing demands of a people growing daily in numbers and wealth and power. The millions of our rural population will be brought into closer relations with the towns and with neighbors, and the loneliness of farm life, which drives so many to the cities, with detriment to all, will no longer retard our agricultural growth, nor prevent a proper distribution of population for the national welfare.

That is the meaning of the automobile, and while the statement may be disputed now, it is made with the earnest belief that when to-day's men of fifty have rounded out their three score and ten years, it will be fully verified.

On the Road ; a Century Run on Long Island.

Good Roads
for the People
(1907)

GOOD ROADS FOR THE PEOPLE

BY W. PIERREPONT WHITE

EVERYONE is interested in the improvement of the ·highways, but the residents of the towns want to put the expense on the county, and the residents of the county want to put the expense on the state, and the residents of the state want to put the expense on the nation; but the nation uses its surplus for the improvement of the rivers and harbors, and so everyone commences all over again, trying to find someone who will stand the expense of road improvement. The men in the cities say that the man in the country should pay for the roads, and the man in the country says that those in the cities should aid in paying for the roads, and with much show of justice.

About twelve years ago a State treasury was first called upon to contribute aid to the country districts in maintaining their roads, on the ground that not a ton of freight comes to the cities which had not at some time passed over a country highway, and since the city consumer paid a tribute to the neglected condition of the country roads, therefore State aid was general aid to all. The streets within incorporated cities and villages are maintained entirely at the expense of the incorporated area, and it is barely thirty years ago that the cities and villages in this country began to improve their streets. Private corporations operating steam roads, trolley roads and steamships, owing to the tremendously increased volume of freight and passengers to be moved by them, have had to build and rebuild, investing more money in terminals, bridges and culverts, heavier iron, better ties, ballasting and the straightening of the roads; the work is still going on, and approved methods of only twenty years ago are all ready to be abandoned. *Our States and counties are rushing into*

highway improvement with the same lack of foresight, not profiting by the common experience of private corporations.

STATE AID

It is only about twelve or fifteen years since New Jersey adopted the proposition of State aid. This means that the State contributes from its revenues a certain amount of money for the improvement of the highways in any locality, on condition that plans as approved by the State Superintendent of Highways are complied with. An examination of the table printed with this article showing the wealth and mileage of your State, will show which States will make the fastest progress in highway development by granting State aid, and which States, while passing the necessary legislation, will find no response on the part of the local communities. "It's money makes the mare go," and there are many years of muddy roads ahead, unless more intelligent work is secured under stronger systems than those now in use, and efforts devoted to spending money almost entirely in securing better drainage

Table I on page 228 treats the highway question as though it were a State issue, and as if the States were responsible for the condition of the highways, when as a matter of fact, the present laws provide that the maintenance of the b.idges and highways shall be a county or a town charge. It shows that even the States with their vast millions of property, could not maintain their highways if they were called upon to spend much money upon them. There is no doubt but that $100 a mile spent upon each mile of highway in your State, would do wonders, but if you will multiply the total mileage of highways in your State by $100 a mile, then

109

Laying a Telford foundation for a hillside highway.

compare this figure with the amount of money that your State is raising for State purposes, and see how much this would increase your State tax, and then make it an annual expenditure, you will have some idea of what the proposition means. It will also show why the railroads are in need of such immense sums of money for the development of their properties.

GENERAL PLAN

No large amount of money should be provided by any town, county, State or the nation, until a general plan is laid out for a completed highway system. The first thing to do is find out the area of square miles to be opened up with highways. Next, the tonnage to be carried over the roads. Third, the population to be accommodated. Fourth, the miles and location of the main highways to be improved, and fifth, the amount of money to be expended annually in the improvement, which amount however raised and made payable, must not create a burdensome tax rate upon the people.

RULE FOR OPENING UP FARMING LANDS WITH HIGHWAYS

The rule established by the Federal Government for making farm lands accessible is, that it takes two miles of highway to open up one square mile of area. That is, in one square mile you have one mile of highway running north and south, and another mile of highway running east and west, the two crossing each other at right angles in the center of the area. This makes each farm 160 acres, and is known as a quarter section. If the country is all farm land, 100 square miles of tillable soil would, under the above plan, require 200 miles of highway to divide it into quarter sections, and make each farm accessible. This rule changes when you come into timber belts, sandy stretches and mountainous sections. Here one mile of highway to each square mile of area is ample development, and frequently a less mileage will do. While the highway mileage per square mile of area is less, the one road running through is of greater importance in carrying tonnage and people, because it is the only method of ingress and egress, through to more settled territory. For instance, New York State has in round numbers 50,000 square miles of area. If it were all farm lands, it would have 100,000 miles of highways. It actually has 74,000 miles of highways, from which the deduction is that one quarter of the State is undeveloped, and the report of the Fish, Forest and Game Commission, which says that one-fourth of the State is still in forest, bears out the correctness of the statement. The highways leading into the Adirondacks and the Catskill sections are called upon to carry an excessive tonnage of freight, and accommodate all the people because everything must go over the one road.

RULE FOR CITIES AND VILLAGES

As the density of the population increases, it requires more miles of highway to the square mile of area to accommodate the wants of the people. And as the miles of highway increase in each square mile of area it is because it becomes thickly settled and then the people lay out a village with

streets, and if the conditions warrant, it grows to a city. The rule in the city of New York after it had grown away from the Dutch village at the Battery, is that twenty blocks constitute a mile, which roughly speaking provides that streets shall cross each other at right angles every 264 feet. In the cities, the concentration of values is so great that few people are able to own more than one lot, with a frontage of from twenty to fifty feet to the lot. They are responsible for the care and maintenance of the paving and repaving in front of their particular property. This permits a city to pave and charge up to the property owners immensely expensive pavements of stone, wood or asphalt, or other suitable material, which, according to the width of the street costs from $20,000 to $50,000 a mile, and this without being particularly burdensome to the lot owner, because it is apportioned upon so many pieces of property and also made payable over a term of years. These conditions do not exist in the country, because in many places, a man owns from a quar-

A decent bit of road for the man in the lead.   An application of crude oil would lay the dust.

ter to a mile of property fronting on one or both sides of the road, and in many instances it is miles of highway that pass in front of one man's property.

PROFITABLE LENGTH OF HAUL OF FARM PRODUCTS

Railroad officials state that in a fairly level country such as Indiana or Ohio, a steam railroad will have sufficient freight to haul to make it a safe financial investment if it receives the freight produced from

macadam and establishing proper grades, each wagon, in place of carrying one ton, will be enabled to carry with the same team three or four tons in less time than the one ton was formerly carried the ten miles to market, and that, too, for the same price of $2.50 for the haul, thus reducing the cost to six cents or eight cents per ton per mile. The following table shows the cost of hauling product five miles, which gives readily to the eye the reason why a longer haul than five miles is not profitable unless

An unimproved highway in Clinton County, Pa.

the farms for a distance of five miles on either side of the steam road, and the road is long enough. In other words, steam roads in rich agricultural sections are profitable investments if located ten miles apart, and will not disastrously interfere with the business of each other in securing local freights. The cost of transportation on dirt roads is figured at $2.50 for the hauling of one ton ten miles, or a cost of twenty-five cents per ton per mile, and by improving the highways with gravel or

the product hauled is of a greater than ordinary value to the usual product carried.

$1.25 will haul a ton	Cost per Mile
5 miles on a common road.	.25
12½ to 15 miles on a well made stone road.	.12
25 miles on a trolley road.	.05
250 miles on a steam railway.	.005
1,000 miles on a steamship.	.00012

It can be mathematically demonstrated and actually shown to the eye by the use of highway maps that the improvement of from 8 per cent. to 16 per cent. of the total highway mileage of a State, being the main highways which follow the natural valleys or are arbitrarily established in level sections, will, when improved, leave no farm further away than five miles from the main highways. Therefore, the improvement of a comparatively small percentage of the total mileage is of a certain and positive value to the entire agricultural interests of the State, and it is proper that these roads should be built and maintained at State expense, as rapidly as may be permitted without

incorporated cities and villages. In other words, the steam and trolley development following the main valleys and thoroughfares through the mountain passes, and connecting the centers of population as shown by our railroad maps of the United States, have done so by the improvement of practically a little less than one mile of steam and trolley road to each thirteen and two-thirds square miles of area. Table II on page 228 will illustrate this.

It has taken nearly eighty years to build

In Crawford County, Pa., after the State Highway Department has been at work.

the creation of a burdensome tax rate upon the people.

TIME IN WHICH TO COMPLETE

There are 2,728,780 square miles of area in the States admitted to the Union, and the agricultural department estimates that this area has 2,745,392 miles of public highways, or an average of one mile of highway to each square mile of area. The same area had in 1905, 199,704 miles of railroad, and 6,816 miles of trolley roads outside of

and develop this system of steam roads. It has taken millions of capital. It has created in that eighty years the best railroad engineers in the world, and in the same period, the burial of the mistakes of these engineers has been enormous. Traffic has doubled and increased so that bridges, trestles and culverts have been abandoned, built and rebuilt again, iron rails converted to steel, and steel rails increased in their carrying capacity more than 100 per cent. Grades have been reduced and curves

Farmington Road, in Connecticut, treated with a coal tar preparation to prevent formation of dust.

straightened. Engines and cars, both freight and passenger have been hurled into the scrap heap at an enormous loss, and yet the ever increasing earning power of the road as tonnage has increased, has permitted the continued increase of the capitalization and the obtaining from the people of additional money to develop and improve the facilities in carrying of freight and transportation as offered to the public. And still at this moment, greater accommodations, and greater carrying capacity is required and additional funds for its creation needed. Looking, therefore, at the millions of money, and the time required for the development of our steam road system, it would seem that starting now, we are approaching a distinctively historical era in improved road building. And this improvement, using the greatest intelligence of each State, and all of the energy and force of the respective sections of the country, can not have the total mileage now in existence (estimated at 2,745,392 miles) completed in less than one hundred years of deliberate, well planned and effective work.

The completion in the respective parts of the country of 6,000 miles a year, not of cheap but of expensive and durable highways, improving the main highways only, would take fifty years to complete and this would be barely more than 10 per cent. of the present total mileage of the States.

MAINTENANCE

Not one cent of money should be expended in the creation of these expensive highways unless, at the same time, a system of careful maintenance and repair is established. Steam roads when first built were permitted to run down, ties to rot, the ends of the iron rails to flatten, bolts in the fish plates to become loose, until a general overhauling was ordered, and an excessively expensive amount of repairs were made, owing to the neglect. To-day well managed roads do not permit this. But each road is divided into sections under engineers, under assistant engineers, under section bosses, with men passing daily up and down the road, giving it constant repair and attention. This we are familiar with. In Europe highways are patrolled in the same way. Men, usually old, patrol the roads under their care, each in charge of a section, each responsible for its condition, and the slightest hole in the wearing surface is detected, repaired and filled in immediately after it commences. Ruts are detected and filled, sluices and ditches kept open, the washing of the sides stopped, and only by this constant care, are roads kept in good condition. This same system must come to this country and be inaugurated at the time that the general improvement is made, otherwise the people's money will be thrown away.

COST

No one can tell what a highway will cost per mile for its improvement, without knowing the actual conditions. The first element is grade, for the nearest grade to a level secures the carrying of the largest tonnage, with the least power, making the cheapest hauling cost. The second element of cost is drainage. The third is the obtaining of the necessary material for construction. The fourth is labor. Railroads that are built and bonded for $30,000 a mile are considered cheap. Some miles cost $125,000 a mile and are cut in solid rock. Stone or macadam roads that are built at an average cost of $10,000 a mile are considered expensive. But every stone road, or road with a hard surface is built for the express purpose of gathering freight from the agricultural products on either side of the highway. And it must be built strongly, because if the road is fifty miles long and receives the freight from a five mile area on either side, it would receive freight from 500 square miles of land. This makes a territory of 320,000 acres, and if one ton an acre should go to market, there would be 320,000 tons going over this highway to market each year. If as much as ten tons an acre should need to go to market, there would be 3,200,000 tons going in a year one way only. If the wagons carry a ton to a load, with a two-inch tire, the wear on the road is less than if the load is made five tons on a two-inch tire, and the road cut to pieces. All of these elements must be considered, because stone roads are for freight, and must be used with wisdom and wide tires.

THE AUTOMOBILE

Arrogant and insulting as some of the owners of automobiles are, still they do not represent the greater part of the class now interested in the running of motor cars. The development of the automobile will shortly bring about its adoption in the carrying of passengers between centers of population, just as the old stage coach was used. It will also be used as a single freight car, going from the cities and villages to take freight to the farm houses, delivering at the door, or being called to receive freight to go to one of the present shipping centers. No resident of a city unless he is on a trolley line, has the privilege of stepping off from the street car in front of his own door. Residents of other streets must walk to and from the cars. No manufacturer has the privilege of receiving freight in car load lots, unless his business warrants it, and he has room and sufficient business to have a switch put at his disposal. The conditions in a country of good roads, capable of carrying automobiles for the transportation of freight and passengers without excessive wearing, will provide the farmers with greater accommodations than the residents of the cities, because the individual automobile can carry its passengers or its freight directly to the point of destination or the source of its origin. The possibilities in the creating of values in the country are beyond conception, because the highways will be built and maintained at the expense of the State, the county or the nation, and the owner of the automobile will differ from the railroad corporation, whose chief expense is the maintenance of its own road bed, and right of way, in that the automobile owner will have his road bed provided for him at the expense of the public, and will only have to provide the vehicle needed.

BEST SOLUTION

Road legislators are running mad with the idea that State aid statutes with State supervision is the solution of the road question. A hundred years ago it was settled in Europe by Napoleon, and followed on the continent and in England, with the result that they have constructed and maintained roads for a century which are the envy of the world. The plan is simple. The main highways are set aside to be

TABLE I

Name of State	Number of miles of public highway, actual and estimated, 1905.	State assessed valuation of fiscal year 1904, or nearest prior year.	Showing in even thousands, amount of assessed valuation liable to taxation to maintain one mile of highway, if cared for by the State.
Nevada........	50,000	$28,391,252	$ 600
Utah.........	40,000	49,663,004	1,000
Wyoming......	45,000	46,696,939	1,000
Florida........	42,000	96,686,654	2,000
Montana.......	70,000	153,412,962	2,000
North Dakota...	70,000	117,204,485	2,000
South Dakota...	77,000	173,206,733	2,000
Oregon........	96,000	173,559,889	2,000
Nebraska......	125,000	294,779,244	2,000
Idaho.........	40,000	67,473,887	2,000
Arkansas......	53,000	249,779,108	4,000
Washington....	69,000	298,460,979	4,000
Kansas........	80,000	378,335,401	4,000
Texas.........	265,000	1,082,587,438	4,000
Mississippi.....	46,810	222,847,525	5,000
Louisiana......	48,000	301,215,222	6,000
South Carolina ..	30,570	204,405,879	6,000
Alabama.......	52,000	322,878,793	6,000
Iowa..........	100,257	641,832,582	6,000
Tennessee......	50,000	351,762,769	7,000
Virginia.......	50,000	423,842,680	8,000
North Carolina..	52,000	433,372,940	8,000
Colorado.......	50,000	465,000,000	9,000
West Virginia...	24,000	242,184,392	10,000
Minnesota......	83,000	870,502,653	10,000
Maine.........	33,000	352,228,897	11,000
Georgia........	46,712	504,647,947	11,000
Kentucky......	60,000	667,056,375	11,000
Illinois.........	101,040	1,083,050,979	11,000
California.....	125,000	1,550,511,761	11,000
Vermont.......	14,019	168,011,776	12,000
Missouri.......	89,946	1,242,842,125	14,000
Delaware......	5,000	76,000,000	15,000
New Hampshire.	13,500	220,624,307	16,000
Wisconsin.....	84,000	1,358,098,346	16,000
Michigan.......	80,000	1,578,100,000	20,000
Ohio..........	80,000	1,968,280,000	24,000
Indiana........	58,000	1,360,445,139	24,000
Maryland......	16,000	643,812,408	40,000
Pennsylvania...	99,224	4,166,330,404	42,000
Connecticut....	15,000	677,396,711	45,000
New Jersey.....	20,000	918,418,741	45,000
New York......	74,074	7,446,476,127	100,000
Massachusetts..	20,000	3,981,876,499	199,000
Rhode Island...	2,240	432,933,610	200,000
Total No. Miles.	2,745,392		

TABLE II

State	No. of miles of public highways. 1905	Area in square miles. 1905	No. of miles of railroad. 1904	No. miles trolley roads outside cities and villages. 1904
Rhode Island...	2,240	1,250	211	102
Delaware......	*5,000	2,050	335	31
New Hampshire	*13,500	9,305	1,261	86
Vermont......	14,019	9,565	1,058	44
Connecticut....	15,000	4,990	1,025	339
Maryland.....	16,000	12,210	1,423	194
New Jersey....	20,000	7,815	2,270	195
Massachusetts...	20,000	8,315	2,122	
West Virginia..	*24,000	24,780	2,700	60
South Carolina..	*30,570	30,570	3,151	25
Maine.........	*33,000	33,040	2,004	228
Idaho.........	*40,000	84,800	1,447	1
Utah.........	*40,000	84,970	1,664	10
Florida........	*42,000	58,680	3,468	12
Wyoming......	*45,000	97,890	1,240	
Georgia.......	46,712	59,475	6,228	100
Mississippi....	46,810	46,810	3,305	3
Louisiana......	*48,000	48,720	3,490	3
Colorado......	*50,000	103,925	4,885	21
Nevada.......	*50,000	110,700	955	
Tennessee.....	*50,000	42,050	3,337	100
Virginia......	*50,000	42,450	3,896	198
Alabama......	*52,000	52,250	4,486	86
North Carolina..	*52,000	52,250	4,071	19
Arkansas......	*53,000	53,850	3,814	2
Indiana........	58,000	36,350	6,830	278
Kentucky,....	*60,000	40,400	3,205	63
Washington....	*69,000	69,180	3,275	47
Montana......	*70,000	146,080	3,217	21
North Dakota..	*70,000	70,795	3,069	
New York....	74,074	50,000	8,242	690
South Dakota..	*77,000	77,650	3,014	
Kansas........	80,000	82,080	8,799	20
Michigan......	80,000	58,915	8,572	559
Ohio.........	80,000	41,060	9,040	1,278
Minnesota.....	*83,000	83,305	7,616	15
Wisconsin.....	*84,000	56,040	6,976	129
Missouri......	89,946	69,415	7,337	139
Oregon.......	*96,000	96,030	1,720	31
Pennsylvania..	99,224	45,215	10,705	1,114
Iowa.........	100,257	56,025	9,541	80
Illinois........	101,040	56,650	11,426	245
California.....	*125,000	158,360	6,099	162
Nebraska.....	*125,000	77,510	5,816	13
Texas........	*265,000	265,780	11,344	80
*Approximation	2,745,392	2,728,780	199,704	6,816

built and maintained from the national treasury. The next most important roads are set aside to be built and maintained by the next strongest department of the nation; that is the Canton. The lesser highways having the least traffic are naturally left to be built and maintained by the towns.

It is doubtful if there will ever be national roads in this country. If you put the discussion of this question to one side, you then have the road issue put squarely in front of each State to solve for itself as follows:

First.—State roads to be built and maintained by the State, being the main highways only.

Second.—The next most important roads to be built and maintained by the counties.

Third.—The remaining roads to be built and maintained by the towns.

In those States having no town government, the county roads should be classed into first and second class roads, and cared for accordingly.

The above plan does not cause a conflict between State, county and town officials over the inspection and acceptance of the roads during their construction and maintenance. It leaves each department of the government to build and accept its own roads without a partnership interest, and exposes the highway work to the keenest kind of competition in its construction and maintenance, in the desire of one department to obtain more and better roads for an equivalent outlay than the other two. It is simply effective; it is practical, and it has been proven successful on the continent.

The Packard Carriage Single Cylinder Motor (1901)

The Packard Carriage Single Cylinder Motor

By HUGH DOLNAR

M R. J. W. PACKARD, of Ohio, feeling a desire to enter the ranks of practical automobile users, and taking a favorable view of the Benz single cylinder driven system once endeavored to place an order with makers willing to incorporate some of Mr. Packard's own ideas with their own practice. This proposition met with no favor from automobile makers, who naturally thought their own established types were good enough for all practical purposes, without suggestions from outsiders, and they advised Mr. Packard to build a carriage himself if he could not be suited with what was to be had in the market. After a few rebuffs of this sort, Mr. Packard picked up the gauntlet, and proceeded to construct a heavy wagon with a single cylinder motor, which now, having been under construction little more than a year, and there having been produced for sale but few more than a hundred vehicles all told, has yet gained for itself a most enviable reputation, all of its users without exception being its staunch friends, many of them not hesitating to assert that the Packard is the very best single cylinder driven vehicle which has yet appeared anywhere.

Mr. Packard writes me that he is making extensive detail improvements in his carriage and is increasing his plant as fast as he can, and will soon be able to have wagons in stock he hopes, although at present he is much behind his cash orders. The Packard factory is at Warren, Ohio, U. S. A., and the New York office managed by the firm of Adams & McMurtry, is at 114 Fifth Avenue.

Since the circumstances in connection with the rapid rise of the Packard wagon into public favor give much interest to this new vehicle, I have prepared the following full description of its mechanical details. As I am aware that a detailed story of the experiences of Samuel Rushmore, a well known manufacturer of electrical work and acetylene searchlights in Jersey City, N. J., in driving a Packard wagon from New York to Buffalo, has been furnished to the AUTOMOBILE MAGAZINE, I feel sure that what I have to offer will be of interest to many readers.

At the outset, Mr. Packard fully understood and recognized the fact that the single cylinder driven motor must have weight, or mass,

far in excess of the demands of actual working strains, to take up the
violent thrust of the widely separated working strokes of the motor.
Whitney, originator of the present type of Stanley steam wagon,
represented by the Locomobile, Mobile, and in fact almost all American steam wagons, made his first wagon to weigh only 650 pounds ;
he gradually increased
his weights, leaving
his motor unchanged,
to about 1,000 or
1,100 pounds, and was
thoroughly satisfied
that this weight of
about 1,000 pounds
for a two‑passenger
wagon was the best
for American roads.

Oblique View of Packard

Stanley, quite to
the contrary, assumed
that every pound of
non-paying load which
could be spared should
be spared, and the
two-passenger wagons
which the Stanley
Brothers are now
building at Newton,
Mass., weigh only
about 500 pounds
empty. Both the
Whitney and Stanley
wagons had the same
type of motor, a pair
of small double acting steam cylinders, and hence gave what may be
called a constant torque on the driving shaft and wheels. With this
type of motor the only possible gain from mere added mass of the
wagon is in making it "stay down on the road better," as Whitney
phrased it. That is to say, weight makes the wagon bounce about
less on a rough road than it would if it was lighter. On smooth
roads, like those about Newton where Stanley Brothers drive all the
time, weight added after the wagon is heavy enough to carry its full

load is incontestibly a blunder, because it costs fuel to move every pound of the wagon weight, and added weight of wagon frame means added load to be carried by the axles and tires, which must be made larger and stronger and more costly, to meet the needless burdens imposed by needless weight.

With the single cylinder fired motor, all this is changed. The wagon must run by momentum, not impulse, three-fourths of the time, and in the working one-fourth of the time the motor must give out a comparatively enormous propelling impulse. Packard uses a cylinder 6 inches in diameter, and the "kick" which it gives a wagon when it works, cannot be absorbed by any weight of fly-wheel, which can be well used, but must go into the mass of the whole fabric, which must be heavy enough to absorb the violent shock at slow speeds to avoid giving great discomfort to the riders.

Plan View of Packard

Packard's weight of 2,005 pounds for an empty two-passenger wagon having 36 circular inches of motor piston area, is not a pound too heavy for the comfort of the passengers.

The general scheme of the Packard is to provide a very substantial tubular running gear, the two reach members being connected to both front and rear axles by globe joints, as fully shown in detail engravings. This tubular frame takes the springs, and the springs carry an angle iron frame of ample strength to which all of the running motor parts are secured, thus giving a reliable motor support. The body is carried above the motor frame, and can be removed by taking out four screws, and uncoupling a few minor connections, almost the entire mechanism being carried on the angle iron frame. The plan and oblique views of the Packard with the body removed show the general arrangement of the principal parts very clearly. Lever steering was first used, but is now abandoned in favor of wheel, tangent screw and worm gear, as the wagon is altogether too heavy to be handled by lever steering. Radius rods are jointed to the running gear and the tops of the springs both lengthwise and crosswise to resist starting and stopping strains.

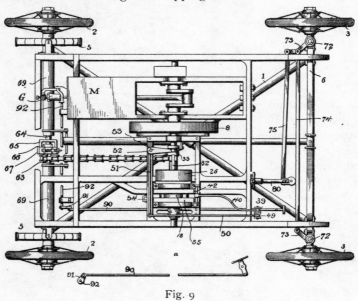

Fig. 9

The Packard Model C cylinder is 6 inches by 6½ inches. The wire spoke wheels have 4-inch pneumatic tires 34 inches diameter, front and rear alike. These tires are made by the Hartford-Diamond-Goodrich Company, weigh 34 pounds each and cost $36 each. The wheel gage is 56 inches. The wheel base was at first 75 inches, but is now changed to 84 inches.

The water jacket is of corrugated sheet copper. The expected compression, maximum, is 80 pounds, and the maximum motor speed is 850 revolutions per minute. The ignition is jump spark, with dry cell batteries, coil and trembler, the spark time of occurrence and the spark time duration being governor-controlled, as described later. The transmission gear is of the epicyclic spur gear order, Figs. 10 and 11. This gear is changed by the substantial hand lever in front, so as to give two forward speeds and a reverse, and also to handle the regular brake, which is a steel band lined with brass blocks. An emergency brake, possibly old, but new to me, is as follows : The rear wheel rims are recurved to the inside, thus forming an internal groove, and to this groove a lever hung brake shoe with a curved face is fitted. This brake is operated by a treadle on the footboard, with wire cable transmission both ways. and will check the wagon so long as the wheels can turn, no matter whether the motor transmission gear is or is not operative. This is highly important. No wagon or

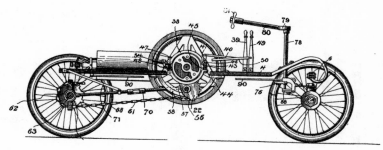

Fig. 10

bicycle should ever be used which is not provided with a brake of ample power in both directions always ready for use, no matter what else gives way. Going forward this emergency treadle has to be held to its work. Going backward the centers are so located that the brake is self-tightening and hence forms a most efficient "sprag" to prevent a down-hill backward runaway.

.The starting crank is applied at the right side of the wagon. Of course, with 6-inch piston and 80-pound compression, a compression release is required when cranking for a start. This release takes the form of a cock tapped into the cylinder and so located as to give only 1½ inches compression travel of piston, making easy starting possible with a hand crank only 7 or 8 inches long. The starting is very certain. The detail half-tone given, showing the cushion flap lifted, will give an idea of the arrangement of the compression release rocker and regulating devices.

This much will give the reader an understanding of the leading features of Packard's general arrangement of driving and controlling elements. The detail of this article and the number of illustrations accompanying make unnecessary a description of the Packard and Hatcher United States patents.

The Packard automobile is built under U. S. Patents No. 667,792, February 12, 1901. J. W. Packard, igniting device. This mechanism is designed to effect three distinct results : (1) To give the spark a constant time duration regardless of the revolutions per minute of the motor shaft; (2) to make the spark occur earlier as the motor runs faster, and (3) to stop the production of the spark altogether when the motor reaches a predetermined speed. Enough of the drawings with this patent are given in Figs. 1 and 2 to show the simple means by which the highly important ends sought are gained.

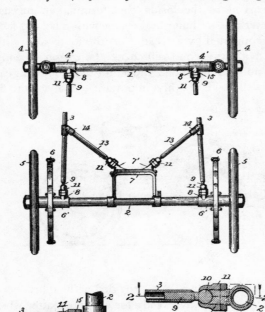

Fig. 5

The horizontal shaft 2 is driven rapidly from the motor shaft, top toward observer, and carries three elements : First, to right a governor of the simplest form, consisting of a pierced block, 9, pivoted to the shaft 2 by the screw 10, so as to swing on the shaft 2, by which this single governor element is pierced. This governor element is in practice made of a single rough grey iron casting, and is held when at rest top to extreme right, by means of a spring collar, 11a, to which one end of the spring 11 is hooked, the other end being hooked to the governing element 9, opposite side to a link eye integral with the governor element, from which eye a link, 8, extends to the left, where the link is pivoted to a cam, 7, splined to slide on the shaft 2. As the speed of shaft 2 increases, the governor element tends to assume a position at right angles to shaft 2, against the influence of the spring 11. The cam 7 carries one wedged shape cam toe, 5, the leaving side of the cam being parallel to the axis of shaft 2, and the meeting side of toe 5 being inclined to said axis so that as the cam is moved by the governor to the left the face of the cam becomes wider with reference to a fixed point.

Cam 7 has a hub extending to the left on which a sleeve, 31, is

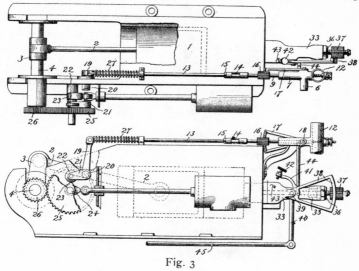

Fig. 3

adjustably secured by the screw 23. The right end of sleeve 31 is formed in a cone larger than the sleeve. The cam 5 operates a V-roller, 35, and the sleeve cone, 32, operates a V-roller, 34 ; lifting the roller 35 (see Fig. 2) makes a contact between the terminals 27, 28, and establishes the spark, which continues as long as the roller is held up by the wedge shaped cam toe face, 5, so that the faster the motor runs the larger the arc of cam revolution affecting the roller position, this resulting in a proper taper of the face of toe 5, giving equal times of spark duration for any speed of motor shaft revolution. When the cam and cylinder 31 are moved a sufficient distance to the left by the governor action the cone 32 lifts the roller 34, and deprives the terminal 27 of its electric current, so that no spark is made, hence no charge ignition takes place and the motor speed cannot be more augmented.

The correct reasoning as to essentials of wagon motor performance, and the extreme certainty, simplicity and cheapness of the mechanical elements employed to effect these motor performance essentials reflect the highest credit on their originator, and this spark regulation alone, if Mr. Packard had originated nothing else in wagon motors, would entitle his work to profound respect.

The spark is the chief faulty point in wagon motors as now made,

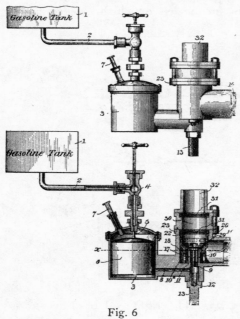

Fig. 6

and this equalization of spark duration time and the provision of elements by which the maximum speed of the motor may be adjustably fixed are highly important steps towards certainty of motor performance.

Packard's U. S. Patent 667,792 embodies nine claims, the first two as follows :

1. An igniting device for hydrocarbon engines comprising, in combination, a sparking circuit, a circuit-closer, a governor, and means, controlled by the governor, for causing the circuit-closer to produce a spark of constant duration at different speeds of the engine, for the purpose set forth.

2. An igniting device for hydrocarbon engines comprising, in combination, a sparking-circuit, a circuit-closer, a rotating shaft, a cam arranged to rotate with and slide on said shaft, said cam having an operative face constructed to control the circuit-closer so as to produce a spark of constant duration as the speed of the engine varies, a governor driven by the engine, and connections between said governor and said cam whereby the cam is moved longitudinally of the shaft as the speed increases or decreases, for the purpose set forth.

U. S. Patent 667,902, February 12, 1901, to W. A. Hatcher, speed regulator for explosive motors, is as follows :

See Figs. 3 and 4.   1 is the cylinder, 2 the rod, 3 the crank and 24 the second motion shaft of the motor, from which the variable stroke plunger 9, working in the fuel pump barrel 7, is made to deliver the liquid fuel in variable quantities to the mixing chamber 11, the virtual length of the screw-threaded pump plunger 9 being changed by means of the pinion 37 and the hand-operated toothed segment 38. From the mixer 11 the air and fuel charge goes to the motor cylinder through the valve 31, fixed in the cylinder head 30, this admission valve being operated by the piston suction against the influence of the

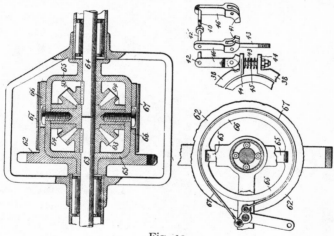

Fig. 12

spring 34, and the lift of the valve 31 being limited by the long pinion 37, threaded on the stem 32 of the valve 31, pinion 37 being operated by the hand-actuated toothed segment 38 so as to advance or retreat on the valve stem 32 and thus regulate the lift of the charge admission valve 31, and so vary the volume of the cylinder charge drawn from the mixing chamber 11 by the piston suction.   Connection is made between segments 17 and 37 so that their individual actions are made adjustably interdependent.

By these means Hatcher first measures an adjustably fixed bulk of liquid fuel into the mixing chamber, and next draws an adjustably fixed quantity of this mixture into the cylinder during the charging stroke.   This mechanism necessitates an unknown residue in the mixing chamber, and hence is not ideal.   It is, however, undoubtedly available for excellent average results, the result of fuel diminution or augmentation being merely spread over several strokes of the motor, instead of being clean cut for each individual motor charge.

The first three claims of this patent are as follows :

1. In a hydrocarbon engine for motor vehicles, the combination with a cylinder and mixing chamber, of a pump discharging into the mixing chamber and having a measuring chamber for the fluid, a valve for controlling the admission of mixture to the cylinder, a stop for limiting the movement of the valve, and means, controllable at will, for simultaneously varying the capacity of the pump measuring chamber and the position of said stop relative to its valve to vary the speed and power of the engine.

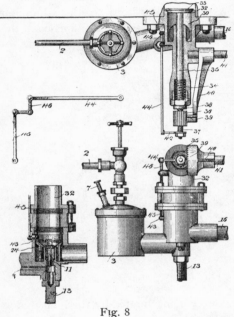

Fig. 8

2. In a hydrocarbon engine for motor vehicles, the combination with a cylinder and mixing chamber, of a pump discharging into the mixing chamber, a valve controlling the admission of mixture to the cylinder, a stop mounted on and movable longitudinally of the stem of said valve to regulate the extent of movement thereof, and means, controllable at will, for simultaneously varying the volume of the charge of fluid delivered by the pump to the mixing chamber and moving said stop longitudinally of the valve stem, whereby the amount of fluid admitted to the mixing chamber is properly proportioned to the amount of mixture admitted to the cylinder.

3. In a hydrocarbon engine for motor vehicles, the combination with a cylinder and mixer, of a pump discharging into the mixer and having a longitudinally extensible piston, a valve controlling the admission of mixture to the cylinder, a stop connected with the valve

for limiting its opening movement, and means, controllable at will, for simultaneously varying the length of the pump piston and adjusting said stop relatively to the valve, to vary the speed and power of the engine.

Patent 667,909, February 12, 1901, to Hatcher and Packard jointly, covers their flexible motor wagon frame, which is so clearly shown in Fig. 5 as to need no description. This patent carries five claims, of which the first is as follows :

1. In a motor vehicle frame, the combination of the front and rear axles, two reach bars extending from the front axle to the rear axle and connected to both axles by universal joints, and two diagonal braces each connected rigidly to an intermediate portion of a reach-bar at one end and connected by a universal joint to an intermediate portion of the rear axle at its other end.

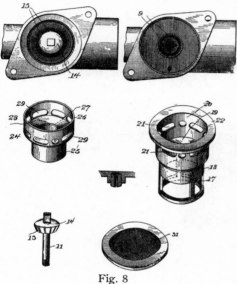

By this construction Hatcher and Packard secure a strong, substantial frame, which is a necessity for American roads, and also that perfect flexibility which is an imperative requisite where a wagon is to be used on uneven road surfaces.

The manner in which Hatcher and Packard attacked the carbureter ogre,

Fig. 8

which up to date devours all both great and small, is fully shown in Figs. 6, 7 and 8, illustrating the specifications of U. S. Patent 667,910, February 12, 1901, to Hatcher and Packard jointly. The specification says :

" The operation of the invention above described is as follows : The gasoline stands at the level of the line x just at the base of the openings 15, and the air valve normally stands in its closed position, cutting off all communication with the air inlet pipe, as shown in Fig. 2. At stated intervals suction is created in the pipe 32 in the usual manner, the effect of which is to draw into the mixing chamber a charge of gasoline, which is sprayed in through the openings 15, and to simultaneously raise the air valve and permit a charge of air to enter at the inner edge of the flange 28, the air and oil coming into intimate contact and being carried up into the mixer together. When the engine is taking light charges of the mixture, the air valve is raised but slightly and the openings 21 are not uncovered. When, however, the draft upon the mixture is stronger, the air valve is raised sufficiently to uncover more or less of the openings 21, so that air may enter through said openings, as well as through the central opening of flange 28. The air valve falls back to its seat and closes all of the air inlets after each charge of mixture is drawn into the cylinder. We have found an apparatus constructed as above to regulate automatically the charges of air and hydrocarbon in a very satisfactory manner."

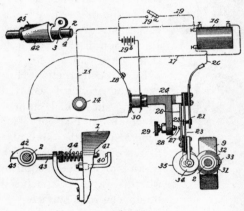

Fig. 2

The word "satisfactory" is well qualified in the last line of this quotation by the word "very." Experts well know that every carbureter must be manipulated by a wise driver to make it work under varying atmospheric conditions in a "very" satisfactory manner, and the readers of this magazine are also well aware that I, personally, expect the carbureter in all its forms, moods and tenses to wholly disappear in the final automobile ; indeed, I have the very strongest reasons for believing that the day is close at hand when it will be well known that the carbureter is a mistake from A to Ampersand.

The Hatcher-Packard carbureter embodies five claims :

The general arrangement of the driving elements of the Packard wagon is covered by U. S. Patent to Hatcher alone. This patent has five sheets of illustrations, which are partly reproduced in Figs. 9, 10, 11 and 12, which are so clear as to need no special text for experts in motor wagon construction. The specification says :

"The power shaft 7 is driven by a suitable motor M, preferably a hydro-carbon engine. Upon one end of the power shaft is a fly-wheel 8, and in line with the power shaft is a countershaft 9, the ends

of said shafts being close together.   Referring to Figs. 10, 14 and 15,
10 indicates a frame or spider, which is fast upon countershaft 9.   The
shaft and frame are supported, as shown, by the bearing 11.   The
spider 10 has a series of lugs 12, which are integral with and in the
same circle with lugs 13 upon the fly-wheel 8.   Through the lugs 12
and 13 passes a circular rod 14, surrounded by spiral springs 15,
which springs keep the lugs 12 centrally located between lugs 13. The
arrangement of lugs and springs forms a yielding connection between

Packard Carriage with cushion flap turned up, showing compression reliei
rocker, carbureter, fuel regulation, electric switch push buttons, vertical
rock shaft, hand lever regulating searchlight, vertical gear controlling
lever and emergency brake treadle

the motor and the driving wheels, which prevents strains iñ the machinery due to suddenly starting the motor or applying the brakes
and also due to inequalities in the roadway.   To prevent undue strain
upon the springs 15, the fly-wheel is also provided with intermediate
fixed lugs 16, against which the lugs 12 abut when there is an extreme
strain upon the motor.

Turning freely on the countershaft 9 is a part 17, which is provided with a power transmitting gear 18, two internal gears 19 and

20, and a braking surface 21, all of which parts are either integral or securely fastened together. The driving gear 18 intermeshes with a gear 22, from which power is transmitted to the driving wheels through devices which will be hereinafter described.

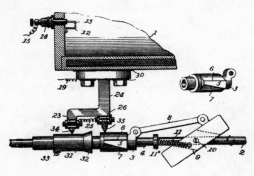

Fig 1

A slow backward movement is imparted to the driving gear by means of a gear 23, Figs. 10 and 11, which is keyed upon the shaft and intermediate gears 24, which mesh with the gears 23 and 20. The gears 24 are carried upon the studs 25 upon disk 26, which is free to revolve upon the shaft 9. Surrounding the disk 26 are brake shoes 27, which may be applied to stop the rotation of said disk, as will be hereinafter described. When the disk 26 is stopped, power is positively transmitted from the gear 23 through the gears 24 and 20 to the gears 18 and 22, giving the vehicle a backward movement.

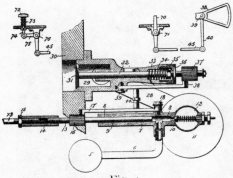

Fig. 4

Integral with the disk 26 is a flange 28, within which are shoes 29 of an expanding clutch, Fig. 13. As shown, the clutch shoes 29 are expanded by means of screws 30, arms 31, links 32, sliding collar 33, and means for moving

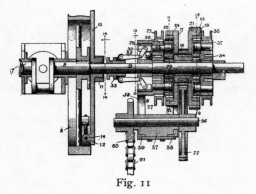

Fig. 11

the collar, which will be referred to hereinafter. When the clutch shoes 29 are rendered operative, the disk 26 and its pinions are carried around positively with the shaft 9 and the pinions 24 lock the gear 23 to the internal gear 20. The driving gear 18 is thus rotated with the speed of the driving shaft 7 and the countershaft 9, giving the vehicle a high speed forward.

A low speed forward is given to the vehicle by means of a gear 34, fixed on the shaft 9, and two pairs ot intermediate gears 35, Figs. 10 and 12, mounted on studs 36, which are carried by a disk 37, loose upon the shaft 9. The disk 37 may be held stationary by brake shoes 38 and when so held the integral gear 19 and the driving gear 18 will be slowly rotated forward, thus cutting down the speed and increasing pull upon the driving wheels for the purpose of climbing hills and overcoming other resistances.

This patent carries twelve specific claims, which need no quotation.

The introduction of the heavy coiled springs between the motor shafts and the transmission elements is an excellent feature. Such springs have long been used in heavy machinery drives between the motor shaft and the first driven element, and have always been found highly conducive to smooth running and long life of the parts. So far as I know, the present is the first example of such use of interposed springs in a motor wagon.

Touring in California
(1901)

Touring in California

By CHARLES FULLER GATES

AUTOMOBILE touring on the Pacific Coast is altogether a different matter from that of tooling about the East. There are, of course, bad roads east of the Rockies but none of the giddy mountain grades, unbridged rivers and wide sand "washes" that make touring with wagon, cycle or automobile a nightmare for hours out here, "where it is always afternoon." California roads have a way of losing themselves in great barley fields or coming out on the remains of a boom town and going no farther. Another un-novel occurrence is often met with along the Coast. A good road gradually deteriorates till it finally comes out on the beach and if it is high tide ends right there. To make this form of joke all the more comprehensive it may be said that some roads will drop from the top of the ocean bluffs with a 40 per cent. grade over a deep sand surface and then plunge into the soft beach sand nearly axle deep. Away off yonder there may be another of those nice little grades to gain a bluff again. Then one works all the afternoon to cover a half mile.

Still there are here and there bits of awfully good road. So much so that one wonders why it is thus. The writer lately returned from a six-day tour in company with E. B. Waterman, of Los Angeles, in a 9 H. P. Winton carriage that gave more pioneer auto touring experience than half a dozen trips from Chicago to Buffalo would do. As he was a pioneer in cycle touring and has traveled the roads between Buffalo and Chicago, when they were much worse than they are now, he speaks from experience. Here in this great State of California we have a number of veritable deserts, rivers that are bottom side up, mountains galore and a greater variety of roads and trails than can probably be found in an equal territory anywhere on earth.

Los Angeles is the metropolis of the southern part of the State, and this southland may in time be set apart as a State by itself. San Francisco is on a narrow peninsula, where touring means crossing the bay, 5 miles wide, and going 10 miles inland to begin real road riding or going down the peninsula, slowly feeling your way through freight yards and the workshop districts of the city for miles until the open country is reached below the glue factory on the narrow bay road.

137

When San José is reached at the south end of the great San Francisco Bay good roads are found, and in the heart of California the same conditions exist, but, with an automobile that will do touring work, distance is soon annihilated and mountains are reached.   North of San Francisco mountains shut in a third of the State, which is still heavily timbered and very thinly settled, outside of the mining country, which of course is quite mountainous.   Thus it will be seen that touring in California means Southern California as a rule.   This climate renders road riding almost equally desirable all the year.   The exception is in

Charles Fuller Gates (in Carriage) and E. B. Waterman After a Six-Day Tour on a 9 H. P. Winton

harvest time, August to October, when heavy hauling nearly destroys the roads.   The rains cease generally long before May and do not recur until October.   As the roads become drier and drier travel becomes heavier and that means parallel ruts sometimes 200 yards wide where the fields on each side of the public road are used by the four to ten-horse grain teams.   The hair of the cycler or chauffeur turns grey from prospecting ahead unless he is already blinded by the finely ground yellow or red dust.

It will be some time yet before California horses will accept the automobile with equanimity. In all the trips of the writer, with all forms of horseless carriages, from runabouts to big livery carriages, whether gasoline, steam or electric, the result was the same as soon as the city limits were left. Horses that paid no attention to bicycles would execute all sorts of foolish maneuvers at sight of the "mobes." Frequently it becomes necessary to unhitch them in order to get by, and even the big hauling teams buck and tangle up and refuse to pass the automobiles. It is, therefore, a sure sign of trouble to see any sort of horseflesh loom up on the horizon.

In one of the snapshot photographs sent with this article is seen a four-mule team trying to tie up in a knot. The engine was shut down and the carriage run to the edge of the road. It was too rough to run the machine off into the field as the locality was on a steep grade in Temescal Canyon, so the only recourse left was to spend a half hour helping the mule "skinner" persuade the team by. Fortunately Mr. Waterman thoroughly understood mules and horses, so these horseflesh incidents of our last long trip were not fatal on either side, although there were some narrow escapes.

Trying to Pass a Team—the Usual Occurrence

Relative to mountain grades—the five-hundred mile run from Los Angeles up to San Francisco means sometimes climbing as many as a dozen long grades in a day. Going south along the one hundred and fifty miles from Los Angeles to San Diégo we climbed five in one day, snailing along all the forenoon up toward the sky on the hill-climbing gear until we reached the summit, on the very backbone of a range ; we then coasted as fast as we dared to and in a half hour attacked another long grade, at the end of which we were confronted by yet another. The last time I was over these San Diego County grades they were hidden by the clouds and I experienced the novelty of wheeling for hours among the clouds, selecting the early morning hours for this purpose, in order to avoid teams. Fortunately we chose Sunday, and so got over the worst grades without meeting a team. This will be better understood when one realizes that for miles and miles the grade is only wide enough for one team and this narrow roadbed is cut out of the side of the mountain, dodging into the hollows and shooting "around the horn" in a way that fairly makes one dizzy if he looks either ahead or behind. Hundreds of feet below defiles the narrow gorge which is a canyon in summer and the narrow bed of a terrific torrent in winter. Above is the rugged mountain covered with scrub timber, and the road or trail leading steadily and steeply up or down, as the case may be.

" Railing " Through a " Sand-Wash "

In automobile touring out here in the land of sundown one thing is necessary above everything else, which is to have a machine able to climb 40 per cent. grades. If your carriage will not do that you must stay in the towns. Of those automobiles that have gone into the Yosemite Valley only two have come out with their own power. One was a little DeDion and the other a big steam carriage made on the original Stanley plan. There are wide valleys that form the beds of rivers part of the year when the waters pour out of the mountains from cloudbursts and sudden winter storms. These are known as "washes" and are really small deserts, some 10 miles wide. To cross these means plowing through sand, with wheels cutting a foot deep, unless a road surface of gravel or rotten rock has been built over them. With an ordinary electric carriage, especially with solid tires, one could never cross one of these "washes." With small power, steam or gasoline, and even with big pneumatic tires a "mobe" could not cross one of these wide "washes" unless pushed on both sides by the passengers, so it is evident that powerful engines are needed for touring here in California and also that the larger the diameter of the tires the better.

The straw roads present another obstacle, especially for steam carriages. At this time of the year the badly cut up roads are covered with straw, sometimes to a depth of nearly 3 feet. This straw packs down, but when newly laid, a steam carriage will get the straw tangled up in the chain if uncovered, and the gasoline flame is liable to set it on fire. While it is a crime to set a road on fire in most of the counties of this State, the immediate loss of a steam automobile

Distant View of a California Mission

would result more seriously to the unlucky chauffeur, if the deep straw reached the fire under the boiler.

Some of the rare sights in automobile touring in California are the old Catholic Mission ruins. These are about 40 miles apart and are scattered throughout nearly the length of the State. On a trip from the metropolis of the North to the metropolis of the South one can visit a dozen of them easily, or even more if short side trips are taken. Once there were small cities about each of these queer old churches and many of these ruins have been partly restored. Most of them cover over 50 acres. The best preserved missions are in Southern California, where the Landmarks Club has looked after them.

Flocks of sheep and herds of cattle must be encountered on California roads as well as frisky horses and mules. Near Pala Mission, on the way to San Diégo, while we were steering through the midst of one of these herds we saw a fight between two huge ugly bulls, one of which carried a barbed fence with him in his charge and soon whipped the other one—so soon, in fact, that a snap shot could not be taken of the thick of the fight.

On the Coast route up from San Diégo all one day was used in crossing a big ranch, and we passed but two houses during that time. This ranch, which is a Spanish grant, is about the size of Rhode Island, and midway across it we broke a front spring. The nearest village was fully 30 miles away with some wretched roads intervening. The day before we had broken the lower leaf of this same spring, so when we pitched into a big hole at the bottom of one of the little can-

Back Country of California : Wild Bulls Fighting at Ranch Line Fence

yons we were obliged to cross, the balance of the spring gave away. These canyons were about 50 feet deep with steep grades descending into them from the level of the table land through which they were cut, leading from the hills to the ocean near by. As the grade was frequently over 35 per cent. it was necessary to fly them. Old bicycle riders will understand what this means from experience.

Naturally, with a broken spring on a 1,600 pound automobile in the middle of the Los Flores Rancho, we were somewhat blue. But pounding on a few miles brought us in sight of the ranch house with its necessary blacksmith shop. By luck an old spring was found that could be made to work if a buffer was used. An odd piece of large sized hose was found, chopped up and wired in place after two hours'

work fitting the spring.   The blacksmith was off to the other side of
the ranch but we were glad to try our own hands at the job, meanwhile bribing the Chinese cook to get us a lunch.   All the crew were
away, part of whom we overtook that afternoon working a 38-horse
combined harvester and thresher.

Khaki suits are the best chauffeur clothing to wear out here and
in warm weather would be very satisfactory back East, I should think.
Here, where there is so much dust and the necessity of doing your
own repairing on the road, khaki seems the best of materials.

One of California's Landmarks

Our biggest mileage on this trip from Los Angeles to San Diégo
and return was 85 miles a day on two different days.   The last
day we made 60 miles in 4½ hours.   On a previous trip, made over
better roads, we covered 160 miles in 10 hours and 12 minutes running time.

The Endurance Test
(1901)

AUTOMOBILE MAGAZINE.

President Albert R. Shattuck, in his 12 horse-power Panhard, ready for start in Automobile Club of America Endurance Test
Vice-President J. Dunbar Wright was his guest

THE AUTOMOBILE MAGAZINE

VOL. III   OCTOBER, 1901   No. 10

The Endurance Test

THE 500-mile automobile endurance test held by the Automobile Club of America and scheduled to be from New York to Buffalo, was commenced Monday, September 9, at New York and finished Friday, September 13, at Rochester, the total distance traveled being 394 miles. The original plan was altered on account of the death of President Wiliam McKinley, Friday evening, September 13, the committee deciding to end the run then. As a result of the President's death the club also abandoned the week of automobile events which was to have been held at Buffalo, beginning, Monday, September 16, and which included the much looked forward to road race between Erie and Buffalo.

The committee having charge of this important and successful test was composed of William M. Power, chairman ; Winthrop E. Scarritt and Harlan W. Whipple ; S. M. Butler was secretary, and Walter H. Stearns was general manager for the outside part.

The result of the run represented about everything the committee had intended, it being, with its machine repairs, truly an endurance test. A ludicrous side of this feature was exemplified by the remark of a driver, that he considered the run an endurance test in every sense of the word, for so far as he was concerned he "had driven on his machine all day and worked under it all night." His experience was typical of many other machines, some being worked on, after reaching the evening control, way into the small hours of the night. This, however, was to be expected, for it would be impossible to have seventy or eighty vehicles go on any kind of a run lasting over a day without some needing overhauling to a more or less degree after the first one hundred miles.

Some vehicles needed only the ordinary examination, adjusting and oiling, such as would be given to any good, healthy machine. Those which needed more than this can in some cases be called unfortunate, for they met with accidents which brought about injuries that were in no way the fault of design or construction. It was quite surprising that so many vehicles stood the test so well, for the conditions attendant upon smooth and easy running were simply execrable.

William M. Power, Chairman of Endurance Test Committee

Even had the weather been pleasant the test would have been a severe one, for the roads were, to say the least, rough. Their surface was not only in this state, but their general contour was up and down hill to such an extent that all features of running, such as using brakes under various exigencies, gears for long and short spells and quick steering, continually occupied the whole attention of the driver. Added to these rigorous conditions, the weather contributed an extra handicap on the third and fourth days, or virtually between Albany and Syracuse. It was nothing but constant rain between these two points, the roads being a quagmire. Not only was much ordinary discomfiture added to drivers as a result of the down-pour, but steering and general manipulation of machines became so uncertain that a fairly straight course could not be kept. Machines veered from one side of the narrow roads to the other, and although in distance this did not mean a variance of over five or six feet, still at each extreme point the outside wheels were liable to quickly slide sideways three or four feet more, it all depending upon the slope of the road.

On certain parts of the route this skidding became a genuine menace, especially where the highway had been cut along the side of

"Red Devil" 12 Horse-Power Panhard
Harlan W. Whipple   Winthrop E. Scarritt   Jefferson Seligman   Loie J. Harris

a hill and the bank on one side was high enough and steep enough to cause an automobile to probably be wrecked should it slide off the road down the slope. There were plenty of such places and several machines did meet with this mishap, fortunately though in places where the slope was not excessively steep or long. One of these machines involuntarily backed straight down into the field, carrying away the insecure fence. Its hind wheels had skidded so much at this part that they slipped sideways off the comparatively level, though mushy, road and the front wheels being turned quickly toward the middle of the road, brought the total position at almost right angles to the road, with the hind wheels still slipping sideways and also downward. The brakes would not act with the wheels going backwards, and down the vehicle went fifty or sixty feet—a team of horses being necessary to get it on the road again. One who has only driven a carriage on an average country road cannot realize what it means when it is raining hard and the surface has been thoroughly softened by previous rains. It is perfectly safe to say that the majority of those who drove vehicles on this endurance run had their eyes opened as to what really adverse conditions are so far as muddy roads are concerned.

All the breakdowns, trying conditions and general misfortunes did the run good from a fraternal standpoint, and as predicted in the AUTOMOBILE MAGAZINE of last issue, the run was worth taking part in, merely from a goodfellowship standpoint if for nothing else. Some of the best known manufacturers and amateur automobilists undertook the journey, and more would have competed had they not wished to reserve their energies for the Erie-Buffalo road race which was to have been held the following week. Those who had set their hearts on this feature did not care to risk straining or breaking down their machines in a 500-mile run over rough country roads, and their decision not to do this was consistent with common sense, for no matter how good the machine was, it would have been sorely tried and more or less abused during that journey toward Buffalo. Among those who thus reserved themselves and their machines were Henri Fournier, Alexander Winton, Albert C. Bostwick, William K. Vanderbilt, Jr., and William N. Murray.

It would be easy to give a large list of many of the casualties that happened on the run, blaming this or that part of the machine's construction, etc., but such information would not be of material benefit to either the trade or user, simply because it is impossible to interpret the real cause of the break-downs. When a wheel or axle is broken it is difficult to say whether it was on account of faulty material or poor manipulation of the vehicle in running it against an object or in endeavoring to get out of an extra deep rut in the road. All that can be seen in such a case is the broken part, the driver alone knowing the circumstances, and in many cases he is not certain. If clutches fail to hold or brakes fail to act it is generally because the parts have either worn or stretched, as the case may be, the trouble being merely local.

Ignition was the usual bugbear, this being especially noticeable during the wet weather. This is such a deep subject that it would be idle to express any opinion on it without exhaustive handling. The machines the writer traveled on had comparatively no trouble in this regard. On one of these occasions F. Walsh, who drove the well-known Gasmobile entered by Albert T. Otto, found one of his three cylinders missing its spark just after leaving the morning control at Herkimer. He went several miles until, concluding the trouble had better be fixed, he gave the outside contact point a three-quarter

Riker 16 Horse-Power Gasoline Touring Car
Whitney Lyon   Jefferson Seligman   Robert Graves   Andrew L. Riker

turn with the pincers while the motor was running, and the missing cylinder sparked properly.

The delay in this case was only about a minute, most of the time being taken in lifting up the front seat and putting it back again, but an ordinary user in such trouble might have gone on until it would have been necessary to lay up and then the machine would have been condemned. Mr. Walsh said that he had not touched the contact point of this machine for some time previous to the Newport races.

When it is considered what little alteration was necessary to produce perfect ignition it would be unfair to claim that the machine was at fault, in case of an amateur driving a vehicle under similar conditions and being obliged to stop, through ignorance of the subject.   This incident tends to further prove that the modern high-class automobile is in the main satisfactory and can be relied upon if the driver is thoroughly cognizant of its workings.   It is needless to say that self-propelling vehicles, like other machines, will never do as much for one who does not understand them as for one who does.

In being afforded opportunities for seeing the workings of this endurance test between controls the writer is indebted to the following well known representatives of automobilism whom he had the pleasure of riding with : Louis R. Adams, President of the Long Island Automobile Club, De Dion-Bouton Brooklyn type Motorette; Cornelius J. Field, De Dion-Bouton New York type Motorette; Edgar Apperson, Haynes-Apperson; Alexander Fischer and F. Walsh, Gasmobiles.

The start from the Plaza, New York, was not only picturesque but also impressive.   Each vehicle of the eighty drawn up on either side of Fifty-eighth Street, and also in front of the Plaza Hotel, glided on as though a steely form of hitherto inert, impassive force were suddenly vivified into power, at the wave of the white gauntlet of Walter H. Stearns, the imposing master of ceremonies, accompanied by his clear, distinct word of command, '' Go !''—at fifteen seconds' intervals. A silent salute from the owner, with hand raised to hat, in half military precision, and alternating from opposite sides of the street in turn, each individual part of this glowing whole rounded the curve up Fifth Avenue, on past the deep rows of spectators with a systematic conduct that lent a touch of magic to this latter-day spectacle of the acme of science.

It was truly the best collection of vehicles ever witnessed in this country.   There have been expositions where many more were gathered together, but then the participants were inanimate, many of them only '' picture carriages '' displayed by firms to complete their exhibit. Here, however, congregated on this morning of September 9, were animate creatures instinct with mechanical life.   Some had been tried for the journey, but those which were not completed in time to allow their makers to test them on the road came to grief, more or less, though since in most of these cases the manufacturers expected it, and were not altogether surprised or disappointed.

At the start the Robinson touring carriage was conspicuous, being driven by J. R. Robinson, Jr., he and his three companions, partly on account of their numbers, making the most conspicuous show along the whole route. No matter what the weather was, they always seemed to preserve their equipoise, taking the trying conditions with a philosophical air that could not fail to cheer anyone speaking with them. During the rain they were all dressed alike in yellow oil-skins, and they and even their vehicle looked so symmetrical and generally shipshape on all occasions that the whole affair appeared like a pleas-

Robinson 16 Horse-Power Touring Car

ure tour for them. Added to this was the fact that their vehicle came through to Rochester in good shape, and although no official figures can be procured at this writing it is known that the vehicle's performance with its heavy load was far more regular than the majority, and was sufficient to place it in the front ranks for efficiency.

The club's president, Albert R. Shattuck, in his nickel trimmed

Panhard-Levassor, took along, as a guest, the club's third Vice-Presiden, J. Dunbar Wright. A mechanic was aboard who preferred sitting in front at the side to occupying the tonneau, which was covered with an oiled cloth. The riding is not only easier for one occupying even that position, but the machine went better, and it also permitted the rear part to be protected from water and mud. Mr. Shattuck's vehicle was unquestionably the handsomest on the run; and the way it proceeded at an even speed up and down hill, accentuated strongly the beauties of automobiling when the vehicle is good. The only time it disappointed its owner was near the top of Nelson's Hill, when two of the cylinders, according to Mr. Shattuck, acted strangely, and he then had to be towed up. He and Mr. Wright, as they went along over the roads, through the mud, passing and repassing different vehicles, looked as though they were at peace with the world so far as easy traveling was concerned. It was quite natural that Mr. Shattuck did not care to extol the good points of his machine too much, but his companion, who knows as much of that vehicle as the owner, felt freer to relate their experiences.

Mr. Wright said in substance: "I never appreciated what Mr. Shattuck's vehicle would do until this trip, although we have toured together in it for several thousand miles in France. It did not seem to make any difference when we left a control for we passed vehicle after vehicle before arriving at the next control, and Mr. Shattuck did not open her up at all. He simply took a gait that was consistent with the rough roads, and we went right along with no hitch whatever. The machine is equipped with a governor which, if used, will make the speed up an ordinary grade just the same as on a level. This is why we passed so many vehicles on hills, although we did not put ourselves out to do so. I am very glad to have had this experience on these roads, for although I have gone through such conditions before in America, still my vehicle was alone when doing so and I could not see how others were affected by it. Now I have seen how others fare."

Mr. Shattuck was one of the most active men during the trip and conferred with the committee continually. At Herkimer quite a mass meeting was held for the reception of the automobilists during the night control. A brass band of about forty pieces played in front of the hotels which harbored most of the contestants and which were almost opposite each other on the street, and Mayor Thomas addressed the assemblage on the subject of good roads and what the persevering automobilists were doing to encourage building them. Mr. Shattuck, on behalf of the club and all automobilists, answered very appropriately, his remarks attracting the concerted attention of the throng. Mr. Winthrop E. Scarritt was also called for on this occasion, and made some brief and pointed remarks on the growing industry and good roads that struck home as decisively as did the two previous speakers' words.

Returning to those who were at the start at the beginning of the run, one could hardly fail to notice J. W. Packard and George L.

Louis Adams in 8 Horse-Power Brooklyn Type De Dion Motorette

Weiss, head officers of the Ohio Automobile Company, who drove together in a 12 horse-power Packard. These two well-known authorities derived about as much enjoyment from all phases of the run as any team could. They seemed to have an ecouraging word for everyone, and even though their carriage met with the misfortune of losing a tire and they were thus forced to go many miles on the rim of the rear wheel, they took their accident as genuine mechanics do and made the best of their bad situation until it could be changed. They were usually near the front when coming into each control ; had a good vehicle and undoubtedly drove it well.   In fact, all of the Packards did well.

Three others who drove Packards, John M. Satterfield, Doctor Truman J. Martin and A. L. McMurtry, made an excellent collective showing, even though the first was handicapped by a broken rear axle, which placed him completely out of the test until a new one could be put on.   Doctor Martin, president of the Buffalo Automobile Club, and the driver of a noticeable 16 horse-power Packard, had his machine rigged as sort of an ambulance, but the fatalities happening to contestants were few and far between, and his services in

J. W. Packard and George L. Weiss in 12 Horse-Power Packard

this line were not needed to any extent.   He was, however, around at the different stopping places making himself generally agreeable, and he thoroughly enjoyed every part of the run.   During the rain he rigged the hind wheels of his vehicle in a clever way for the slippery roads ; the tires were covered with sole leather strips about two inches wide and about four or five inches apart.   These strips passed cross-wise over the tire and were fastened to two strips, which in turn were laced to the spokes near the rim.   It prevented his machine from skidding, to a great extent, and it did not wear out as so many of the hurriedly arranged ropes around the rim and tires of other vehicles, and which cut through in a short time, leaving whirling ends to be taken off when they grew too troublesome.

A. Ward Leonard started in a Knickerbocker car and at 58th street looked as though he expected nothing to interfere with his getting through safely, but before even reaching Yonkers he met with a serious mishap in the shape of a bent or broken axle, and had to abandon the run. Robert P. Scott, who drove a Gladiator voiturette of French make, also came to grief near where Mr. Leonard did, and was forced to discontinue.

Robert P. Scott in 3 Horse-Power Gladiator Voiturette

Andrew L. Riker started in his 16 horse-power gasoline touring car, with Mrs. Riker, Robert Graves and a mechanic as passengers. The machine had just been taken out of the shop, in fact its completion was so much in doubt that Mr. Riker did not know until the last day whether he would start. Many were of the opinion that he showed considerable courage to take the untried machine on such a long and hard journey, but the owner was not concerned much over the probable fate he would meet. The machine started from the Plaza with its handsome load of passengers and moved up Fifth Avenue, giving the general impression that there was nothing that could surpass it in ease of action and general style. Mr. Riker had not gone far before he saw that the machine's rear springs were altogether too light for the extra load of passengers and luggage. With the three people in front, the mechanic sitting on the floor, representing a weight of 560 pounds and Robert Graves and four dress suit cases occupying the tonneau, with other accessories of over 500 pounds, it can readily be seen that the total extra weight was considerable. New rear springs were put on at Albany, they having been telegraphed for and sent there; but

Mr. and Mrs. Andrew L. Riker leaving Plaza

later on, with the mud and rain, several bad short circuits were developed and Mr. Riker was forced to give up, the exact reason for his not being able to continue not being officially known. The plucky and determined way he tried to overcome adverse circumstances was remarked on by many, and the majority were hoping that he would be able to reach the destination.

The White steam machines proved to be surprises, especially to those who previously were not acquainted with their good points. Four of these vehicles started and all finished in good shape. Paul H. Deming, who with R. H. White acted as leader of their coterie, remarked to the writer that had the performances of their machines been different, he would have been surprised. Mr. Deming made his debut East with one of his machines last Spring in an Automobile Club of America run to Tuxedo, and hung close for the thirty miles to Cornelius J. Field's De Dion racer. Those who remember his performance then are not surprised at the good showing the White quartette made on this later test.

The Pierce machines, with their De Dion motors of small power,

Paul H. Deming in 6 Horse-Power White Steam Stanhope

were among the novelties on the run, they taking their two passengers apiece along, as well as did the majority of the heavier and more expensive vehicles. This make will undoubtedly be heard from in the development of the extreme light class of gasoline carriages, and for the price they are listed at there is no four-wheel vehicle that can beat them for general service.

The Haynes-Apperson's did not attract very much notice from a spectacular standpoint, but they were absolutely unbeaten in point of performance when lack of adjustment and lack of repairs are considered. The two Apperson brothers, Edgar and Elmer, came through with what might truthfully be called clean records. They easily maintained the desired speed, and their stops were hardly worthy of notice. One of their machines had a new steering knuckle put in, the break of the old one being foreseen by Edgar Apperson, who predicted to the writer that the steel casting would not last, but that the same pattern in a drop forging would do all that was required. It came out as he said. The Haynes-Apperson Surrey driven by Wm. H. Browning and carrying Mrs. Browning and one other passen-

Edgar Apperson in 8 Horse-Power Haynes-Apperson

ger, with the necessary luggage, did a performance proportionately as good as the two Stanhopes of the same make driven by the two above named experts: Mr. and Mrs. Browning went over the fearful roads and through rain in a style that showed they were fearless of the terrors of extreme jolting and constant splashing with mud and other corresponding inconveniences connected with a tour of this description. Mrs. Browning was the only woman who survived the journey, and she has made a name in adapting herself pleasantly to conditions that were enough to try the even tenor of masculinity.

E. B. Gallaher with his three Searchmonts had the misfortune of breaking an important joint in his steering apparatus close to the hub, which made his own machine useless until a new part was obtained. The break showed a clean fracture completely across the one inch and one-eighth steel. One of his other machines was forced to relinquish the run, and the one that kept on was fortunate enough to meet with no accident that required anything that could not be taken from the stock in hand. Like Mr. Riker's machine, these Searchmonts were absolutely untested, and thereby suffered. They are strongly built,

Elmer Apperson in 8½ Horse-Power Haynes-Apperson

good appearing vehicles, and with more development should have a different experience on the next tour.

Bradford B. McGregor, in his 12 horse-power Winton, took as his guest Albert C. Bostwick. Neither one went on the run further than Albany, Mr. McGregor returning to New York on account of business engagements, and Mr. Bostwick continuing on to Buffalo by train, where he had sent his 40 horse-power Winton racer for practice over the Erie-Buffalo course. Mr. McGregor and David Wolfe Bishop who drove a 30 horse-power Panhard had considerable quiet sport in racing during the two days up to Albany. There was enough of this feature to give the impression along the line that the endurance test was a race, but the bad effects of it were not lasting when it was seen at what a harmless speed most of the contestants traveled.   Mr. Mc-Gregor's machine at Albany was taken by Percy Owen, who continued with it until meeting with several bad accidents, chiefly caused by skidding, which put the machine out of business.   Mr. Owen's own machine had been driven up to Albany by H. L. Owesney, who came through to Rochester without the slightest mishap.   It was not the one originally entered and was only 8 horse-power.   Alexander

E. B. Gallaher in 12 Horse-Power Searchmont

Winton went on this machine during the first day and then left to go quickly to Buffalo to prepare for the road race there.   It had been his intention to drive his 40 horse-power car in the endurance test but it was lost by the railroad company during its shipment to New York city and did not arrive in time.

David Wolfe Bishop, on account of always arriving first at controls, received a great deal of advertising by the daily press along the route.   He did a good performance with his powerful machine, but he was armed *cap-a-pie* for the fray.   He not only took a mechanic alongside of him but he sent two mechanics ahead so that they were waiting at the controls for him, they being reinforced with a kit of tools which needed a box about 4 feet long and 3 feet wide to hold them. These two men went over the vehicle each night, adjusting it and putting it in the same shape each morning that the locomotives of the Empire State Express are generally in at the start of the journey. Mr. Bishop's elaborate preparation caused a rumor to easily gain credence that he had made some arrangement with the Panhard-Levassor Cie to represent them on the run, mostly on account of the two French mechanics who arrived in this country only a week before the start.

Colonel John Jacob Astor drove his Gasmobile to Albany with all

Bradford B. McGregor in 12 Horse-Power Winton

the zest which was necessary to land him at that control in the fourth position, he being headed only by Mr. Bishop, Mr. McGregor and Mr. Packard. The Colonel then discontinued the run, returning to his country place, letting his carriage be taken on by Alexander Fischer, who made a showing with it which reflected only credit to the owner, manufacturer and driver.

Cornelius J. Field was very much disappointed on account of his being unable to start his 15 horse-power DeDion Motorette, but like Mr. Riker's and Mr. Gallaher's machines it was completed only a day or two before the start, and he concluded not to risk running it. The illustration shows some of the vehicles he started, and they had more or less vicissitudes. This was bound to happen on a run of this nature where many different drivers had control. His Brooklyn type, which the writer rode in with Mr. Adams, although the latter was not a contestant, merely going along to get some experience, furnishes as nice riding as anyone could desire. This type of vehicle should be a most popular one. It is similar in general shape to the foreign Darracq, Renault, and the domestic Knickerbocker.

The two committeemen, Winthrop E. Scarritt and Harlan W. Whipple, started in the striking looking '' Red Devil,'' the Panhard, which at that time belonged to Mr. Whipple, but which has since been sold to A. L. McMurtry. Mr. Whipple's party went as far as Yonkers when, on account of breakdowns, he had to '' break up '' and come to Poughkeepsie by train. The committeemen then took turns in riding with different machines and arrived at Rochester, having passed through similar experiences to all. It was pleasant to have these two automobile enthusiasts at the controls, their presence lending an enjoyable atmosphere on all occasions.

At this writing no official figures can be procured regarding the result of the test, but the AUTOMOBILE MAGAZINE expects to lay before its readers full information on this part in the next issue. The following 41 vehicles arrived at Rochester in time for the control: C 55, C 23, A 47, B 5, C 24, B 80, B 12, B 78, B 70, C 31, B 35, B 13, B 86, A 11, B 4, B 28, C 2, B 32, C 77, B 14, C 79, A 37, A 72, A 8, C 1, C 30, B 34, B 81, C 65, A 82, A 75, A 63, A 38, C 56, C 18, C 59, B 27, B 22, B 20, B 39, C 61.

The De Dion-Bouton Group—J. Peck   Cornelius H. Tangemann   Kenneth A. Skinner   Leslie Rand   Cornelius J. Field

AUTOMOBILE CLUB OF AMERICA—ENDURANCE CONTEST.

New York to Rochester Sept. 9–13, 1901—List of Starters from New York.

*Entered but did not start.

Official Number.	Class, and General Description.	Name and Address of Manufacturer.	Entered by	Driven by	No. of Passengers, including Driver	Motive Power	Horse-Power.	Weight, including fuel supplies and equipment, Lbs.
1	C Touring Car	Robinson Motor Vehicle Co., Hyde Park, Mass.	J. R. Robinson, Jr.	J. R. Robinson, Jr.	4	G	16	2425
2	C Panhard Tonneau Body	Panhard-Levassor, Paris, France	A. R. Shattuck	A. R. Shattuck	2	G	12	2400
3	A Knickerbocker, No. 19	Ward-Leonard Electric Co., Bronxville, N. Y.	Ward-Leonard Electric Co.	A. Ward Leonard	3	G	5	700
4	B 2-Passenger Carriage	Haynes-Apperson Co., Kokomo, Ind.	Haynes-Apperson Co.	Edgar Apperson	2	G	8	1800
5	B 2-Passenger Carriage	Haynes-Apperson Co., Kokomo, Ind.	Haynes-Apperson Co.	Elmer Apperson	2	G	8½	1800
6*	D Motor Bicycle	Stratton Motor Bicycle Co., 7 Wall Street, N. Y.	Edmund F. Stratton	. . . .	1	G	1¾	78
7	A Runabout	Geo. N. Pierce Co., Buffalo, N.Y.	G. N. Pierce Co.	D. Ferguson	2	G	2¾	590
8	A Runabout	Geo. N. Pierce Co., Buffalo, N.Y.	G. N. Pierce Co.	P. P. Pierce	2	G	2¾	590
9	D Motor Bicycle	E. R. Thomas Motor Co., Buffalo, N.Y.	E. R. Thomas Motor Co.	G. W. Sherman	1	G	1	95
10	A Gladiator—Voiturette	Clement, Paris, France	R. P. Scott	R. P. Scott	2	G	3	750
11	A Runabout	White Sewing Machine Co., Cleveland, O.	White Sewing Machine Co.	R. H. White	2	S	6	995
12	B Stanhope	White Sewing Machine Co., Cleveland, O.	White Sewing Machine Co.	A. J. Southworth	2	S	6	1350
13	B Stanhope	White Sewing Machine Co., Cleveland, O.	White Sewing Machine Co.	Morris Hughs	2	S	6	1350
14	B Stanhope	White Sewing Machine Co., Cleveland, O.	White Sewing Machine Co.	Paul H. Deming	2	S	6	1350

166

No.	Class	Type	Maker / Entrant	Representative	Driver		Power	H.P.	Weight
15	B	Runabout	Overman Automobile Co., 81 Fulton St., N. Y.	Overman Automobile Co.	E. E. Degonin	2	S	6½	1200
16	B	Runabout	Overman Automobile Co., 81 Fulton St., N. Y.	Overman Automobile Co.	D. E. Rienhard	2	S	6½	1200
17	E	Light Delivery Wagon	Baldwin Motor Wagon Co., Providence, R. I.	Baldwin Motor Wagon Co.	L. F. N. Baldwin	2	S	7	2240
18	C	Phaeton	Holyoke Automobile Co., Holyoke, Mass.	C. R. Greuter	Chas. R. Greuter	2	G	9	3000
19	E	3-ton Steam Truck	American Bicycle Co., Toledo, O.	Am. Bicycle Co.	A. W. Doe	3	S	20	7000
20	B	Stanhope	American Bicycle Co., Toledo, O.	Am. Bicycle Co.	H. W. Curtis	2	S	6½	1550
21	B	Stanhope	American Bicycle Co., Toledo, O.	A. R. Townsend	H. H. Lytle	2	S	6½	1450
22	B	Semi-Racing Car	Winton Motor Carriage Co., Cleveland, O.	Alexander Dow	Alexander Dow	2	G	12	1700
23	C	Packard, Model "C"	Ohio Auto. Co., Warren, O.	Ohio Auto. Co.	J. W. Packard and George L. Weiss	2	G	12	2100
24	C	Packard, Model "C"	Ohio Automobile Co., Warren, O.	Ohio Auto. Co.	Wm. A. Hatcher	2	G	12	2100
25*	C	Racing Car	Winton Motor Carriage Co., Cleveland, O.	Albert C. Bostwick	....	2	G	40	2600
26	B	Semi-Racing Car	Winton Motor Carriage Co., Cleveland, O.	Bradford B. McGregor	Bradford B. McGregor	2	G	12	1600
27	B	Autocar	The Autocar Co., Ardmore, Pa.	Louis S. Clarke	Louis S. Clarke	2	G	8½	1100
28	B	4 Passenger Surrey	Lane Motor Vehicle Co., Poughkeepsie, N. Y.	Lane Motor Vehicle Co.	O. K. Raymond	2	S	9.99	1650
29	C	Phaeton	Automobile Co. of America, N. Y.	John H. Flagler	W. Owen	2	G	9	2100
30	C	Surrey	Automobile Co. of America, N. Y.	Sid. Dillon Ripley	F. Walsh	2	G	9	2100
31	C	Phaeton	Automobile Co. of America, N. Y.	Albert T. Otto	....	2	G	9	2100
32	B	Semi-Racing Car	Winton Motor Carriage Co., Cleveland, O.	Percy Owen	Percy Owen	2	G	12	1700
33	B	Phaeton	Winton Motor Carriage Co., Cleveland, O.	H. Rogers Winthrop	H. Rogers Winthrop	2	G	8	1700
34	B	Gasoline Carriage	St. Louis Motor Carriage Co., St. Louis, Mo.	St. Louis Motor Carriage Co.	John L. French	2	G	7	1400
35	B	Touring Wagon	Foster Automobile Mfg. Co., Rochester, N. Y.	Foster Automobile Mfg. Co.	S. D. Waldron	2	S	6	1400
36	A	Runabout	Locomobile Co. of America, N. Y.	Loco. Co. of Am.	J. W. Page	2	S	3½	999
37	A	Runabout	Locomobile Co. of America, N. Y.	Loco. Co. of Am.	—— Mitchell	2	S	3½	999
38	A	Runabout	Locomobile Co. of America, N. Y.	Loco. Co. of Am.	—— Knowles	2	S	3	999

Official Number.	Class, and General Description.	Name and Address of Manufacturer.	Entered by	Driven by	No. of Passengers, including Driver.	Motive Power.	Horse-power.	Weight, including fuel supplies and equipment, Lbs.
39	B Large Runabout No. 102	Locomobile Co. of America, N.Y.	Loco. Co. of Am.	Thos. W. Clarke	2	S	4½	1100
40	B Touring Carriage	Locomobile Co. of America, N.Y.	Loco. Co. of Am.	R. S. Davis	4	S	10	1700
41	B Touring Carriage	Locomobile Co. of America, N.Y.	Loco. Co. of Am.	W. F. Murphy	4	S	10	1700
42	E Quick Delivery	Locomobile Co. of America, N.Y.	Loco. Co. of Am.	Ashley	—	S	10	1700
43	B 4 Passenger Carriage	Haynes-Apperson Co., Kokomo, Ind.	Wm. H. Browning	Wm. H. Browning	3	G	8	1850
44	C Dos a dos	F. B. Stearns & Co., Cleveland, O.	Hy. K. Browning	Hv. K. Browning	4	G	—	2000
45*	A Open Stanhope	Grout Brotherss, Orange, Mass.	Grout Brothers	B. L. Wright	2	S		800
46*	C Mercedes	Daimler Mfg. Co., Cannstatt, Ger.	W.K.Vanderbilt,Jr	C.Arthur Benjamin	2	G	35	2400
47	A Open Runabout	Locomobile Co. of America, N.Y.	C.Arthur Benjamin	Wm. Morgan	2	S	3½	900
48	B Autocar	The Autocar Co., Ardmore, Pa.	Wm. Morgan		2	G	8	1050
49*	C Panhard	Panhard-Levassor, Paris	Dr. J. G. Lyman		2	G	12	2500
50	A Runabout	Geneva Automobile & Mfg. Co., Geneva, O.	Geneva Automobile & Mfg. Co.	W. K. Hadley	2	S	5	900
51	B Touring Car	Searchmont Motor Co., Philadelphia, Pa.	E. B. Gallaher	E. B. Gallaher	2	G	12	1500
52	B Touring Car	Searchmont Motor Co., Philadelphia, Pa.	E. B. Gallaher	L. P. Chadwick	2	G	12	1500
53	B Touring Car	Searchmont Motor Co., Philadelphia, Pa.	E. B. Gallaher	V. V. Torbensen	2	G	12	1500
54	B Runabout	Stearns Steam Carriage Co., Syracuse, N. Y.	Stearns Steam Carriage Co.	Henry L. Trebert	2	S	6	1300
55	C Panhard	Panhard-Levassor, Paris	D. Wolfe Bishop	D. Wolfe Bishop	2	G	30	2800
56	C Packard Model C	Ohio Automobile Co., Warren, O.	A. L. McMurtry	A. L. McMurtry	2	G	14	2400
57	B Touring Buggy	Milwaukee Automobile Co., Milwaukee, Wis.	Milwaukee Automobile Co.		2	S	2	1450
58	C Gasmobile	Automobile Co. of America, N.Y.	H. R. Taylor	H. R. Taylor	3	G	9	2500
59	B Gasmobile	Automobile Co. of America, N.Y.	John Jacob Astor	John Jacob Astor	2	G	12	2500

No.	Class	Name	Manufacturer	Agent	Driver	Seats	Fuel	H.P.	Price
60	C	Panhard	Panhard-Levassor, Paris	Harlan W. Whipple		4	G	12	2200
61	C	Packard Model C	Ohio Automobile Co., Warren, O.	John M. Satterfield	John M. Satterfield	2	G	12	2150
62*	A	Autocar	The Autocar Co., Ardmore, Pa.	H. B. Baruch, M.D.		2	G	6	900
63	A	Phaeton (3-Wheel)	Duryea Power Co., Reading, Pa.	Duryea Power Co.		2	G	8	900
64	D	Orient Motor Bicycle	Waltham Manufacturing Co., Waltham, Mass.	C. H. Metz	C. Metz	1	G	2¾	175
65	C	Surrey	Century Motor Vehicle Co., Syracuse, N. Y.	C. R. Woodin	C. R. Woodin	4	S	9	2100
66	A	Knickerbocker No. 20	Ward-Leonard Electric Co., Bronxville, N. Y.	Ward-Leonard Electric Co.	C. W. Wridgway	3	G	5	900
67	D	Indian Motor Bicycle	Hendee Manufacturing Co., Springfield, Mass.	Hendee Manufacturing Co.	Oscar Hedstrom	1	G	1¾	85
68	B	Gasoline Runabout	Electric Vehicle Co., N. Y.	Electric Vehicle Co.	E. H. Cox	2	G	4.5	1675
69	B	16 H.-P. Touring Car	Electric Vehicle Co., N. Y.	Electric Vehicle Co.	A. L. Riker	3	G	16	1950
70	B	Touring Wagon	Foster Automobile Mfg. Co., Rochester, N. Y.	Foster Auto Co.	Park Densmere	2	S	6	1400
71*	C	40 H.-P. Racing Car	Winton Motor Carriage Co., Cleveland, O.	Alex. Winton		2	G	40	2500
72	A	H. P. Motorette	De Dion-Bouton Motorette Co., Brooklyn, N. Y.	DeDion-Bouton Motorette Co.	J. Louvenez	2	G	5	900
73	A	H. P. Motorette	De Dion-Bouton Motorette Co., Brooklyn, N. Y.	DeDion-Bouton Motorette Co.		2	G	5	900
74	A	H. P. Moterette	De Dion-Bouton Motorette Co., Brooklyn, N. Y.	Kenneth A. Skinner	Ken. A. Sninner	2	G	8	880
75*	B	15 H.-P. Motorette	De Dion-Bouton Motorette Co., Brooklyn, N. Y.	C. J. Field		4	G	15	1500
76	B	Stanhope	Steam Vehicle Co. of America, N. Y.	L. Schermerhorn	I. D. Lengel	2	S	6	1200
77	C	Phaeton	Automobile Co. of America, N. Y.	Alex. Fischer	Alex. Fischer	2	G	9	2100
78	B	Columbia Runabout	Electric Vehicle Co., N. Y.	J. Seligman	H. P. Maxim, Jr.	3	G	4½	1700
79	C	Packard	Ohio Automobile Co., Warren, O.	T. J. Martin	T. J. Martin, M.D.	3	G	16	2800
80	B	Columbia Runabout	Electric Vehicle Co., N. Y.	G. B. Pettingill	Geo. B. Pettingill	2	G	4½	1640
81	B	Stanhope	U. S. Long Distance Auto. Co.	F. E. Lewis, 2d	F. E. Lewis, 2d	2	G	7	1500
82	A	Runabout (3-wheeled)	Knox Auto. Co.	Knox Auto Co.	F. H. Fowler	2	G	4	700
85	B	Voiturette	Darracq et Cie.	J. Peck	J. Peck	2	G	6	1020
86	B	Hydrocar	American Bicycle Co., Toledo, O.	M. H. Winters	M. H. Winters	2	G	—	1780
87	D	Regas Motor Cycle	Regas Vehicle Co., Rochester, N. Y.	J. H. Sager	J. H. Sager	1	G	1½	110
88	D	Regas	Regas Vehicle Co., Rochester, N. Y.	George D. Green	George D. Green	1	G	2¾	160
89	D	Regas Motor Cycle	Regas Vehicle Co., Rochester, N. Y.	J. H. Sager	W. L. Stoneburn	1	G	1½	110

The hill-climbing contest on Nelson Hill was the only part of the whole route where the management was not up to standard, the trouble being that too many vehicles were allowed on the hill at one time. The total distance of this control, which was timed separately, was 2,914 feet, the main slope between surveyed points being 2,372 feet. The extra 542 feet was prefixed to the slope so as to give vehicles a distance on which to gather momentum. The total rise in the 2,372 feet was 226 feet, which showed a little over 10

Mr. and Mrs. Wm. H. Browning in 8 Horse-Power Haynes-Apperson Surrey

per cent. grade. Parts of the incline were 5 and 6 per cent. steeper than this. The surface of the hill had been greatly improved over the way it has been for years. All the loose stones and also much of the loose sandy surface had been taken off. The artificially made ridges, generally known as "thank-you-ma'ams," had not been touched, but they did not hinder the ascent of any vehicle, except those that were unfortunate enough to slow up just as the crest of one of these miniature extra hills had to be taken. These parts would have given much trouble to vehicles descending this slope at speed on account of the abrubt side facing them, but any vehicle could have taken them the reverse, or uphill way, at even more speed than most of them did, on account of the ascent presenting the easy side of these "thank-you-ma'ams."

Although this was termed a "hill-climbing contest," it would have been a little more appropriate to have called it an obstacle race with an extra handicap of being run uphill. The slope itself was enough of a barrier to give drivers considerable apprehension as to getting through safely, but the stalled vehicles made greater obstacles.

The mix-up of carriages on the hill was caused by the attendants not signaling properly with the flags that divided the course into seven blocks. On account of the hill not being straight these blocks were necessary to show the managers at the bottom when the course was clear far enough ahead to justify allowing a vehicle to start. The signal men at the intermediate portions had red and white flags accordingly, but they were either inexperienced at using them or else they misunderstood or could not see the upper flag signals. They were supposed to take their signals from the top of the hill, causing the signs to be worked down toward the foot. It was done in this way. If at the top the course were ready, the first block from the top displayed a white flag, which was in sight of the one who held the signal for the second block, this latter being in sight of the one who signaled for the third block, and so on down, the blocks being divided according to the curves of the road and the large overshadowing trees, which made it difficult to see for much distance, even if the road were straight. It can readily be seen that by the time the seventh block received the signal down the line from the first block, many seconds would elapse. If a vehicle became stalled half-way up, the signalman of the block just below it was forced to use his own judgment concerning whether the vehicle constituted an obstruction great enough to justify showing a red flag.

Most of these signalmen were natives of the adjacent rural country, and they either did not know how or they were in no position to use any brains in doing their duty, for it was but a little while before their services were almost useless. The vehicles that started later had about as much chance in getting through without being impeded whether or not signals were displayed, for those having the flags in charge became so confused with the quickly changing orders and signs that there was no concert in their actions. There were times when the second block displayed a red flag, meaning that a stoppage had occurred there, when several blocks below there was a stoppage of three or four vehicles, which precluded all possibility of anyone getting by ; then the second block stoppage would be cleared and the white flag would again appear, but no vehicles came up, simply because they could not get around the stalled ones. The fifth and sixth blocks, the ones below the bad stoppage, were also blocked on account of the displayed red flags stopping vehicles which had already started on the incline.

To make matters worse, it may be mentioned that brakes in some cases proved to be unreliable in preventing the vehicles from running backward down the hill when the power was insufficient to make them go forward. Very few vehicles were equipped with a pick, a pointed piece of iron trailing behind, which takes hold on the ground, when the vehicle starts to go backward. In many cases, bystanders helped contestants by wedging stones under the rear wheels, and there were plenty who jumped from their carriages and did all necessary pushing to get over the worst spots. It is safe to say that all carriages that consumed more than 7 minutes in getting up, had troubles of one kind or another, lack of power, failure of the clutches to hold, or too heavy a load.

To sum the situation up briefly, it may be said that the hill was alternately clear and completely blocked five or six times, and the vehicles that happened to get a clear road, or not be sufficiently impeded to interfere materially with their time, should be called lucky. The only proper way to manage a contest of this kind where the course is crooked and narrow is to have only one vehicle on it at a time. This would mean the consuming of a great deal of time, but it is the only correct way. As it was, when starting vehicles as often as possible, consistent with signals, there was in some cases considerable delay at the start, an instance of this being the time the winner of Class A was forced to wait, which was about half an hour. If the course had been given up alone to each vehicle and they averaged five minutes apiece from start to finish, including signaling back from the top for the next one to come on, this contest would have taken about four hours to finish for forty-seven vehicles competed.

The method of timing this contest was the same as that used in timing between controls, viz.: Records of the time when the vehicle started and finished were made and the difference between them was the actual time consumed in negotiating the journey. The vehicles

commenced arriving at the hill control a little after noon, the first at
the scene being President Albert R. Shattuck in his stunning looking
Panhard. There was some delay at the start, not so much though as
happened afterwards during the middle part of the contest on account
of blockades on the hill. Mr. Shattuck started with his pick dropped
behind and took the first part of the grade steadily. He went over
several bumps in a matter-of-fact way and everything seemed to be

Henry K. Browning in Stearns Gasoline Dos-a-dos

doing well until he struck some of the lighter grades above, when he
stopped on account of a derangement in the working of two of his four
cylinders. He subsequently had to be towed up. Next to him came
Charles G. Wridgway, in a Knickerbocker, but it became stalled at
the first steep grade and badly impeded a steam vehicle. The fourth
was A. L. McMurtry's Packard, which took the whole grade in good
shape, going around the several stalled vehicles easily, they not making
enough of an obstacle to cause trouble. Then came the steam surrey

of the Lane Motor Vehicle Company, closely followed by the winner of Class A, the Grout Brothers' Steam Stanhope. Then came several of the White Steam Stanhopes, and in a few minutes the hill was alive with contestants.

It can readily be seen that a stoppage or even a slight slowing down of the leaders on such a narrow road would be apt to end in complete stoppage of those following. It would be impossible to determine the merits of all claims of interference in this contest, they being so numerous that it would be useless to try to find witnesses who knew enough about the subject to determine which vehicles were absolutely retarded through no fault of their own. One instance mentioned to the writer shows the philosophy with which some probably took their mishap. Edgar Apperson says that a vehicle backed down on him before he could get out of the way, and although the collision was not hard, still it was enough to make him come to a dead stop, and many seconds were lost in his backing away and getting up momentum again to go around the one in trouble. "But," as Mr. Apperson said, "I did not make a formal protest because there were others more seriously impeded than I, and besides I did not wish to consume any time or thought on the subject, for I started in the whole contest to get to Buffalo in good shape, the hill climbing being only a side issue."

Although it made no difference in Mr. Apperson's case, an opposite condition exists with one machine that lodged a formal protest, this being a locomobile driven by J. Murray Page, which was but two seconds behind the best time in its class. Mr. Kingman of the Locomobile Company claims that two of his carriages in Class A were impeded from 20 to 50 seconds, and as their official times were 2 minutes 47 seconds and 3 minutes and 49 seconds respectively, it can be seen that had there been no impediment the results would have been quite different.

This hill climbing contest for the heavy class was won by David Wolfe Bishop, in the remarkable time of 2 minutes 13 seconds, which shows an average of just about 17 miles an hour for the total distance. There was no part of the hill which was taken by Mr. Bishop at a less rate of speed than 10 miles an hour, for he passed most others just as though they were not competing, and at one part he was compelled to do unusually clever steering on account of almost being pocketed, he being forced to cross from ditch to ditch on each side four times in a short space of about 200 feet in length to get away from stalled vehicles.

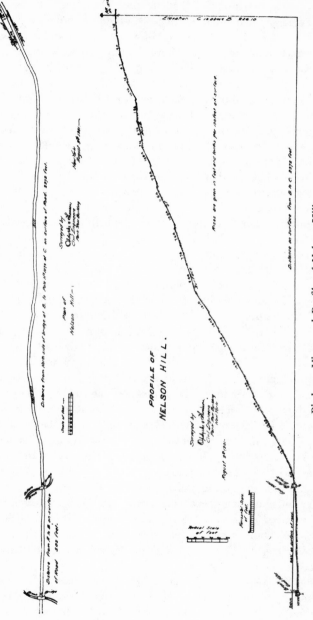

Birdseye View and Profile of Nelson Hill

When it is remembered that he did this at a rate of speed of about 12 miles an hour his dexterity can readily be imagined. He did not suffer from impediments on the hill as much as some of the others, it being a mere coincidence that there did not happen to be a complete block on the slope while he was running up. When Manager Stearns saw the threatened stoppage just as Mr. Bishop entered the foot of the hill at a speed of about 25 miles an hour he made a special effort to clear the way. Had it not been for this there would have been a complete mix-up of vehicles three-fourths of the way up and Mr. Bishop would have had to come to a dead stop, as half a dozen did. Mr. Bishop's vehicle went over the "thank-you-ma'ams" in a way that caused its wheels to land on the upper hollow side with a jump that would have wrecked the springs and axles of many an automobile. This winner told the writer that he could not have taken the hill any faster, even if he had had a clear road, the artificial ridges preventing his doing so.

The speed Mr. Bishop showed is remarkable when the slope is considered, and it was faster than even the most sanguine automobilist had dared to predict. The winner of the next weight class was William Morgan, on his Autocar, his time being 3 minutes 17 seconds. The winner of the light class was the steam Stanhope made by Grout Brothers and driven by B. L. Wright, his time being 2 minutes 45 seconds. A good many of those who drove steam vehicles up the hill made the mistake of racing hard for the preliminary 500 feet, thereby somewhat reducing their steam pressures just before commencing the arduous part of the distance. It is questionable whether the time they gained in the first 500 feet made up for the time lost on the 2,300 feet.

On this point the opinion of Mr. Wright, the Class A winner is interesting, he giving the writer a few facts concerning his steam pres-sure and how it varied. He started at the beginning of the preliminary 500 feet with 300 pounds pressure, but by the time he reached the foot of the hill his gauge registered 280 pounds, having lost 20 pounds in the insignificant distance of 500 feet. Mr. Wright says it was not because he raced to the foot of the hill that caused his pressure to go down so much, but as he was forced to wait for about half an hour at the start, his engine grew cold and much steam was condensed and wasted accordingly.

During the journey up the slope Mr. Wright had a comparatively free course. It was not so good as though there had been no vehicles on it, for he had to go around a number before reaching the top, but he was not impeded to the extent that some were. At the top or end of the hill climbing control his steam gauge registered 180 pounds, but after traveling for ten minutes the pressure went back to 300 pounds.

SUMMARY OF NELSON HILL CONTEST.

(Steam = S.   Gasoline = G.)

CLASS A.	Passen-gers.		Horse-power.	Weight. Lbs.	Time. M. S.
A 45 Grout Bros.	2	S	—	800	2 45
A 36 Locomobile	2	S	$3\frac{1}{2}$	999	2 47
A 63 Duryea, 3-wheel	2	G	8	900	3 16
A 38 Locomobile	2	S	$3\frac{1}{2}$	999	3 48
A 47 Locomobile	2	S	$3\frac{1}{2}$	960	4 2
A 37 Locomobile	2	S	$3\frac{1}{2}$	990	4 10
A 73 De Dion-Bouton Motorette	2	G	5	900	4 59
A 11 De Dion-Bouton Motorette	2	G	6	995	7 2

Jefferson Seligman in $4\frac{1}{2}$ Horse-Power Columbia Gasoline

CLASS A.		Passengers.	Horsepower.	Weight. Lbs.	Time. M. S.
A 75 De Dion-Bouton Motorette	. .	2	G 5	880	9 40
A 66 Ward-Leonard Electric Co.	. .	3	G 5	700	10 40
A 72 De Dion-Bouton Motorette	. .	2	G 5	930	11 58

CLASS B.					
B 48 Autocar	. .	2	G 8	1200	3 17
B 39 Locomobile No. 2 . .	. .	2	S 4½	1280	3 55
B 54 Stearns Steam Carriage Co.	. .	2	S 6	1470	4 02
B 4 Haynes-Apperson . .	. .	2	G 8	1910	4 35
B 32 Winton Semi-Racer . .	. .	2	G 12	1700	4 38
B 86 Am. Bic. Co. "Hydrocar"	. .	2	G —	1780	4 50
B 28 Lane Motor Vehicle Co.	. . .	2	S 10	1600	5 00
B 78 Columbia Mark VIII. .	. .	2	G 4½	1800	5 31
B 80 Columbia Mark VIII. .	. .	2	G 4½	1640	5 40
B 5 Haynes-Apperson . .	. .	2	G 8	1940	5 41
B 50 "Geneva"	. .	2	S 5	900	6 00
B 12 White Sewing Machine Co.	. .	2	S 6	1350	6 00
B 52 Searchmont . . .	. .	2	G 12	1500	6 06
B 16 Overman Auto. Co. .	. .	2	S 6½	1270	6 10
B 27 Autocar	. .	2	G 8½	1150	6 12
B 81 U. S. Long Distance .	. .	2	G 7	1520	6 21
B 15 Overman Auto. Co. .	. .	2	S 6½	1200	7 29
B 21 Toledo Stanhope . .	. .	2	S 6½	1450	8 09
B 13 White Sewing Machine Co.	. .	2	S 6	1350	8 15
B 14 White Sewing Machine Co.	. .	2	S 6	1350	8 33
B 76 "Reading" . . .	. .	2	S 6	1200	10 53
B 20 "Toledo"	. .	2	S 6½	1630	11 41

CLASS C.					
C 55 Panhard-Levassor . .	. .	2	G 30	2500	2 13
C 59 Columbia Mark VIII. .	. .	2	G 5	1900	3 44
C 56 Packard (A. L. McMurtry)	. .	2	G 14	2410	3 50
C 31 Auto. Co. of America .	. .	2	G 9	2240	5 22
C 30 Auto. Co. of America .	. .	2	G 9	2230	5 45
C 65 Century Surrey . .	. .	4	S 9	2100	5 50
C 77 Auto. Co. of Am. . .	. .	2	G 9	2100	5 52
C 44 F. B. Stearns & Co. .	. .	—	G —	2000	6 03
C 61 Packard.	. .	2	G 12	2350	6 20
C 18 Holyoke	. .	2	G 9	3300	7 00
C 79 Packard	. .	3	G 16	2350	8 15
C 58 Gasmobile	. .	3	G 9	2410	9 12
C 29 Auto. Co. of America .	. .	2	G 9	2100	9 42
C 2 Panhard-Levassor . .	. .	2	G 12	2550	16 40

The prizes for this contest were silver cups presented by Winthrop E. Scarritt, Class A ; Harlan W. Whipple, Class B, and Albert R. Shattuck, Class C.

The Newport Races
(1901)

The Newport Races

THE second race meet of the National Automobile Racing Association of Newport was held at Aquidneck Park, Newport, Friday, August 30. It had been the intention of the association to hold the meet on several of the highways in Newport proper, the chief road to be used being Ocean Driveway. The association circulated a petition in favor of the road races some weeks before the

Infield Near Judges' Stand

selected day, and received signatures of the great majority of property owners along the roads to be used. In addition to this there was almost a unanimous sentiment all over Newport that the races should be held on the public highways. In response to this feeling the city council granted permission to hold the races on the roads selected, subject to proper police surveillance. There were, however, a few people, residents along the selected roads, who did not approve of the idea of turning the public thoroughfares into a race track even for such an insignificant time as three hours once a year. Among the objectors were estimable people, and although the stand they took was a most unpopular one and brought on them much adverse criticism, still they not only had the law on their side but in several ways their protest was not so narrow-minded as it seemed to be.

In speaking seriously with several of the objectors as to the true inwardness of their opposition, it was learned that ever since the public roads had been chosen for the races dozens of automobilists, most of whom had no intention of competing in the races, had commenced using the selected roads as a place for holding speed trials, with the result that a horseman never knew when an automobile would come upon him at a rate of speed anywhere from twenty to forty miles per hour. If only intending competitors had used the highways for speeding it would not have been so bad, for their numbers were insignificant ; but according to general report almost everyone in Newport, including visitors, who owned a self-propelling vehicle, commenced to use the selected roads for testing their machines weeks in advance of the race day.

It was also learned that had the objectors been a little more diplomatically handled, enough of them might have been won over to favor the races on the roads ; but the executives of the National Automobile Racing Association felt so confident the protests would not take on the strength which they eventually showed, that they went ahead and made arrangements for the road races and almost completely ignored the feelings of those who had at first refused their sanction. Then the objectors proceeded in an organized way and obtained a court injunction restraining the promoters from using the highways as planned.

It was just as well, so far as a showing of speed was concerned, that the races were not held on the drives, for in the proposed 9-mile circuit there were three or four bad turns which would have made it necessary to slow down very materially, so much so that some time would have been taken up before full speed could again be resumed on the straights. Ocean Drive, the most picturesque part of the proposed course and that having the best road surface, would have been an excellent place to try speeding on—up and down slight grades and around a few short turns having a radius large enough not to necessitate slowing down much. But taking the course as a whole, just as much speed can be shown on the comparatively small half-mile track that the races were held on, although the complete change was a disappointment to all who had expected a finer day's sport than was served to them.

It was not known until three days prior to August 30 that Aquid-neck Park would have to be used, but it was then quickly put in shape.   The course was scraped, but on account of not having been much used, there were tufts of grass on it which the scraper could not dislodge without making a hole large enough to offset the advantage gained by getting rid of the grass.   It had been announced that the track would be sprinkled in order to lay the dust ; this, however, was not done and it resulted that there was dust galore.   The atmosphere was brown with it, and just why the track was not watered and thereby

Clarence Gray Dinsmore and Foxhall P. Keene in Latter's 50 H.-P. Mors

made more pleasant for everyone concerned is difficult to understand when other arrangements were so complete.   Too much water on such a course would have resulted in more skidding by the machines around the turns than did take place on the loose, dusty surface, but a little water would have helped the general speeding, especially so on the part of competitors who were not so fortunate as to be the leader and were thereby more or less blinded.

The only competitor of note who did not take part was Albert C. Bostwick, who was so disappointed at the races being transferred to a

half-mile track that he shipped his 40 horse-power Winton back to
New York the day before the races.   No one can blame him for feeling this way, since the contests for such large machines as his would
have been more or less of a scramble had the competitors been closer
together than proved to be the case.   The risk of accident on such a
sized track with big machines is great enough to debar anyone from
competing who values his machine or his life.   If, for instance, two
such machines as Mr. Bostwick's Winton were about even in entering
a turn, both would be forced to slow up before they could get

William N. Murray and Frederick G. Bourne in Former's 40 H.-P. Winton

around the curve safely.   It does not need much stretch of imagination to determine what would be the result in the case of two such
machines meeting in such a coincidence.   Neither driver would feel
like slowing up, fearing that the other would continue with full power
for a second or two longer, and the result is that if the inside one
skidded a little more than usual—as would surely be the case if
full power were left on—its wheels would be locked with the other
vehicle, and there would be a fine mass of overturned, tangled metal,
going at anywhere from forty to fifty miles per hour.

If the machines did not come together, one or both would go off the outer side of the curve, or capsize if the driver made too much of an effort to hold the turn. As is afterwards explained, none of these big machines were let out to their fullest extent. Racing under such conditions should not be honored by that term. The traveling is merely a matter of negotiating the turns as expertly as possible, and otherwise feeling the way almost for the full distance. The driver is in a constant state of uncertainty as to whether the machine should be slowed down at all, little or much. At best, such traveling can be called

Louis Stern's Son in Panhard

more or less experimental, little of the race feature existing so far as its being a true showing of speed.

The afternoon's sport interested most of those assembled, for the speed shown was great enough to open the eyes of whoever had been unfamiliar with automobile racing. The attendance was very large, completely filling the stands, and gathering along the course on the infield to make a solid mass around the important points. The infield was filled with equipages of all kinds, both horse and horseless. The picture entitled "Infield Near Judge's Stand" gives a good idea of how coaches and drags were lined up, making fine places to view the races from.   In this picture are Bradish Johnson, William K. Vanderbilt, Jr., in the foreground, walking toward the course, Foxhall P. Keene, who can be recognized by that celebrated hat he wore, he standing at the fence between the grass and the course, looking at the latter, and Oliver H. P. Belmont and Theodore Havemeyer on the coach.   At this same part of the infield at times were other notables, including Chauncey M. Depew and Frederick G. Bourne.

Wm. K. Vanderbilt, Jr., in His DeDion-Bouton Voiturette

The judges and timers were Victor Sorchan, J. Dunbar Wright, Albert C. Bostwick and Arthur T. Kemp.   All races were started by pistol shot with machines at a standstill.

The races opened with a 3-mile contest for bicycles and tricycles. It was won by Kenneth A. Skinner on a De Dion-Bouton tricyle in 5 minutes 40 seconds.   G. M. Holly on a gasoline bicycle was second and U. G. Scott on a gasoline bicycle did not finish.   During the first mile of this race it seemed as though the eventual winner would not be anywhere near the first at the finish, this state being caused by the failure of his machine to spark properly, but after a mile and a half had been passed Mr. Skinner showed by his actions that the difficulty had been fixed and his machine went ahead and took the lead in a fashion that clearly showed its superiority. Then the result of the race was never in doubt.

The 3-mile race for electric vehicles resulted in rather a fizzle on account of its slowness, no time being taken. It was won by Lispenard Stewart with Dennison Hatch second.

The special 3-mile race for De Dion-Bouton motorettes resulted in a win for Oliver H. P. Belmont's vehicle, it being driven by the owner's chauffeur. Wm. K. Vanderbilt, Jr., was second. Kenneth

Wm. K. Vanderbilt, Jr., Racing in His Mercedes.

A. Skinner was third. Augustus Jay and John R. Livermore, who also started, did not finish. Time, 7 minutes 35¼ seconds. This race created a great deal of interest on account of the published names of the drivers being well known. A glance at the accompanying picture entitled "Infield Near Judges' Stand" reveals Mr. Belmont reclining carelessly on the middle seat of his drag. This is where he was when some of the crowd were cheering him, he supposedly being on his vehicle as it led the others in the race. Mr. Vanderbilt did start in this contest, the picture entitled "Wm. K. Vanderbilt, Jr., in his De Dion-Bouton Voiturette" representing him as he was waiting back of the starting line. The chief of the Newport police had just made a remark to him that made him relinquish the very intent look he wore

for most of the afternoon.   He started in this race not for the purpose
of filling it with competitors, as many thought, but to see if his
De Dion-Bouton machine was as good or better than the others.   It
was proved conclusively that on this day Mr. Belmont's was the best
vehicle, for the latter won by a handsome margin.

The 3-mile race for steam-propelled vehicles was run in heats ;
the first bringing out Colonel John Jacob Astor in a Toledo, Baron
Pierre de Morogues in a Locomobile and J. McMillan Hamilton in a
Locomobile.   Paulding Fosdick in a Locomobile did not finish.   It

Col. Astor   Baron de Morogues   J. McMillan Hamilton

was won by Mr. Hamilton, with Baron de Morogues second and Colonel Astor third.   Time, 6 minutes 25½ seconds.   This was a case of
at least one man competing not with the idea of winning but merely
to see how his machine would compare with others'.   Colonel Astor
drove his vehicle with this thought, but the onlookers did not understand the situation and made merry with his ability as a chauffeur
If the same people had seen the Colonel several weeks later in the
500-mile endurance test skilfully and speedily driving his heavy
12 horse-power Gasmobile up and down the rough roads between
New York and Albany, their conclusions would have been changed.

The second heat in this class was won by Henry Howard on a Howard machine. J. A. Mitchell on a Locomobile was second, and Paul H. Deming on a White vehicle was third. Time, 6 minutes 30 seconds. This race was devoid of feature, the Howard vehicle taking the lead and increasing it easily to the end. The picture entitled "The Howard Machine Being Pushed In" represents how this vehicle crossed the line in the final heat, and it also shows the unusual gear for this style of automobile. Attention is called to the large wheels both front and back, the rear ones being 3 feet 6 inches in diameter, this measurement being in great contrast with other steam vehicles in the race. Although the Howard machine crossed the finish line first in the final heat, the judges were forced to disqualify it on account of

The Howard Machine Being Pushed In

its not coming in under its own power. It had a great lead on all the others in the final heat, which was five miles in length, but on entering the last quarter mile the chain broke, and the occupants, finding what the trouble was, commenced a vigorous athlethic exercise by pushing their carriage at a run. Even though they were about a lap ahead of the second carriage when the chain broke, they only succeeded in passing the finish about seventy-five feet ahead of Mr. Hamilton, whose machine had quickly overtaken them. Mr. Hamilton was awarded the race. The photograph reveals the broken chain, both ends of which are trailing the ground. The distance between the crank shaft and the rear axle is unusually long, which accounts for the chain being long enough to drag both ends.

The first heat for gasoline vehicles developing not more than 12 horse-power brought out Frederick H. Benedict and F. Walsh both driving Gasmobiles, and Lieutenant H. L. Willoughby on an Autocar. It was won by Mr. Walsh, who covered the three miles in 6 minutes 6¼ seconds. He easily took the lead, and increased it as he chose. The second heat was won by C. Macey on a Gasmobile, with Mr. Stern, the son of Louis Stern, on a Panhard, second. George McFadden, of Boston polo fame, drove a Gasmobile but did not finish. Time, 6 minutes 45 seconds. The third heat was won by Clarence Gray Dinsmore on a Panhard in a walkover. The fourth heat was won by Rudolph Myer on a Gasmobile, with James L. Breese on a Panhard, second, and I. Townsend Burden, Jr., on an Autocar, third.

Lieut. Willoughby   F. Walsh   F. H. Benedict

Time, 6 minutes 17¼ seconds. The feature of this race was the easy way in which the Gasmobile disposed of the celebrated French machine. Some well-known authorities among the judges and onlookers were of the opinion that the winner's machine had considerable more than 12 horse-power. Mr. Breese did not drive his own vehicle, his chauffeur doing this. The owner sat on the inside seat and went through the usual gyrations, while taking turns, of the one who is generally given that position. The picture entitled "Rudolph Myer and James L. Breese in Trial Heat" shows Mr. Breese sitting down on the left seat of the inside vehicle ready for his part of the race.

The final heat was 5 miles and was won by Mr. Myer easily in 9 minutes 37 seconds. Mr. Dinsmore was second. Mr. Macey did not

finish.   As was the case in the trial heat, the Gasmobile never was
headed and won as it liked.

The next race was the first heat of the event of the day, it being
a 5-mile race for gasoline vehicles developing more than 12 horse-
power.   The first to line up were Foxhall P. Keene in a Mors vehicle
and David Wolfe Bishop in a 30 horse-power Panhard.   There was considerable quiet speculation as to the outcome of the meeting between
these two celebrated amateur automobilists both driving such world-
renowned machines.   Mr. Keene's can develop over 50 horse-power,
it being the one he started in when taking part in the Paris-Berlin

Rudolph Myer and James L. Breese

race.   Mr. Bishop's was also in that contest, it being driven by a Mr.
Heath, who sold it to its present owner.   Mr. Bishop changed the
machine's appearance somewhat before bringing it to this country,
elevating its motor and body five inches so that it would be better
adapted to running on American roads.   The picture entitled " David
Wolfe Bishop Rounding a Turn " shows very conclusively that this
vehicle could not hug the rail the way Mr. Keene's could.   It was
noticed that Mr. Bishop all through the race was nearer the outside of
the track than even the middle of it, especially so in passing the
grand stand, where on each circuit he caused a scampering on the part
of the many who were near the stand on the track, who showed no
desire to run the slightest risk of being within touching distance of

the powerful machine as it thundered past them.   The description of
this heat can be brief, Mr. Keene taking the lead and never being
headed, he being one hundred yards ahead at the end of one lap and
over one lap ahead at the finish.   The time was 8 minutes 2 seconds.

This meeting between these two well known sportsmen was extra
interesting on account of its being the first occasion of Mr. Keene's
taking part in this country in an automobile race.   This gentleman
has previously been associated with almost every kind of amateur
sport, he in his younger days being a good runner, base ball and ten-
nis player.   Those interested in amateur sports well remember that it
was only half a dozen years ago when Mr. Keene suddenly loomed

Foxhall P. Keene in His Mors Ready On Track

up as a golf player by winning the amateur championship of this
country.   His favorite pastime is polo, which he still follows successfully, he being rated with several others as being in a class by themselves at this game.   His polo team since he competed in these
Newport antomobile races won the polo championship at Boston.
Mr. Keene is a medium height slender type of man, weighing 152
pounds.   In automobiling he displays the same slow movements that
have characterized him in sports requiring much physical activity.
When the occasion requires he has always put all necessary life into
an exercise, but controlling it all, in a cool, confident manner.   Should

he continue taking part in automobile events, he will undoubtedly make the same name in that sport as he has in others.

The second heat brought out William K. Vanderbilt, Jr., on a rated 40 horse-power Mercedes, which is without doubt "a thing of beauty," and William N. Murray, of Pittsburgh, who drove a 40 horse-power Winton exactly similar to Alexander Winton's own car, Albert C. Bostwick's and Captain Larz Andersen's. The picture

David Wolfe Bishop Rounding a Turn at Speed

entitled "W. K. Vanderbilt, Jr., and W. N. Murray Ready for Trial Heat" shows them as they waited while the starter adjusted their machines prior to firing the pistol. It will be noticed that Mr. Murray is still a few feet back of the line. Mr. Vanderbilt had given a clever exhibition of coming up fast and stopping within a few inches of the line, the dust at the rear showing that his machine had been in quick motion momentarily before.

The start of this heat impressed many that there had been a misunderstanding on the part of Mr. Murray in getting ready for the pistol shot. He did not have his motor well speeded or else he did not dare put the clutch on as fast as Mr. Vanderbilt did. Whatever was the trouble it caused Mr. Murray to lose at least two hundred feet before he got his big vehicle under way properly. When the pistol was fired Mr. Vanderbilt shot forward just as though something had come up from behind and given him a tremendous push, in fact it was even more than this—it looked as though a blow had been given. Almost simultaneously with the pistol Mr. Vanderbilt's vehicle was jumped or driven—both terms will do—eight or ten feet, and slowing down for about five feet more, it then shot ahead at a rate not far away from full speed.   Mr. Murray's clutch was not even on and when his vehicle did begin to move Mr. Vanderbilt was one hundred feet away from the finish, which lead he increased to fully two hundred feet before Mr. Murray's machine commenced to show real life.   After this the race was quite exciting, in fact it was the best of the day, for it did not take but about two laps to show that Mr. Vanderbilt had not gained anything worth speaking of after his opponent's machine was thoroughly under way.   As there were ten circuits to be made, the crowd had the pleasure of being fully alive to the situation for eight circuits, after arriving at the conclusion that the machines were about equal in speed.   Mr. Murray was at a fearful disadvantage in being forced to take the dust on account of being so close to his leader.   No one who has not witnessed a contest of this kind on a dusty track can realize what it means.   It is something that is beyond description, and unless an automobilist is thoroughly used to it and knows how to follow the vortex, as Henri Fournier says, it is impossible to see where one is going.   Although the popular feeling seemed to be with Mr. Vanderbilt, this being quite natural on account of his being so well known at Newport, there were plenty of expressions of admiration for Mr. Murray, for in spite of the great handicap of dust, he prevented the winner from materially increasing his lead after both machines were in full speed.   The winner's time was 7 minutes 43½ seconds.   Mr. Murray was but five seconds behind, which computed in distance shows that he was 285 feet in the rear, he traveling about 57 feet per second.

The final heat of this race was by a long way the event of the afternoon.   Even though there was quite a difference in the times of their respective heats everyone was on edge when Messrs. Vanderbilt and Keene lined up for the final trial.   The picture entitled "W. K. Vanderbilt and Foxhall P. Keene Preparing for Final Heat" shows their machines on the starting line nearly ready for the pistol shot. Mr. Vanderbilt is adjusting his goggles and Mr. Keene is doing something with his levers.   It will be noticed that Mr. Vanderbilt had the outside and that his adversary had the pole.   If there were any significance to this such as either one having an advantage, it would be in favor of Mr. Keene, but as it turned out the big start which Mr.

Vanderbilt obtained enabled him to take the pole immediately. When the machines were sent away Mr. Vanderbilt took the lead and was fully 100 feet ahead when taking the first turn. The positions did not change after that, Mr. Keene never being able to overcome the advantage. Mr. Vanderbilt won easily in 7 minutes 36¼ seconds, which shows an average of about 1 minute, 31 seconds for each mile. His best mile was done in 1 minute 28 seconds.

It was rather amusing to notice the feeling of the majority of the onlookers, they showing unmistakably whom they hoped would win. Each time Mr. Vanderbilt rushed past the stands there were any quantity of opinions expressed concerning his superiority as a chauf-

Wm. K. Vanderbilt, Jr., and Wm. N. Murray Ready for Trial Heat

feur over Mr. Keene. This popularity is presumably due to Mr. Vanderbilt's long conspicuous life in Newport. For half the race he was compelled to take Mr. Vanderbilt's dust in the very way that Mr. Murray was forced to, and after the race he said his eyes were so blinded that he could scarcely see for several minutes. He acknowledged that on this day he was hardly a match for Mr. Vanderbilt.

The last race of the afternoon was a so-called 10-mile championship for all classes. It was won by Mr. Vanderbilt, in his Mercedes, who simply let his machine out to about the limit he showed in his previous races and lapped competitors in a most unconcerned way. Several times when he was on the point of passing a machine he was forced to take dust in the same fashion that he had given it to others, but on account of the great speed of his machine he did not have to submit to this handicap long enough to interfere with very fast traveling. He won this race in 15 minutes 23½ seconds, second place being taken by Kenneth A. Skinner, on the DeDion-Bouton tricycle, which he drove to such signal victory in the first race. Rudolph Myer, on the celebrated Gasmobile which had taken him in first in several previous races, was third. Mr. Skinner, although no match for Mr. Vanderbilt, showed surprising speed around that track, he maintaining a position of leaning his body toward the pole for the whole 16 minutes, which showed more than average determination and fortitude.

On account of Mr. Vanderbilt's automobile reputation given him by the immense amount of newspaper notoriety he has attracted, it is not amiss to describe his doings when on a machine. He is without doubt an unusually competent driver so far as concerns getting speed and handling his machine easily and quickly. All kinds of stories have been published about him regarding the risks he has run and the utter disdain in which he holds the rights of other people when on the public highway. He is a nervous, quick-acting young man, but gives the impression that on nearly every occasion he knows what he is about. One scene alone which was witnessed by the writer shows conclusively how thoroughly at home he is on his powerful racer. This machine was resting under the tent that he had provided for the entertainment of his friends, and when the time came to take the inappropriate object away from its close association with punch bowls, champagne, lemonade, etc., the owner entered the canvas covering, quickly jumped on the driver's seat, gave a couple of quick instructions to his chauffeur, who immediately went to the front and set the motor going. Then Mr. Vanderbilt took charge of the wheel and levers and moved the apparently cumbersome vehicle backward and forward in quick succession, edging it toward a very small opening, made so by stakes and ropes which held the tent, and backed it out as expertly as anyone could imagine it to be done. Once free from the tent, he backed it at greater speed over some thick fence rails which were on the ground that in turn momentarily sent the rear part of the machine in the air long enough to cause the hind wheels to race with a deafening racket. When on the track, he veered his machine around still backing at speed and then sent it forward in a confident way that could not fail to impress anyone.

Just what his abilities are as compared with, for instance, Albert

C. Bostwick and Messrs. Keene, Bishop and Murray, when all would be on a course broad enough, smooth enough and long enough to enable their machines to be let out to their fullest extent, remains to be seen. The track at Newport was a ridiculous place to have automobile races for high-powered cars. It was all right for small machines, but for speedy and heavy vehicles was most unsatisfactory. It would not be fair to compare Mr. Vanderbilt's racing abilities with such renowned foreign drivers as Fournier, Charron, Girardot or even Alexander Winton of America, who although not having had

Mr. Vanderbilt and Mr. Keene Ready for Final Heat

nearly so much experience in racing as the Frenchmen is enough acquainted with this branch of automobiling to probably outclass, if the machines are equal, any driver of Mr. Vanderbilt's set.

To show how foolish it would be to form convincing opinions from the Newport races as to the relative merits of Messrs. Vanderbilt, Keene, Murray and Bishop it may be said that none of these men kept their full power on at any one time for over a dozen seconds. Only on coming up the home stretch which is practically level or a trifle up hill were things opened up wide. When the turn was reached Mr. Vanderbilt would cut off a cylinder and not put it on again until the home stretch was again met. The back stretch being a little down hill, gave all machines such momentum that in some cases they had to be braked before the turn could be entered with safety. Mr. Vanderbilt's machine held the pole better than any, probably mostly on account of the way his attendant was trained when taking curves. This man just before a turn was reached would suspend himself outward from the machine with his feet on the step and his hands clinging to two straps fastened to the fore and aft part of the machine respectively. His body in this way was inclined at an angle of about 30 degrees and his head was about 4 feet away from the seat. This counterbalance enabled the machine to be sent a little swifter around the curves than it otherwise could.

———————

One of the neatest air cooled motors we have seen is the one built by the Dieble-Cox Manufacturing Company, of Philadelphia. In appearance, it reminds one of the Knox, at first glance, but further examination shows the difference. Instead of pins fastened into the cylinder, there are rings with radiating arms, which are shrunk on the cylinder casting. These present more radiating surface than we have ever seen in a similar space and the results in practice seem to indicate beyond doubt that it is effective. Altogether, it's a neat little runabout and is making friends among those who want a light, low-priced runabout.

———————

Perhaps most of us are too prone to talk about our mishaps and overlook the many pleasant miles where nothing whatever occurred to mar our ride. Mr. Walter Creber writes to the *Motor Car Journal* that he has driven a Glasgow built car about 3,000 miles without any trouble since the first week when he was learning to run it. Few can present such a record, and if tires are included, this part can be attributed to good fortune as much as to the make of tires or the management of the car.

Vagaries of a Vermont Automobile (1902)

Vagaries of a Vermont Automobile

By W. D. WOOLSON

AMONG the many interesting articles that appear upon the pages of the AUTOMOBILE MAGAZINE, none are of more interest to me than those narrating the experiences of that ever increasing army of automobile owners and users ; perhaps this is because in moments of reflection I feel as if I too belong in that army, or perchance it is because reading these articles partially convinces me that there are others beside myself who do not know it all.

Possessed of these ideas, I make bold to pay an installment on my debt of gratitude to these writers of experience by giving a few experiences from life with the automobile up here in the woods of Vermont, where macadam roads are as scarce as golden streets, and the art of the road-maker consists in periodically scraping the sods and stones into the center of the path, and making water bars across the highway at every conceivable opportunity.

My first vehicle was a steam one and I had sold it. I lived upon investigations for the next month. No buyer of a horse ever examined the teeth or the hoofs of his intended purchase more carefully than did I the workmanship and the material of the various makes of vehicles. I believe there is an old legend of a man who felt so strong that he elected to fight the devil. I did not select the devil as a thing to wrestle with, but I did choose a gasoline vehicle, and I often think may be the other chap had the softest job in his devil beating.

After my previous experience with a steam vehicle, the confidence with which I tackled that gasoline one was simply sublime, you couldn't possibly call it anything else. My second choice was a single-cylindered, model C, Packard, weighing a ton. It was delivered at Boston, and at the beginning of a bright July day, just after a rain, I started for my home in central Vermont with a representative of the

makers to aid me.   That ride was a dream.   Not even the adjustment
of a nut was required on that trip of 136 miles, even though it was
over a very hilly country and roads which were not of the finest.

We made the trip in a running time of 8 hours and a quarter,
and that with a vehicle just out of the factory, with the paint not yet
dry on it, certainly was phenomenal.   Once we were sent out of our
way, and had to run up a mountainous road near Keene, N. H.,
using our hill-climber continuously for 1½ hours.   That was the only
time I ever saw the cylinder cooling water get hot enough to boil.
Coming down the other side of this mountain, my companion seemed
to think it a religious duty, as well as a real pleasure for him to go as
fast down that mountain as the combined forces of gravity and the
engine could drive that heavy carriage.   I finally persuaded him to
bring the speed down to a modest 40 miles an hour at least until we
had reached a road which had a few less water bars (thank-you-
marms), and a mile or two more of straightness in it.   I never rode
a jack rabbit, but the way the vehicle jumped those thank-you-marms
was as near the sensation as ever I care to come.

In my stable, my horses took the arrival of that automobile much
to heart. and five of them almost died with some form of distemper
the next month.   Time cures all things, even horses, and now those
faithful beasts of mine have so far recovered that they are occasionlly
kind enough to haul their rival in, when it has a bad attack of heart
failure.   My hostler did almost as much kicking as his four-footed
charges.   He insisted that he had to hunt for the horses in the hay
loft, because they invariably went up the feed spout every time I started
the engine in the stable ; and when I asked him to wash that automobile, he fainted dead away, and revived only enough to give
notice of his departure.

Being thus left to my own devices, I had many pleasant rides in
that vehicle, and some mighty unpleasant experiences under it.   One
thing I have had duly impressed upon me, and that is, unless you
have an urgent engagement in the road directly in front of the dasher,
you don't want to throw in your low gear when the carriage is running
at any speed.   This is a simple matter.   It is so simple, in fact, that
any one would know it if he stopped to think about it, but I pre-
sume I must have been as dense as a door mat, since I nearly disem-
boweled myself on the steering column in finding it out by experience.

My first real trouble was with the friction clutches, which being
enclosed and the oil hole plugged, got to cutting before I was aware

of the trouble ; but on returning them to the makers of the carriage, they sent me new ones gratis. Right here I want to say that the treatment the makers have invariably given me has in every instance been courteous, liberal and efficient. It is worth the price of the carriage to know that there are some manufacturers who are interested enough in the successful operation of their vehicles, after they have

got your money, to do what they can to remedy any dissatisfaction on the part of the owner. My experience with my first vehicle had almost made me doubt this.

The next jar to my routine of pleasure was experienced in a neighboring town, after an eight or ten mile run. I had my wife and our three cherubs on board, when suddenly sundry noises from beneath the cushion made me head the vehicle for a side street. I had a vague feeling that the motor was about to have a spasmodic attack of indigestion.   Scarcely had I gained the coveted seclusion of an unfrequented thoroughfare when, with a rip and a groan, the motor stopped.   It only took a glance at the engine-cavity to show that one of the bolts holding the cap of the crank-pin box had worked back about a turn.   This play had broken the other bolt off at the juncture of the cap and the box, allowing the cap to swing around and release the piston, which, at the next explosion, shot through the lower casing, but fortunately doing no other damage.   It was an easy matter to transfer my erstwhile passengers and unwilling deserters to the next home-bound electric car, and after this to secure some new bolts, replace the cap, and arrive home two hours late for dinner.

Up to this time I had had no ignition troubles of any account. Of course, as a matter of physical development, I had at times turned the crank to the amusement of the crowd, but never had run the carriage very far by this method.   Nevertheless, it came at last.   I had started early one morning to run to a fair in a neighboring town.   I never saw the carriage do better than it did for about ten miles through the beautiful scenery along the Connecticut River.   Suddenly all my interest in the beauties of nature ceased, and with sundry skips, the engine stopped dead.

I went over the wiring carefully, and took out the spark plug, but no spark ; tested the batteries, found the voltage all right. Pushed the vehicle off the road and into the shade, just to gain time to think, tried the spark again, and got a good one.   Started the engine, and got back into the road, and incidentally into the sun, when another skip, and another stop.   Took out the spark plug, no spark; made a few oral observations, there being no one in earshot.   Took off my coat, and turned the crank about nine hundred and ninety-nine times without a response from the engine.   Fearing I would develop a hot box, I discontinued that form of motor improvement for the time being.   In short, I worked all that day with the same results—nothing.

Went home that night by four-legged horse power.   Came back the next morning with a man, and together he and I fooled away another day.   Same result—nothing.   When it got dark enough we hitched the old horse on and hauled that automobile home.   Somehow it leaked out that we were coming, per hay motor, and several friends met me in the village square with an ovation that was entirely uncalled for.   This two days' experience was a severe shock to my moral as well as motor growth. The third day, however, I found the cause of my troubles. The jump-spark coil had a break in the inside wiring, where two wires were joined together in the coil. These had come apart so that the vibrations of the engine would occasionally bring them in contact. This was when I would get a spark, but the constant vibration would soon throw them apart again, and that was when I didn't get a spark. The next day when everything was going lovely once more I went down with the automobile and drew back the horse wagon, just to show the farmers along the route that this hauling busi-

A Russian Motor
Sleigh

ness was a reciprocal one in which the automobile asked from the horse no aid it could not return.

Frankly, I have not had the success with the jump spark that I would like, doubtless, on account of my lack of grey matter, but from my experience with both systems, I would much prefer a simple form of touch spark, and current furnished from a dynamo, with a small storage battery in circuit. This arrangement is simpler to maintain, and can be put in shape more quickly than the other when it gets out of order on the road. If tripped by a spiral cam, you can also get the automatic or manual advancement or retarding of the spark.

The carburettor was the next thing which taught me mental

humility.   Up here in the primeval forests we get from the local
dealers as gasoline any liquid that has ever in the course of its existence been anywhere near a gasoline barrel, with the very natural
result the amount of water and other extras in the fluid give no end
of trouble where float feed is used.   Eventually I found I had less
trouble if I used a hybrid device, which was a cross between an
atomizer and a carburettor, wherein a constant level was maintained
by a pump of comparatively large capacity.   With this arrangement
I can burn anything, even the backwoods fluid the sellers call ''gasoline'' and the buyers call — well, no matter what.

I have only run up against one condition with this device of
mine which gave me trouble and here it is.   Being called in haste to
a town about 16 miles away, I did not stop to fill the gasoline tank
from my own supply.   So upon arrival at my destination, my tank
being nearly emptied by the run over, I bought 5 gallons of so-called
''engine gasoline,'' and with the stuff filled the tank.   It was a bitter
cold day, with a strong wind blowing, and everything frozen hard,
but as I had taken the precaution to fill the water in the cooler full of
calcium cloride, I let the vehicle stand exposed to the weather for 3
hours, while I completed the business which was the cause of my
journey.   When I started at about 6 o'clock in the evening for home,
the motor wheezed and fussed considerably, but went along after a
fashion for about 3 miles, then stopped.   I got out and tried the
spark, it was O. K., looked into the carburettor, and found it almost
empty, tried the pump, and found it would deliver nothing but air,
disconnected the supply pipe, and found it was frozen full of ice.
The thermometer was steadily dropping, and my courage and temperature were racing with the thermometer for the zero point.

I finally thawed out the pipes over a carriage lamp.   It was a
delightful experience.   I never remember but one other occasion, and
that was last winter when I was trying in vain to get warm in a hotel
in England, that the lurid fires of the nether world seemed so enticing
as they did on that pipe-thawing job.   But now the pipe was clear,
I was unable to get any gasoline from the tank, although the gauge
showed the tank was nearly full.   Finally I got desperate, punched a
hole in the top of the tank, and found about an inch of solid ice
completely covering the bottom of the tank.   We took turns in
thawing that supply pipe, and breaking the ice in the bottom of the
tank with a stick thrust through the hole we had made, until 2 o'clock
in the morning, when we finally got home.   If any one had offered

me a recipe that would keep country (Vermont) gasoline from freezing, I would have paid high for it that night.

The only thing that I have found radically wrong with my gasoline carriage has been the exhaust cam, which did not allow the valve to open soon enough, and permitted it to close too quickly on the stroke. By changing this I made a great difference in the ability of the engine. There was also a weak place in the design of the axle which caused it to break. This, with the trouble I have had with the exhaust valve stem unscrewing, so that the cam will not allow it to seat, completes the list of the shady side of my automobiling experiences. The last two troubles I have named are especially exasperating, because the appearance of either means a long delay usually, where farming tools and free advice abound, but nothing else.

An English Idea for a Removable Top

I am often asked as to the cost of repairs and maintenance. This always seems to me a good deal like asking a fellow how much it costs him to live? or what his doctor's bills are? since it all depends upon where and how he lives. On these hilly Vermont roads I figure that I average about fifteen miles on a gallon of gasoline. The cash cost of maintenance has been with me exceedingly small, because I have a man from my factory who takes care of the vehicle, and keeps it in running order for the use he is allowed to make of it when I have no need of it. He also does the repairing, which has for the past season only been the changing of the clutches and a new axle and brake castings, which all told have not cost me in money over $10. I have doubtless spent between two and three hundred dollars in experimenting and trying to perfect some devices which I thought would be improvements in the vehicle, but which were *not* in any way necessary to either its maintenance or its operation. I have had no tire troubles excepting the collapsing of the inner tube of one of the rear tires, which was replaced by a new tire from the factory free of charge. I think the way I am situated one hundred dollars would cover. all my expenditures for maintenance and repairs for another season, providing I did not have a collision with something, or did not get so far from home as to be at the tender mercies of city repair shops.

When I placed the order for my present carriage a member of the firm wrote that he was glad to have it go into the hands of a manufacturer. I replied that it was the worst possible place he could put the vehicle, as it was all I could do to keep from tinkering with it. I have, at the cost of some effort, refrained from giving you all the joys and sorrows that came to me in connection with said improvements. They are not worth much to those who build automobiles, but they have been a great aid to character building, and while I think I know something more about a gasoline engine than I once did, I can with equal certainty, take my oath that there are a great many things about the engine that I don't know, though I certainly thought I did at the start. Neither have I gone into detail regarding the endless source of pleasure that the conveyance as a whole has been to me, or the peculiar joys that have been mine in connection with its use. The enjoyment of the first Boston trip has been repeated many times since, with just variations enough to make it intensely interesting. As to this particular make of vehicle which I was fortunate enough to select, after Summering and Wintering it, I can swear by it and by the men who built it too, and the vehicle is not for sale either.

I send you herewith a couple of pictures which will show you how I am endeavoring to inculcate in my family an early knowledge of the automobile. If enthusiasm and anxiety to learn count for anything, I feel confident that I have in training the finest batch of automobile experts Vermont or anywhere else has ever seen, though it will be some time yet before the young man you see in the picture will be allowed to pilot a big racer. He's like his father, though, in being pefectly willing to undertake the job even now.

I am not fortunate enough to be the possessor of a degree given by any institution, so that I cannot follow my name with even an M. E. or an M. D., but in view of all the many fool things I have done with an automobile, I feel that it is no more than fair to the motor vehicle industry that my name should be followed by D. F. in large letters.

Road Description
of the 500 Mile
Endurance Test
(1901)

Road Description of the 500-Mile Endurance Test

FOLLOWING are maps, road description and general instructions, as compiled by the committee having charge of this important contest.

MONDAY MORNING, SEPTEMBER 9

RECORD SHEETS MUST BE FILLED IN HERE

Start: Club House, 58th Street and Fifth Avenue, 8 a. m. The carriages will form on the east and west sides of Fifth Avenue south from 58th Street, close to the curb, according to their official numbers, the even numbers on the east and the odd numbers on the west side, with an interval of ten feet between carriages in each column.

Fifth Avenue to 112th Street ; turn left into 112th Street to Seventh Avenue ; turn right into Seventh Avenue to 154th Street ; turn left one block to Central Bridge ; over Central Bridge, straight ahead into Jerome Avenue, which follow to Woodlawn Cemetery gate; turn left at first road beyond Cemetery gate (Mosholu Avenue) to Broadway, which follow straight ahead to Getty Square, Yonkers.

8 M. P. H. THROUGH YONKERS CONTROL

From Getty Square into Warburton Avenue, following street railway four and a half miles to Hastings, and the road is then called Broadway on to Dobb's Ferry. At the stone church turn sharp to the left (still Broadway), on to Irvington and Tarrytown.

At Florence House Stable, Tarrytown, *water* can be obtained. Still follow Broadway to a brick church and bear to the left down a hill, across Horses Head Bridge, passing the stone gateway of the Mobile Company's plant on the left, and up the hill, 10 per cent. grade, past Sleepy Hollow Cemetery to the Aqueduct. After passing under the Aqueduct the road is called Highland Avenue, and there is a short hill with a 9 per cent. grade. One and a quarter miles beyond the Aqueduct, opposite a stone church, is public well (*water*) which is on the corner of Scarboro Road and Broadway and Highland Avenue. Continue straight ahead to Ossining (Sing Sing.)

8 M. P. H. THROUGH OSSINING CONTROL

Continue north through this town and take road to left of Sold-

211

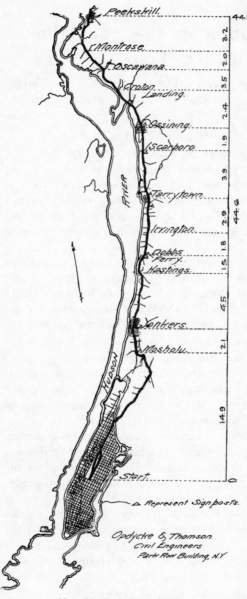

△ Represent Signposts.

Opdycke & Thomson.
Civil Engineers
Park Row Building, N.Y.

New York to Peekskill

iers' Monument down a hill, crossing a brook (*water*); then up a short hill, 7 to 10 per cent. grade, to a fountain three quarters of a mile beyond Ossining; bear to the left to a school house and turn sharp to the left. The road is very good all the way to this school house, but from here on to Croton the road is sandy. Cross the bridge over Croton River and turn to the left about a quarter of a mile after crossing the river. Just north of this town is a short hill of 12 per cent. grade. Continue one and a half miles to Oscawana (*spring* on the side of the road). One and a half miles from Oscawana is a short hill, 15 per cent. grade; then keep the road to the left across railroad bridge, continuing on to hotel at Centerville (*water*). Turn sharp to the right into Washington Street, passing under railroad bridge and following railroad for about a half a mile, continuing on Washington Street to South Street, Peekskill.

8 M. P. H. THROUGH PEEKSKILL CONTROL

On arriving at Peekskill turn sharp to the left into Nelson Avenue and go one block to McCoy and Best's yard, where time will be taken for the *noon control*.

RECORD SHEETS MUST BE FILLED IN HERE

Peekskill.—Lunch at Eagle Hotel.

MONDAY AFTERNOON, SEPTEMBER 9

RECORD SHEET MUST BE FILLED IN HERE

The first carriage will be started from Peekskill at 12.45 p. m. In leaving Peekskill continue one-half block on Nelson Avenue, then turn to the right into Main Street for half a block, then turn to the left into North Division Street as far as water fountain and take road to left which is Highland Avenue. About a mile further on, go down a long hill, 20 per cent. grade, and cross the bridge over Peekskill Creek ; after crossing the bridge curve to the left and cross Spout Brook ; keep straight on to a little settlement called Annsville and up a short hill, 15 per cent. grade, to a brook which can be crossed or forded, then up another short hill, 13 per cent. grade. One and a half miles beyond Annsville take road to the right at the forks and a short distance beyond cross a brook and *STOP* at signal of approach to control for Hill Climbing Contest on Nelson Hill.

RECORD SHEET MUST BE FILLED IN HERE

Hill Climbing Contest on Nelson Hill for description and profile map see page 838.

Record sheets of contestants who do not compete in Hill Climbing must be filled in at control at top of Nelson Hill.

Proceed straight ahead. One-half mile beyond the top of the hill take road to the left at the forks and cross Kendrin's Brook (*water*) at the four corners at Garrisons ; one-half mile after crossing brook turn sharp to right and continue on two miles, passing cemetery and stone church on the left, crossing Indian Brook and passing a stone water trough, *water* just around the bend. At the forks, one-half mile beyond this, take road to the right, passing a cemetery and crossing a stone bridge, bear to the right a short distance to Main Street, Cold Spring, and turn to the right. At the fork near wheelwright's shop, take road to the left for Fishkill, cross a rustic bridge over brook (*water*) and in about a mile cross or ford another brook to three corners near a church and take road to the left, passing a brick school house on the right, and a little later a small cemetery in the middle of a corn field, also on the right. *Water* in a trough half a mile beyond ; bear to the right at red barn and cross or ford a brook and go on, keeping to the left and crossing a rustic bridge over another brook, about two miles to Springside Hotel, *water;* then past a small granite monument on the right to mark some Revolutionary event ; cross red bridge over Fishkill River one-half mile before coming to Fishkill Village.

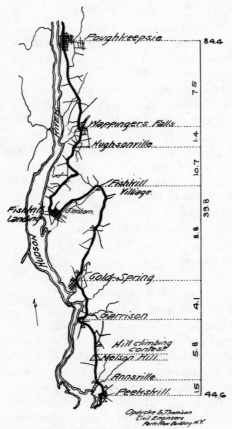

Peekskill to Poughkeepsie

8 M. P. H. THROUGH THE FISHKILLS

Follow street railway track through Glenham and Matteawan direct to Fishkill Landing (Griffith & Howe, hardware store, have *gasoline*). Turn to the right on North Avenue for Wappinger Falls, passing Belle Isle Road House on the right, and about 2 miles from Fishkill Landing is a sharp hill, 12 per cent. grade ; keep to the right at the forks, passing a red school house on the right, and at the next forks take road to the left through Hudsonville to Wappinger Falls ; then down the hill past a *water* trough. At the foot of the hill turn sharp to the right into South Avenue, and follow street railway track 7½ miles to Nelson House, Poughkeepsie, where the time will be taken for the night control.

RECORD SHEETS MUST BE FILLED IN HERE
(The night storage station is on Main Street.)

TUESDAY MORNING, SEPTEMBER 10

RECORD SHEETS MUST BE FILLED IN HERE
8 a. m.   Leave Nelson House, which is on Market Street, and

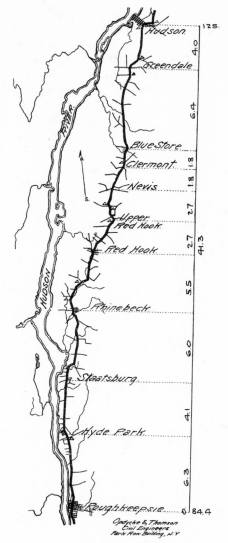

Poughkeepsie to Hudson

go to Main Street, turn to the left one-half block, then turn sharp to the right into Washington Street, continue 1½ miles and then take left road at forks. In about a mile you come to a hill 5 to 13 per cent. grade, then on through Hyde Park, which is 6 miles from Poughkeepsie, going down a short hill 12 per cent. grade, *before* reaching Hyde Park, and passing a pump (*water*) on the left about 1½ miles *after* leaving this village. Country is rolling but roads are very good. In about 4 miles you come to Staatsburg and there you will find a stone *water* trough on the left. Two miles beyond this place take the right road at the forks for Rhinebeck (*water* here).

8 M. P. H. THROUGH RHINE-BECK

Keep on and over the hill ; at the forks take road to the left. One-half mile from Rhinebeck cross or ford a brook (*water*), go up a hill and at top of the hill at forks take road to right for Red Hook. At the next forks, which is just after crossing railroad track, take road to the left. In about one-half mile you will come to a hill 7 to 15 per cent. grade, keep to the left at the next forks for Red Hook, where *water* can be obtained at hotel. One-half mile from here cross or ford a large brook (*water*) ; take left road at forks ; take left road again at next forks after leaving Upper Red Hook for Blue Store. At three forks take road to the right and keep straight, passing Hotel Nevis on your right through Clermont. Take road to the left at the next forks after Clermont and continue to Blue Store, where you turn sharp to the left for Hudson (*water*). Keep to the right at the next forks, and 4 miles from Blue Store there is a spring (*water*) on the left, then on through Glendale which is four miles from Hudson. Two miles from Glendale there is a red *pump* on the right. Continue on the Post Road into Warren Street, Hudson.

8 M. P. H. THROUH HUDSON CONTROL

Continue as far as Fifth Street, to the Hotel Central, where time will be taken for noon control.

RECORD SHEETS
MUST BE FILLED
IN HERE

Lunch at Hotel Central.

TUESDAY AFTERNOON, SEPTEMBER 10

In leaving Hudson go up Warren Street to the Square and turn to the left side into Columbia Street, then to the right into Green Street. At the *water* trough bear to the left passing the Fair Grounds on the left. Take road to the left at the next forks for Stottsville, passing a cemetery to the left, and on arriving at a slate-colored church, turn

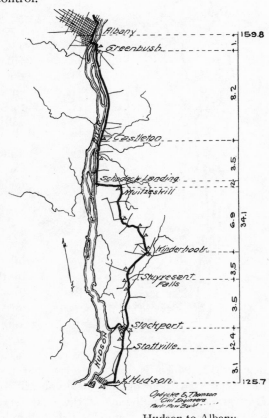

Hudson to Albany

to the right, go down a long hill ; at the foot, turn to the right and cross bridge over Kinderhook Creek, bear to the left and cross railroad track, go over a small hill and there is a *water* trough on the left.   Keep to the right and go up a short hill 12 per cent. grade and then a long hill into Stuyvesant Falls (*pump* on the right in front of what was once a store).   Go on down a hill across a bridge and keep to the right ; then up a hill across a railroad track. At the next forks take road to the right, then bend to the right and cross railroad track at Sunnyside, keep to the left after crossing railroad track into Kinderhook.   (Stone trough on the right—*water*). Turn to the left, passing by cemetery on both sides of the road, to sign post "*Castleton 11 M.*" and at sign post "*Greenbush 18½ M.*" turn again to the left to sign post "*Albany 17 M.*"   At sign post "*Castleton 6½ M.*" (Muitzeskill) turn left down to the river to Schodack Landing and to the right and along Hudson River & New York Central Railroad track, north, to sign post "*Castleton 1 M.*"   Continue from here on River Street to Castleton.   At sign post "*Albany 8 M.*" leave Green Street at your right and follow Albany Post Road, keeping to the left ; straight ahead to sign post "*Albany ⇒*" in Greenbush, which is 1 mile from Albany, beginning of Albany control.

8 M. P. H. THROUGH ALBANY CONTROL

After crossing two bridges over railroad tracks, keep straight on until you reach asphalt pavement ; turn here sharp to the left into the bridge and cross into Albany toll, 15 cents.   At the Albany end of the bridge make a slight jog to the left into Ferry Street, go up this street three blocks and turn to the right into Green Street, to the end of the street, then turn to the right into State Street one block, then turn left one block to Stanwix Hall on the right, where time will be taken for the night control.

RECORD SHEETS MUST BE FILLED IN HERE

Night Storage Station is at Empire Curling Rink on Lake Avenue.

WEDNESDAY MORNING, SEPTEMBER 11

RECORD SHEETS MUST BE FILLED IN HERE

In leaving rink at Albany go out to Lake Avenue as far as State Street, turn right on State Street into Knox sometimes called Northern Boulevard, continue straight north to the Van Rensselaer Boulevard over railroad bridge for about two miles, then turn to the left into Menan Road in front of a cemetery gate and later turn to the right into Louden Road for Latham Corners which is about three miles distant. Turn to the left and take main road for Schenectady; one mile

beyond take road to the left at the forks and at Verdoy which is three miles from Latham Corners, there is a pump on the right side of the road in front of a store (*water*).

One-half mile beyond is Niskayuna. Then on down a short hill, 15 per cent. grade, passing soon brick church on your right ; the road is quite rough along here for a mile or so; then you go down a very steep, rough hill, with a bridge at the foot. *Great caution* must be used at this hill as it is *dangerous* on account of its curve at the bridge.

Go up a long hill leading to the outskirts of Schenectady.

8 M. P. H. THROUGH SCHENECTADY

Go into Union Street, on which continue, crossing railroad track, and then on to Washington Avenue, where turn to the right and cross bridge over Mohawk River; bear to the left after crossing bridge, passing Scotia, bear to the right at Mohawk Avenue. After leaving Schenectady

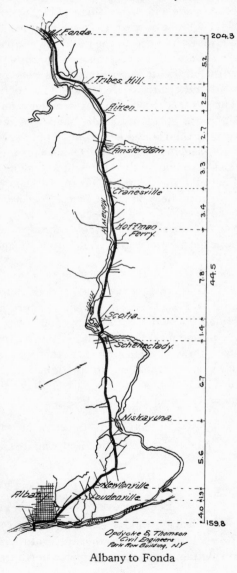

Albany to Fonda

the road is sandy for about two miles, then good for some miles. A yellow house on the left known as Rectors, five miles out, has a pump in the yard and there is a pump beside the road a few yards further on.

Go up a short hill, 16 per cent. grade, and in three-quarters of a mile go up a short rise, 14 per cent. grade, to the approach of railroad bridge, keep to the left down the hill, red house to the left, then up a hill of 10 per cent. grade. Seven miles from Schenectady go down a hill and across a small bridge into Hoffman's Ferry (*water*), pump in front of store on the left. Three-fourths of a mile beyond here go down a sharp rocky hill, 12 per cent. grade at Crane's Village, *water* trough on the right side of the road. At the beginning of railroad track is Amsterdam; *water* is on the right side of the road.

8 M. P. H. THROUGH AMSTERDAM

Continue on Main Street, Amsterdam, as far as Market Street, turn to the right into Market Street for one block and then turn to the left into Division Street and at end of brick pavement turn to the right into Clinton Street for a short block and then to the left into the boulevard and go on towards Fonda which is twelve miles away. Cross the railroad track at end of boulevard and in three miles arrive at Akin (*water* on the right). Road from end of boulevard to Akin is bad, then for half a mile it is better to Peppers Hill, which is very rocky and sandy with 7 per cent. grade. Then follow along New York Central track for about two miles on very fair road. Five miles from Amsterdam is Tribes Hill, which is one-fourth of a mile long, rocky and quite poor road, 5, 12 and 15 per cent. grade. At the top of the hill is a well (*water*) on the right. Bear to the left, passing school house on the right, keep to the right at the next forks near a small church, which has a cross for a steeple, on the right then down a hill over a white bridge, and it is a good road for three miles. Two miles before reaching Fonda there is a *water* trough on the left. Continue on to Hotel Roy (Fonda), formerly Snell House, where time will be taken for *noon control*.

RECORD SHEETS MUST BE FILLED IN HERE

WEDNESDAY AFTERNOON, SEPTEMBER 11

RECORD SHEETS MUST BE FILLED IN HERE

In leaving Fonda bear to the left opposite Farmers Hotel and cross the bridge over the creek and one railroad track, then follow

New York Central for a long distance. Six miles from Fonda is a water trough on the right opposite railroad pumping station; two miles beyond this go over a rocky hill, 15 per cent. grade on both sides, and a short distance beyond foot is a *water* trough on the right. The road from here for the next ten miles is much better. Two miles from the last water trough is another trough (*water*) on the right and at Palatine Bridge a little further beyond, is a stone trough on the right. Four miles beyond is Nelliston; go down a hill and at the foot is a *water* trough on the right, then up a sharp hill, 19 per cent. grade. Two miles beyond Nelliston is a *water* trough on the left. In another mile pass Palatine Church on the left, the oldest building in this section of the country. Three miles beyond comes St. Johnsville, which has a *water* trough on the right at the edge of the town and another in the square.

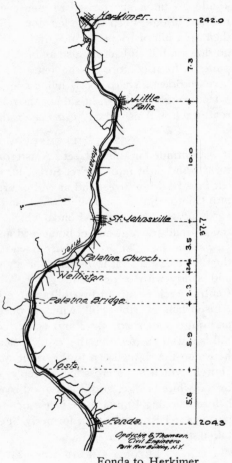

Fonda to Herkimer

8 M. P. H. THROUGH ST. JOHNSVILLE

Three miles beyond this is East Creek, where there is a *water* trough on the right. Cross a covered bridge and continue to Little Falls, seven miles beyond. Going into Little Falls under railroad bridge there is a hill of 12 per cent. grade (*water* a little beyond this) and again at the end of the Main Street.

8 M. P. H. THROUGH LITTLE FALLS

Continue straight on toward Herkimer, seven miles. After leaving

Little Falls the road is quite rough for about two miles, then good for two miles, then down a little hill, then begins an ascent of a hill a mile long, 5 to 8 per cent. grade.   Then for two miles a series of small hills with road in fair condition.   At the top of a hill on the right is a water trough, where a danger signal will be displayed as a caution in descending a winding hill at the foot of which is a long bridge, over West Canada Creek, and thence into Herkimer.   The name of the street after crossing the bridge is Albany Street, on which you continue as far as the depot, and then turn to the right into Main Street and continue 1½ blocks to the Palmer House, where time for night control will be taken.

RECORD SHEET MUST BE FILLED IN HERE

THURSDAY MORNING, SEPTEMBER 12

RECORD SHEETS MUST BE FILLED IN HERE

In leaving Herkimer go down Main Street, cross New York Central Railroad and follow street railway through Mohawk and Ilion to Frankfort.

(*Water* on left of lumber yard).   Road rough until a mile beyond Frankfort, then a fine road for a mile, then sandy and rough to Utica.

Turn to right, go under a railroad bridge, and in half-mile cross or ford a brook.

Turn to the left where the cinder path crosses the road, and go toward the Masonic Home (which is on the outskirts of Utica).

8 M. P. H. THROUGH UTICA

Crossing bridge over canal and two railroad tracks, bear to the left just a little, and sharp to the right through the Masonic Home grounds.   Keep to the left after passing the house, and go down a hill, and up another in the grounds to the asphalt, on which continue for two miles.

Turn to left into Genesee Street, and go toward New Hartford, which is four miles away; and *water* on both sides of the road in front of hotels.   Take road to the right after passing hotels.

Cross railroad track in about a mile and take road to right at next forks for Kirkland, which is four miles away, passing a cemetery on the left.   At the next forks take road to the right, and just beyond is a *water* trough on the right.   Good road from here for about a mile, then fair or poor to Laidsville, then improves ; the road is rolling but in good repair.

Five miles from Laidsville is Vernon, and just beyond is *water* trough on the right. Again in about a mile *water* on left in a farm yard.

Go under railroad bridge near the silk mills of the Oneida Community and turn sharp to right following West Shore R. R.; then go under West Shore railroad bridge again and keep to left again for Oneida, three miles.

8 M. P. H. THROUGH
ONEIDA

After crossing railroad track at Oneida Castle take first street to right, which is Main Street, and continue as far as Madison Street. Turn to right into this street, and Madison House is half-block on the right, where time for *noon control* will be taken.

RECORD SHEETS MUST BE
FILLED IN HERE
Lunch at Madison House.

THURSDAY AFTER-
NOON, SEPTEMBER 12

RECORD SHEETS MUST BE
FILLED IN HERE

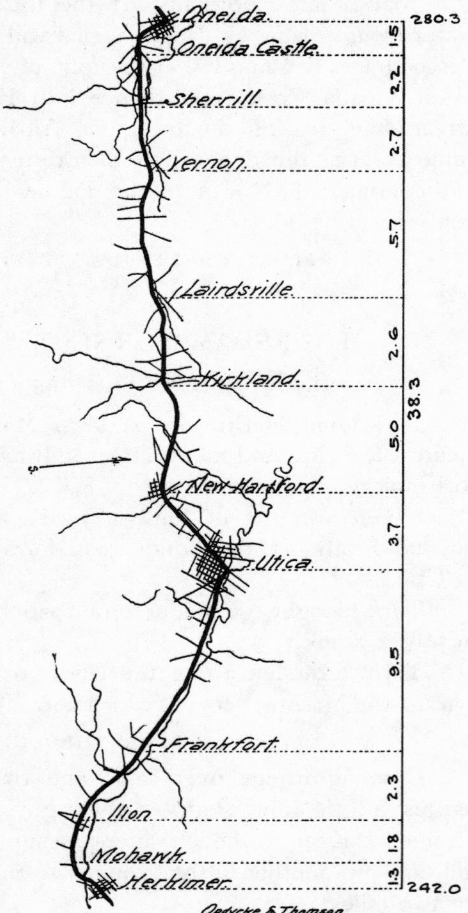

In leaving Oneida go out on Madison Street, turn to the left into Main Street, for one block, and then to right into Lenox Avenue, and continue toward Chittenango, twelve miles away. The roads from Oneida to Syracuse are poor.

At the forks take road to the right, go down a short, rocky hill

Herkimer to Oneida

of 10 per cent. grade, and a little beyond up a short hill, 6 per cent. grade, passing through Wampsville, which is about 3½ miles from Oneida.   Water trough on the left half a mile beyond.

Then up long hill, 8, 9 and 10 per cent. grade and down a long hill across Lehigh Railroad track, through Quality Hill, passing on the right a white school house with a large bell ; then down a long hill, at the foot of which is a brook (*water*) ; half a mile beyond is a water trough on the left ; then over a long hill, continuing on through the village of Sullivan.

Take road to the right at forks and go on through Four Corners, Chittenango for Fayetteville, crossing a bridge and up a short hill, 12 per cent. grade.

Continue straight on at the foot of hill following through telegraph poles, passing a cheese factory on the left (*water* trough here).

Then comes a short hill, 12 and 14 per cent. grade, and then a series of hills 9 to 5 per cent.   At the forks on a hill, take road to the right, and go down a rocky hill.   One-half mile beyond is a *water* trough on the right under a windmill in barnyard.

Oneida to Syracuse

Continue through village of Mycenae ; cross or ford a brook ; then up a hill, 6 per cent. grade, passing a stone school house on the left at the top.   At the top of a hill, one mile beyond, there is water on the left at a red barn.

Cross railroad track at the Fayetteville station one-half mile before arriving at the village.   (Stone water trough in the square.)   Two and one-half miles beyond is a toll gate (toll 8 cents).   In 1½ miles you come to Orrville (*water* in front of the hotel) ; 1½ miles beyond stone *water* trough on the left.

Four miles from the first toll gate is a second one (toll 8 cents). One-half mile beyond is Syracuse city line where asphalt pavement commences. This is Genesee Street, on which continue to Yates House, where time will be taken for *night control*.

RECORD SHEETS MUST BE FILLED IN HERE

The night storage station is at Convention Hall.

FRIDAY MORNING, SEPTEMBER 13

RECORD SHEETS MUST BE FILLED IN HERE

In leaving Syracuse cross Swing Bridge on to West Genesee Street, and continue on asphalt and brick pavement two miles to the road for Camillus.

Go up several small hills, and finally go down a long, winding hill, very crooked and covered with sharp rubble, and cross railroad track into Camillus, and after passing through the village go up a very long, stony hill, 17, 14, 10, 7, 9 per cent. grade. This hill is about a mile long ; then go down a long hill, and after this there is a series of hills, but quite good roads for a few miles. Two miles before arriving at Elbridge is a *water* trough on the right, and also a stone *water* trough on the left as you enter the town. Continue straight, passing a thick row of willow trees, on the left is a *water* trough a short distance beyond which, at the second forks, take road to right for Weedsport, four miles beyond. Keep to the left near old house and barn.

Just a little beyond another forks take the road to the right for Weedsport, which is three miles beyond.

Up a long hill, 9, 4 and 9 per cent. grade. Cross or ford a brook just on outskirts of Weedsport.

8 M. P. H. THROUGH WEEDSPORT

Cross railroad track into Weedsport (at one *water* trough on the left) and cross the canal bridge just beyond the town, and keep straight on to Port Byron, which is three miles away.

Go under railroad bridge, bend to the right and cross a red bridge. (Two miles beyond, *water* trough on the left.) Then cross canal bridge and enter Port Byron. At the flagstone crossing turn sharp to the right for Montezuma. Cross bridge and turn to left at blacksmith shop, and in 50 feet turn to right, passing school house on the right, then keep to the left at the next forks.

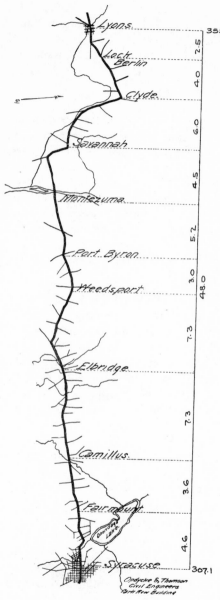

Syracuse to Lyons

Go up a few short hills, then down a long, sandy, rocky hill, then over one-half mile of sandy road, and over a short hill, 10 per cent. grade, and still another 14 and 18 grade, then down a rough rocky hill, and go over the worst road on the route.

Cross canal bridge and turn sharp to the left off the bridge and cross the red bridge over creek.

Keep straight on through the four corners, passing the village of Montezuma a few rods away on the left. Go through an old toll gate, and cross bridge over creek, and very soon cross another bridge.

The roads through Port Byron and Montezuma through the salt marshes are very bad, but from Savannah to Lyons are better.

At the forks beyond the marsh take road to right for Savannah (*water* trough on the left a little beyond).

After passing the stores in Savannah, turn sharp to the first left into West Church Street for Clyde. Keep to right at railroad bridge at top of hill, then to the left at the forks, and it is a straight road to Clyde.

At the forks just beyond an old blacksmith shop take road to right, over a small hill, 12 per cent. grade, and down a long hill and pass through a long swamp, and over a bridge.

Then over a short hill 10 per cent. grade (*water* trough on the right about three miles from Savannah) and school house on the right a little beyond, and continue straight on into Clyde.

8 M. P. H. THROUGH CLYDE

On reaching Clyde turn to the right into Main Street for one-half block, then to the left past the park, and at the end of the park turn to the left again for Lyons. Go over a hill 10 per cent. grade and over another 7 per cent. grade and pass through the village of Lock Berlin. Take road to the right at next forks.

Entering Lyons through Montezuma Street, turn left into William Street, one short block, then turn to the left into Water Street, and cross canal bridge to the fair grounds, where time will be taken for *noon control*.

RECORD SHEETS MUST BE FILLED IN HERE
Lunch at Congress Hall.

FRIDAY AFTERNOON, SEPTEMBER 13

RECORD SHEETS MUST BE FILLED IN HERE

In leaving Lyons go out Water Street and at the top of the hill take road to left for Newark, which is nine miles away.

Keep to the left at Canal Locks, cross bridge and then go to right, following canal and passing County Alms House on the left, Then over the canal again, 16 per cent. grade, at approach and turn sharp to the left, following the canal on the other side and passing school house on the right. Roads from Lyons to Rochester fair except few miles through Egypt.

Follow telegraph poles and turn to left, crossing railroad tracks, then under a railroad bridge.

At the forks beyond take road to the right into Newark.

8 M. P. H. THROUGH NEWARK

Turn left at the hotels and cross canal bridge, turning sharp to the right after crossing bridge, and proceed to East Palmyra, four miles away.

Take road to the left at the forks near the canal bridge, and follow canal. At the next forks take road to the right and cross canal bridge, keeping to the right on either side and crossing railroad track. At the next forks take road to the left.

At the next forks take road to the right, passing through long rows of maple trees on each side. Keeping to the left at the brick churches, and then down a small hill into East Palmyra. (*Water* trough on right near the stores). About a mile beyond is a *pump* and trough on the right.

At the forks keep to the right, crossing bridge over creek and then a railroad track, passing a school house on the right.

8 M. P. H. THROUGH PALMYRA

Cross canal bridge into the center of the town of Palmyra. (*Water* trough on the left, just before coming to Powers Hotel).

Keep straight on for about two miles, turn to right and cross bridge at the yellow mills, and a few rods further on cross canal bridge and take the first left for Macedon, which is four miles from Palmyra. Less than one-half mile after crossing canal bridge there is a *pump* and a trough at the foot of a hill, 9 per cent. grade. *Water* again on the right in another half mile.

Pass Canal Lock No. 60 on the left and one-half mile beyond turn to left across canal bridge into outskirts of Macedon. Straight through Macedon and at the forks beyond the town take road to right (which is known as Rochester and Palmyra Road) for Rochester eighteen miles away.

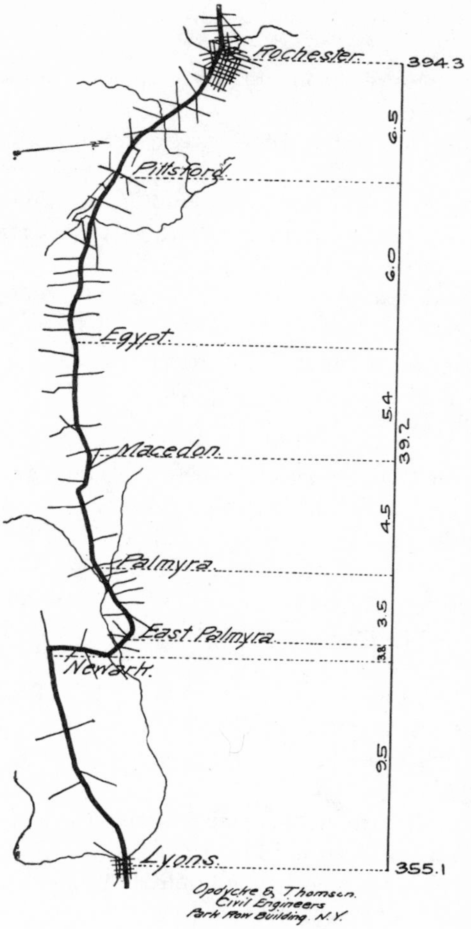

In about a mile go over a hill, which has 18 per cent. grade on

Lyons to Rochester

the up side, and is long, rough and rocky on the down side.   Near
the foot cross a brook (*water*) and go up a long hill, 12, 9 and 14 per
cent. grade, and then down a long hill, and soon pass through the
town of Egypt, which is only a post office.

At the forks beyond, keep to the right and go up the hill towards
Pittsford.

At Pittsford (*water* trough on the left in square) keep straight on
for Rochester, which is about seven miles.

In about four miles at twelve corners there are *water* troughs
in two places on the right.

The asphalt pavement is Monroe Avenue, Rochester, on which
continue for two miles, and then turn to right into Clinton Avenue, for
several blocks ; and then turn to the left into Main Street.

Follow Main Street for a dozen blocks to Hotel Powers, where
time will be taken for *Night Control.*

RECORD SHEETS SHOULD BE FILLED HERE

SATURDAY MORNING, SEPTEMBER 14

RECORD SHEETS MUST BE FILLED IN HERE

Leaving Rochester, go out Main Street over Central Bridge, and
at the fork near Orphan Asylum, take road to the right.   The name
of the street after crossing bridge is West Avenue.   In about four miles
go through Gates Center, passing brick school house on the right and
keeping on toward Chili, another hamlet six miles away.   One mile
from Gates Center there is a pump and trough on the right, in front
of road house.

Pass a school house on the right, and take road to the left at the
forks beyond.   Pass Methodist Seminary on the right, and soon come
to Chili.   At the forks take road to right for Churchville, four miles
beyond.

Go up a series of hills, which are not difficult as the roads are
good.   *Water* on the right in front of store in Churchville.

Keep straight on for Bergen, two miles beyond railroad bridge ; at
the next forks take road to the right into Bergen.   Water on left in
the town.   Pass through the town and follow New York Central for
about a mile, then turn to the left and continue for a mile in sort of a
curve and cross railroad, passing school house on right, and heading
toward Byron.   (Pump in the town on right).   Cross brook at the
edge of the village; keep straight on for Batavia, ten miles away.
Take road to left at forks near railroad crossing and go towards a red

barn on the left.   Keep to the right at the bend in the road, and at forks near school house take road to left.   Cross a bridge by an old mill and go up a little hill.   At the forks near stone blacksmith shop take road to the left and go up a series of hills.   One mile beyond, *pump* on right in front of a house.   At the forks take the road to the left for East Main Street, Batavia, and continue to Hotel Richmond on the left, where time will be taken for *noon control.*

RECORD SHEETS MUST BE FILLED IN HERE

Lunch at Hotel Richmond.

SATURDAY AFTER-NOON, SEPTEMBER 14

RECORD SHEETS MUST BE FILLED IN HERE

In leaving Batavia, keep up West Main Street to Walnut Street on the bridge and turn sharp to the right into South Main Street.   At the forks take road to the left, which is Pearl Street, for West Batavia, six miles away.   Cross a railroad track in about two miles, and about two miles further on pass a white school house on the left.   *Water* at road house on the left, six miles from Batavia.   At the forks near white school house, take road to left for Corfu, which is six miles from West

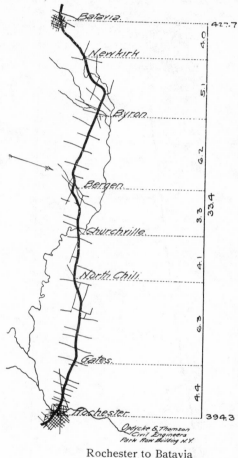

Rochester to Batavia

Batavia.   Pass through Corfu at the forks two miles beyond, take road to the right, and in one-quarter of a mile cross a single railroad track, and soon go through Crittenden, which is four miles from Corfu. Keep straight on to the forks, and take road to the right for Mill Grove, which is three miles from Crittenden.   *Pump* on the left in the town. Keep on, passing an old cemetery on the left, and over a few small hills, and go through the village·of Wilhelm. Post Office on the right and school house on the left. This hamlet is four miles beyond Mill Grove. Continue straight on for three miles to Bowmansville. Pass through Bowmansville (*pump* on right in front of hotel) and it is six miles to the city line, and ten miles to the center of Buffalo, passing through a toll gate (toll, 5 cents). From the city line the road is called Genesee Street, on which continue as far as Chippewa Street (hay scales on the corner of Chippewa Street). Turn to right into Chippewa Street for four blocks, then to the right into Delaware Avenue as far as the tunnel, where time will be taken for *night control*.

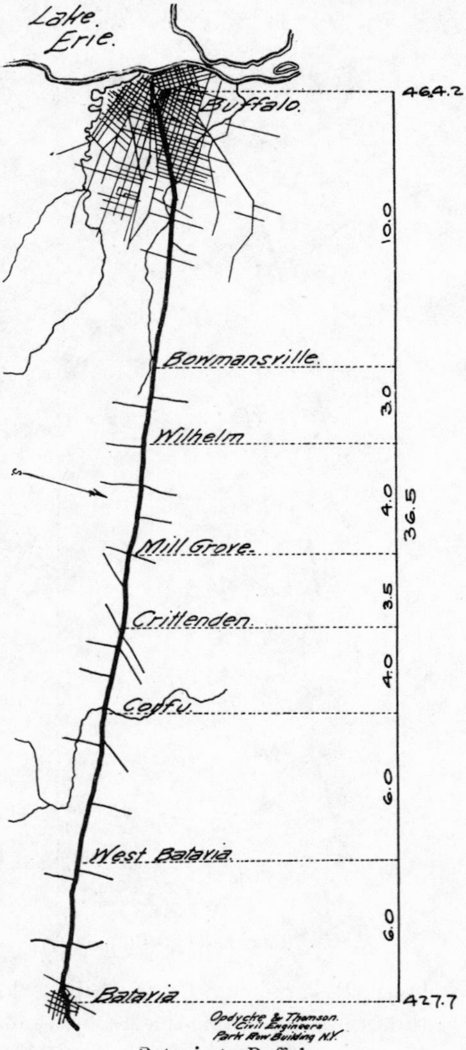

RECORD SHEETS MUST BE FILLED IN HERE

HILL CLIMBING CONTEST ON NELSON HILL

MONDAY SEPTEMBER 9

Nelson Hill is about three miles north of Peekskill.

The following special rules and conditions will apply to this contest:

1. A vehicle in climbing the hill, on being signalled by an overtaking vehicle, shall drive to the extreme ·right of the road.

Batavia to Buffalo

2. If it becomes necessary for a vehicle to stop on the hill, it must take a position on the extreme right of the road as nearly as practicable.

3. Vehicles, on arriving at the signal of approach to control for hill climbing contest, will stop; those which are going to compete in the contest, on the right side of the road; those which are not going to compete, on the left side of the road.

4. The control for the Hill Climbing Contest will open at 1 p. m., and remain open for half an hour until 1:30 p. m., during which time those vehicles which desire to compete in the contest will be started up the hill at 30 seconds intervals. From 1:30 p. m., to 2 p. m., those vehicles which do not desire to compete in the contest will proceed up the hill to the beginning of the next control on the summit, where their time will be taken and they will proceed toward Poughkeepsie. This procedure will be repeated in alternate half hour until 4:30 p. m., when the control at the bottom of the hill will close. The control on the summit of the hill will be closed at 5 p. m.

The official time of vehicles which have climbed the hill will be taken at the summit *without stop* and will be the official time for the beginning of the next control. This time will be entered on contestants' record sheets at the night control at Poughkeepsie.

This trial is a separate contest. The time occupied from reaching the control at the base of the hill to leaving the control at the summit *will be deducted from the general running time.*

Stop at red flag, signal of approach to control for hill.

RECORD SHEETS MUST BE FILLED IN HERE

Contestants who desire to compete will drive to the right side of the road 500 feet beyond to control for Hill Climbing Contest, in order of their arrival, allowing 10 feet space between vehicles. Other vehicles will drive to the left side of the road.

Record sheets for hill climbing contests will be filled in here, and vehicles will be started at 30 seconds intervals.

Proceed at full speed up the hill to signal at summit at telegraph pole No. 1,079, which is end of Hill Control, where time will be taken *without stop*, which will constitute the official time for the beginning of the next control.

Proceed straight ahead toward Poughkeepsie.

The President of the Club, Albert R. Shattuck, Esq., has presented a Cup to be awarded by the Committee to the automobile carrying two passengers and running on four wheels which makes the best time in climbing Nelson Hill.

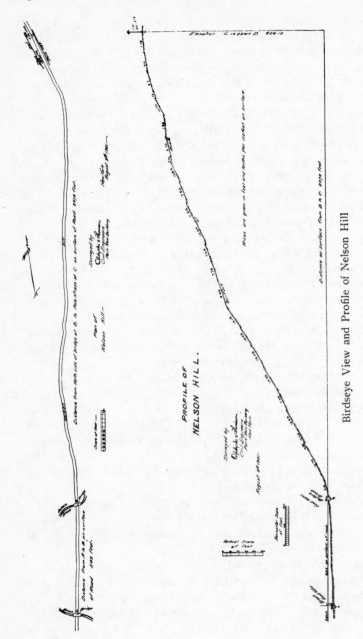

Birdseye View and Profile of Nelson Hill

The Automobile and its Mission
(1902)

A farmer of Farragut, Iowa, making the rounds of his big farm.

THE AUTOMOBILE AND ITS MISSION

BY HERBERT LADD TOWLE

FIFTEEN years ago the automobile was only a traveller's tale and the hobby of a few crack-brained experimenters. Five years ago the automobile factories of the United States produced about 100,000 cars. This year about 500,-000 cars will be built, whose total value will exceed $600,000,000. One city alone will produce 300,000 cars—one factory, 200,000.

In 1905 the lowest practical price for an automobile was $900; to-day a better one costs but $600. Cars equal to those costing $1,500 and $2,000 five years ago, cost $1,200 and $1,500 to-day; and $900 buys a car better than the $1,200 car of the earlier date.

In 1908 about 300,000 of our citizens owned automobiles; before summer there will be an automobile for every 100 persons. In 1908 our export motor business was not worth mentioning. Last year it exceeded $25,000,000.

Five years ago this country had but a sprinkling of motor-trucks. They were poorly built; their advantages were doubtful; the only thing certain was the enormous latent demand. To-day there are some 40,000 motor-trucks giving satisfaction to 18,000 owners, and the percentage of growth in this business exceeds that in the pleasure-car field.

To-day the invested capital in the automobile business in this country alone rivals that of the United States Steel Corporation. Most of the employees are skilled, most of them work in modern, wholesome factories, and all are well paid.

Five years ago the automobile was a transcendent plaything—thrilling, seductive, desperately expensive. Its oldest devotees could view with patience neither abstention from its charms nor the bills which followed surrender. To-day the harrowing alternative is mitigated at both ends. The bills are less and some of the excitement has worn off. Neighbor Brown, who sensibly refused to mortgage his house to buy a car in 1908, is now piling his family into a smart little black-and-red car, and is starting out on a four-day run to the Water Gap and return. And you know that he can do it now without the mortgage.

Fifth Avenue, New York, looking north, seven years ago.
Photograph taken from opposite the Windsor Arcade.

your daily life as your walk to the office.

What does it all signify? This tremendous industry that has grown up almost overnight, and has made itself so necessary that a million owners of cars are giving food and roofs and clothing to another million—wage-earners and their families —for supplying them with the new means of locomotion—what does this new industry portend? How many more people are going to buy cars? Are automobiles a permanent development or a temporary fad? If permanent, how do they justify themselves—in mere pleasure, which a few can afford but more cannot, or in genuine service? Are they at bottom a liability or an asset?

Neighbor Brown, the effervescent novice, cannot teach

You yourself have seen the Water Gap, have explored every sunny road and leafy by-way within a hundred miles of your home, have seen the speedometer needle hang at 50 or 60, and have come unscathed through adventures which, when you think of them in cold blood, bring a creepy stirring to your spine. Your present car is good, but not showy; you keep it in a little garage behind your house and use it soberly—you and your family—nearly every day; and your motoring costs about half what it did five years ago. You seldom drive now for the mere pleasure of driving; yet your car is as much a part of

us much. The bicycle, twenty years ago, had just as fervid votaries, but to-day the bicycle is used chiefly for getting about. How is it with you, the seasoned motorist? If you had no car, in what respect would your life and your family's be changed?

You and I—all of us—used to choose our homes for their nearness to train or trolley. A mile from the station, half a mile from the trolley, was our immutable limit. The gates of Paradise would not have tempted us further. Rents soared; the lucky first owners of land near a new transportation line retired from business and lived in luxury on the fruits of their good fortune; still we cheerfully paid tribute, and dotted the map with little disks and bands of high-priced real estate. Horses were expensive and a nuisance, and we did not know that we might become each his own motor-man.

But to-day your home is in a suburb, handy for the motorist but otherwise dependent on trolley service. Were it not for the automobile, your wife's need of companionship would compel removal either to the city or to a more central part of your village. Part, at least, of what you saved on the car would go out in higher rent. Then you would need some other forms of exercise and recreation—golf, weekends at the shore, or the theatre. More money! When you visit friends in the next town, you take

Fifth Avenue to-day, from about the same point, showing the change in the character of the traffic.

The new home of SCRIBNER'S MAGAZINE, under construction, is the white building in the middle distance.

your maid to visit *her* friends. Without the car she would have to shift for herself. And the children—you can already hear the lamentations when they learn that they have seen the last of Green Pond, and that these Saturday picnics by the babbling Wanaque River will be no more! You moved to your country home after you began motoring. Dare you say that that change was for the worse?

Perchance you have no car—as yet. But you have friends living five miles away by road. To visit them by rail, you must go half a mile to the station, ride ten miles to a junction, wait an hour, and

travel a dozen miles more to a station half a mile from their home. How often do you see your friends?

Or you are a nature-lover and a busy man. The city stifles you and the daily ordeal of strap-hanging is a horror. Yet your wife declares that she will be "buried alive" if she goes where houses are more than a hundred feet apart. She has a right to her view, too. How shall yours and hers be reconciled?

Or you have children. Shall they be reduced to "tag" on the streets and in a bric-à-brac-filled apartment, or shall they have green grass, a sand-pile, trees, and a

Automobiles gathered at a hotel in the suburbs.

swing? Or perhaps you are a farmer, seeking means to relieve the monotony of farm life and hold your sons from the dangerous lure of the city.

For hundreds of thousands of families the automobile is at last supplying the happiest of answers. Bridging as it does the gap between rail travel and the horse, at a possible cost less than that of the latter, it has added threefold or more to the habitable areas outside of our cities. Double a certain radius and you quadruple the enclosed area. Make three miles your limit and the area becomes nine. Think what this will lead to in the course of a generation or two, and you will realize the transformation which the low-cost automobile is working.

What has wrought this change? Not merely improvements in mechanism, though those have been essential. Rather, it is the ingenious reduction in both first cost and expense of maintenance to figures which a few years ago seemed utterly impossible.

For a dollar a day and a little spare time any one who will may now keep a small but serviceable car and use it daily and for week-ends. For five or six hundred a year one may have a "real car" with sliding-gear transmission and all the similitude of luxury, and if it is used only for week-ends, not for daily business trips, a few dollars a week will cover the ex-

Arriving at the opera in automobiles, Philadelphia.

pense even of such
a car.

At the other end
of the scale, one
may purchase a high-
grade car of thirty
or forty horse-power
at a price material-
ly lower than five
years ago, equipped
with electric horn,
electric lights, en-
gine-starter, and
other conveniences
then unthought of;
and this car will be
so well built, so dur-
able, and so simple
to manage that the
high-priest of the

The motor fire-engine which is crowding out the much-beloved fire-horse in New York.

The new high-pressure motor hose-wagon.

The efficiency of the fire service has been greatly increased by the adoption of the motor-propelled
hose-wagons because of the great speed obtained and greater carrying capacity.

The difference in
rental will be, at 8
per cent, $160. Add-
ing the theatre,
club, and vacation
expenses, you have
$460 to apply on a
new programme.

The country house
is a mile and a half
from the village, and
your wife or son will
go to the station
with you and drive
the car home. Six
miles a day, plus
week-end trips, will
make about 4,000
miles a year. A fair
average for gas-
olene, oil, tires, and
repairs is five cents
a mile for a $1,200

steering-wheel—the chauffeur—is now only
worshipped if one has a stable of several
cars. Even chauffeurs demand the ritual
of the check-book less often, and sacrifices
and burnt-offerings of wrecked cars are
seldom required.

Let us suppose a case. Your city house
is worth, say, $9,000. Included in your
recreation budget are $100 for theatre,
$150 for vacations, and $50 for club dues.
You can get a neat suburban home, with
an acre of ground and a garage, for $7,000.

car—$200 for the year. Depreciation, if
averaged over four years, will be about
the same. Insurance and extras will
amount to perhaps $50.

Thus far, the saving and expense about
balance. Whether they do so in practice
will depend largely on the outlays for
commutation, extra fuel, and servants'
wages. But one thing is certain: you will
spend only a fifth or a tenth as much on
doctors! I could name men who date
their first real grip on business from the

Two types of Fifth Avenue motor-bus, New York.

ing and evening trains are met by scores of motor-cars. In a few years there will be hundreds.

Did space permit, I could say much about the private suburban garage. It must be more than four walls and a roof, especially if the car is to be used in winter. The first essential is room to work; the second, fireproofness; the third, abundant light; the fourth, double walls

time when they began building up their physical energies by motoring—conservative motoring, mind you, not extravagance in either speed or spending.

The logic of the situation points to the growth of motor colonies. It is the exceptional city family that removes outright to the farming hinterland, and in most cases distance from transportation has hitherto produced an inferior neighborhood. That latter condition is visibly giving way to the new order; already the cities have many automobile "commuters," and in every large suburb the morn-

that will mitigate the heat of summer and the rigors of winter; and the fifth, if the car is to be used the year round, is a heating system, preferably by hot water. With these things provided, plus a bench and a fair tool equipment, the details can be arranged to suit the taste and purse of the owner. If the chauffeur's quarters are above, they should be wholly separated from the place where the cars are kept, and should be reached by an outside door.

Turn now to the great rural districts, and what do we see? For two generations agriculture has lost ground in the competition for men and brains. Manufacturing has been over-stimulated; city life has been made attractive by countless modern appliances, few of which

A motor police patrol wagon, Chicago.

have reached the farm. As a class, farmers have been more intent on improvements for haymaking than for homemaking. Furnace heat, running water, sanitary plumbing, fireless cookers, kitchen cabinets, aluminum ware, hardwood floors, and rugs—how many farms to-day have these devices to ease the burden of the farmer's wife?

Yet the pendulum is ready to swing the

The truth is that macadam depends on the constant abrasion of hoofs and steel tires to supply fresh bonding material, and when the dust bond is sucked up and flung over the fence by pneumatic tires, the rest of the road soon follows—squaring accounts, meanwhile, by cutting the tires to rags.

In the end the motorists will have to pay for the damage they cause—or, better, for

A now common sight at all out-door sporting meets—the family motor party.

other way. Too many of us are making luxuries and paying the farmer to feed us. The next decade will see a tremendous growth in the rural demand for home comforts. And one of the things that will keep the boys and the help on the farm will be the modern distance-shortener and reducer of rural isolation.

Is not the next step plain? Heretofore the farmer has improved his roads reluctantly, and has complained with bitterness (and justice) when they were damaged by automobiles. When he owns a car he will improve his roads without urging, and will do it right. And he will make due provision for their maintenance.

That matter of road maintenance, it must be said, has become acute of late and is growing worse. Millions have been laid out in highway improvement, and have been wasted for lack of adequate system in repair. Motor traffic demands both a smoother surface and a stronger bond than horse traffic; it tends inherently, at touring speeds, to ravel a loosely bonded surface like macadam.

the upkeep of roads suitably bonded for motor traffic. Crude oil, if rich in asphalt, makes a fair temporary bond; tar is far more durable, but needs watching to correct hollows and waves; calcium chloride, as a treatment for the foundation, appears to be useful for its property of retaining moisture. Recently a new chemical bond derived from blast-furnace slag has been suggested. Whatever the method, it is cheaper to pay well for good roads than to pay for the damage done by bad ones to mechanism and tires.

At this point I hear the reader (who has for some minutes been vainly trying to check my flow of prophecy) interrupt to say: "That is all very well, if your figures are correct and if these low-priced cars are really good. But five years ago a thousand dollars—spent on a new sliding-gear car—would buy nothing but a travesty on good construction. The man who could afford that sum or less had to buy at second-hand in order to get a run for his money. Are these present cars really so much better? And, if so, how is it done?"

Let me begin by saying that, for the experienced buyer, there is no value so good as a high-grade car from one to three years old. In the light of its total life, its wear is trifling. Paint and tires, and a few such parts as brake linings, transmission or front-wheel bearings, and possibly the

fallen less than those of the cheaper cars, they are well worth their cost to those who can afford them.

But, even so, how is it possible to build plain utility cars, that shall not yearn each week for the ministrations of the repair man, for less than a thousand dollars? How is it possible to build a really good forty-horse-power car for even twice that sum?

A visit to almost any of the larger factories would answer the question. Cleveland, Indianapolis, Toledo, Lansing, and many other cities boast plants which for size, efficiency, and scientific method would have astonished the expert of ten years ago. But to get the story in one volume, we cannot do better than to visit the automobile capital of the country and see for ourselves what the new industry has done.

Ten years ago the first automobile factory was moved to Detroit from an Ohio town. Other factories followed rapidly. In ten years Detroit's population has grown from 300,000 to nearly half a million. It has twenty-seven automobile factories, the value of whose output last year exceeded $200,000,000. Still others

Packard Motor Car Co., Detroit.

Forging the front axle of a truck under the steam-hammer.

first or second speed gears, may need to be renewed. But depreciation otherwise should be small, and the vital elements—design, materials, workmanship—are certain to be superior to those of the cheap new car of the same price. But the buyer must be a judge of cars!

The higher-priced cars—the old, well-known makes—are smoother-running, better-proportioned, longer-lived, simpler to manage than ever before. Their prices represent, not mere ability to get over the map, but convenience, freedom from care, high mileage without repairs—the luxury of motoring. Though their prices have

manufacture parts—axles, radiators, engines, bodies—some used in Detroit, some elsewhere. North of the business section are miles of cottages, the last word of modernity, each surrounded by lawn and shrubbery and having—perhaps one in five—a neat garage in the rear. Shade trees line the streets; at frequent corners stand white sanitary drinking fountains, and everywhere are automobiles! Hardly one vehicle in twenty is horse-drawn. Naturally the streets of Detroit are clean.

And the motor factories! To north, east, and west they radiate, nearly all new, imposing structures, all steel and glass, with just enough brick or concrete to give a semblance of walls, themselves the last word of modern factory engineering. No dingy loop-holes for windows, no haphazard ventilation here! The mark of the efficiency expert is seen even in the buildings, and we shall find it everywhere in the work itself.

Some of the factories make everything possible —even wheels—under their own roofs. Others design cars and contract with specialists for the various parts, which they inspect and assemble. Since we cannot visit all, we will select a few of the most typical plants. One factory for high-priced cars in which everything but tires, rims, and ignition specialties is made; another, building a medium-priced car and likewise manufacturing nearly all its parts; a third factory, which designs and assembles—these are excellent examples, each of its class. Lastly, we must see the one wholly unique factory in the world for building low-priced automobiles.

In the first plant the most notable feature is the attention to matters which, with a lower selling-price, would have to be passed over or managed by short cuts. For instance, the cam shaft gears of the engine, instead of being bronze, have silent teeth of muslin. The oiling system is so controlled that opening the throttle acts also to increase the supply of oil to the pistons. Another feature is a valve, which supplements the electric engine-starter, for letting acetylene gas into the intake manifold. Our present gasolene does not vaporize well in freezing weather, and the first explosion is sometimes hard to get unless ether, acetylene, or a similar agent is used.

A trip through these shops is full of fascinating glimpses. Here is a big machine at work on eight pairs of cylinders at once,

finishing the flat top and side surfaces. Here is another, smoothing the top or bottom surfaces of an aluminum crank case. On a curious swivelling table are clamped eight pairs of cylinders, all with their bottoms outward; two pairs of tools, working from opposite sides, bore two pairs of cyl-

Packard Motor Car Co., Detroit.

Milling the tops and sides of cylinders; seven milling cutters working at once.

inders at once, while the operator removes others already bored and clamps fresh ones to the table. Elsewhere is a vertical boring mill, bristling with tools, which attack a heavy truck hub at three points at once, and shape it with automatic precision. Everywhere—on iron, aluminum, and alloy steel—are used the modern high-speed cutting tools, which eat through the toughest steel as if it were soft brass.

Many trucks are built here, and a separate building is provided for their assembling. Altogether, the factory comprises thirty buildings, having thirty-seven acres of floor space and extending three-quarters of a mile across the Boulevard. Seven thousand men are employed, most of them the year round.

The factory for medium-priced cars, though less pretentious, is an even better example of intensive production. Machines and men are closely packed, boys are pushing hand-trucks filled with castings, forgings, finished parts or assembled

The assembling is as carefully planned as the manufacture. Crank shafts are fitted to their bearings, run by pulley and belt to "limber" them, then cleaned and again put together. Different men assemble the various elements of the motor. Others assemble the steering gear; still others, the front and rear axles, the transmission, and the frame members.

In the contracting-engineering field, motor-trucks are doing the work of from eight to sixteen horses as a general average.

The picture shows a motor-truck of the Pittsburg Contracting Co., one of the builders of the big Catskill Aqueduct, that has displaced twelve teams.

"groups"; a system of exhaust-piping overhead supplements window ventilation.

The familiar engine, lathes, planers, and other plodding jacks-of-all-trades are conspicuously absent. Instead, we see special tools everywhere. Where several surfaces are to be finished, tools are set working simultaneously on as many as possible. Where a certain operation, like cutting gear teeth, can be done on several pieces at once, it is done. Piece rates largely prevail, and seem to work well.

With all the seeming hurry, time is found for accuracy. The bevel driving gears, for example, whose quietness depends on their true form and alignment, are elaborately tested before and after hardening, and again for noise when finally assembled.

Then these several units are brought to the chassis-room, where picked squads, each with its own task, put them together; first the frame, then the springs, then axles, motor, transmission, steering gear, radiator, piping, and wiring in about the order given. Twenty or thirty chassis are in process at once, and as each nears completion it is wheeled, with the last squad still working, into line for the testing-room.

There are really two tests, one for the motors, and one for the complete chassis. In the former some thirty or forty motors are made to drive as many dynamos, first at light load, then at full load, for several hours. The power developed is measured, and the current goes into the main circuit of the factory. In the chassis test-

The contractor's motor-truck and trailers.

ing-room—said to be the only one of its kind—the rear wheels are raised off the floor, and dynamos again receive the power (this time through the transmission gears and axle) and convert it into current for the factory. The energy thus conserved amounts to some 800 horse-power—a good example of the care with which waste has been eliminated, to the ultimate benefit of the consumer.

As the third factory does not manufacture directly, a brief visit will suffice. It turns out as many cars as the preceding —some fifty or sixty a day—but in much smaller compass. The special features of interest are of design rather than process—a pressed-steel floor, riveted to the frame, which takes the place of a wood body floor; the ingeniously compact transmission, built in one case with the engine, saving weight and expense; the low-priced yet serviceable pressed-steel bodies, and so on. All these things, by simplifying manufacture, reduce the cost and enable people to own larger and more able cars than they could otherwise afford.

But the greatest sight of Detroit is the huge plant for low-priced cars. Here, as nowhere else, may you see automobiles turned out veritably like sewing-machines, brass beds, or shoes. Here, literally, the raw material comes in at one end and issues from the other a finished product. One unloading platform, to which are pushed daily train-loads of pig-iron, brass, aluminum, rough forgings, pressed-steel parts, and bodies; two long shipping platforms, each with two tracks, into whose box-cars are stowed every working-day half a thou-

sand automobiles or more! The iron pigs unloaded to-day will become cylinder castings to-morrow. The next morning they will enter the machine shop; by night they will be fully machined, the valves ground in, the crank shafts fitted, the motors assembled. Next morning the motors will receive a bench run under their own power. After lunch they will pass to the assembling-room, and in a few hours the finished cars will go to the shipping platform. A hundred cars being assembled at once; an hour or so for the job; a hundred cars an hour, if need be!

The main building is 840 feet wide— nearly a sixth of a mile—and 500 feet in depth. Around three sides it has three stories; the central machine shop is one story high, with " saw-tooth " roof. In front are the administration building—itself 300 feet long—and the power house, with one 1,500-horse-power gas engine running and another of 3,500 horse-power under erection. Behind are the foundry and the heat-treating department, and a wide expanse whereon new buildings are already going up. The present plant covers sixty acres of floor space and employs 9,000 men.

The real marvel of this marvellous plant is not its bigness, but the fact that it is able to produce from 500 to 750 cars a day. Even to the expert, unless he has seen the methods used, the reality seems incredible.

When these methods are studied, they are found to consist largely of three elements: (1) elimination of useless handling; (2) the use of special machinery to perform many operations simultaneously; (3)

A thirty-foot girder carried on a five-ton truck, the body of which has been removed and the girder supported on a timber cradle.

The motor-truck for this service is valuable in that it prevents the traffic congestion incidental to the carrying of heavy steel girders by the horse method, using a trailer and carrying the girder in a sling.

they emerge, fresh ones are put in their places, so that when the table has finished its travel it is ready at once to start again. A similar machine finishes the top and side flat surfaces.

Other machines first bore, then ream, the four cylinders at once. Three castings at once have their front ends smoothed for the cover plates—a matter of ten minutes, requiring only two machines to handle the entire output. Later, a machine with forty-five drills, all working at once, makes the bolt and stud holes in the top, both ends, and bottom flange. One and one-half minutes per casting, including blowing away the chips (by a compressed-air jet) and setting up the work! There is a second machine, but for emergencies only.

A year ago two shifts were run, of ten and twelve hours. Then the length of the shifts was reduced. By dint of planning the output was greater in nine hours than it had been in ten, and wages remained the same.

The multitudinous small time-savers must remain unmentioned. One stands out in my mind—a socket wrench attached to a small suspended air motor, by whose aid two men are able to screw up twenty-

the use of fixtures which, so far as possible, automatically insure accuracy. Thus the machines may be operated by men of small skill, paid well but still much less than skilled machinists; and a highly skilled force of tool-makers insures the quality of the product.

These principles are not novel, but they are seldom carried into effect so thoroughly. For successive steps on a given piece, the machines are so placed that parts dropped into a box by one operator are handy to the man at the next machine. Milling-machine, boring-machine, reamer, drill press, and tapping-machine consort amicably in rows, and the piece which starts as a rough forging or casting at one end reaches the other fully finished.

The most complicated single piece is that comprising the four cylinders and upper half of the crank case. Twelve of these are clamped, bottom up, on the table of a milling-machine, and the bottom flats and half-round bearing seats are milled in one operation by different sets of cutters. As fast as

Large six-wheel coal-truck with four-wheel drive.

A gasolene engine runs a dynamo and charges a storage battery. Individual motors drive the four front wheels. The body with the two rear wheels is practically a trailer.

four oil-pan flange bolts in less than three minutes.

While the motor has been taking shape, other departments have been at work on transmission, axles, radiator, and frame. When the assembling-floor is reached, the parts already form groups—motor and transmission, frame, steering column and dash, and so on; and trained squads move from chassis to chassis, each doing one thing only. Hand-trucks in a steady

In France, which until recently set the automobile pace for the world, the rise of the small car has been equally impressive, though in another way. The engines are even smaller, ten to twenty horse-power being the usual range, with four-cylinder types favored. What these small cars lack in power is largely made up in efficiency; they are very light, very able, and with their four-speed transmissions they get the utmost from their engines. Owing

The motor at work upon the roads.

stream bring the parts; wind-shields and bodies come from upstairs, and every few minutes a finished car is cranked up, given a run around the yard, and wheeled to the shipping platform.

Only a portion—possibly two-thirds—of the output is assembled at the factory. The rest is shipped in "knockdown" to the large distributing centres and there put together. The resultant saving in space reduces freight rates on these cars almost to one-third of the assembled-car tariff.

In the radiator department, ingenious machines force 95 quarter-inch tubes through 74 copper fins at one operation; yet, even so, 300 men are required to turn out 250 radiators. For painting and varnishing, the wheels are dipped bodily into vats of pigment and whirled to throw off the surplus paint.

The factory has a "hospital" in which are treated not only accidental injuries but all ailments whatsoever, and it is found cheaper to do this gratis than to lose the workmen's time in seeking (or avoiding) outside medical aid.

partly to the difference in methods of manufacture, their prices are materially higher than those of our small cars, but it seems certain that before long there will be a market in this country for cars on similar lines, extending the principle of the multi-speed sliding-gear transmission to smaller sizes than hitherto. Both here and abroad the outstanding fact is that the main incentive for buying high-power cars—the excitement of speed—is losing its force, and the rising cost of fuel is wielding its influence to the same end.

The fuel problem, by the way, seems to be solving itself in a measure by devices which burn heavy oils successfully. Our gasolene is getting heavier every year, yet the carburetor makers seem able to keep pace with it. At a pinch, alcohol is possible, though not very probable. Straight kerosene is used in certain recent high-compression automobile engines, and a recent inventor has found a way to gasify and burn small coal directly in the engine, thus eliminating the "producer."

If utility is increasingly the motive for

owning pleasure cars, it is wholly so with the motor-truck. A problem far more difficult, because the incentive for spending is absent, the truck has logically been the slower to develop. Its design is even yet not wholly standardized, but already we can define certain classes of service wherein motors show better economy than horses. Notable is the entire class of "long hauls," wherein stops are few and the truck runs steadily most of the day. The reason for this lies in the inherently high first cost of the motor vehicle. It earns nothing when idle, hence the cost per ton mile is least when interest, depreciation, and wages are distributed over a continuous haul. Express companies, coal dealers, department stores, furniture movers, wholesalers in many lines, and manufacturers of all kinds are finding it cheaper to move goods by motor-trucks than by horses. Even when hauls are short, as in most city deliveries, the quickness and handiness of the motor vehicle often give it the advantage.

Since loading and unloading time is counted as waste, many ingenious devices are used to shorten it. False bodies packed at leisure and pushed bodily on the truck platform are common. Quick-dumping bodies, much like those of railway cars, are used for sand and coal. Garbage may be loaded into a loose body, which is picked up by a derrick, swung over a scow, and dumped like a tin cup. Some department stores have suburban distributing centres, to which packages are carried overnight by large trucks, and transferred to "mosquito fleets" of light wagons for house-to-house delivery.

Operation—a vital matter with drivers paid $15 to $20 a week—has been greatly simplified. For each day's run, at least, such matters as lubrication, carburetion, and ignition adjustments have been made either fixed or automatic. The driver has only to learn the rules of the road and the knack of the levers. Time was when every motor-truck was merely a training-school for private chauffeurs; happily that stage is past. Nowadays the proper plan is to have all skilled work done, not by the drivers, but by a separate force after each day's run, and one man can thus keep about five trucks in order.

If the motor-truck were only a mechanical substitute for the horse, its significance would be small. But, like the pleasure car, it is opening a new field of possibilities. No longer twenty miles a day, but fifty to eighty, is the economical limit. By changing drivers, a motor-truck can be kept going twenty hours out of the twenty-four. The practical radius is no longer half a day's horse travel, but is solely a question of expense and profit. If the profit warrants going fifty miles and back, the right sort of truck will do it. A wholesale grocer, adding both to radius and promptness of delivery, doubles his business in a year. A furniture house saves money on freight and express charges, and delivers regularly in hot weather that cripples its horse-using competitor. A coal dealer gains a name for quick delivery in bad weather; a brewer, using five trucks to replace fifty horses, reduces delivery cost one-half.

For suburban use the gasolene truck is the logical choice. In cities the simplicity of the electric truck causes it to be frequently preferred. The electric light and power stations, which long held aloof from the new movement, are beginning to offer complete facilities for charging, storage, and repair of all electric vehicles, including pleasure cars. Their object is to increase the sale of current in light-load hours, but the public gains the benefit, and with this support the urban use of electric vehicles of all sorts is certain to increase largely. My lady's town car, which for years has eked out a precarious existence on the border-land of real motordom, appears at last to be coming into its own, swept into a new lease of life by the expansion of electric trucking and by recent improvements in storage batteries.

Has not the automobile proved its mission? Greater liberty, greater fruitfulness of time and effort, brighter glimpses of the wide and beautiful world, more health and happiness—these are the lasting benefits of the modern motor-car. Its extravagance is passing with the novelty of speed; the rational balance of service and expense will ere long be struck, and cars built in conformity thereto. And then we shall thank God that we live in the Motor-Car Era!

Motoring to the Jamestown Exposition (1907)

MOTORING TO THE JAMESTOWN EXPOSITION

BY WILLIAM N. PARKER

PHOTOGRAPHS BY N. LAZARNICK

ERHAPS ho one but a motorist thoroughly understands the abysmal difference between consulting a train schedule and examining a road map, though on the face of it the latter is the more complex. The fine simplicity of the former is at best a tainted thing in which intellect and free will have no place and slavish dependence becomes a necessity and almost a virtue. Just so many hours to travel, with no delightful deviations five minutes here and there "allowed"—save the mark—for changing trains or making connections. But the map with its glorious intricacies fills one with a sense of freedom; true it may be the freedom of the lost sheep, but we felt that Norfolk would rejoice over us more than over the ninety-nine who had never strayed from the sanctity of their parlor-car.

In this cheerful frame of mind and accompanied by a forty horse power machine, well stored with tools and supplies, we left the Battery by the Staten Island ferry en route for Philadelphia, the first night's objective. We had provisionally decided on the new direct route to Cape Charles as out of the beaten track and considerably shorter than by the main roads, the distance being only a little over three hundred miles from New York to that point. The ninety-two miles to Philadelphia is of course well-known ground.

As the skyscrapers of Manhattan faded into the summer haze across the Bay we discussed the merits of the rival routes through Staten Island and decided on the southern road from St. George via New Dorp to the Tottenville ferry, a distance of about fifteen miles. The road winds pleasantly through numerous small villages, the undulating surface is good and with the exception of several grade railroad crossings there is nothing to fear from traffic. A half-hourly ferry service operates between Tottenville and Perth Amboy and we made the six mile run from there to Metuchen over New Brunswick Avenue with fine paving all the way. Another five miles brings one to New Brunswick itself and the rest of the run to Trenton, about thirty-two miles, is over one of the finest roads in New Jersey, which means that it is very good indeed. On this Cranbury Turnpike we managed to infringe the speed laws without exciting comment, propitiating the fates meanwhile by calling down blessings on the shade of old Scotch Macadam, whose good works have truly followed him and who, it is to be hoped, is in blissful ignorance of the state of our New York streets to-day. This route is about four miles longer than that via Princeton, but the latter road is far from good in parts. This was confessed even by our Princetonian on board, who is at all times a motorist first and a 'Varsity man afterward, and treats his tires "as though he loved them," to misuse the words of Isaak Walton. True sign-manual of your real motorist.

It may be news to the provincial New Yorker to hear that hunger can be appeased, nay, satisfied, at Trenton, but such is the case; there are a couple of excellent hotels and a garage where we took on a supply of gasoline and got an expert opin-

On the road to Wilmington—in happy ignorance of other roads to come.

ion on the choice of routes to the Quaker City. "Keep to the Jersey side of the Delaware," said the expert; "Go via the Bristol Turnpike on the Pennsylvania side," said the map. The latter looked much shorter certainly, but the blessed word macadam turned the scale in favor of the former. The expert declared that the Bristol Pike was sandy and rough in parts; he was born in Hoboken, he said, and he knew. After this Washington himself could not have induced us to cross the Delaware, at this particular point at least, and we set out for Philadelphia by Burlington and finally through Camden, taking the Market Street ferry over the river and so completing our first day's run.

The wheel at times had been relinquished to our amateur; like all amateurs he took it with avidity, and equally like all amateurs he had a somewhat checkered career. We watched him crank the motor with mixed feelings; he touched the carburetor needle and flooded the chamber in a highly professional manner—the result came promptly but not quite in the

way he expected, for the ignition had been left somewhat far advanced and when the inevitable back-fire did take place he received a staggering shock which dampened his enthusiasm for several seconds. Once fairly started things went well as long as the clutch was engaged, but only then; at every re-engagement there was a bang which literally drove the tires into the road surface. Some little time was lost in explaining to him that clutches, even of the metal-disc variety, are constructed to slip as well as hold, and that spur gears are the work of mortal hands and therefore liable to extinction unless the left foot is pressed well down before handling the change-speed lever. Traces of his driving education were also noticeable in his free use of the accelerator pedal, which with amazing perversity he always advanced before putting in the clutch, "so that the engine would take up the load," he said. "That's all right for ten horse power," we informed him, "but you've forty under you now"; he smiled and understood.

Our first real *contretemps* arose shortly

252

after leaving Trenton, when two of the cylinders began to miss. "Are you monkeying with the clutch?" said a warning voice. "I am not," said the poor amateur, "'tis the engine." The motion became more and more irregular and we finally stopped to locate the trouble. Guessing the real cause from the first we nevertheless, with the motorist's usual fatuity, went through a general process of diagnosis, assisted by the amateur who performed his original stunt with the carburetor without effect; we tried the coil—the vibrators were certainly all right, so were the wires and terminal connections, then the commutator came in for more than a passing notice—nothing wrong there. Finally, having begun at the wrong end of the alphabet we worked our way back to the A B C of the question and traced the trouble to the plugs, two of which had become so sooted up that no spark passed the points. "Too much oil" was the immediate verdict. It was then that the amateur confessed he had felt it his duty to give a couple of left turns to the oil-feeds

while we were lunching and had hoped for better results. Then it was conveyed to him that lubricating oil, though an excellent thing in moderation, carbonized if fed to excess, sooting up the combustion chamber and plugs and destroying the insulation of the latter.

Meanwhile we received five distinct and separate lessons on the amenities of the road from as many motorists, who, when they saw us apparently holding a post-mortem, slowed up and proffered their help in resuscitating the corpse. This brotherly offering of first aid to the injured is still sufficiently novel to excite comment, but the day is evidently at hand when all good motorists will also become good Samaritans. It is only the boor who passes by on the other side when he sees others in trouble. The morals of motoring will some day demand a volume to themselves in the library of our social ethics.

Leaving Philadelphia next morning we started for the South, with Wilmington, Delaware, as our first stop, some twenty-

Near Harrington, Delaware—where real ruts are to be found.   Photograph by N. Lazarnick.

eight miles distant. The road as far as Chester via the Darby Pike is finely macadamized and though the surrounding country is flat the scenery is far from monotonous; broad cultivated acres and tree-sheltered farms spreading contentedly away into the middle distance, with stretches of river coming into view every now and then. The route here skirts the Delaware for some miles to Chester, where it leads into the broad Wilmington pike. By all accounts this was to be our last

question. We had brought only two spare inners with us and the worst of the journey was yet to come. . Grudgingly we fished one out from its dust-proof receptacle, as men who are drawing a check against half their earthly possessions and do not know how soon the other half may have to go too. The precious tube was soon pushed inside the cover with an all too liberal allowance of French chalk administered by the irrepressible amateur. It was shaken out in time, however, the tube partially

A Maryland lumber wagon—part of the team is not easily frightened.   Photograph by N. Lazarnick.

stretch of good road and we determined to make the most of it. But man merely proposes, the car is the real arbiter. Down went a tire on the off driving-wheel and we were in for a repair. Off came the cover, a stiff brand-new cover it was too—but the inner tube lay revealed at last and we set to work to find the puncture. We blew the tube up, filled it with water even, in our effort to find where the trouble lay and finally discovered it lurking close to the valve where a patch was out of the

inflated and in a few moments the beaded edge was safe within the rim, the tire blown up, the wing-bolts tightened and we were ready for the road again.

What is there in a puncture that exhilarates your true motorist? Nobody but a motorist can explain the paradox and he will not tell; perhaps one is grateful that worse has not happened—a broken ball-bearing or a cracked cylinder for instance. However that may be we started off in the highest spirits and made record time into the little town of Belleview, thence across the Brandywine Creek bridge to Wilmington, without further mishap, though we did have a narrow escape in the town itself where the pavements had just been watered and we side-slipped heavily on a down grade corner. The expert at the wheel, however, managed to "keep her head in the wind," by maneuvering the wheel dextrously with one hand while he threw out the clutch and touched on the hand-brake just sufficiently to check

of historic Delaware where close by the present Wilmington, Peter Minuit, the Swede, first settled and built and held Fort Christina until Peter Stuyvesant came over from the Battery (New York) about 1671 and turned it into a Dutch colony.

Steering south from Wilmington the country spreads out to the horizon flat on every hand, dotted here and there with cultivated farms, picturesque, and far from monotonous, with every now and

Near Eden, Maryland—where soft sand is cheap and plentiful.　　　Photograph by N. Lazarnick.

the differential action. Not even a lamp was touched and a few minutes later we were seated at lunch discussing our itinerary which was now for the first time to diverge from the beaten track and take us direct to Cape Charles by comparatively unfrequented ways.

We finally settled on Dover, as our stopping place for the night, a total run of about seventy-five miles from Philadelphia; an easy schedule, but time was unimportant and we wanted to see something

again a tree-bordered canal threading its way sleepily through low-lying lands. Umbrageous little villages crop up by the roadside with their inevitable "general store," and signs of rural industry are everywhere apparent. The fields are cultivated right up to the road which meanders through meadows without fencing in many parts. The roads themselves are mostly bad, the surface heavy with loose sand and worn into deep ruts by the farmers' wagons which follow their channels faithfully for miles. To steer clear of these ruts, straggling along as they did in irregular lines, was a task far from easy and one always successfully accomplished with a resulting heavy strain on the distance-rod and knuckles. Moreover, we had forgotten to cover the steering joints with leather and the grit ground into the open joints to such an extent that by the time we reached Cape Charles the wheel had a "backlash" that five thousand miles of ordinary road would not have given it.

Under these conditions we naturally made no attempts on road-records and reached Dover late in the afternoon, with dust covered car and a pinch of sand in the carburetor, as we half suspected, for we had been firing rather irregularly, but the dead level of the roads enabled us to pull through on a mixture which was far from perfect.

Dover will never be found written on our hearts. After a short delay employed in cleaning the carburetor and fitting it with

Nearing Cape Charles—a breath of the pines in old Virginia.   Photograph by N. Lazarnick.

Evidently cars as yet are few and far between in this part of the country, for the honk of our horn brought folks to their doors and horses and mules resented our approach by backing away and performing other antics discreditable to their sagacity. We often stopped in deference to their feelings while the driver made a detour into the fields to avoid us or stood at their heads while, with a maximum of caution and a minimum of gasoline, we slowly passed.

a rough and ready dust shield, we started for Seaford about forty miles further on, and made first acquaintance with the perfectly even and almost dustless surface of the shell road. Its construction is simple—oyster shells and plenty of them, spread evenly over the road. Time and traffic do the rest. Passing over the border into Maryland the scenery became more diversified and we now began to run through fine stretches of pine timber, which was welcome after the monotony of plowing through the flats under a pitiless sun. Here we initiated the amateur into the mysteries of "coasting," with clutch out and the engine running free, and also showed him how to save his brakes on a down grade by cutting off spark and gas and running against the cylinder vacuum, leaving the clutch in engagement; a practice which seemed to afford him intense gratification.

The quaint and colonial little town of Princess Anne was our next stopping place

you can—vary the throttle instead of the speed-lever.

A ten horse power car takes more handling than a Vanderbilt racer; it's like a small income and wants ekeing out.

Be very sure to push your clutch well out when changing from a low to a higher gear—the reason is obvious.

In changing back it is not so necessary for reasons equally obvious — think it over.

If you can run "free" over a rough bit

A shell road in the making—it pays to wait for the finished product.   Photograph by N. Lazarnick.

and a delightful one it proved. We ambled happily about the decorous streets and what we heard of our route convinced us we could go farther and fare worse, so we decided to spend the night here, and, having dined, occupied the evening in drawing up and presenting to the amateur a list of driving instructions:

Don't drive on too rich a mixture, the hotter the day the more air your motor needs.

Keep in your top speed notch as long as

or a patch of new metal, do so—tires are expensive.

Don't put your reverse in till your car has come to an absolute stop, even steel has an ascertained breaking-point; it may be too low to meet the occasion.

Don't run on half-inflated tires or you may have to run on a deflated one before you get home.

Don't let your tires stand unprotected in the sun—Solar heat does not improve vulcanized rubber.

A peaceful invasion of old Fortress Monroe.   Photograph by N. Lazarnick.

The rule of the road is the same as the rule of the sea—the slower and weaker has the right of way.

Don't lean desperately over your wheel —the policeman will add ten miles an hour to your speed.

The fact that you have a couple of brakes fitted to your car does not in itself annihilate the laws of Momentum—"*Festina lente*" is an excellent motorist's motto, though it is antique.

Don't break speed laws; respect the local restrictions you encounter; slow down at all cross roads; come to a stop at all unguarded railroad crossings.

Lubrication is the second law of Nature. You are not likely to forget the first.

Man sometimes forgets but Machinery never forgives. Don't outrage it.

Some fifteen miles south of Princess Anne, over indifferent and very crooked roads we crossed into Virginia which necessitated our hanging out a new license number. We passed a number of small villages on our way, most of them monotonously alike and merely interesting as milestones to show that the end of our journey was

approaching. The country again grew low-lying and flat and the roads varied greatly, sometimes heavy and sandy and occasionally showing a mile or two of excellent surface. Luckily from time to time we came upon stretches of shell road which improved our average speed and our spirits at the same time.

We finished the ninety mile run between Princess Anne and the Cape, with an hour's stop-over for lunch at the little town of Bellehaven, arriving in time to catch the afternoon boat for Norfolk. The car was stowed on board and we disembarked at Old Point Comfort, which we finally decided to make our headquarters.

This is beyond question the best spot from which to visit the Exposition; Norfolk, Portsmouth and all spots on Hampton Roads being readily accessible by ferry. Fortress Monroe lies close by and the great shipbuilding yards at Newport News are but a few miles to the west along the coast. As to the Peninsula itself there is Jamestown to see, Yorktown—the scene of Cornwallis' surrender, the charming old Colonial town of Williams-

Jamestown at last—the Pennsylvania Building at the Exposition.   Photograph by N. Lazarnick.

burg and a hundred spots famous in Revolutionary times and in the later days of the Civil War. With Old Point Comfort as a base these are all easily reached, most of them in a short day's run.

Our amateur left us here, called back "to Wall Street and worry," as he expressed it. His last words had reference to speed-levers and clutches—"I've got it bad," he said.

We laughed and bade him a cheery "Good-bye."

That was a week ago. Yesterday he was arrested, pleaded guilty and was fined ten dollars for exceeding the speed limit in Fifth Avenue. He sent us the wire himself.

"He'll win the Vanderbilt Cup yet," said the expert.

"He will," said I, "Let us drink his health."

What a Woman Can Do With an Auto
(1910)

WHAT A WOMAN CAN DO WITH AN AUTO

by Robert Sloss

Illustrated With Photographs

ON posters and programmes of motor meets, shows, and tourneys, and even on the catalogues of the makers, the favorite device is a female figure with hands airily touching the steering wheel. Sometimes her garb is a cross between that of a Greek goddess and the Statue of Liberty; sometimes it is of a wasp-like modernism. Always it is altogether decorative, and if people think about it at all, they are inclined to set it down to the pretty symbolism of artists who invariably paint a figure of a woman to represent " Progress," " Commerce," and most of the things with which women are supposed to have nothing to do.

Yet the woman at the wheel is no allegory. Already her intuition has put her in touch with the automobile. Its delicacy of adjustment, its vagary of moods, she has come to understand as those of a sister organism, for what enthusiastic motorist does not refer to his car as " she." This will seem a flight of fancy to many. Some may even see in it opportunity to apply an old joke and assure us that the lady motorists' tool kit is confined to a hairpin.

In sober seriousness, however, let us make the surprising statement that woman not only can do but has done with the automobile everything of which man can boast—in some respects she has done it better. Shake your head at that all you like, remembering first of all that the car is a mechanism and denying that woman has any mechanical ability. Did you ever see a woman fixing her sewing machine? If you have, and possess any imagination, it will not be hard for you to look into the future far enough to see the automobile working as marvelous, though quite different, a change in the life of a woman as the sewing machine is credited with having brought about.

Let us hasten from the realm of imagination, however, for the man who has not seen her do it and the woman who has not tried it herself will never be convinced of what she can do with a car, unless we set down the cold facts. At the very start we are confronted with such an array of evidence as can be no more than hinted at in limited space. New York City boasts at least one regularly licensed woman chauffeur who tools a big private car through the city streets for her woman employer, and it is not uncommon to see in country districts, especially in the West, women drivers of public automobile stages. This can justly be described as a phase of the modern development of woman in industry, but it is as the private owner and operator of her own car for her own pleasure that woman has achieved her most interesting motoring records.

There is scarcely an organized competitive tour nowadays that starts without the entry of at least one woman driver, and it is no longer surprising if she makes an enviable score for herself. As long as two years ago a number of women automobilists organized a run of their own from New York to Philadelphia and back. The result demonstrated completely their ability to manage and care for their own machines *en route* without any assistance from the stronger sex. One of them, Mrs. J. W. Ramsay, the following year, started with three women passengers from New York for San Francisco and made an enviable record.

Two years ago Miss Alice Potter, of Chicago, drove unaided from that city to New York. We might swell the list of women motorists and their achievements into a volume. It should convince even the skeptical if we select two typical women motorists, at opposite ends of the continent, and tell just a little of their experiences.

Mrs. F. J. Linz, of San Francisco, since she learned to manage a car more than five years ago, has driven over every road in both California and Nevada. Her husband was a dealer in automobiles, and that circumstance brought her quite naturally into touch with motoring. She had little more than learned to drive when her abilities were put to what would seem even to a man quite a crucial test. She accompanied her husband in a car which he was delivering to Shaw Hot Springs, Nevada.

The purchaser was an Italian, who kept the roadhouse at the Springs, chiefly frequented by miners. The man saw an opportunity to make money by running a car regularly between his hostelry and Carson City, a mile and a half distant, bringing passengers over at a dollar the round trip, including a bath at the hot springs.

The run out from San Francisco to Carson City through the mountains was no child's play in those early days of motoring. No sooner had Mrs. Linz, her husband, and the Italian completed it than Mr. Linz was summoned back to San Francisco. In the emergency Mrs. Linz volunteered to take her husband's place in putting the automobile into operation. It was the first automobile ever seen in Carson City. Not a man there knew a spark plug from a carburetor, and most of the miners were rather shy of the noisy motor.

No Easy Job

Plucky little Mrs. Linz, however drove the car for three weeks on schedule time between Carson City and the Springs, carrying a greater number of passengers every day, as confidence in her ability grew. She not only drove but washed the car, oiled and adjusted the machinery, and repaired punctures —which she says occurred at the rate of about one an hour, owing to the extremely bad roads and excessive heat. That was before the days of " quick detachable " tires.

" I came back to the Springs many a dark night alone," she says, " and stalled my car in an old barn three hundred feet from the roadhouse, with no light but a lantern. Then I went in and went to bed in a room with no glass in the windows and no lock on the door. The only others in the house were the Italian proprietor and a Frenchman who acted as bartender. They went upstairs to bed, each with a rifle under his arm, as the Italian had his money secreted somewhere about the house. The last night I was there they killed a rattlesnake just outside my door. It probably had the intention of sharing the warmth of the room with me."

That was surely enough to develop the motoring nerve of any woman, and since then Mrs. Linz has had her share of the exciting experiences which the Far West provides for the automobilist. Not the least of these was brought to her by the San Francisco earthquake, when, with only a thin waist and petticoat over her underclothing, she drove steadily for two days carrying women and children and even exhausted soldiers to shelter. It is little wonder that, as the only woman contestant in the San Francisco-La Honda Mountain Endurance Run of a hundred miles hard driving she made 995 points, the five short of perfection being lost through the necessity of adjusting a new spark plug four miles from the last control. Mrs. Linz organized the first American motor club for women, is an honorary member of the Royal Club of Great Britain and Ireland, and was president and general manager of the second San Francisco automobile show in 1908.

Not Alone in the West

Lest you conclude that only the freer and more rugged conditions of Western life can produce the woman motorist, you must be reminded of Mrs. Andrew Cuneo, of New York City, who, in competition with men, has won more motoring prizes for speed, endurance, and skill than any other woman alive. In July, 1902, Mrs. Cuneo took a notion to buy a small second-hand steamer. She had never before even sat in an automobile. After a driving lesson of an hour and a half in the morning, she took her two babies and their nursemaid for a ride through Central Park the same afternoon. The next day she drove alone all the way down Fifth Avenue, and while making a call left the car too long and burned the boiler out.

This impressed upon her the fact that driving is not the only thing to learn about a motor car. For a year she devoted herself to learning how to care for her machine and to drive it through the crowded streets of New York City and around the adjacent country. In 1903 she bought a steam tourer, and after using it almost daily for two years, replaced it with a 1905 model of the same make. With only a week's practice in the new machine she entered her first tour, the famous Glidden run to the White Mountains and back to New York.

Here Mrs. Cuneo met her first serious accident. Near Greenwich, Connecticut, on the narrow Put's Hill, the automobile just ahead of her, being warned of a blast, began to back rapidly, the driver not even looking behind. Mrs. Cuneo had to choose between letting this car smash into her own, or backing down against the temporary wooden railing on a narrow bridge.

She took the latter chance; the railing broke and her machine went upside down into the creek below. By some miracle she and her three friends escaped without serious injury. With the help of her fellow tourists the car was righted and put back on the road. Undismayed Mrs. Cuneo not only drove on to Hartford, the first night's stop, but completed the entire tour with the others.

In September of the same year she did some fast exhibition driving at Atlantic City. Subsequently Mr. Al. Reeves, the automobile association manager, asked her to repeat the performance at the Poughkeepsie, N. Y., Fair. There she competed with Barney Oldfield, Cedrino, and other famous men drivers and did an exhibition mile in the then splendid time of 1 minute and 24 seconds. The following November she drove an exhibition mile in 1 minute and 14 seconds at the Empire track in New York City. The next year in Atlantic City she won her first race in competition with men drivers, doing a mile in 1 minute and 12 seconds. At the same time she made a record for small cars— 1 minute and 22 seconds.

It was not till the spring of 1907 that Mrs. Cuneo bought her first gasoline car, a seven-passenger tourer. The fol-

MRS. LINZ, CALIFORNIA'S MOST FAMOUS WOMAN MOTORIST, RECEIVING THE
FIRST PRIZE CUP FROM THE KING OF PORTOLA.

"DON'T RIG YOURSELF UP IN A LOT OF SPECIALLY DESIGNED APPAREL FOR
THE 'LADY AUTOMOBILIST.'"

WOMAN MAY TAKE THE WHEEL ON A PLEASURE TOUR—

lowing summer she entered it in the Glidden Tour from Cleveland to Chicago and back to New York. The distance was covered in two weeks. Near Baltimore one of Mrs. Cuneo's tires burst and threw her car into a ditch, badly bending the front axle. With no better repair than could be secured in a blacksmith's shop, she made the hard drive over the Blue Ridge Mountains, along strange roads with not even a kerosene lamp to mark the way. At the finish she was at the head of the procession of travel-stained tourists who crawled up Broadway. They all united in presenting her with a handsome silver loving cup, one of her highest prized trophies.

In the summer of 1908, in a new car, Mrs. Cuneo realized her ambition of finishing the Glidden Tour of that year with a perfect score. The following fall in the same car she entered the Long Island mechanical efficiency tour, from New York City to Montauk Point and back again, carrying four women passengers and finishing with a perfect score. In the women's run to Philadelphia and back, February, 1908, Mrs.

Cuneo was prevailed upon to drive the famous Lancia Lampo in which Hilliard had won the Savannah light-car race. The result was an easy winning of a perfect score.

She was now being urged constantly to drive cars with which men had made records. In the Jersey jubilee tour of 1909 she took part, driving the famous Bluebird. Later she did some exhibition speeding with this big racer, and in 1909, at the New Orleans Mardi Gras celebration, she entered the races with a famous car which had competed for the Vanderbilt Cup and had won several hill climbs. Racing with such experts as De Palma, Robertson, Strang, Burman, Ryall, and others, she beat the last named three in every event she entered, and beat Robertson in all but one. She thus won the national amateur championship and five other valuable prizes.

This would never have been the end of Mrs. Cuneo's racing victories over male competitors had not the American Automobile Association shortly afterwards adopted a rule that no woman should in future be allowed to drive, or even ride, in a car in any of their con-

OR DRIVING FOR RECORDS ON THE TRACK.

tests. Though she had been a member of the association since 1905, Mrs. Cuneo raised no protest against this piece of masculine discrimination. Nevertheless, it was merely her sex and not her record as an automobilist that furnished the excuse for barring her out. She says jocosely of the incident:

"Would that I could cultivate some suffragette tendencies and fight for my rights. But I can't—having instead always tried to keep the woman's end in automobiling sweet, clean, and refined. I drive and race just for the love of it all."

She contented herself with purchasing a duplicate of the car in which she had won at New Orleans. A close-coupled body was fitted to it, and she continued to drive for pleasure, entering such contests as were open to her, mostly tours, and making exhibition records on various tracks. At Atlanta on the two-mile motordrome she drove the distance in 1 minute and 45 seconds.

The achievements of these two typical women automobilists, though remarkable, need not be in any sense exceptional. The majority of women will not, per-

haps, be inclined to emulate the roughing-it experiences of Mrs. Linz nor the racing proclivities of Mrs. Cuneo. The striking fact is that it was no special physical prowess that enabled either of them to do what they have done. Mrs. Linz is a slight, willowy little woman whose appearance would never suggest either strength or endurance. As for Mrs. Cuneo, once at a ladies' day of the Automobile Club of America in New York another woman guest who had heard of her record was introduced to her. Towering above her something more than a foot, this liberally built woman gazed down at Mrs. Cuneo through her lorgnette and exclaimed, "Well, my dear, I expected you to be at least as big as I am."

Evidently unusual physique is not necessary for the woman motorist. Neither sex needs extraordinary muscular development in automobiling, and almost any woman not an invalid can master its mysteries quite as well as a man, provided she has the will and patience to acquire the know-how. Certainly in the sphere of patience woman by nature is equipped to give man a long handicap. The woman motorist is not half so likely as man is to swear and call loudly for a tow when anything goes wrong with the car. She will more probably set quietly to work to find the trouble and remedy it quite as thoroughly as if she were cleaning out the kitchen range.

Remember, nevertheless, that though sex and slight physique are in no sense disabilities to the woman who wants to do her own motoring, and though her feminine patience and intuition stand her in good stead, she must not expect to succeed by intuition alone. I asked Mrs. Cuneo to tell the readers of this magazine to what, most of all, she attributes her remarkable expertness.

The Secret of Success

" To my taking the trouble to learn everything I could about my car myself," she said, promptly. " I was towed home only once; that was when I let the boiler burn out in my first steamer. Right after that I had a little garage built back of my house and determined to care for my car entirely with my own hands. I soon learned how much I didn't know about the mechanism, but I persisted in wanting to ' see the wheels go round,' till I found out what every funny little thing was for. Even to this day I am as much of a crank about my car as the proverbial New England housewife is about her kitchen. I am not so particular about a few splashes of mud on the body, but regularly one morning a week I give the machinery such a house-cleaning that it shines like a baby after its bath."

There you have the secret of success for any motorist, man or woman, and there feminine patience will enable the latter to progress the more rapidly in motor lore, provided she begins with a real love for the sport and a determination to take the slight trouble necessary to enjoy it to the full. For the rest there is no special advice for the woman motorist that can be added to what has already been given in these pages to motorists generally, except this: " Don't rig yourself up in a lot of specially designed apparel for the ' lady automobilist,' and don't drive as though it were hard work." Those are the only special cautions for her sex which Mrs. Cuneo could think of, when I asked her for some.

" I never wear anything more than an ordinary skirt, shirtwaist, and hat in warm weather, or perhaps a duster, cap, and goggles on tour," she said. " Add the necessary coat and wraps in winter, and you have all the special costuming any woman needs.

" There are two compliments I prize very highly," she continued. " One was from a woman to whom I had just been introduced. ' Why,' she said, ' you're the woman I saw driving down the street the other day; I thought at the time you looked as if you just grew in that automobile. Most women have such a hunched-up, worried look, just as when they drive horses they lean forward anxiously as if pushing on the lines.'

" The other compliment was from Caruso," went on Mrs. Cuneo. " I took him for a drive one morning, when he surprised me by saying in his impulsive way:

" ' I say to you, Mrs. Cuneo, that I have never ridden in an automobile till this day!'

" ' Why,' I said, ' you have one of your own, haven't you?'

" ' Ah,' he exclaimed, ' I have three, but now I know that I have never really ridden in any one of them. I see that my chauffeur does not know how to drive them at all. He starts with a jerk that nearly throws me forward from my seat; he stops with a bump that almost breaks my neck over the back of it. He should run a trolley car—nothing else! But this—this is like sailing on the ocean or in the air!'

" I quietly slipped in the high speed then," said Mrs. Cuneo, " and scared him into silence, as I once scared Barney Oldfield into yelling, ' Slow down!' when I drove him around the wet track at Poughkeepsie before the races."

It is a curious fact that, if she goes at motoring seriously, woman's natural intuition puts her into closer touch with her car than a man seems to be able to get with his. She acquires the " feel " of the mechanism more readily, she detects more quickly the evidence of something out of adjustment, and altogether she drives more gently and with more delicate technic—all of which adds peculiarly to her pleasure and satisfaction in motoring.

Those who have never tried it will be inclined to ask whether it is worth while for a woman to acquire this ability to run her own car. The unanimous reply of all women motorists is strongly in the affirmative, and the reasons are simple and not far to seek. In the first place motoring, seriously undertaken, is not only the most pleasurable but the most healthful outdoor sport for woman. It gives her immediately a larger interest and takes her out of the monotonous round of household duties quickly and conveniently, whenever she requires respite.

" Whenever I feel nervous or out of sorts," says Mrs. Cuneo, " I get into my car and drive off my troubles. Since I have motored, I do not know what the inside of a doctor's office looks like; and as for pleasure, there is not only the exhilaration of actual driving, but the joy of being able to share it with other people. If I kept a car for nothing else,

it would be worth while to have it so that one could join in taking the poor little orphans from the asylum on their annual outing to Coney Island."

Mrs. Linz also testifies to her pleasure in taking out the inmates of the charitable institutions of San Francisco and avers that the happiest hours of her life have been spent behind the wheel.

On the purely practical side, when the average family comes into possession of an automobile, it is well worth while for the woman of the household to acquire the ability to run it. In the vast majority of instances it is the modern medium light car which is chosen, and it presents the minimum of difficulties for the woman to master. Once she has learned to drive it and to help her husband care for it, the family's use and pleasure in the car are increased several hundred per cent. If the head of the house is the only motorist and the services of a chauffeur cannot be afforded, the car is probably idle three fourths of the time. As soon as the woman makes friends with it, it becomes an indefatigable source of health and pleasure to her, her children, and her friends.

The Automobile as a Means of Country Travel (1905)

THE AUTOMOBILE AS A MEANS OF COUNTRY TRAVEL

By H. P. BURCHELL

DRAWINGS BY EDWARD PENFIELD

TO the owner of an automobile its greatest charm lies in the countless opportunities it furnishes for convenient travel. The touring-car has truly become a fixed type of the horseless vehicle. The ponderous, dust-raising, loud-snorting, racing cars, that look more like a troublesome gift from the devil himself than a beneficent gift from the gods, may have their devotees, but the joys of making a mile in several seconds less than a minute possess no charms for the man who bids his wife and little ones clamber into his neat, compact touring-car and then, with a twist of the wheel, starts off noiselessly and easily on a trip of some hundred miles through picturesque bits of country. Where is he going? Where will he stop over night? How many miles will he run a day? To such questions, perhaps, the owner himself could give no answer. He may have a fairly clear idea regarding his terminus, but there is a pleasant vagueness about the intermediate stations, contributing something of that spice of curiosity to his tour, that, in larger measure, forced the pioneers of old to push on into unknown regions wondering what they would see or find next. This freedom, this independence, this being in the largest possible degree completely master of one's self, constitutes one of the greatest charms of country travel by automobile. That horrible fiend, the railroad time-table, is banished to the far woods; no longer does the early morning "tramp,

tramp" and sharp "tap, tap" of the hotel bell-boy rudely disturb one's quiet sleeping with the peremptory summons, as articulate as if spoken in words, to get up or miss the train; no longer does the perspiring traveler on the slow-moving local hurl anathemas at unseen and unknown foes because of interminable delays, soft-coal dust, soot and a long absence of ice water from the receptacle that tantalizingly bears those words. No, the steel rails with their varying degrees of speed have ceased to be a necessity to the summer tourist, who, with a little means and unlimited capabilities of enjoyment, is willing to intrust himself to the mercies of the country roads, good, bad or indifferent, as they may be, and plain but usually substantial living in the village tavern. He can travel as slowly and sometimes as fast as he pleases and can run off the main road, here and there, visiting little-known places of historic or picturesque interest which would ever have remained to him as a sealed book had he been restricted to the undeviating pathway of the steam road.

The great network of trolley roads has contributed enormously to country travel within recent years, but even the electric roads have their limitations. Years ago the bicycle was hailed as the great emancipator from the railroad and the trammels of city life, offering to thousands of persons the benefits of healthful, open-air exercise in the rural districts. The bicycle did a great work, but naturally its use was restricted, very largely, to those of the younger and more athletic age. Bicycle tours in Europe, where good roads were more numerous than in our own free land, were all the rage, and the historic inns and ale-houses that had been languishing since the decline of the old coaching days became wonderfully popular and active. Indeed, a trip to Europe was not considered complete unless the visitor spent at least a night in some quaint out-of-the-way English pot-house and imagined all

The passengers.

sorts of gay things having taken place within its walls in the days of good "Queen Bess."

The bicycle had its day as a popular means of travel and touring. An interregnum followed. The ale-houses again sank into desuetude and scores of them were not aroused into wakefulness until a year or two ago when the prolonged *toot*, *toot* of the automobile horn told them that good times were coming around once more. And, as the automobile has benefited many trades, so it has, in the country districts, contributed wonderfully to the improvement of the typical village tavern. The last two years has witnessed a great

transformation in this respect throughout the smaller towns of New England, and the same is probably true in other parts of the country where automobilists are frequent and good paying visitors. In fact, the automobilist is looked upon by the Yankee inn-keeper as a very desirable customer. The stories of the cost of these wonderful horseless cars have not been lost upon the shrewd provider of victuals and drink, and the stopping of an automobile party at one of these old-fashioned resorts usually means an increase in prices. It must be confessed that, if over-taxed, the motorists themselves are generally to blame. The influx of moneyed tourists who appear anxious to spend their money always works a hardship to the parties of more moderate purses who follow. However, these little things usually find their proper level, but if they lead to better accommodations and a few necessities, if need be, for his machine, the automobilist is perfectly willing that the price should be commensurate with his own comforts.

Not alone has the automobile caused the minor hostelries to spruce up a bit, but in the large country hotels automobile gar-

Showing them how it works.

An addition to his sign.

ages are now to be seen completely equipped, often employing several expert mechanicians who can repair over night any little trouble to the machinery and start the car off as good as new in the morning. The big hotels now give as much attention to the perfection of their automobile conveniences as they used to and still do to their stabling quarters. Indeed, many of the leading hotels in New England keep several automobiles to hire out by the day or longer periods. All of the prominent summer hotels in Lenox, Pittsfield, Great Barrington, in the popular resorts along the Sound and even in the White Mountains are completely equipped for all ordinary automobile needs. The change in this respect has been remarkable, but it simply illustrates the wide area covered by the automobile.

Native animosity has also been worn down and frequently stamped out entirely by the steady invasion of the rural districts by the motor-car. The opposition of the backwoods farmer to the appearance of this strange, self-propelled car among his barnyard "critters," has more than once given careful and law-abiding tourists not only a moment of anxiety, but the opportunity of studying human nature under its most crotchety conditions.

"Better arbitrate and conciliate than dispute and aggravate," is the sound legal advice of James B. Dill, who belongs to that delightful band of automobile enthusiasts who do not believe that business should stand in the way of a motor-car. Mr. Dill conciliates not only by the persuasiveness of his voice but, to the ordinary farmer, by the more potent influence of a good Havana cigar.

"Cigars are as necessary as gasoline to insure a successful automobile trip," is one of Mr. Dill's axioms, and he ought to know, for he has gone with his machine in some portions of Maine and Canada where no automobile ever went before or since. Mr. Dill lays out for his trip a liberal supply of good cigars, no five-cent Raines Law Hotel variety, but the kind that will go straight to the heart of any smoker.

"A gentle word backed up by a good cigar has made more than one cantankerous farmer meet me more than half way and pull out into the ditch in the narrowest road so as to allow me just enough room to go by," adds Mr. Dill in confirmation of his claim.

Mr. Dill made one of the most ambitious automobile tours of the year last season. He did not try for a record, and few people would have heard anything about it had not his friends talked so much about the hardships he encountered in cutting his own way from Quebec to the Rangeley Lakes, Maine. This was a distance of about two hundred and fifty miles, and Mr. Dill with some members of his family in his big steam car virtually established an automobile route between those two places. One reason why Mr. Dill undertook this arduous trip is because he believes that if the motor vehicle is good for anything it ought to be serviceable for hunting and fishing trips as well as for pleasure runs. This principle he carries out in practice. On this memorable route through the Maine woods, Mr. Dill's party saw many deer, while they frequently feasted upon trout, partridge and other small game of their own catching. Fair roads were encountered, but in many cases they were very rough and very narrow. The trusty axe proved a friend in need on more than one occasion, when the overgrowth of brush was so dense as to seriously retard the progress of a heavy motor-car. But it was great fun and

Mr. Dill enjoyed every experience of the trip, even to the primitive lodging in the various places that went by the names of hotels in the Maine backwoods.

"I don't know as I can recommend one kind of automobile any more than another as most suitable for an automobile country tour," said Mr. Dill when asked what requirements he considered necessary. "I want a machine for that purpose which will go out with me and bring me back at the proper time, and will not, upon the road, call for an excessive expenditure of energy, activity or profanity by breakdowns or permanent stoppage. I look for a machine which is a concomitant to my rod, my gun and my dog and will carry all three. I look for a machine which I can call to my door in July and start for the woods, to the extremes of Canada, if necessary, and which will take the requisite passengers, guns, rods and all the essentials of sportsmen's life in the woods, without the resources and supplies of near-by civilization."

And every automobile tourist, who has in his veins the slightest drop of sporting blood will re-echo, "Them's my sentiments."

Every part of New England offers delightful opportunities for pleasant touring. The journey from New York to Boston is a favorite one and is traveled by hundreds of automobilists every season. Some take it leisurely, passing through New Haven and Hartford and then skirting the Connecticut River to Springfield, from where some delightful short tours may be made, then continuing on through Worcester and so into Boston. The roads around Boston are admirable for day trips and the interesting historic associations with which every one of these routes is filled adds materially to the charm of the run. Taking the road rendered famous by Paul Revere's ride, for instance, with its warlike associations of Concord and Lexington, in which are also mingled some of the most hallowed literary reminiscences of New England, one can appreciate the perfection of motor-car touring, for the roads are excellent, the scenery delightful, the points of interest brimful of patriotic fervor and the country inns fully up to the standard of New England's best hospitality.

New York also presents many admirable tours for the automobilist. The run up the Hudson to Albany will discover good roads and accommodations, but between Albany and Buffalo are many sections that have been the *bete noir* to hardy motorists, the roads, especially in wet weather, resembling beds of mud more than civilized highways. But the automobile is changing all this, and another and perhaps the most important of its benefits to humanity is the impetus given to the good-roads movement by the advent of the horseless carriage.

New Jersey contains many good roads, and fair touring routes may be found to the Far West. The run to Chicago has ceased to be a novelty, and the memorable tour of the American Automobile Association last

The old and the new.

summer to St. Louis, over one thousand five hundred miles being traveled successfully by many members from New York and other Eastern cities, demonstrated more conclusively than ever before the complete reliability of the motor vehicle of the present day and its all-around possibilities. The American continent has been crossed more than once, all of them experiments and with an eye to business, to be sure, but their success again demonstrated the capability of the automobile to go anywhere that it is possible for a horse-drawn conveyance or a railroad train to go. The record for the trip from San Francisco to New York stands at present at thirty-three days, made last August by a light touring car of ten horse power and weighing but twelve hundred pounds.

Rivals.

Colorado has become a popular State for the automobile tourist. The picturesque grandeur of the country intensifies the attractiveness of the tour, the roads for the most part are good, and if one is careful to select proper routes he can avoid severe mountainous hills. But hills no longer terrify the motorist. A few years ago a hill of more than ordinary steepness gave the tourist cold shudders. The demand in recent years has been for cars of moderate horse power, built so strongly and yet lightly that they can stand the strain of thousands of miles and climb hills at a pretty fast clip in the bargain. The manufacturers have succeeded in turning out such machines and they have found a ready sale. A close student of automobile growth in America has stated that there is now in use one automobile to twelve hundred inhabitants. Two years ago the ratio was one to six thousand five hundred inhabitants and four years ago it was one to one million five hundred thousand inhabitants. A whole story is contained in these figures, and the high average of the present day means continued touring in country districts and a

larger ownership of automobiles by country residents.

Automobile tours in Europe have become so common as to give no excuse for comment. It is now possible to hire cars with responsible chauffeurs in London for a tour of a week or a month outside of London, extending up into Scotland if required. and even the rougher roads of Ireland have been traveled by automobilists. In France, of course, every one expects good roads just as he does good cooking, and a disappointment in either case is so surprising as to be remembered ever afterward.

The crowning glory of automobile touring, however, lies in the demand it has created, in all parts of the world where motor-cars are being used for pleasure or business purposes, for good roads. Here in America the good-roads movement, within recent years, has become a question of national importance. With the exception of a few States, notably New Jersey and Massachusetts, the subject of better roads was the last thought that gave the legislators the least particle of trouble. The Automobile Club of America, in its younger days, expended a tremendous amount of argumentative energy in endeavoring to convince the lawmakers of New York that money expended on good roads was a good business investment. Their appeals brought out a few thousand dollars, somewhat grudgingly given. Finally the generous sum of one hundred thousand dollars was appropriated, and at the forthcoming election a constitutional amendment will be presented to the voters providing that the State may bond itself for five million dollars for ten years for the building of improved wagon roads.

Agitation has been productive of similar good results in other States. Governor Dineen, of Illinois, gave a marked illustration of the growing demand for better roads in the West when, in his last message, he made a strong plea for the expenditure of more money and careful thought upon road building. His statement that barely two per cent. of the Illinois roads were suitable for traffic at all periods of the year was no exaggeration, and scores of other States could show no higher average. Departments of highways have been established in California, Idaho, Minnesota, Mississippi, Missouri, Oregon, Tennessee, North Carolina, Nebraska and in several of the Eastern States in which the good-roads movement has languished. Florida recently appropriated five hundred thousand dollars for good roads, and it is confidently predicted that within a short time there will not be a State in the Union that will not manifest a just pride in the increasing mileage of its serviceable roads good all the year round.

Reasonable credit must be given to the automobile for bringing about this condition of affairs. While legislators have been busy, ever since the motor-car began to assert itself as entitled to the ordinary privileges of the road, in enacting laws regulating its speed and compelling the affixing of license tags and other marks of easy identification, the motor-car has been steadily demonstrating its purposes of utility, and perhaps unconsciously has paved the way for lasting benefits to all classes of citizens.

With the speed of an express.

How to Avoid Automobile Accidents
(1905)

HOW TO AVOID AUTOMOBILE ACCIDENTS

FIFTY MILLION DOLLARS FOR GOOD ROADS

THE $50,000,000 appropriation for good roads in New York state certainly will, if all spent for roads and not for politics, insure this state the best roads in the country. The amount spent by towns, counties and state for road improvement since 1898 was $11,508,133. There are in this state 74,097 miles of highway, of which 38,000 miles are repaired and maintained under the day's work system—working out taxes at $1.50 a day instead of paying taxes in cash.

Already there are 16,000 miles of good roads in this state made at an expense of about eleven and one-half millions. In ten years—the time allowed for the spending of the $50,000,000—New York should have perfect roads from one end of the state to the other, and hundreds of thoroughfares improved from the Hudson River to the Long Island Sound.

A portion of the appropriation could be

advantageously spent upon the men who work out their taxes by appointing a man in each county to teach the rudiments of road building, especially the inexpensive, practical and effective split-log method, which has been so successfully used in the Western country.

New York state spent in 1904 over $300,000 more than did New Jersey, Massachusetts and Connecticut combined; but this is in a measure accounted for in the fact that these three states have spent nothing to speak of in improvement or building, all their appropriation having gone for maintenance, while New York built nearly seven hundred miles of highway in 1904.

State Engineer Henry C. Van Alstyn, under whose administration New York state's road improvement has been rapid, is responsible for the statement that to build properly one mile of road costs about $7,000. At this figure $50,000,000 would build 7,500 miles, approximately—or one mile in ten throughout the state. This would bring every farm in the state within five miles of an improved thoroughfare, while sixty per cent. of them will either be directly on or within three miles of a macadam road. This brings out the truth that the farmer, and not the automobilist, will be the great gainer through the investment of the $50,000,000.

DO AUTOMOBILES INJURE ROADS?

The charge has been made in Elizabeth, N. J., by a committee of citizens, that automobiles injure the roads. This is ridiculous from the state engineer's viewpoint, inasmuch as wide tires on wagons allow the owner a reduction in his taxes. There is no doubt that skidding around curves throws the top dressing into the ditch, but the man who shoots around curves violates the speed law, so he may easily be reached.

The Iowa State Highway Commission has taken a step in the right direction. It has opened in the State College in Ames a fine course in road building and improvement.

THE COMMERCIAL MOTOR VEHICLE

Beyond doubt the motor vehicle for commercial purposes has become indispensable, not only for delivery purposes, but more especially for handling passenger traffic and for long Western stage lines. This particularly is true in the case of vehicles used the year round. The problem of heating and lighting has been solved—or can be—and in this wise, if the motive power be gasoline: The heat from the exhaust gases or the cooling water may be utilized by installing radiators along the floor of the car. This heat naturally would go to waste, so that the problem of heating is solved at almost no cost — none, in fact, other than the cost of radiators. The lighting question is not much more difficult of solution. A small dynamo driven direct from the engine, together with a storage battery, furnishes an electric power plant which may be depended upon at all times. Many of the up-to-date stage lines in the West—notably the longest line in this country, between Torrence and Roswell, Mexico, a distance of 105 miles—is having this sort of stage built; and while one travels across the prairie in the coldest of weather he is as comfortable as in a Pullman, and traveling at twenty miles an hour and at a cost of ten cents a mile. The same lighting and heating proposition may be applied to delivery wagons, and for the matter of that, to limousine and landaulet. Then, too, the baggage wagon that will carry 5,000 pounds at a load and bring it round to us at ten miles an hour will enable us to go out of town and have our trunk sent to the depot on the same day. This in itself makes the automobile baggage wagon a boon to humanity, and will take much imaginary trouble from the minds of the Haines Society, for all the troubles will be tire troubles, with no hatrack horses and cruelty to animals.

ANOTHER ANTI-FREEZING SOLUTION

With the coming of cold weather a formula for a good anti-freezing solution to be used in motor vehicle radiators may not come amiss. One of the best solutions for this purpose is: glycerine, forty-nine per cent.; sodium carbonate, two per cent.; water, forty-nine per cent. One filling of the water system will last indefinitely, as neither water nor gasoline will evaporate to any great extent. The mixture is comparatively cheap, and thorough testing has proved that it has no effect on galvanized iron or rubber hose, and very little action on copper. A mixture of equal portions of glycerine and water shows up very well, but is not quite as good as the formula above. A solution of calcium chloride and water having a density of about twenty-six per cent. Baumé is sometimes used, but the one objection to it is that it attacks galvanized iron, and must be carefully kept at nearly the same density all the time to give it good anti-freezing qualities. Another mixture sometimes used, and one which has practically no action on any of the metals, is: alcohol, twenty-five per cent.; water, seventy-five per cent.; or alcohol, thirty-five per cent.; water, sixty-five per cent. When either of these solutions is used the water system must be kept enclosed and perfectly tight in order to keep the solution at the proper strength.

AUTOMOBILE ACCIDENTS—AND REASONS

Of course automobile accidents cannot be attributed to any one thing, but certain it is that the long-suffering and much-abused term "recklessness" is not by any means the chief offender, as generally is charged.

If one will substitute inability, the truth more nearly will be reached. Inability not alone to expertly run a car, but inability to realize the power that is placed in one's hands, and the great responsibility attached to that power; inability to realize the fact that others have rights on the highways, though they may prefer to drive a horse instead of an engine. These seldom are the kind of persons who have courage to protect their rights afoot. They have no physical courage, but the sensation of having strength that belongs not to themselves momentarily turns their heads, and they relapse into their natural selves and contract "greedomania."

A reckless man in any sport is not dangerous, for he generally has courage, and with that courage some judgment; and even when he suffers through his recklessness, generally he suffers alone.

It is the "road hog" who is to be feared in automobiling, and, thank Heaven! there is only a small percentage of this variety in the motor world, as is shown in the fact that with nearly twenty-five thousand automobiles in New York state only five hundred persons were injured by motor cars during the year just past, and many of these must be charged to the injured persons and stupidity of the street-crossing public, for even with automobiles there are some few unavoidable accidents. In London and Paris together there were fewer automobile accidents than in the city of New York, which may be accounted for in the fact that the people in Europe are more used to running cars and seeing them, but it is more likely because of the severity with which offending chauffeurs are dealt.

It is shown that horse-drawn vehicles were responsible for many more accidents than automobiles in a dozen cities; which, however, proves little because of the predominance of the former in every city in the world, in addition to which the injuries in almost every case were less severe.

One of the best accident preventives for insane drivers would be an example such as was recently made of a well-known American in Paris—a jail sentence and a heavy fine payable to the family of the person killed. The fear of jail is held by wealth and poverty alike, whereas a fine means only a mild protest from the intemperate driver. Three months in jail for a few "deserving Americans" would save time and money spent in legislation, and be an everlasting benefit to the motorist who runs a car like a sane gentleman.

License the man and not the car, and before any license be granted the applicant should be compelled to pass a practical examination and then granted a sixty-day probatory certificate, which should not be made permanent unless the holder had a clean record. No license should be granted to children, as now is done.

HOW TO TAKE CORNERS

Taking corners at a high speed is dangerous, not only to occupants of the car but to any one else who happens to be near the turn. To this particular form of "road hog" three out of every four out-of-town accidents are accountable. This is especially true of New Jersey.

It is impossible for a driver to see down the street until he has negotiated the turn, which generally is too late to avoid a collision with horse, car, or pedestrian traveling the hidden road.

A little common sense will enable the motorist to avoid this contingency. First of all he should reduce his speed to a minimum. Then, if approaching from the left instead of continuing to the narrow road on his own—the right—side of the main road, he should run over to the left, and when abreast the treed way, so that he has a clear view of it for a distance, turn straight in. He should adopt the same tactics in passing these narrow, treed roads—swinging to the left until he has passed, then run back to the right. In approaching from the right he has only to stay on that side, and when opposite the narrow way turn in.

DON'TS THAT WILL PREVENT ACCIDENTS

Don't allow your chauffeur to drink liquor while in charge of your car. If running your own car avoid rum yourself.

Don't run on the wrong side of the road except at narrow, intersecting streets.

Don't try to see how close you can run to pedestrians. Give them even more room than they require. Many walkers have heart trouble.

Don't take any kind of a turn or curve at twenty miles an hour; better go four miles and be able to do it again.

Don't put oil on your registration number and throw dust on it. An honest man isn't afraid of identification.

Don't toot your horn in passing horses unless approaching from behind, and then not unless absolutely necessary. There still are some spirited animals.

Don't blow your Gabriel horn continually in a city street. A little of it is music; too much is a disagreeable, irritating racket.

Don't forget to light your lamps one hour before sunset; then you will have more chance than the wagon ahead without lights—and be within the law.

Don't grab at the things that concern the chauffeur, and don't ever take a passenger again who has grabbed once—if you ever are able to go out again.

Don't run away after running down anybody; you'll stand a better chance if you stay.

Don't ever act like anything but an intelligent gentleman.

The Promise
of the Automobile
in Recreative Life
(1900)

THE PROMISE OF THE AUTOMOBILE IN RECREATIVE LIFE.

By Robert Bruce.

THE extension of the domain, and the multiplication of the means of pleasure-life, which so markedly characterizes the present age, is due, perhaps, not more to an unexampled awakening of the recreative instinct than to the increased opportunities afforded for wider personal participation in the many forms of accepted sport. A broad-gauged, far-reaching change is in process. The old idea of physical exercise merely for its own sake has long been losing its hold. Here, as elsewhere in contemporaneous living, consciousness of some underlying, actuating incentive, and the realization of pleasant and profitable auxiliary results, has been needed to lead the way to healthful, cheerful and invigorating performance of well-sustained interest, and to endow with vitality that which the conditions of the times might otherwise narrow to feeble insignificance.

Incentive finds more or less expression in all recreations worthy of encouragement and support. To some there has been lent the enthusiasm and interest of friendly rivalries conducted in true and dignified spirit ; while others are linked with the progress of some modern invention. The latter 'have already afforded the devotees of outdoor life some efficient means of pleasure travel, by the use of which the radius of individual movement has been sensibly lengthened, and freedom, ease and comfort in so doing, favorably redefined.

Two types, both exclusively modern—the bicycle and the automobile—stand at the head of the list of mechanical accessories to sport and recreation ; the first-named credited the most in achieved results ; the second—the special contemplation of the present paper—showing from this view point the brightest promise for the future.

Those who best know the motor carriages of to-day—more especially clearsighted and hard-headed inventors and manufacturers—are, as a rule, the most conservative of their proven capabilities and the least ungenerous to their remaining faults. The professional boomer, in whatever form appearing, is the worst possible enemy to a movement the success of which must ultimately be measured by ability to satisfactorily meet a number of severe mechanical requirements. Already some of those responsible for wide-of-the-mark utterances are formulating humble apologies to the public whose interests they have been pretending to serve, and whose confidence they have rightfully forfeited. The publicity radiating from this industry is either well-founded or withering ; that of OUTING's publishing may be depended upon as solely of the safer type.

One refreshing fact confronts the friend of automobile development in whatever way his observation may be turned—the serious thought of designers and makers finds utterance in the construction of models first for pleasure and afterwards for commercial uses. That this has not been the result—as some profess to believe—of a desire to solve the easier problem first will be apparent when it is understood that the most bothersome of all structural requirements are those called for by carriages adaptable to such highways, loads, powers and speeds as are contemplated for private ownership.

Neither the ponderous omnibus nor the lumbersome autotruck call for equal nicety in unity and detail of outworking as compared with the self-moving surrey,

or phaeton, or even the roundabout. To combine strength and durability with reasonable lightness and speed, high efficiency and endurance of propelling forces, with symmetry of outline and ease of management, grade ascending power, with ample carrying capacity, and so following—these are but a few of the special difficulties to be overcome in the construction of pleasure types of automobiles. No more arbitrary array of fixed requirements could easily be formulated to vex designers and builders.

And, yet in at least one important respect the motor vehicle industry is greatly favored over all other of the developments of modern mechanics. The purchasers of its earliest products are almost without exception men and women of means, of patience and personal enthusiasm for an ultimate, rather than immediate, satisfactory outcome of their investments and efforts. Many are themselves, indeed, amateur designers and constructors of no mean order. Not a few have suggested, and in extremity demonstrated, various devices and improvements already indispensable to the operation and control of accepted models.

Whatever may result from the combination of explosive gas and compressed air as a propelling resource for automobiles—and the possibilities of success in this direction grow with the progress of daily experiment—will ever stand credited, first of all, to the courage and perseverance of an American, who has for years backed his belief in the worth of this system with his time, labor and fortune, and is now equipping a factory for the manufacture, on an extended scale, of vehicles brought to promising efficiency in his private service. Whether

or not these models secure that share of public favor expected for them, it is admitted that their possibilities are being searched to the uttermost. This instance, although the most notable of all, is but one among the many known to the current records of the trade.

There are perhaps two scores of improvised laboratories in the United States to-day designed solely for automobile experiment, and doubtless one-half that number of completed vehicles assembled on individual lines from working parts made to special single order. The sum-total of value of such outside coöperation is beyond easy calculation at this particular stage of the movement.

Were it possible to select a goodly number of the best models of each of the three practicable types of carriages, namely, those propelled by (1) electricity, (2) the hydrocarbons, and (3) steam, place them in the hands of persons of active and varied pleasure-searching inclinations, and afford them full and free opportunity for the all-round use of these machines, a comprehensive summary of their experiences would form a fair reflection of what we may confidently expect in due time from the addition of the automobile to the means of recreation. New possibilities in track and road racing, in general pleasure riding and touring would be demonstrated before our eyes. We would be fully justified in availing ourselves of this improvised index to future probabilities, for the reason that the certainty of far-reaching improvements in contemporaneous types would lend extreme conservatism to any calculation of such matter.

Another margin of safety would be afforded in the likelihood that selling prices will in some degree decline with the multiplication and further perfection of the facilities of production, thus materially increasing the number of machines, which coming years will place in commission. Whatever has already, through vexatious trials, been accomplished, even one by one, will be but primary practice for multitudes under conditions which will be brought about so swiftly as to become commonplace with us, before the end of the decade upon which we are soon to enter. We are therefore privileged to foreshadow the future position of the automobile in sport and pastime by means of the account it has already rendered of itself.

Competition on the road and track alike divides itself into two broad classes: contests between (1) motor cycles and tricycles (both commonly known as "motocycles,"), and those between (2) motor vehicles as such. The lines separating these classes are drawn much more distinctly in Europe, and especially in France, than in the United States, owing largely to the more advanced state of both industry and sport in that country. Motocycles are of many types, constructed after the manner of heavier bicycles and tricycles, and ingeniously fitted with various motive powers. Racing with these machines has come to be very popular on the Continent, and more so in Great Britain than with us. At a tournament held at the Crystal Palace, London, on July 1st, 1899, five events were run, and each one was well contested, notwithstanding that Mr. S. F. Edge, formerly a champion middle-distance cyclist, swept every event on the programme. He won the mile handicap in 1:50, the two miles handicap in 3:38, and the five miles scratch in 8:55 2-5, while in the hour race he covered 34 miles 540 yards, and finally, with Jarrott for partner, beat Stocks and Ridgeway in the mile tandem in 1:43 4-5. There were six starters in the mile, six in the two miles, seven in the five miles, and five in the hour competition.

The road record between London and Edinburgh has always been much sought after by British long-distance men, with the result that the figures have been gradually reduced for the bicycle to 25 hours, 20 minutes. Recently Mr. J. W. Stocks, on a motocycle, undertook to eclipse the cycle record, which he did very effectually. Leaving the Scottish end at 6 A. M., he reached London at 2:35 the next morning, covering the route in 20 hours, 35 minutes, and averaging, including all stops, nearly 20 miles per hour for the entire journey. The superiority of the latter performance more clearly appears when it is remembered that the cycle record was, like the automobile record, practically a single dash from start to finish, which a trained cyclist is able to sustain for that number of miles like an animated machine. And yet the time of the motocycle, notwithstanding all the perils and

drawbacks of management at high speed by night, was 4 hours, 45 minutes less than the cycle time.

In the last annual race over the Paris-Bordeaux course, Bardin's average time for the 565 kilometers was 42¼ kilometers per hour. In the "Tour de France" (motocycle division) Teste sustained a uniform speed of 41½ kilometers per hour over a distance of 2,-291 kilometers. Paris-St. Malo was won by Renaux on the motor bearing his name, his time for the 372 kilometers giving the high average of 52 kilometers per hour. The winner of the Paris-Dieppe race averaged 42 kilometers per hour, and Teste was victorious in the shorter Paris-Trouville course of 175 kilometers, making 57 kilometers per hour. Baras scored three brilliant victories in the Paris-Lille (258 k.), Paris-Ostend (323 k.), and Paris-Boulogne (330 k.) races, his respective average times per hour being 48½, 52½ and 45¾ kilometers.

The last-named figure is perhaps the most meritorious of them all, inasmuch as it was made on a quadracycle, carrying a passenger instead of the usual stripped tricycle. The last of the big races for 1899, Bordeaux-Biarritz, was productive of high averages, and Bertin's time for the 281 kilometers reached the record mark of 60 kilometers per hour. Mention must also be made of the shorter distance performances of Beconnais, at Acheres, in September. On the famous "route du Parc d'Agricole," this motoclycist covered two kilometers in 1 minute 50 3-5 seconds, and made the kilometer with flying start in 48 seconds, equaling a speed of 75 kilometers (about 47 miles) per hour. This

feat, coupled with his hour record of 42 miles 337 yards, on the track, go far to compensate Beconnais for his comparative lack of success in the longer road races.

Motor vehicle speeds average somewhat less than the speeds of motorcycles, owing principally to the heavier weights necessary to be carried and the difficulty of handling a large machine with the same ease and quickness of controlling movement as a small one. Notwithstanding these facts, however, the average of the winner of the Paris-Ostend race (Levegh-Girardot) was 52 kilometers per hour, and in the Paris-Boulogne, 54. Tourist vehicles have averaged 24 or 25 miles per hour for upwards of 200 miles, carrying three or four passengers in a heavy touring body.

The personal mount of the Hon. John Scott Montagu, M. P., has per a recent communication to the *Motor-Car World* (England), as a matter of record averaged 29½ miles per hour between Paris and Amiens, a distance of about eighty miles of rather hilly country, and 30.3 miles on the comparatively level highway in Belgium between Dunkerque and Ostend. These are averages from end to end of distances named, and, of course, on the favorable level or slightly down-hill portions of a speeding effort, forty and fifty miles per hour are sometimes maintained for miles at a time.

In the "Tour de France," briefly noted in the automobile records department of the OUTING for January, 1900, René de Knyff, on a 16 horse-power Panhard-Lavassor, averaged 51 kilometers per hour over a route 2,291 kilometers long. The Paris-St. Malo was won by Anthony, with a 16 horse-power Mors vehicle, at an average speed of 50 kilometers per hour for the course of 372 kilometers. The same equipment gained the Paris-Trouville race, making an average of 58 kilometers per hour for 175 kilometers. Levegh, on a Mors, and Girardot, on a Panhard-Lavassor, who finished the Paris-Ostend race in a dead heat, averaged 52 kilometers to the hour for 322 kilometers. The 330 kilometers between Paris and Boulogne have been covered by Girardot at an average speed of nearly 54 kilometers per hour.

An interesting comparison of moto cycles and motor vehicles, in the matter of recorded speeds over identical courses, may be made by placing certain items in this and the preceding paragraph against each other. Omitting those where the comparison would be from any cause incomplete, we have the following :

	Motorcycle average.	Motor vehicle average.
Tour de France, 2,291 kilometers.....	41½	51
Paris-St. Malo, 372 kilometers........	52	50
Paris-Trouville,175 kilometers........	57	58
Paris-Ostend, 322 kilometers........ ..	52½	52*
Paris-Boulogne, 330 kilometers........	45¾†	54‡

    *Levegh-Girardot competition.
    † Quadracycle machine with passenger.
    ‡ Girardot's record time.

It will be noticed that in three instances here noted the motor-vehicle speed exceeded that of the motocycle, and of these, one event was the longest of all, and the lower average of another is accounted for by the footnote marked with the dagger. The short distance records are uniformly to the credit of the lighter types of machines.

In the summaries of both motocycle and motor-vehicle performances here briefly given, the promise of future competition plainly appears. A two-wheeled, three-wheeled or four-wheeled power-driven machine, capable of negotiating various distances at upwards of forty miles per hour to-day, carrying weights ranging from 100 to 1,000 pounds, possesses possibilities which the untamed inclinations of sport-loving people in the United States will hardly overlook beyond the time required by manufacturers to produce the machines. Road courses suitable for these contests will become many, and the use thus made of them ought to be surprisingly great and widespread. Tournaments and track competitions will come, and grow into deserved popularity. And it may here properly be said that the personnel of contestants in automobile events must form a pleasing contrast to any oft-met type of cycle racing enthusiasts.

The supreme test in speeding consists in the management of the machine. The success of the operator depends upon his getting the utmost power and swiftness out of his motor; in knowing how to best supply it with fuel, and in the thousand-and-one precautions against being taken unawares or caught by accident. He must be perfectly cool at all times, have plenty of nerve force, and be an utter stranger to fear. When one has no misgivings either about himself or the mechanism under his hand, he is less likely than otherwise to meet with misfortune.

Many of the famous French motocyclists have been brought up in the workshops, and have therefore a thorough acquaintance with the practical side of their machines; but the best amateur management does not materially suffer from point-and-point comparison therewith. The latter displays infinitely more tact and resource; the former more mechanical dexterity. Since the skill of the operator counts for so much, and the liability to accident must always be taken into account, there is considerable glorious uncertainty about racing with automobiles; and, in fact, it is extremely rare to find the same person winning in consecutive events. All this tends to lend especial interest to the sport, and is helping to create a popularity for it.

Touring by motor vehicle, the social interest in general and the motor club interest in particular, already centering about this new form of transportation, are developments of the greater movement intimately related to the topics constituting the present paper, but impossible to comprehensively treat in the same connection. They will be subsequently discussed in OUTING.

The spirit in which the automobile has been seized upon by those to whom we must chiefly look for support of its further development, is the best possible, as well as the nearest available index to its likely position in the recreative life of the approaching century. That spirit can at this moment be credited

with having accepted and improved to the utmost every advantage vouchsafed it by the industry, and with a surplus of wholly rational energy and enthusiasm for the opportunities denied to-day but promised to-morrow.

These things are very largely in the hands of those who have brought real strength to the sport of to-day. The older need not necessarily suffer by the addition to the list of a newer one of only far-distant kin; for, vital and vigorous in growth as it promises to be, it is in conflict with none other that can be named. It may, indeed, serve the ultimate best interests of those who innocently fear its power and tendency to somewhat eclipse their favorite recreations. The self-propelling carriage will take one not to the depths of the forests but to the suburban traps and ranges; it

will find the river road, seldom the river; it will carry home only what the automobilist-angler succeeds in catching; the leg-weary cannot pursue fugitive golf balls mounted upon it, but it will find the way home before the enthusiasm and hilarity of the game has suffered sensible decline.

Observe with what refinement of conscience this new form of transportation stops short of interfering with anything in the recreative world that flourished before its day, and how modestly content it is to contribute to the means and resources of the practice and enjoyment of many of them! This is the last as well as the very first of the premises of this paper. By thus furthering the purposes of rational pleasure-seeking, the automobile must likewise confer upon life a long line of especial benefits and blessings.

The Place
of the Automobile
(1900)

THE PLACE OF THE AUTOMOBILE.

By Robert Bruce.

FIRST impressions of the self-moving carriage are apt to be unsympathetic, if not, indeed, acutely disappointing. You cannot help admiring the audacity of whosoever fastened his ideas of sport to the road motor; yet only on the plea of a proven capacity for distance-covering and burden-carrying can you justify its position. To the inexperienced eye it is merely brother to the trolley-car, released from scheduled service and able to follow, within its limitations, the will of the owner and driver.

This unkindly feeling is due in some measure to prejudice. It is a far step from the innate intelligence of the horse and the companionship of the dog to the blind power and mere possession of the machine.

You can share the ecstasies and the dangers of your outing with the fleet four-footer; relax attention now and then; feel that the responsibilities of the ride are not wholly yours; and trust to a discrimination in avoiding the perils of street and highway too marvelously clever to be merely automatic. But the power-driven vehicle is wholly and directly in the care of your head and hand. You are the most independent and absolute monarch locomotion ever produced—until something happens; then no wayside beggar is so poor or so helpless.

The liking for travel by motor thrives best on a groundwork of genuine interest in engineering and mechanics. Most of our successful automobilists would make daring locomotive engineers with half a chance.

Who has not stood beside a modern greyhound of the rail, and thought a kingdom all too small a price to pay for the privilege of just once being engineer?

In real life, comparatively few of us can handle the throttle, and mow down the miles over glistening rails as the reaper passes the grain stalks behind him. But the willingness for such adventure is present in ever-increasing numbers of our people.

A very large proportion of the men and women now enrolled in the ranks of the automobilists owe their intimacy with the new sport to personal and persistent liking for just that sort of ambition. Mere pleasure-seeking in novel forms is not enough to explain all they are doing to-day. They are simply allowing a natural instinct to assert itself.

There is constant need for vigilant nerve to make good progress with the automobile. And when mishap does come—which is frequent enough to bar monotonous driving—the personal intelligence and mechanical resource of the operator will often enable a crippled vehicle to finish its trip. Exasperated profanity in such cases is never any good—at least, not to the machine.

A love of sustained

Mrs. George B. De Forest in her Electric Park Phaeton.

Mr. H. H. Hunnewell in his Steam Automobile.

with the measured sway of the yacht.

Above all else in point of real enjoyment is the feeling of being lifted up and along—carried away — rather than that of being drawn or pushed. The absence of the horse from in front emphasizes the difference for a while; then it becomes a mere matter of course. The mechanical capacity to negotiate from fifteen to thirty-five miles an hour on favorable stretches is the smallest part of it. Mere distance-covering has long since been dismissed from the list of recreations.

The best that is in automobilism comes as the reward of experience, not the first fruit of half-hearted apprenticeship. Nor is it equally divided between passenger and capable driver. The latter is the favored one at all times. To him is the certain control of the lever and foot-button, as well as exhilaration of rivalry based on confidence in one's own familiar type of machine.

At the very outset we find the enthusiasts of two continents dividing themselves into groups according to the types they drive. It is a rivalry without distances or tapes, handicaps or rules. Lines are withdrawn from among kindreds, nationalities, and creeds, and re-established according to motive powers and operating details.

To come across the owner of a machine different from your own is inevitably to pitch a battle-ground on the spot, and thereon deepen the already unalterable convictions of each. No thought of working a change—no; only of rendering a change more than ever before impossible.

This is due more or less to the fact that the intelligent use of a motor vehicle—especially to-day—calls for vastly more than a familiarity with road rules—more

speed and endurance of motive force enlists many to whom the automobile would otherwise be unattractive and its operation tame, for outside of those named in laws and regulations there are practically no speed restrictions. The horse and span are challenged at the first mile, and left hopelessly behind in middle and long distances. The racing automobile does not become tired or diminish in pace so long as quick change of batteries or continuous fuel supplies are arranged, while its total distance capacity for twenty-four hours multiplies that of the fleetest and strongest horse at least by four.

There is a superb luxury about far-and-wide travel by motor. All other means for movement in which there is delight seem to have contributed to its being.

That feeling of independence which so consciously possesses the cyclist is present with the seasoned motorist, though, naturally, to a lesser degree. Driving strength necessary and ample to make play of the ups and downs of the ways traversed—the sensation of gliding down and of bounding up—suggests the full coach behind fresh and spirited teams. And the well-hung and properly managed land machine has something in common than a close study of books of instruction in care and management.

A considerable knowledge, if not indeed a technical command, of the principles of construction individualized in a favorite type is essential to so complete a mastery as will insure confidence in competition, and this can be gained only at the expense of earnest personal application. In such soil enthusiasm takes root.

Electric, hydrocarbon, and steam powers are already successfully established in use. But their specialization is only beginning. Each has highways and byways to be explored, theories to test and sift, and principles to be demonstrated. This important work falls not only to the professional designer and builder, but to all whose interest prompts either suggestion or co-operative effort.

Individual enthusiasm may take hold where it wills, and go where it chooses. Recognition quickly follows the practical, and the rest is soon smothered in good-natured candor. And that difference in opinion which among sportsmen means a vigorous rivalry on existing lines, with now and then a distinct forward step in the perfection of mechanical forms, has free course.

The willingness to meet and the will to overcome any and all troubles—real or imaginary—are so marked among enthusiasts, that features of questionable worth are not, in many cases, discarded as soon as they might well be. There is, especially on the European Continent, a general liking for those types of machines which depend most upon the skill of the operator, and the least upon handling by rule, for their successful speeding. A premium is placed not only upon mental and mechanical dexterity in management, but also upon careful and accurate judgment in such prosaic matters as equipping and refueling.

In very truth, one reason why the electric vehicle has not been developed in France as rapidly as it has in the United States is because of a decided preference there for propelling powers more directly under the eye and care of the operator. Within the strength of its batteries, this type of machine needs far less personal attention than any other—a feature appreciated by many, but not by all.

The summer of 1900 may be said to have marked the entry of the automobile into the ranks as an important factor in recreative life in and about the popular resorts of the North Atlantic coast. Favored by vastly increased interest in their construction and operation, and encouraged by roads much better than the average in this country, there has been a veritable multiplication of machines of all kinds within the past twelve-month.

In addition to the numerous models of American production, one or more representatives of every approved European type have been brought over by enthusiasts, so that our assortment of self-propelled vehicles has now become the most complete in the world. The high-speed motor purchased in France by W. K. Vanderbilt, Jr., for $9,000 was designed expressly for record-making on Conti-

Mrs. Clement C. Moore in her Electric Automobile.

nental highways, and is unlike anything heretofore used on this side of the Atlantic. Among other accessions have been winners of some of the most important automobile racing events abroad.

It is a notable fact that our importations are principally racing vehicles, and our exportations principally pleasure carriages. Naturally Newport, being the most fashionable summer gathering-place of our wealthy and leisured classes, would contain all the most varied and advanced specimens of the automobile, and by the courtesy of their owners OUTING is able to reproduce the accompanying illustra-

Mr. Foxhall Keene on his Motor-Tricycle.

tions of some of the most important of them. But Newport is simply in the van of a large procession. At the New England and Jersey coast resorts, at Saratoga and Lake George, by the side of the Great Lakes, and in the mountains and country East and West, this new form of pleasure travel is gaining rapidly in popularity.

It must necessarily be some time before automobilism finds its sure and proper place among the sports of the times. Even those to whom its progress is to-day indebted for the best and most healthful of

its impulses have constant need for that quality of faith which confidently strives toward results not yet specifically foreshadowed. The leaders in the effort are to a large extent men and women of experience and training in wholesome pastimes, worthy of being trusted to do in a sportsmanlike manner whatever they undertake.

To them the new types of road machine clearly appear as valuable accessories to all outdoor life, to be developed as much for their possibilities of useful ministry to other sports as for their own sake. They know the limitations as well as the main certainties in the development of the automobile.

It is certainly under a favorable sky that another means of pleasure transit is being added to our already known list. To precede a new departure with a deep popular conviction that it is due to come, and certain to broaden to many-sided usefulness, is to endow it with that strength and vitality which lends wings to progress. The wheat is sooner separated from the chaff, standards more opportunely adopted, and less breeding-ground for unhealthy growths exposed.

The road motor is saved in advance nearly all the adverse conditions which greeted the advent of the bicycle, and all the forces of advanced and diversified industry are at the command of the designer and builder who calls upon them to reinforce or exemplify his work. With rare openness of mind, suggestion and offering are alike received; only the crude and the ridiculous fail of respectful attention.

The automobile has already earned its right to be classed as another of our means of recreation.

The position of the automobile and its relation to society uses are at present in a stage of uncertainty, but its solid advantages assure it a place of importance as part of the establishment of every man of means. Exactly what position it will ultimately occupy it is only now possible to speculate on. Possibly it may in the end be the distinguishing mark of social

Master DeForest in his Electric Runabout.

able them to be traversed in safety, then we may witness a return to them of undreamed-of magnificence, and our people of wealth and leisure may move from country seat to country seat and tour from city to city, or from one social resort to another in all the pomp and circumstance that lavish expenditure can buy and emulation spur them on to.

This seems to me to be by no means a far-fetched imagination, because it should be noted that the old-time aristocracy did not adopt the railroad because they liked it, but because the road inns on the old coach routes died out when the railroad took other routes. The automobile will circumvent this, because by its increased capacity to cover distance it will enable travelers by it to reach towns farther apart and provided with hotels capable of appropriately entertaining such guests. For instance, in going south from New York, Philadelphia and Washington would be by no means out of the capacity of a day's trip between each, and so on in many other directions.

grades and affluence, much as the private equipages and cavalcades of the early centuries were the outward and visible signs of the rank and wealth of their respective owners.

Much will depend upon the condition in which the main high roads of the country are kept. If these are brought, over wide areas, into a condition which will en-

Indeed, given good roads there is no apparent limit to the use, or usefulness, of the automobile; for if every mile of a long journey could be performed with the comfort that comes to one at the end of a dusty, hot, stuffy, foul-smelling ride by train, when the railroad carriage is exchanged for the private landau, who would submit to the conditions which are inseparable from the commercial locomotive?

Mr. Royal Phelps Carroll's Gasoline Phaeton.

The Beginner and His Automobile (1902)

THE BEGINNER AND HIS AUTOMOBILE

By LEON VANDERVORT

IN theory, at least, we should have been prepared for the coming of the automobile, for men had prophesied of the day of the horseless carriage from time immemorial. Besides we knew that dreamy men with overalls, in grimy machine shops, were working day and night on problems mechanical, which ninety-nine out of every hundred of their fellows looked upon as folly, problems which the dreamy ones said would give the world horseless carriages and a horseless age. If one of us stopped to think at all of the worker and his prospects, and undertook to understand his progress, he was met with the theories of combustion and bevel gear differentials and designs for a divided axle shaft; whereupon he retired in confusion and went away to rest.

But all at once we awoke to the fact that the dreamy men in overalls had accomplished something, for upon our city streets and our country roads appeared vehicles that dashed about without horses or track, by a motive power within themselves, and they went at wondrous speed. If Saint Paul should arise and attempt to characterize us as he did the Athenians, he would say, not that we lived for the purpose of learning and telling some new thing, but that our chief delight is to know some new sensation. When we saw this new selfpropelling, wondrous swift machine in our midst we wondered how it must seem to be its controlling power. So the American public, that part of it which

"Has pushed when he should have pulled."

had money to spend, sought the factories and ordered automobiles, and the factories worked, and are working overtime to fill orders; and out upon our highways and byways go new carriages of the horseless type every day, and with them go new operators, men who have never before handled anything more complicated in the mechanical line than a bicycle or a telephone. It is a mighty ripple the machine has made on the surface of things, a ripple that will not lessen until the automobile has adjusted itself to its place in our economy and until we have adjusted ourselves to the automobile. There are two sides to this adjustment, that of the automobilist and that of the public.

The former saw in the machine a new means of gratifying the longing for fast motion inherent to humanity. He straightway investigated the merits of steam, gasoline, and electricity, came to a conclusion, and then drew his check. Now it behooved him to learn to use his new possession. So he went down to the shops, determined to face even theories of combustion and bevel gear differentials.

He took off his coat, hung it on a nail, and, sometimes, borrowed overalls with an apron. He studied his machine, learned what will happen if you turn this lever this way and what if you turn it the other, and what may happen if you do not turn it at all. He learned how to fire up a steam machine, to charge the motors of an elec-

"The grimy shop was brightened by light feminine attire."

tric, and came to know that a gasoline carriage is not one that burns gasoline to heat water, but that it does without water and has its piston driven by the explosion of a bit of gasoline in the cylinder. He learned that the gasoline is exploded by electricity but that the machine is not, therefore, an electric motor. He learned that by pushing a lever you make the sparks faster or slower and that your own speed corresponds.

His wife or daughter or sister now and then determined to learn, and accompanied him, and the grimy shop was brightened by light feminine attire. And not infrequently the man was put to shame by the superior rapidity with which the feminine mind grasped the principles underlying the use of the selfmoving vehicle.

The learner who would run an automobile is usually surprised to find how very little he is obliged to learn. Much has been said of the need that the operator of a steam-propelled automobile should be a steam engineer and that one who would use the electric vehicle should be a graduate electrician. In the shops the learner finds that he must know the general prin-

ciples which underlie the workings of his machine, but beyond these and a knowledge of which lever to press for a given purpose he need not go. He may have entered upon his training with fear and trembling for some of those numerous bogies of childhood, a boiler or gasoline explosion, but he soon learns that automatic devices have reduced these to practical, if not absolute, impossibilities. He knows that to neglect keeping a proper amount of water in the boiler of the steam vehicle means that his boiler pipes will "burn" and release the steam and put the machine temporarily out of business, but that there can be no explosion. He knows that gasoline is shut off by an automatic device in case of fire, and that so far as explosions go the new machine is as safe as a bicycle.

The different degrees of readiness with which men grasp the principles and methods vary from zero to infinity. A man entered a New York shop one morning recently and before dark went away his own operator, on his own machine. Another went to the same shop and worked faithfully for two weeks before he could be trusted on the road.

When the learner has passed through his baptism of machine oil and starts out upon the road he has entered upon a new stage of his existence. He has ridden rapidly before, but never when he could look directly down on the onrushing road, with no horses or engine to interfere, nor when he rushed about in a carriage drawn by nothing and with no tracks or trolleys.

But his first ventures outside the shop are not the most exhilarating. The young millionaire who is not used to taking orders, and the society queen whose will is law, must sit by an operator who says "do this" and "don't do that," and says it sharply, sometimes, in a tone that makes one want to throw him out of the carriage. And the operator insists at first on keeping the speed down to a snail's pace and putting on and taking off power himself while his pupil merely learns the use of the steering lever, which seems uncomfortably like holding the lines while some one else does the driving, and is humiliating when one's friends dash by.

Then the operator gives both levers to his pupil, who must steer and control the power at the same time. Now the latter finds there was reason for the operator's caution. His task is that of using both hands at once and moving them in different directions at the same instant. The new automobilist meets a carriage and turns out. He is just turning back into the normal direction when another carriage cuts across in front. He realizes that he should turn toward the curb again and that he should slow up. He pushes sharply at the steering lever, but his hands do not yet work automatically nor do they move in opposite directions of their own accord; and the beginner suddenly awakens to the fact that he has pushed when he should have pulled, has thrown on power instead of turning it off. There is a mighty jump, and the machine is climbing the curb when the professional operator gets his hand on the lever and his foot on the brake.

But a day comes when the beginner's hands work unconsciously, when he turns to right or left and puts on or takes off power or reverses as the case may demand, and does it without thinking. Now he bids a glad farewell to the shops and the operator and goes forth into the highways. He is still a beginner, however, and one can best learn of his adventures by coming in touch with the great factories and listening to the complaints and requests that come in. One New York man went into the country on a gasoline carriage. When well toward the upper limits of Westchester his machine stopped. He turned every lever and stopcock that he knew, but no explosion came, therefore no power. Around a bend in the road was an automobile station, but he never thought of applying there. His only thought was of the factory where he had received his instructions. So he walked to the nearest telephone, called the factory, hurled over the 'phone some sulphurous language, and sat down to await the coming of a promised repair man. The latter appeared some two hours later. His first move showed him that the gasoline tank was empty. The owner had utterly forgotten that his tank had to be filled. Similar was the experience of another beginner. He went into a New England town where the machines are manufactured, took instruction, and bought a steam carriage. He started for New York city. When he arrived at the city offices of the company from which the machine had been purchased he was white with rage. He ran the automobile into the barn and then began an invective against autos in general and that carriage in particular. Men tried to interrupt, but it was no use. After he had cursed himself wellnigh breathless an operator, who had gathered from his disconnected explosions that the automobile had not shown any speed whatever, beckoned him to examine the gasoline cutoff, and the angry one saw that he had it so nearly closed that only the least bit of fuel could find its way to the burner. When it dawned upon him that one turn of his hand would have given him speed enough to lift the wheels fairly off the ground, and that he had never thought of making that turn, he grew suddenly silent. He thought for a minute. Then he said: "Gentlemen, I beg your pardon. I thought I knew it all, but I'm just a plain d——n fool."

"Turned every lever and stopcock * * * but no explosion came."

I have spoken of these accidents, or rather experiences, of the beginner as affecting primarily himself and his fellow automobilists. They affect the public also, tending to make mankind in general afraid of the machine as something treacherous and unreliable, which is likely to fail its owner in time of need and leave him stranded in whatever place it may happen. To a certain extent this is true, for no machine in the world is perfectly reliable. The locomotive gives out now and then. The steamship loses a rudder or propeller, or breaks a bolt in the engine. The bicycle has proven its fickleness to every rider. Perhaps the automobile fails oftenest of all nowadays because its operators are beginners who forget something, and who become confused, like a man lost in the woods, at the first sign of trouble, and do absurd things, leaving undone those that would seem perfectly obvious to a man in his senses. I once saw a young man in a hurry to secure a marriage license stand ten minutes with the telephone receiver at his ear trying to call a hackman. He cursed the telephone, and then remembered that he had forgotten to ring. And there is the Ballad of Little Johnny,

> Who looked into his gun,
> And saw the bullet coming,
> But hadn't time to run.

Telephones and guns are good things for all that. The trouble is with the excited bridegrooms and the little Johnnies.

After the beginner has made one or two such breaks his wisdom increases, and he seldom does a similar thing again. Then it is that automobiling becomes a passion. When a man can sit in his own carriage and fly over the country roads at a speed limited only by law, when he comes to feel the machine a part of himself which he can control to the second, in speed, and to the inch, in direction; when his body sways with the carriage as the corners are turned and the mile posts fly past; when he comes to swear by his machine because it is as silent as night or because he finds comfort in the " puff-puff " of its vibrations; when whatever belongs to it is good; then he knows that his days in the machine shop and his early humiliations upon the road were a tiny price with which to purchase a sport fit for kings.

Right here come the temptations of the automobilist which most affect the public. There are in the world, alas, too many individuals who, not content with the possession of a giant's strength, must needs also use it like a giant. They must fly at full speed on roads where other men travel by slower motive power, and now and then one dashes into the rear of a wagon going around a curve, or frightens a pair of colts into doing acrobatic feats in harness. Once in a while the meanest man in the world goes abroad in his automobile. He meets a carriage and turns to the left to avoid the mud. The carriage turns the same way, which it should do; but the auto has no fear of the horses, while the horses have of the auto; so the former begin to dance and the disgusted driver has to take the left side and the mud. Then, too, there is nothing to prevent the automobilist from taking a drink, and then another and another like the young man who recently struck a New Jersey hitching post while running thirty miles an hour. A policeman picked him up and the automobilist, full of disgust, complained that, " Streets widenuff thish mornin', but thish aft'noon theysh s' narrow can' go between posts."

This sort of thing makes the country very angry with the automobile and its driver. And quite righteous is its wrath. But it is well to remember that the beginner in all things which have thrill and dash to them is tempted to recklessness and that there are some who will not act like gentlemen till they are shamed into it. But the scorching bicyclist, who raced on footpaths, knocked down meditative old gentlemen on Sunday afternoons, and frightened horses, has become a law abiding citizen, partly from the force of public opinion and partly because, at bottom, he was really a sensible and manly fellow who saw in time the difference between right and wrong and preferred the right. So, too, will it be with the automobilist when he ceases to be a beginner and his carriage ceases to be an innovation.

Faster than the
Locomotive
(1901)

FASTER THAN THE LOCOMOTIVE

THE FLIGHT OF THE AUTOMOBILE

By Ritchie G. Betts

CURIOSITIES of yesterday are the commonplaces of to-day. While it can scarcely be termed a commonplace, the automobile is certainly no longer a curiosity. To-day, on the city streets at least, it causes no more head-turning than the jingling trappings of a spanking team.

The twelve-month which effected this result has been marked by substantial progress in all that pertains to the self-propelled vehicle. Those who make them, those who use them, those who intend to use them, those who legislate for them and those who merely view them, the great general public, have each and all advanced in information, diverse in its ramifications though it may be. There is not lacking even the highly technical scientific sharps, whose bulging brows have advanced them so very far that they have been able to picture and discuss more or less profoundly the automobile of the future. Pen-painted visions of the sort are, however, more interesting than intelligent or valuable. It is easier far to picture the influence of the automobile on the

Photo by G. B. Bain.

KENNETH SKINNER TURNING A CURVE ON A
MOTOR TRICYCLE AT FULL SPEED.

future than even to hint at the future vehicle itself. The one is profitable and probable; the other profitless and impossible.

If we are but in the kindergarten of electrical wonder-working—and one of the world's most renowned wizards has given voice to the assertion—there is need only for a featherweight and inexhaustible battery, or one which may, by the twist of a wrist or the pass of a hand, draw power, and be recharged from the skies or the atmosphere or the whatnot, and lo! all problems are solved! The ideal automobile is at hand, and not only steam but gasolene must seek elsewhere for victories. This is mightily like imagining the vehicle of the future. Let it serve, at least, as a "horrible example." *En passant*, and as a mere flash of fancy, it is more plausible than not a few of the creations drawn to compass and reduced to writing by mathematical seers.

But the inexhaustible electric battery is not of to-day, and it is mainly to-day that must be dealt with. The show which held the boards at Madison Square Garden, in athletics on the scholarship and discipline of the cadets has often been brought up. A good many opponents of athletics who are not at all familiar with the true situation have assumed that scholarship is deleteriously affected —the facts show the contrary. From the report of the superintendent for December, '93, we find the following based on data furnished by the heads of the Academic Departments: "The figures given out are not to be taken in any individual case as a direct measurement of the effects of football. The greater or less aptitude of the student for the new studies taken up in September always causes many variations in class standing. But taken as a whole they indicate that the general effect of the games upon the scholarship of those taking part in them is in general not injurious. * * * If not injurious to these then the general net result to the entire corps of cadets must be beneficial if my assumption be correct that complete distraction from work during the hours for recreation is beneficial."

The effect on discipline can not be better illustrated than by comparing the conduct reports of the present athletic season with those of previous months. This comparison shows that the number of cadets for each class in the first grade has been doubled during the athletic season.

The athletic event in which the army at large is most interested is the Army and Navy football game. This match was interdicted in 1894 but through the kind offices of Dr. J. William White and the Athletic Association of the University of Pennsylvania it was renewed in 1899 under the most pleasant circumstances. Franklin Field, Philadelphia, was then and every year since has been placed at the disposal of the teams from the two National Academies and as now played all the cadets from both institutions are enabled to witness the game each year and return to their respective academies in a single day. This game is a glorious athletic event and when the novelty wears off it should be most beneficial in bringing the members of both services to a fuller appreciation of that good old song:

> May the service united ne'er sever
> But hold to their colors so true
> The Army and Navy forever,
> Three cheers for the Red, White and Blue "

Capt. Treat.

WEST POINT POLO TEAMS AND THEIR COACH, CAPT. C. G. TREAT.

Copyright photo by C. M. Hays & Co.

ALEXANDER WINTON, IN AN AMERICAN GASOLENE, MAKING ONE MILE IN 1.06 (A WORLD'S RECORD AT THE TIME) OVER THE DETROIT TRACK.

November 2d to 9th last, may be accepted as the first milestone in American automobile progress. The show of the year before will serve as the starting point.

The milestone stands for material improvement, and yet nothing had occurred or was in evidence to alter the respective status of the three rival motor powers, steam, electricity and gas, gasolene or hydrocarbon, whichever you prefer to term the gaseous power. The advocates and followings of each were in about the same ratios as the year before, with the advantage, if anything, favoring the gas-propelled vehicle.

of action. A year ago twenty miles was its limit, now it is forty miles, and each day brings promise of better things. Indeed, one of the newer batteries, in a trial performance, maintained its power for more than 150 miles.

Steam, too, which at one time threatened to envelop itself in a cloud of its own making, has developed apace. New systems of generation have evolved that have refreshed the laurels of "the world's standard power." Indeed, of the automobiles that are truly American in design and invention, and not merely adaptations of foreign

Copyright photo by George G. Bain.
HENRI FOURNIER SPEEDING ONE MILE A MINUTE OVER THE PROVIDENCE (R.I.) TRACK.

Its general principle remains the same, and, paradoxical though it may appear, while steam is the most powerful propelling agent of general commerce, it does not obtain in automobiles; in these, hydrocarbon gas is paramount as the agent of greatest power; it is the power applied to all the swift and massive vehicles. All of the marvelous speed records established since automobiles began stand to its credit, whether for long distances or short ones. But its rivals have not stood still, if they may be said to stand.

The electric battery has doubled its range

ideas, it was a steam carriage which upheld the prestige of American ingenuity. The remarkable and uniform performances of four of these "boilerless" steam vehicles in the trying New York-Rochester endurance run constituted the automobile sensation of the year.

The rest of the world appears to have gone daft on gasolene vehicles. France, Germany and England have devoted but the very minimum of attention to "steamers" and electrics. As a result, America easily leads the world in vehicles of those powers. In "gasoleners," France undoubtedly sets the fashion. The latest American models of that type all reflect the influence of the French designer. The influence of the horse on automobile design has waned correspondingly.

Heretofore, the average self-propelled vehicle has been in appearance little more than a shaftless reproduction of the vehicle designed to be drawn by "man's best friend." As dictated by France, the automobile, as a particular type, may be best described as "a long, low, rakish craft" with "a narrowing and piratical prow"; it is guided by wheel instead of lever, and the man at the wheel is ensconced "amidship" in, rather than on, an upholstered seat. It is further distinguished by having its motor or engine located forward, and by the latticed hood or bonnet which encloses it, not to mention the bristling, cooling flanges or radiators which form the nose of the vehicle and give it an aggressive, hands-off appearance. It is a type which suggests the speed and power which is contained within itself.

France also has contributed the so-termed *tonneau* body—the body with luxuriously cushioned individual seats for each occupant—the seats, three or more, being arranged vis-à-vis, tête-à-tête, or at any other unstilted and conversational angles. The unversed would probably term the automobile with *tonneau* body a family vehicle and the description would not be inapt. But fortunate the family in such a vehicle! No horse has ever drawn one so invitingly suggestive of individual ease, comfort and elbow room. It almost creates the picture of an unroofed lounging room, mounted on wheels. When the touring spirit possesses the automobilist—when he fully realizes, as he surely will, that at last there is a vehicle which enables man and his family to get close to nature—to go far afield and view the country as it should be seen, the *tonneau* should become a familiar sight to even Si and Hiram.

While other countries, not excepting the United States, have frowned on speed contests, France, if it has not encouraged them of late, has not wet-blanketed the sport. The fact has contributed immensely to the development of the automobile and to the dominance of France and Frenchmen and French ideas in all that pertains thereto. The world has fairly gasped at the marvel-

ous and long-sustained flights which official France has made possible.

Paris to Bordeaux, 327 1-2 miles, in 6 hours, 11 min., 44 se .—an average of 53.3 miles per hour! Paris to Berlin, 744 1-2 miles, in 16 hours, 6 min.—equivalent to more than 1,000 miles within the limits of a day!

The world marvels at the nerve—the lion-hearted courage—of the engineer who sits in his cab and manipulates the throttle and levers of the locomotive that speeds fifty, sixty, or more miles per hour; and the engineer deserves his meed of praise.

But what of the man who, without smoothest of rails to guide it, sits at the wheel of an automobile, and, exposed to blinding dust and the elements, steers it at fifty, sixty, or more miles an hour over the common highways, up hill, down dale, around corners, over crossings, across bridges none too smooth, and through lanes of craning, surging, nervous humanity, miles in length? Who will say that the courage, the superb skill, the clear-headedness of the chauffeur does not pale that of the locomotive engineer? Who can fail to share the admiring appreciation of such chauffeurs as Henri Fournier, the victor in the three most notable flights of speed since the world began? Three—for to those other prodigious feats has Fournier added the fastest mile ever compassed on unrailed earth, not to mention unrailable air and water—a mile in 51 4-5 sec.

But Fournier has not all of the skill and daring to himself. Others across the sea have accomplishments but a whit less wonderful to their credit, and here in America the automobile has served to convince the masses that the Vanderbilts, the Keenes, the Bostwicks and other so-called "pampered pets of fortune" are not lacking the eye, the head, the heart, and the hand that such feats call into play.

Unlike his others, Fournier's bedizening record of 51 4-5 sec. was made on American soil—on the Coney Island Boulevard, Brooklyn, N. Y., November 16, 1901, which certainly will stand as the speediest day the world has yet known. It witnessed the upset of all previous and preconceived standards; the two rival powers, gasolene and electricity, each fairly smothered its previous record; steam however failed to equal or better its record of 1 min. 6 sec.

Never since man first reveled in speed

MR. ALBERT C. BOSTWICK AND THE 40 HORSE POWER AMERICAN GASOLENE MACHINE IN WHICH HE COVERED ONE MILE IN 56 2-5 SECONDS OVER THE CONEY ISLAND BOULEVARD.

Photo by courtesy N. Y. Tribune.

MR. FOXHALL KEENE AND HIS 40 HORSE POWER FRENCH GASOLENE MACHINE IN WHICH HE RODE ONE MILE IN 54 2-5 SECONDS
ON THE CONEY ISLAND BOULEVARD.

A. L. RIKER AND THE ELECTRIC MACHINE WHICH HE RAN ONE MILE IN 1 MINUTE, 3 SECONDS OVER THE CONEY ISLAND BOULEVARD.

had such speed and so much of it been crowded into such short flights of time. Four times was the minute mark beaten— twice by Fournier, in 51 4-5 sec. and 52 sec., once by Foxhall Keene in 54 2-5 sec., and once by Albert C. Bostwick in 56 2-5 sec.— all these with gasolene vehicles. Little less remarkable was A. L. Riker's mile in 1 min. 3 sec. in an electric skeleton—remarkable because it was the first flash of real speed ever credited to the electric conveyance.

"To your own doorstep in Harlem in less than fifteen minutes" or to your shooting-box in thirty, and in one's private conveyance, does not appear particularly unreasonable!

The world loves speed. All mankind would in some form indulge in it, if it but could. He who cannot, finds zest in watching him who can and does indulge. The thousands are ever ready to turn out and view the one. The love of speed is inherent and increasing in intensity. The automobile is spreading and will continue to spread the desire for swift and exhilarating flight through space. With the self-propelled vehicle, eight miles per hour is the merest dawdle, fifteen but a canter. As its numbers increase, its speed must be reckoned with. Of course, legislators, who themselves make laws only to break them, have already enacted measures of limitation, but there will come a time, and it is not far removed, when other laws must see the light. The human desire to save time, to annihilate space and that inherent love of swift flight must be taken into account and be heeded. The result? Speedways—exclusive routes for automobiles—subterranean street crossings, elevated roadways, bisected roads, each for particular conveyances! Let individual man permit his fancy to paint his own picture. None can speak with assurance. But the power—the pace of the self-propelled vehicle—will compel changes now too difficult of conception.

Ten years hence or less, the action of the mayor of Gannat, France, who recently decreed that "the speed of an automobile must not exceed that of a horse walking," and who further invited the citizens of Gannat to lend aid to the police, and "even protect public security by stretching across the road at the approach of these vehicles chains, ropes or strong iron wire" may appear as foolish as those who saw in the

locomotive only an instrument of death and damnation. We all know what locomotives and steel rails wrought. Who will undertake to say what may be wrought by the locomotive which requires no rails and which will be within the means or at the disposal of every farm and family?

Only the performance of Charles M. Murphy, who on June 30th, 1899, maintained his equilibrium on a bicycle in the vortex of a Long Island Railroad train, and in that manner rode or was swirled one mile in 57 1-5 seconds, is comparable with the speed of the automobile.

Murphy's mile, however, was made under exceptional circumstances and with abnormal aids, and is, herefore, a thing apart; it occupies a peculiar niche of its own, and while interesting for reference, it is not a speed-standard in any sense. Perforce, there is nothing that runs on unrailed road or unrailed track that has records permitting of fair comparison with the automobile.

The horse may be dismissed from the discussion with the words that constitute the dismissal. The bicycle supplies the only records that even by courtesy may be said to begin to approach the whirlwind flight of the self-propelled vehicle on foreign roads, and these records—one mile, 1 min. 19 2-5 sec.; 5 miles, 7 min. 26 sec.; 10 miles, 14 min. 49 3-5 sec.; 20 miles, 30 min. 11 sec.; 25 miles, 37 min. 44 sec.; 50 miles, 1 hour 17 min. 44 sec.; 100 miles, 2 hours 45 min. 20 2-5 sec.; one hour, 41 miles, 1495 yards; 25 hours, 634 miles, 774 yards—were all made possible by the use of motor-driven tandem pacemakers. Compared with the track performances of the automobile, these records indicate, however, that, aided by pacemakers, the bicyclist is not so far outclassed as the uninformed are apt to believe is the case.

The records of the automobile itself are in unsatisfactory, if not chaotic, shape, and it is rather difficult to faithfully follow its development of speed. The causes are twofold: In this country practically no attention has been devoted to road racing; abroad, no attention has been devoted to anything else. Thus America may lay claim to all track records and short distance records, only to have them put to blush by the average pace maintained for long distances in the notable contests on the roads of France.

It was only in the fall of 1900 that the automobile established a track reputation, so to speak. In that year, five race meetings were held; this year, eight meetings were conducted. The results, coupled with a mile in 1 min. 11 sec. made in France, afford the only comparisons on which the speed development of the vehicle may be based. Let the figures speak for themselves:

GASOLENE.

	1900.	1901.
1 mile,	1 min. 11 sec.	51 4-5 sec.
5 miles,	7 min. 43 4-5 sec.	5 min. 33 4-5 sec.
10 miles,	15 min. 9 1-5 sec.	11 min. 9 sec.
20 miles,	30 min. 30 1-5 sec.	25 min. 25 2-5 sec.
50 miles,	....	1 hour 17 min. 50 sec.

HENRI FOURNIER, WHO DROVE HIS FRENCH GASOLENE MACHINE ONE MILE IN 51 4-5 SECONDS OVER THE CONEY ISLAND BOULEVARD.

STEAM.

	1900.	1901.
1 mile,	1 min. 6 sec.	1 min. 6 sec.
5 miles,	10 min. 45 1-2 sec.	9 min. 40 3-4 sec.
10 miles,	21 min. 13 sec.	19 min. 5 4-5 sec.

ELECTRIC.

	1900.	1901.
1 mile,	2 min. 34 sec.	1 min. 3 sec.
5 miles,	10 min. 44 sec.	10 min. 28 sec.

The truest measure of speed development is furnished, however, by the records of the classic Paris-Bordeaux road race, (327½ miles), of which four have been held, as follows:

1895, 22 hours 25 minutes.
1898, 15 hours 15 minutes.
1899, 11 hours 42 minutes.
1901, 6 hours 11 minutes.

Words cannot add to the impressiveness of the astounding development told by these figures. From 22 hours, 25 minutes in 1895, to 6 hours, 11 minutes in 1901! It would be a sacrilege to say more.

With road racing tabooed or greatly restricted, even the French are making for the establishment of tracks, or motordromes as they style them, and a year or so hence it may be possible to say that automobile sport, to fetch the term, has really taken root. While the horse tracks which have been made to serve, lack the necessary banking to insure high speed with safety, it will require more than a banked course to make automobile racing either attractive or exciting. Not even its most devoted friend can hold to the contrary. The several contests held on American tracks have been devoid of even a suspicion of the elements that arouse the fine frenzy or warm the blood of the sports-lover. In truth, they have been little more than straggling processions, without life or dash or anything else calculated to evoke enthusiasm. It is for those concerned in its development to so classify or handicap the many horse-powers and weights and other whatnot, that genuine racing, not "runaways," may be the rule.

Regardless of what the future may hold, the present is crammed with actualities—with automobiles of every size and form and power, with automobiles at every price from $500 upwards, and capable of every speed from 20 miles to—shall we say—100 miles per hour? We at least have Fournier's assurance that a mile in 35 seconds is not improbable.

Of the three motive powers, electricity stands for safety and cleanliness, but for limited radius of use; gas stands for unlimited pace and power and range of action; steam is best described, perhaps, as the middle layer in the automobile cake.

The Winton Touring Car
(1902)

Winton Touring Car

THE new Winton $2,000 touring car has a motor built on the same general lines as the Winton racer, but it is better adapted for touring on account of its being simpler. The motor has two cylinders and is rated at 15 H. P. The car complete, with all tanks filled and tonneau attached will weigh less than 2,000 pounds.

Winton Touring Car—W. N. Murray at wheel, George A. Ballantine beside him, W. C. Carnegie in tonneau

It will carry two people comfortably on the front seat and two in the tonneau. The seats are 4 inches higher than in other models, but the center of gravity is lower than is the case in any of the previous styles.

This new car has a decidedly improved system of gearing but holds absolutely to the Winton first principles. The low gear frictions are of increased size. Plates are made of steel. The gears are of bronze and steel. It has an entirely new type of steering gear, very sensitive, easily manipulated and in direction is absolutely positive. Should the forward wheels meet with a forceful resistance—a stone fence, telegraph pole, or the like—the steering wheel will yield and the gear absorb the pressure instead of remaining rigid and endangering the axle.

All the tanks—gasoline, water and lubricating oil—are forward, back of the radiating coils, within sight and easy of access at all times.

The gasoline tank has a 10-gallon capacity, water tank 8½ and lubricating oil 2. Ten gallons of gasoline will, under almost any adverse road conditions, be good for 150 miles of travel. Where road conditions are better than the average the possible mileage on one filling will be nearer 200 miles.

An early Winton Motor Carriage Company production. On May 30, 1897, Mr. Winton sent this car a track mile in 1 minute 47 seconds

This car is equipped with wooden wheels, each wheel having twelve 1½ inch spokes, artillery hubs and steel clincher rims holding clincher tires. The car frame is made of riveted angle steel and is supported by semi-elliptic springs. There is an absence of under reaches and consequently no cause there for the slightest noise or rattle. Brakes are the very best ever made. Shoes operate on large inside hub flanges. They will hold the car, forward or back, on any grade. Wheels are run on ball bearings forward and roller bearings rear.

Carbureter, gasoline float and inlet valve are in a solid piece. This whole part may be removed by the unturning of four visible nuts. With this part out the exhaust valve is in sight. This valve may be removed without the trouble of taking out piston.

A jump spark is used for ignition. The rear axle has the benefit of a tri-truss support. There is a spur differential—bevel gears in this being omitted.

An automatic air governor controls and insures a minimum motor speed when car is standing still. Having two cylinders the counter-balance and eccentric are no longer necessary. The muffler is the very best ever placed on any gasoline car. It is equipped with a cut-off, useful when fast work is desired.

Mr. Winton's Opinion

ALEXANDER WINTON is not at all alarmed over the fact that so many Americans are driving foreign built automobiles, for, according to his Auto Era, he says there is quite a change of sentiment on the part of American users on this subject. Mr. Winton's words are : "The desire to get hold of foreign machines and the disposition to think they are better than American made have been overcome. The foreigner does not hold one-fifth of the ground that he did a year ago. It has been discovered that the American machines have been built to meet the needs of Americans and to run upon American roads. The foreigners are beginning to admit this."

Mr. Winton's company has given charge of its New England interests to Harry Fosdick of Boston. Mr. Fosdick is not new at automobiling and there are few agents anywhere who have a larger acquaintance.

The Winton Motor Carriage Company has increased its capital stock from $200,000 to $1,000,000, to meet demands occasioned by the growth of its business. It is the company's intention to open branches in several of the chief cities during the coming year, to properly care for its distributed customers.

Resume of the
New York
Automobile Show
A Talk on Gasoline
(1902)

THE AUTOMOBILE MAGAZINE

VOL. IV   JANUARY, 1902   No. 1

Resume of the New York Automobile Show

By ALEX SCHWALBACH

BEFORE looking forward to the Chicago show in March, let us look backward at the New York exhibition last November and use this view "to point a moral and adorn a tale" for ourselves and to guide the historian of the future as regards its most striking mechanical characteristics and tendencies. A great deal has been published about the New York show, both before it opened, during its progress, and since it closed. That which was written before the opening was necessarily largely composed of reading notices compiled by the manufacturers, and from the nature of its sources had no comparative value ; that which was written during the show was done hastily, and the larger mass published since the close had for its main purpose the demands of the business office. Having read all of these and the catalogues of the makers and "chewed the cud" of reflection on them, in addition to my own work, a work of exploration and interview covering the whole period of the show, a résumé is timely.

SOME STATISTICS

Let me begin by noting a few statistics. Had good old Mrs. Partington visited the show she certainly would have repeated her famous remark about "statistics being odorous," because the bulk of the figures that follow are mostly concerning gasoline—used directly as a power and indirectly in making steam. Forty American manufacturers exhibited 145 vehicles, of which 62 were gasoline, 60 steam and 23 electric vehicles, and of these makers, divided into classes, 21 make gasoline vehicles only, 12 steam and 3 electric exclusively, 1 gasoline and electric, 1 steam and electric, and 2 gasoline, steam and electric.

Of these, 16 showed single-cylindered gasoline motors, *viz:* the Packard, Winton, Peerless, De Dion, Crest, Pierce, Knox, Searchmont, Stearns, Warwick, Long Distance, Knickerbocker, Holland, Olds, Desberon and Automotor.

Thirteen makers showed double-cylindered gasoline motors, among them the Winton, Haynes-Apperson, Gasmobile, Riker, De Dion, Knox, Searchmont, Long Distance, Holland, Automotor, Peerless and Autocar.

Six makers showed multiple-cylindered gasoline motors having

A. S. Winslow and W. A. Hatcher in Packard Dos-a-dos

more than two cylinders, viz.: Gasmobile three, four and six cylindered, Duryea three, Robinson four, Long Distance three, Riker four, and Peerless three and four cylinders.

Water-cooled motors were shown by 19 makers, *viz:* De Dion, Pierce, Duryea, Robinson, Stearns, Gasmobile, Long Distance. Winton, Packard, Haynes-Apperson, Riker, Knickerbocker, Holland, Olds, Desberon, Automotor, Peerless and Autocar.

Air-cooled motors were shown by the makers of the Knox, De Dion, Warwick, Crest and Pierce.

Steam vehicles shown were the Locomobile, Mobile, Foster,

Stevens, Overman, Reading, Toledo, Century, Prescott, Lane, Elite, Milwaukee and Geneva.

The electrics were those made by the Electric Vehicle Co., Baker, A. B. C. Waverly, Fanning and the Vehicle Equipment Co.

Among the 145 vehicles there were 82 that had one brake, 43 that had two brakes, and 20 with three brakes ; 90 vehicles had wire suspension wheels, 50 had wooden wheels, and 5 tubular metal wheels.

Five hundred and forty-four pneumatic tires were shown, and

2¾ H. P. Pierce motorette, weight without passenger 500 lbs., low speed 4 miles, high speed 22 miles, gasoline supply 100 miles, wheels 26 inches

thirty-six solid tires. The pneumatic tires were divided into two classes, the hosepipe and the inner tube detachable, the hosepipe leading with 375 tires, and the detachable following with 136 tires.

DEDUCTIONS AND TENDENCIES

To the critical observer of the progress of the industry these figures are instructive ; the most striking tendency shown is the getting away from the use of single-cylindered gasoline motors, notwithstanding their past and present popularity, and the growing desire for the use of double and multiple-cylindered engines. Indeed, this tendency has been the means of revolutionizing the whole design of the gasoline vehicle. In the single-cylinder type the construction usually placed the motor, the fuel, water coolers, gears and the mass of weight compactly together in the rear part of the vehicle. This construction made hill-climbing difficult, caused side slip and skidding on muddy roads and greasy asphalt streets, and the parts were difficult of access. Besides all of this the single-cylindered motor must be heavy to stand its own thrust and the vehicle must run by momentum three-fourths of the time. In the double, and especially so in the multiple-cylindered motor vehicles, all this construction is changed. The motors and water coolers are placed in front, usually over or nearly over the front axle, the gears and fuel in the rear and the weight of the passengers in the middle. The net results of this change are long wheel bases, low center of gravity, angle-iron frames, plain spring, running gears without reaches, the comfortable tonneau body, freedom from vibration, good traction, great hill-climbing qualities—almost total absence of side slip, and easy access to all parts, the motor being covered only by a detachable metal hood or bonnet. All of this new style of construction has been copied from the French. Some question has arisen whether this type has come to stay. Expert opinion thinks it has, but that it must evolve itself in lighter and more graceful forms, say one hundred pounds of weight to every horse-power.

IGNITION AND STARTING DEVICES

Hot tube ignition which never was common in this country has dropped out of sight altogether. There is, it is obvious, a strong tendency to abandon the use of batteries, and substitute dynamos and magnets for ignition purposes on gasoline motors. Winton uses a dynamo operated by a round belt from the same shaft that drives his water circulating pump, using a set of batteries only as an auxiliary to start his motors. Haynes-Apperson, Robinson and Duryea use a magneto— the two first named using, like Winton, a battery as a starter ; Duryea, however, does not, he using a naked copper wire to carry the current until it wears out—insulation not troubling him. Winton has a mechanical spark advancer, which is very popular in France, and which will be in vogue here, slight as the call for it is now, for it certainly is a great help to the motor when more speed is wanted. The automatic air governor, however, still controls and reduces the speed of the motor when the vehicle is at a standstill. The struggle for supremacy between the make-and-break, and the jump spark for ignition, seems to show preference towards the use of the latter.

Our old troublesome enemy the carbureter is evidently being, pushed to the scrap heap by the atomizer and direct-feed systems of supply.

James S. Mitchell in Toledo carriage

AIR COOLED MOTORS AND POSITIONS

The air-cooled motor is only used on the light types, a variation of it on the Knox consisting of a series of projecting pins, which give it the appearance of a porcupine, cover the cylinder, being cooled there by a rotary fan operated by a belt. A most decided tendency is shown towards the use of upright or vertical cylinder motors, nearly all the makers of double or multiple-cylinder motors showing them in this position.   Haynes – Apperson, however, still use the double-cylinder motor of the horizontal opposed type, and Winton's new 15 H. P. motor is of the same style.

TRANSMISSION GEARS

In the present state of the industry some form of transmission gear, or rather change-speed gear, is necessary in a gasoline vehicle. Heretofore two speeds forward and one reverse seemed to have filled the bill.   The present custom is three speeds forward and one reverse. Bevel-gear transmission with live rear axle and universal joints are noted, but a strongly developed tendency to use driving chains on both rear wheels with a rigid rear axle and the differential in the counter-shaft is to be highly commended.

Some of the transmission gears were so clumsy and so full of friction that it took a horse-power or two to run them alone, to say nothing of moving the whole vehicle.   A wholesome tendency is that of driving directly on the high gear without moving the rest of the transmission gear.   The epicyclic method used on the Packard is a good one.   The well known Upton gear is largely used, in some cases however, modified to suit the makers' views.   Nearly all the gears used are modeled after well known lathe forms and others used in machinery practice, with trains of either fixed, loose, or sliding pinions and clutch mechanisms.   The change-gear problem is a difficult one and nothing seen at the show indicates a solution of it.

STARTING DEVICES

Several efforts have been made to do away with the need of a hand-crank in starting a gasoline motor.   The Crestmobile showed a ratchet, spring and pawl device, operated by a flat strap from the seat.   The Searchmont has something similar, but in the rear of the vehicle, and which is not an improvement on the crank-handle.   The De Dion and the Gasmobile have their hand-cranks permanently fastened to the shaft, an effect not altogether pleasing.   Maxim's idea of an extra sparking device, operated by a button from the seat, the motor being left in the proper position for starting, seems to be a taking suggestion.   However, there is room here for other suggestions and ideas for this purpose.

RUNNING GEARS AND BODIES

The tubular running-gear, costly in construction and delicate in use, has been abandoned for the channel-steel frame, which carries all the mechanism, with semi-elliptic front and rear springs, making a running-gear as strong and as simple as is generally seen in daily use on platform spring business trucks ; also, like them, a side-brace rod from the rear axle to the frame, and which also serves a double purpose now, by being made adjustable to adjust the chains.   This drawing towards the wagon and truck builder, rather than to the carriage-maker, to whom the trade first turned, is all the more remarkable.   In doing this the trade abandoned the regulation carriage body

Century Steam Surrey

and running gears and took something more suitable to its needs and wants, still keeping the aid of the carriage-maker in building, finishing and upholstering the body.   Dividing the bodies into three classes seems to be in vogue ; the tonneau, big and little, the phæton and the runabout.   Black is the main color.   The Winton wine color is distinctive, the Robinson green car was superbly finished, the Packard red was attractive, as were the Peerless white and the canary-colored De Dions and Searchmonts.

The big Gasmobile, with its hood and aluminum sheet metal fenders, was a contrast to the quiet, black metal trimmings of the Winton.   It is evident, though, that brass trimmings, brass horns, brass lamps, brass hub caps on wooden wheels, rather than nickel-plated trimmings, are *comme-il-faut*.   Brass work has the merit of being solid and, while more difficult to keep clean, will not rust, as nickel-plated iron does.   Here the trade differs from carriage-makers, who always prefer to use silver-plated trimmings.

THE TIRE PROBLEM

It is evident that we have reached the limit of size and weight-carrying capacity of single tube pneumatic tires, the use of detachable inner tube tires being strongly indicated.   They are lighter, faster, more resilient, and while it is true that they are more easily punctured, it is also true that they are more quickly repaired.   The single tube tire can only be plugged as a temporary expedient—the puncture finally needing vulcanizing, which takes time and is expensive.   In fact the only solution of the problem is to cut down the weight of the vehicle, so that a 3-inch tire weighing not over 20 pounds, will be the maximum—the weight of the vehicle at present acting as a trip hammer to drive in puncturing materials.   The use of solid tires for pleasure vehicles seems to have had its day, although some splendid specimens for business use were shown.   I was very much impressed with the metallic tire, although I did not think much of it for bicycle use when first shown two years ago. Its workings were thoroughly described in The AUTOMOBILE MAGAZINE last November.

WHEEL CONSTRUCTION

The French invasion has brought with it the adoption of wooden wheels—a popular style called the artillery, leading the others. The use of this wheel became almost a necessity in France, where chain driving is done by sprockets on both rear wheels on a rigid axle. This need arose from the difficulty of fastening a large sprocket on the wire-spoked suspension wheel—the wooden artillery wheel with its flat spokes set in a vertical plane with the hub lending itself more readily to this form of construction.   All that was necessary to do was to drill holes in about every other spoke, and bolt the sprocket to these spokes.   The wire suspension wheel with its naked spokes does not afford so ready a means of fastening the sprocket.

All these wooden wheels are not of one design, the leading one shown being made under Archibald's patents having straight wooden spokes, with an extra knob turned on them where it is intended to fasten a sprocket to them, the spokes being inserted by hydraulic pressure in a long tapering metal-flanged hub of two sections which are bolted together before the square shoulders of the spokes, which

Foster steam touring carriage

touch each other, are inserted.   So far these wooden wheels have stood up well in this country and in France.

A strong effort is being made to introduce metal wheels of a tube spoke construction, one called the Midgely being prominent, the spokes being made of brazed oval taper tubing, brazed to thimbles or sleeves in a double hollow rim, and also to a metal hub in the same manner.   After being assembled in jigs the whole wheel is brazed together at one operation by a dipping process in a crucible of molten spelter, making a compression spoke wheel of great strength.   Another type shown was the Pittsburgh, a suspension tube spoke wheel with a metal hub, the spokes being threaded to a short threaded stud which is in turn threaded into the hub. The spokes are fastened to the rim by a set screw threaded in them through the rim, a washer being placed between the spokes and rim to prevent them from being sheared off. The merit in this wheel consists in the chance to remove and replace broken spokes. A novelty was the "wheel within a wheel" described in the previous issue of the AUTOMOBILE MAGAZINE. Summing up the situation it may be said that there is no better wheel, taking weight for weight, than a well-made wire suspension tangent spoked wheel under every kind of strain.

ELECTRIC VEHICLES

In some way the impression has obtained that the electric vehicle has not kept pace with steam and gasoline construction. In fact it has always been ahead of the others, electric construction lending itself so easily to the art of the carriage maker. The Waverly and Baker runabouts, with their piano-box bodies, are models of neatness and style. In the larger types the influence of gasoline shapes has prevailed and an electric tonneau was a real novelty at the show. Batteries have been improved, giving a larger distance radius. They have also been lightened and a better distribution of weight has been made by carrying one-half of the batteries over the front axle in place of the dashboard. The electric motor is an ideal one producing an almost constant torque, and it only needs still further improvement in the batteries to make it take the same premier position for city use that the gasoline vehicle has for touring purposes.

The single-motor drive with a chain is not as popular as it was, two different forms of two-motor drives being more largely shown. In one form the motors are hung directly on a solid rear axle and driven by gears connected to the driving wheels. The other form has the two motors at the center of the rear axle which is divided and each motor drives one-half of the axle to which the wheels are fastened, so that a differential gear is not required as in the single motor drive system.

STEAM VEHICLES

The steam vehicle, like the electric vehicle, is a distinctly American product, and again like it, has reached its highest development here because we lead the world in steam engineering. Upon its long familiarity its popularity as a vehicle power is based, and also because of the lightness of its construction—following so closely the designs in gears and bodies of the horse-drawn vehicle.   But the body designs have not wholly escaped the influence of the gasoline type of body.   The leather dashboard is gone, and in its place is an extra seat, giving a box-like front.   The bodies are made larger and more comfortable, and running gears widened, lengthened and strengthened. The trouble has been, in designing steam vehicles, that too much attention was given to elaborate tubular gears and springs, copying the mistakes of carriage builders, who mixed good wooden-wheel practice with a new problem when pneumatics came in.   A pneumatic-tired vehicle does not need all of this.   It depends mainly upon its tires for its ease of riding, as the bicycle does.   Every pound of weight added to running gear construction means so much power wasted to move it.

The simplicity, strength and low cost of the running gears now used on the big gasoline tonneaus are the features to follow.

Speaking of steam machines, it may be said that no visitor to the show could look at the imposing displays made by the large and small makers of steam vehicles without being impressed with them.   If the electric vehicles have their city use defined, so has the steam vehicle, with the added capability of making long runs to near-by resorts, leaving to the ponderous gasoline tonneau the pleasures of touring with large parties aboard, the smaller gasoline type of vehicle filling in between them all.   No one familiar with the advanced state of the industry expected to find any very radical departures in steam vehicles at this show.   The custom is to still use the vertical fire tube boiler, but to increase its size and also the size of the gasoline and water tanks, which now have about reached their limit.   The net result of this is, of course, more power and a greater radius of action.   An effort is noted to depart from the detachable torch vaporizer, such as is used on the Locomobile, the pilot light seeming to be most popular.   Like the boilers, the engines are made larger and all are of the two-cylindered vertical type, except the Reading, which has a four-cylinder engine with a rotary valve and which is used to reverse it, the others reversing by the well-known Stevenson link motion.   The Elite reverses by moving a rotary piston valve.

The Stearns, a compound engine, can be run as a single engine, if need be.   On the Stearns and Toledo engines piston-valves are used. In nearly all the types, the crossheads are adjustable, and a few of them use ball-bearings.   On the Toledo a superheating coil was seen, and on the Prescott a superheating dome.   A few of the boilers and engines have automatic devices attached, but it cannot be said that their use is growing. The Victor pump is slowly worked by an eccentric on the rear axle, and this tendency to get away from the troublesome crosshead pump, with its high speed, is to be commended. A number of the makers show independent pumps, operated either from the crosshead or by steam, for keeping up the air pressure on the gasoline tanks. A good feature is the growing tendency to heat the water before it goes into the boiler. Wire wheels are universal, but

Geneva Steam Carriage

heavier and stronger than last year, and the sizes and weights are increasing, but not out of proportion. The Century uses a bevel-gear drive—the others all using a single chain without a gear case. Among the hundreds of little detailed improvements, but which are of no general interest, save to the operator, I noticed that on the Toledo, the gasoline, water, air and steam pipes were painted different colors to distinguish them. The Toledo and Lane also had a syphon and rubber hose water filler—a handy thing anywhere.

BUSINESS VEHICLES

Few of the makers show a disposition to go into the manufacturing of business vehicles, and if they have the show did not reveal it. It is to be conceded that business vehicles alone could not make a show attractive to a pleasure-seeking clientele, but the big electric truck with an electric windlass hoisting a safe had a crowd about it at all times when in operation. Not a gasoline business vehicle was shown, the steam and the electric wagons having the field to themselves, here again showing their adaptability for city use. The high-powered, strong running-geared gasoline pleasure vehicles shown must, however, eventually, with wagon bodies and truck platforms, come into general use for business purposes and present a great and lasting field for the makers who develop them and who will produce a wagon that will be reliable and cost little for repairs.

IN GENERAL AND CONCLUSION

Not a freak was seen at the show, and what was more remarkable, motors using heavy oils, compressed air, carbonic gas, alcohol, combinations of electric and gasoline motors, all of which are so dear to the hearts of the daily space fillers, were conspicuous by their absence.

When Automobiling Becomes General

SOONER or later, Progress, which nothing arrests, brings to even those who have wished to bar her way, unexpected compensations, which would serve as lessons, were it not that mankind is inconsistent, to the point of condemning to-day for his neighbor that which he loves passionately to-morrow for himself! Ten years ago a fabulous price, comparatively, was paid for a Humber that was not comparable to the ordinary bicycle of later times. Great was the outcry against it in the name of public safety, until every person was able to possess one ; then they ceased to be dangerous ! And when the automobile becomes democratic, in its turn, public opinion will turn, acclaiming against the blindness of those who formerly opposed the motor.

A Talk on Gasoline

By R. H. McNALL.

ON Tuesday evening, November 26, Mr. R. H. McNall gave an informal talk on gasoline, in the club rooms of the Automobile Club of America, to the members of that organization. He went step by step in describing this interesting product from the time the well was driven, to when the gasoline was lost among the vapors of the muffler or boiler flues. Mr. McNall's description of the way a well is driven, and what happens when oil is struck under pressure, enlightened many who had not given much thought to the early stages of gasoline. The lecturer's connection with the Standard Oil Company enabled him to treat the well-driving part in a thorough manner. Mr. McNall went into many details, telling them in a plain and interesting way.

The part where the product commenced to assume a gasoline appearance held his listeners to the extreme. He gave the information that stove gasoline was the best all round product to use in a gasoline motor, and also for getting a flame in a steam automobile. He exploded the idea that 76-degree gasoline was the best. Stove gasoline ranges around 70 degrees—it sometimes being 1 or 2 less or more, which fact he says is immaterial, so long as it is stove gasoline. This product is something quite separate from other grades of naphtha, it being the result of a demand a few years ago throughout the country for a fluid which would give a good flame without clogging the burners of gasoline stoves, which came into vogue so extensively then, and which are now largely used. The lecturer did not say that 76 degree fluid would not be good under certain conditions—he for instance, speaking of atmospheric changes where a higher or lower degree would give a greater explosion, and thereby add to the efficiency of the motor.

Mr. McNall's words concerning the manufacture of stove gasoline were practically as follows :

The crude petroleum is pumped into what are termed stills, with a capacity of about 1,000 barrels. These stills are like large boilers in appearance, except that they have no tubes, being shells only. Under them a slow coal fire is made and the oil gradually heated. As

340

the oil becomes hot it gives off vapors which are collected and pass through a series of pipes or coils which are kept cool by water. The first vapors are non-condensing. After these have been removed, the next vapors passing through the condenser coils are cooled and reduced to a liquid, and are collected in the crude naphtha tanks. This crude naphtha contains all of the various naphtha products with which consumers are more or less acquainted. The crude naphtha is then pumped into what are termed steam stills, for the reason that the distillation is there carried on by the use of steam instead of direct fire.

Mr. Struckoil, who has run out of oil 17 miles from nowhere, is thinking of his 9 oil-wells he owns in Pennsylvania

As the distillate comes from the steam still it is divided up into the various products known as light gravity gasoline for illuminating purposes, 76 naphtha, stove gasoline and benzine. This distillate, although perfectly water white in color, has a disagreeable odor, which unfits it for some uses. It is, therefore, necessary to deodorize it. The process by which this is carried on is as follows :

The product to be deodorized is pumped into what are termed agitators, which are large upright cylinder tanks lined with lead. Into this agitator, with the naphtha, is also pumped a small quantity of sulphuric acid, that has an affinity for certain impurities that the naphtha and stove gasoline now contain.   Air under moderate pressure is forced in at the bottom of the agitator and the contents, naphtha and acid, are thoroughly mixed together.   When this result has been obtained the air is cut off, and the acid being of much heavier specific gravity than the naphtha immediately sinks to the bottom and is drawn off.   In order to remove all trace of the acid from the naphtha, water is then sprayed in and the naphtha is thoroughly washed, after which the water, which is also heavier than the naphtha, sinks to the bottom and is drawn off.   The contents of the agitator is now a deodorized product and is pumped to storage tanks to be distributed to general trade.

As above stated, however, in making stove gasoline the process does not end here, as this material has to be subjected to a further treatment to make it suitable for use in engines, either stationary or marine, or for automobile use, and for burners of all kinds.

Mr. McNall went into a complete description of how carefully stove gasoline had to be made, saying that it was very easily contaminated by the slightest particle of dirt, oils, or any extraneous matter.   He put great emphasis on the necessity of users keeping their tanks or receptacles absolutely clean, for, as he said, stove gasoline as a fluid went looking for bad company and would take on with anything so readily that it had to be watched to keep it by itself. This is looking at it from experts' view point, and as Mr. McNall said, common users such as plumbers, cleaners of clothing, and others who use the fluid in only ordinary ways would laugh at the idea of keeping stove gasoline so absolutely pure and apart from the rest of the world, but motor car users or any who rely upon the fluid for giving quick and reliable explosions should jealously guard the gasoline that is put into the receptacles of their cars.

Mr. McNall told some enlightening points about using the fluid in various climates and also went into a comprehensive description of what the autoist should do when starting his carriage in cold weather.   It being well known that gasoline will volatilize quicker against warm parts than cold ones, was reason enough for autoists to see that their connections leading from the reservoir were of a temperature that would encourage gasoline to do its duty.   Mr. Mc Nall gave the following ideas regarding this part.

In considering the use of petroleum products for power purposes two things must be taken into consideration : efficiency, i. e., power, and economy.   As petroleum products contain motive force or heat units in proportion to their weight per gallon, it will be seen that the lower the gravity the less goods will be used or the greater the power given therefrom.   It might be contended from this that refined oil, or as it is commonly called, kerosene, would give better results as far as power is concerned, than stove gasoline.   This is true if only the question of motive force be taken into consideration, but you must also bear in mind that for engine use a product must be used that is volatile enough to form a gas without artificial heat ; therefore a product must be found which will be heavy as possible and yet which will also volatilize readily.   After careful tests the product known as Stove Gasoline has been found to combine these two properties to the greatest extent possible, and a product of 70 gravity contains over 4,000 more heat units per gallon than 76 gravity, and lower gravities contain proportionately more.

In reply to questions as to the best methods of storing stove gasoline, Mr. McNall suggested that owners of motor carriages should provide themselves with a steel storage tank, having a capacity of something more than a barrel.   These tanks are made for such purposes by a number of reliable manufacturing concerns.   Where possible, the receptacle should be buried in the ground, the supply being pumped from it as required.   The reservoir of motor carriages should never be filled, except in the day time, and never in the presence of exposed flame or fire of any kind.

The numbers by which some grades of naphtha are distinguished, such as 62°, 70° and 76°, etc., do not refer to the fire test of the material, but to its weight, as compared with water, by the Beaume hydrometer.   He discouraged the use of hydrometers by parties unaccustomed to the use of this delicate instrument, as the results obtained in other than expert hands are deceptive, and frequently result in unfounded complaints.

There were a number of questions of a hypothetical nature asked by half a dozen of Mr. McNall's listeners, which were answered by him and Mr. C. W. McGee, a chemist and expert refiner, who accompanied the lecturer.

Harlan W. Whipple's
Napier and
Other Machines
(1901)

AUTOMOBILE MAGAZINE

Harlan W. Whipple's 16 Horse-Power Napier.

Harlan W. Whipple's Napier and Other Machines

HARLAN W. WHIPPLE left the Waldorf-Astoria Thursday, August 1, at noon, for a trip over the road to Buffalo as laid out by the Five-Hundred-Mile Endurance Test Committee of the Automobile Club of America. He was in his "Green Dragon," a new 16 horse-power Napier machine. Martin A. Devitt, of the banking firm of Devitt, Tremble & Co., of Chicago, and W. J. Hitchcock, of Youngstown, Ohio, occupied the rear seat. Col. Caleb B. Wick, of Youngstown, had intended leaving New York with the party but circumstances prevented him doing so, but he joined them at Buffalo, whence the trip continued to Youngstown. Alongside of Mr. Whipple, who is at the wheel in the accompanying picture, is the owner's mechanic, who in addition to making the tour pleasant for all concerned by always having the vehicle shipshape, also relieved Mr. Whipple much of the time at the wheel during times when conversation with his guests was more interesting than steering, which state it is necessary to say mostly predominated. The object of the trip was to examine the course and check places and notes on the map as made by Walter H. Stearns, who had been employed by the committee to go over the route and record features and places of interest and importance on the road. Mr. Whipple took his time on the journey and made it a combined gratuitous tour for the club and one of recreation for himself.

This Napier machine is the first one seen in America. In coloring it differs very much from the usual foreign-built automobiles. It is dark green with no brasswork at all outside of its lamps. Its levers and metal trimmings are nickel finished ; but there is so little of this that the whole effect of the machine is quiet and subdued. One noticeable feature is its apparent chunkiness, it being a little shorter appearing than the French automobiles of that power. It really is not shorter, for its wheel-base is 6 feet 9 inches, but it merely looks so perhaps on account of its solid build and its short tonneau. The owner admits that he is a little disappointed regarding the foot space of the rear seats, it being too small for a long ride. However, he says this is a trivial matter, for more ample proportions can be put there at

any time. Mr. Whipple also thinks that the wheel-base is too short
for the comfort of those riding behind, but this is so with almost every
machine built with the same style of body. No more comfortable
riding can be imagined than that which one gets on the main or front
seat. All the little points mentioned by the owner as being a base
for finding fault are, so he says, comparative trifles.

The car is driven by a four cylinder gasoline motor, the cylinders
being 4-inch bore and 6-inch stroke. Vaporization is effected by a
float feed vaporizer, similar in essentials to the DeDion type. A static
spark ignites the gas, a plug of DeDion or similar pattern being employed, but the vibrator is on the coil, operated magnetically, and not on
the motor and actuated by it, as on the DeDion and other motors of
that type. The fly-wheel is 18 inches in diameter with a 4-inch face,
its weight being about 250 pounds. A cone fly-wheel clutch, leather
faced, drives the vehicle, the transmission being of the usual gear
type, enclosed within a large aluminum case.

In a ride in this machine with the owner on Fifth Avenue the impression was received that even though nothing like speed could be
tried, yet the vibration amounted to hardly anything. The lack of
noise was a revelation and Mr. Whipple says that when going faster
the noise is still less. This feature is in marked contrast with other
foreign machines and it was quite a delightful sensation to ride along
crowded Fifth Avenue in an automobile that made little more noise
than the average electric cab. There are a number of American built
high powered cars the vibration and noise of which are not noticeable
when the vehicle is running at good speed, but few can show anything
like the results and lack of noise when travelling slowly as Mr. Whipple's Napier.

Accompanying him to just outside the city limits were the well-
known "Red Rover" the product of the Automobile Company of
America and a handsome Panhard-Levassor machine now owned by
Mr. Whipple and which has had quite an eventful career so far as ownership is concerned since it reached these shores several weeks previously. This automobile was imported by a Mr. Langeman and was
seized by the Custom authorities for undervaluation. The machine
figured in the newspapers for many days and finally it was sold to
Winthrop E. Scarritt, who is on the 500-mile endurance contest committee, of the A. C. of A. Mr. Scarritt named it the "Red Devil"
and turned it over to the Automobile Touring Company and with
the "Red Rover" it did good service, it being very fast, although no

"Green Dragon."   "Red Rover."   "Red Devil."

reflection is meant here on the "Red Rover" for that is fast enough for practical purposes. The evening before Mr. Whipple started on his trip to Buffalo he bought this machine from Mr. Scarritt and it was fortunate he did for he met with an accident on his "Green Dragon" that resulted in this machine being sent back to the DeDion works for repairs. Mr. Whipple was bowling along Broadway near Tarrytown, on the day he started for Buffalo, when he took a rough spot in the road a little faster than usual and the rear spring gave way. He and his friends took the train back to the city and started the next day on the "Red Devil" for Buffalo, where they arrived in good shape. Mr. Whipple is loud in his praises of the varied performances which he put the "Red Devil" through on the 500-mile trip. It is not his intention to keep two such powerful cars as this one and his "Green Dragon" and he is yet undecided which will remain in his posession.

His Panhard car is an unusually attractive-looking machine, its predominating color being red. The panels are of ash finished in the natural color and they, combined with the other rich red finish and the usual amount of brasswork found on these machines, make a very striking appearing vehicle and one that from the point of looks alone could hardly fail to capture the gaze of the casual onlooker. The accompanying picture shows the three vehicles just before Mr. Whipple put his clutch on to lead the way on the first day. The occupants of the "Red Rover" were the driver, Mrs. Edmundson and Mr. Belden (both of Chicago) on the middle seat, and Mr. Edmundson, William B. Smith and the editor of this magazine on the rear seat. Louie J. Harris, the manager of the Automobile Touring Company, which runs the "Red Rover," drove Mr. Whipple's Panhard machine, some friends accompanying him. The vehicles continued in good shape until the upper part of Seventh Avenue was reached, when the "Red Rover" turned around and started back, leaving the "Red Devil" to accompany the "Green Dragon" a little further. Just as the "Red Rover" had turned on broad Seventh Avenue the tire of the right hind wheel burst with a report that caused people within 200 feet of it to look apprehensively as to what it was. The machine was immediately stopped near the curb and the driver and the assistant who occupied the rumble left their perches with a matter-of-fact, business-like air that showed they knew exactly what had happened. The driver nonchalantly remarked, "She's at last gone. I thought she would this morning." Off went the coats of both even before the passengers had disembarked, the two men giving an excellent example of getting to work without unnecessary standing around or talking the thing over. The wheel was jacked up quickly, and as the passengers bade the men "Good-bye and good luck" it seemed, judging by the latter's actions, as though it would not be but a minute before the machine would be ready to run again.

The rubber parts of the "Red Rover" have been the stumbling block to the regular running of this popular vehicle. The driver told the writer that he would not have the slightest complaint or feeling

Louie J. Harris and Father on "Red Devil"

that any trip would not be successful were it not for the tires. On this particular morning, before the machine was taken out, the tire that burst was found to be cut near the rim, but it was thought it might last through the day. The immediate cause of the rubber giving way was the fact that the machine was turned quite speedily and the centrifugal force put the usual increased side strain on the outer hind wheel. The probabilities are that if the machine had been turned so that the strain were on the left side the tire would not have given way;

or if the machine had been sent along without any turning at all the rubber might have lasted for many miles more, for it gave way just at the end of the half-circle turn when the radius had to be made a little smaller to get the machine straight again, thereby bringing an unusual extra strain on the outer wheel.

The "Red Rover" is almost a perfect riding machine so far as concerns the comfort of the passengers. Its long wheel base takes away much susceptibility to the jumping or throwing motion in taking any bumps or elevation on the road. The only detriment to pleasure riding on any part of it is the fact that on days when there is little air stirring, the heat from the motor under the rear seat is carried up and forward by the vortex of air made when the machine is moving so that those occupying the rear seat get a great deal of it around their necks and even on their faces. When the machine is not running but the motor is going this trouble is not noticed very much except by the occupant of the rumble, but when under headway the hot air comes up with a forward swoop that would make one almost think he were sitting with his back to a fair sized blast furnace. The attendant on being questioned what share this hot air gave him when the vehicle was running fast said that he did not notice it except during unusually hot weather but he naively remarked that he thought it was mostly because he was used to it.

The "Red Rover" has been making regular trips to the Oriental Hotel, Manhattan Beach, and generally with a full complement of passengers which includes one on the seat with the driver, and three on the middle and rear seats, making in all with one on the rumble nine persons. Its freedom from breakdowns except from tires is shown by the fact that up to the 15th of August it had made consecutively wenty-nine round trips without the slightest mishap.

Owners of all automobiles crossing from France to Germany during the Paris-Berlin race and the tour held just previous to it had to deposit 12 per cent. of the value with the authorities as a guarantee that the vehicle would be returned to France. The large sum of $265,000 was deposited in this way, the smallest declaration being for a motor cycle valued at $180 and the largest $8,000. The total value of the machines declared was over $2,250,000.

New York-Boston Route
Looking Toward Boston
The Place of the
Mile Record Trial
(1902)

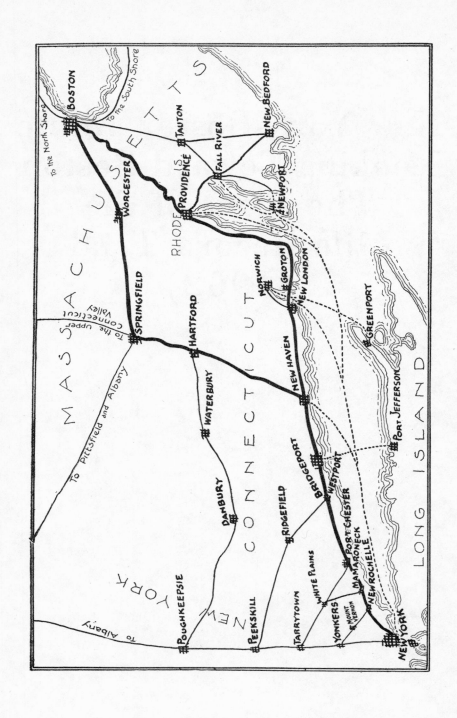

Touring Department

New York - Boston Route

PART I: THE METROPOLITAN-LOWER HUDSON-NEW
HAVEN DISTRICT.

OF the various ways out of New York to the North and East, few are continuous good thoroughfares for automobiles; and concerning these opinions will differ. When, therefore, one comes to the task of naming a certain definite route in preference to all the rest, he is bound to provide that which is not only worthy of itself but well-placed with respect to the others. So the base-line of the first stage of the present association of tours (not one but many in one), is established well up, with a recognition of the good roads leading to or past it, instead of following one chosen exit and its connections into the country.

Fordham Road and Pelham avenue form a continuous, though at times a "jointed" thoroughfare east and northeast from the Harlem River at Fordham Landing until near to New Rochelle on the Sound. Either one or the other is crossed by every through route into the northern suburbs, and together they are a complete connection between the Albany Road and the Boston Road, almost entirely within the limits of Greater New York. Beginning at the water's edge close by the little railroad station, Fordham Road comes up immediately to (a) Sedgwick avenue, just below Webb's Academy and Shipbuilders' Home, intersecting there the New York-Albany route (No. 1 of this series, published May), which leads up past this building, on to Kingsbridge, Yonkers and the north. Within five minutes' of riding it cuts across a number of streets and avenues, among them (b) Aqueduct avenue, from the upper West Side, via Washington Bridge; (c) Jerome avenue, from Central Park and above, via Central Bridge, and (d) Webster avenue and its straightaway connections from lower Harlem points.

This long cross-road is all clear except that for the space of one or two blocks, One Hundred and Eighty-ninth street comes into the same thoroughfare, and for the moment usurps its identity in so far as lamp-post signs are concerned. Here the first impulse (particularly if going eastward at speed), is to continue with One Hundred and Eighty-ninth street. Nevertheless, keep to the left, in which direction a special large sign points the way to the Zoological Park. This will bring up and into Pelham avenue, over the lowered tracks of the Harlem railroad (Fordham station), and under the elevated railway. Immediately to the left are the buildings and grounds of St. John's College, while straight ahead the outlines of Bronx Park appear. Continue to the Park and cross without break or turn, noticing at once as you go out a roadway leading diagonally off to the left, not so wide or as pretentious as the one which opens up even broader and better straight ahead.

This point—officially Bronxdale, in reality not much of anything—is a parting of the ways for about fifteen miles. The diagonal road to the left, the straighter and shorter of the two, is the Boston Post Road, the all-inland way to New Rochelle; the other, the more modern, parkway-and-shore (Pelham Bridge) route to the same place. If you wish to exchange the town for the country at once, and to throw directions to the winds for awhile, take the Boston Road, which is fair-to-good going. In this event you are all right into Main street, New Rochelle, except for the single care to keep right ahead where the double car tracks come over from Mount Vernon into your road.

The outside and more picturesque road is straight ahead out of Bronx Park, although it gradually bends eastward and brings up into Pelham Bay Park, thence by a broad turn to the bridge over East Chester Bay. The Department of Parks has this section now in hand, and there may possibly be some little interruption in getting through, but nowhere a stoppage. Across the bridge (Bartow station over to the left), the road to City Island leads east. Do not take this, but finish Pelham Bay Park on the same road, passing Hunter's Island and going over the Greater New York line into Pelham Manor. All the summer long, the nearby waters are alive with pleasure craft. It is now a stretch of rock-bound coast-line, leading past the entrance to Traver's Island, the country home of the New York Athletic Club. The Pelham Road finally gives way to Center avenue, which take, by a turn left, into Main street, New Rochelle.

In an earlier paragraph it was shown how (a) Sedgwick avenue, (b) Aqueduct avenue, (c) Jerome avenue, and (d) Webster avenue—all through connections from Manhattan—cross the Fordham Road. Likewise, its other self, Pelham avenue, intersects the (e) Boston Post Road which, with a stretch of Third avenue, reaches back to the Harlem River. A little farther on, the (f) Williamsbridge Road crosses nearly at right angles, connecting with Williamsbridge, Westchester and intermediate points. Finally the whole Westchester district (including Unionport and Fort Schuyler), is linked with Pelham Bridge Road by (g) the Eastern Boulevard and its connections. These last connecting routes were not listed with the first series for the reason that one would not ordinarily take any of them out from Manhattan, since the facilities for reaching them from below are inferior. However, there are many automobilists living in Westchester and thereabouts who, by starting from their homes, avoid the cross sections below and enter the Pelham district on equal terms with those who come up on the Fordham Road. The same thoroughfare across the upper city—our original base-line—sooner or later accommodates them all.

Once in New Rochelle, by either the Boston Road or by Pelham Road and Center avenue, go straight through the city on Main street to Larchmont and Mamaroneck. Entering Mamaroneck, turn right at the fountain, immediately over a short stone bridge and up an easy grade, again clear of car tracks. Two or three miles out, there is a fork where one signboard points left for the "Old Post Road," and right for the "Boston Post Road," the latter of which take (down-grade) toward Rye. It is possible—and on the whole best—to cut Rye out entirely. This is done by another right turn at the edge of the town, going uphill and around; but if you do down, take Purdy avenue out. In either case, cross over the railroad tracks immediately above Rye, at the same point where the electric cars out from Purdy street turn back into the country. The highway, however, continues straight on, entering Portchester (twenty-

eight miles) by a left bend under the railroad tracks and up into the center of the city. All the way it is splendid countryside, with ever-increasing promise of open country beyond.

Though direct from New Rochelle, the road has been winding and rolling. The going is good, except that here and there a stretch of macadam has been improperly put down with the result that bushels of small, sharp stones work loose. Brick pavements are more or less in evidence, particularly between car tracks, even where there is macadam alongside. For little of the time in sight of the water, it is still plainly a shore road, now and then a piece of it cut through solid rock. Of cross-roads there are legion—many of them better posted than the main thoroughfare. Pay no attention to them, however, except, perhaps, as a means of "placing" other points and routes. Likewise ignore the directions the street cars take.

The building of the Mutual Trust Company of Westchester stands at the parting of the ways in Portchester, with the road to the Connecticut line leading out to the right of this building. The Byram River, a small stream—not only the interstate boundary but the end of the Westchester road system—is soon crossed. A half mile beyond Portchester, take the right fork toward Greenwich (left fork leads inland to Glenville). There is one bad spot on the way to Greenwich where the snow and ice from the rocks above come down and carry away the surface improvements, closing the road altogether at times in winter. This stretch is soon to be put in permanently good shape, however.

It is straight on to Greenwich, through the upper part of the village, down "Put's Hill," so-called in honor of General Israel Putnam who, on February 26, 1779, cut off from his own soldiers and pursued by British cavalry, galloped down its steep side to freedom. This hill—the worse one on the run—has been graded down at the top and built up at the bottom within recent years, and can now be taken by most automobiles either way. East-bound, one has its grade in his favor anyhow; and if there is any apprehension of difficulty the other way, a short detour nearer the shore will avoid it altogether. Take either the direct road to Mianus or else turn right to Cos Cob and come up to Mianus alongside Cos Cob harbor. The latter is the most attractive of the two and is but a short distance farther. Cross Mianus bridge, go up hill (good dirt roads in place of macadam), over good roads direct to Stamford, thirty-six miles. Enter by East Main street, and at the very center of the city pass over into West Main street, which keep until it brings up to the

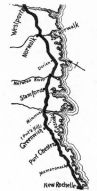

Noroton River. In so doing you bend through the eastern section of Stamford, cross under the railroad tracks and pass many fine country homes.

After crossing the Noroton River, it is straightaway to the Norwalk River, through Darien and Norwalk. South Norwalk, the better-known railroad point, is not touched. The roads—principally Connecticut avenue, as this particular portion of the Boston Post Road is locally called—though fair going, are not so good as the ones left behind. There is an exceptionally fine view just before entering Norwalk. From the last hill on Connecticut avenue (its passing none too good), you look down upon this trim New England city, also to South Norwalk below, with the Sound and the Long Island shore in the farther distance. The actual entrance into Norwalk is perfect going and one to be remembered. Connecticut avenue brings you from the country into West avenue, which follow into Wall street and (by right turn) over the arch across the Norwalk River. Once across, bend left at once on East avenue, only to turn right in two or three minutes into Westport avenue, straight to Westport, over fair-to-good country roads. This town, of scarcely any importance or interest in itself, is yet a sort of hub for local routes, besides being the point where the connecting road from the Hudson (Peekskill its western end) comes into the route along the shore.

Go straight over the bridge at Westport and on to Southport. Here the road makes a right turn, goes under the railroad, running more or less parallel with it to Fairfield, through which it makes a broad bend. One is by this time on Fairfield avenue which (after another crossing under the railroad near the western end of the track elevation) leads into the center of Bridgeport, across Main street and down to the New Haven depot. For the past twenty miles the roads have been mostly of dirt, in fair condition, about equal for automobile riding to the average of country macadam. Small signs, put up by an enterprising dry goods house, point the way.

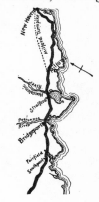

Within a few months the vicinity of the

depot in Bridgeport will be greatly changed, and a handsome stone viaduct will carry the road over from the foot of Fairfield avenue into Stratford avenue, then more clearly even than now, one thoroughfare except in name. At the present time, cross the many tracks at grade, go over the bridge and straight ahead onto Stratford avenue. The railroad tracks are to the left and the Sound to the right. After about three miles, the road turns left, which follow up to but not into Stratford. Instead, turn right at the fountain and go on five miles or so over somewhat poorer roads to Milford, crossing the Housatonic River in so doing.

A system of street railways connects Bridgeport with New Haven, and the signs of these termini are boldly displayed on each car. There is an element of temptation in this for the unacquainted tourist who may be weary of watching where he is going. Nevertheless it would be well-nigh impossible to find more trouble with less difficulty than to yield. Though at times on the highway, these lines take in all the shore resorts, going over trestles, through woods and around every kind of obstruction native to the district. Indeed, in case of doubt, the safer proposition is to go away from rather than with the trolley.

Coming straight into Milford, the highway divides on either side of a narrow street park. Once in the town, there is another parting of the ways, which determines one's course for the rest of the way to New Haven. The least often used and the roughest, though a perfectly straight road, is reached by passing under the railroad tracks and up to the Milford turnpike. This leads overland direct into Congress avenue, New Haven, by a line shorter even than the railroad mileage. However, the shore road, with its added distance and many crooks and turns, is most universally used by automobile tourists, to whom miles are of less moment than road conditions. To reach the shore road, do not cross the railroad tracks but, when down town in Milford, turn right, up to the Memorial Bridge (the names of distinguished citizens cut in stone blocks), uphill and straight out. Again you go for a short distance with the trolley line, but leave it where it turns off into the country. Farther on, where the condition and appearance of two forking roads would confuse, a large sign directs left for New Haven. Woodmont village—a collection of small houses—nestles close to the shore, about three miles out from Milford. The railroad station is off to the left, but in sight. Avoid going down into Woodmont village by making a bend to the left. From this point the road into West Haven is very near the waters, and one cannot miss it if he will only hold to the shore road through all of its windings to Savin Rock, West Haven's Sound resort.

Enter Savin Rock by the road which leads upward between the two largest hotels and bends around into Savin avenue. From here into New Haven the roads suitable for automobiles are far from straight, and none too good at best. Take Savin avenue to Main street, to First avenue, to Elm street. Follow Elm street until it brings up into Kimberly avenue. The latter takes you over a road (largely a built-up road), over the lowlands of the Sound. Keep Kimberly avenue until it comes into Howard avenue just at the crossing of the bridge over the New Haven tracks. Keep Howard avenue into Congress avenue (the New Haven County Hospital on the northeast corner); then Congress avenue direct into Church street and up Church to the corner of Chapel street and the center of the city. As an alternative, keep the shore through and beyond Savin Rock, around to First avenue, into Elm street and on as before. From Elm street the route is almost entirely alongside street car tracks and over variously paved streets. Nevertheless it is the best way to reach New Haven from the western end. It is one hard days' run, or two easy days tour from New York or lower Hudson points. The distance is eighty miles, but rather more than less. Stamford, (thirty-six miles), Norwalk (fifty-four miles) and Bridgeport (sixty-two miles) are cities with suitable accommodations for men and machines en route.

Looking Toward Boston

HELPS IN PLANNING THE EASTERN TRIP

THE outline map of the routes from New York to Boston in this issue show the two principal all-highway trunk lines between the two cities, as well as the main connections from the lower Hudson country and Long Island Sound. It will readily be seen from this that one who is starting eastward from Poughkeepsie or below may do so without coming to New York. This is an item of useful interest not only to automobilists living in the northern suburbs, but also to others wishing to change over from the Albany Road to the Boston Road or vice versa, bridging over, as it were, the Metropol-

itan district. Yonkers, Tarrytown, White Plains and their environs
are at least on equal terms with the metropolis in this respect, since
it is possible to go from any one of them across to New Rochelle,
Mamaroneck or Portchester over good roads; and from Tarrytown
the distance is even less.

From Peekskill across to Bridgeport is about fifty-four miles,
and fair-to-good going, through Yorktown, Somers Center and
Purdy (N. Y.), Ridgefield and Westport (Conn.) This is a safe
enough trip in case one wishes to start from the Peekskill district,
but it would not ordinarily be made an object in itself. One notable
feature of this cross-route is that it really ends, not at Bridgeport,
but at Westport; but as usage has established Westport as a way
station rather than as a terminus, less confusion in terms will result
from allowing it so to stand—especially since one is necessarily
brought by it into the shore road.

The overland run from Poughkeepsie connects with the Hart-
ford-Springfield-Worcester route only, since it enters Connecticut
above New Haven. It is about eighty miles from Poughkeepsie to
Hartford, and the route is through Hopewell and Pawling (N. Y.),
Danbury, Newtown, Naugatuck, Waterbury and New Britain,
Conn. It is a good day's run in fair weather, but one must take
his chances on supplies. This is the end of advantageous routes
from the west entering below Springfield—in itself a big hub of
routes with spokes reaching to the Upper Hudson and Albany.
These belong, however, to another series, the Berkshire connections
to the east.

Long Island offers two connections toward Boston, by boats
which run, none too frequently, between (1) Port Jefferson and
Bridgeport and (2) between Greenport and New London. Port
Jefferson is a trifle less than forty miles from College Point (ferry
from Ninety-ninth street, New York). Greenport is 120 miles or
so, being situated near the end of the island's North Shore road.
It is better reached, however, via Patchogue and Moriches to River-
head, thence east by north to Greenport. This makes the shortest
of all routes to Boston.

It may sometimes happen that one may wish to use his automobile in and around Boston, or on the North or South shore,
without riding the entire distance from New York, or going to the
trouble of sending it as a separate shipment. The same is apt to be
the case with people having summer homes at Narragansett Pier,
Newport, Buzzard's Bay, Martha's Vineyard and round about. Not

very long ago it was different, but now one may take his machine nearly anywhere his handbag may go, in so far as steamboat lines are concerned. The problem with the railroad is different, but an automobile may be run aboard almost any kind of watercraft above the grade of hand ferryboat. There is no trouble except to run it off again; and the revenue has grown to be considerable. So the clerks in the steamboat ticket offices and the captains no longer shake their heads when you timidly admit having an automobile in your equipment; they quote you the stated charge therefor as a matter of course. The lines controlled by the N. Y. N. H. & H. R. R. (Marine District) have established a charge of $8.10 for carrying vehicles seating two persons from New York to Fall River, Providence or Newport. For vehicles seating four, the charge is raised to $10.80; more than four, it is $13.60. Rates to other points will be quoted on application in person or by letter to Pier 19, North River. It is a great convenience to know what you may expect before starting out. The coöperation of a steamboat, like a gun in old-time Texas, is needed only at long intervals—and then badly!

REFERENCE TABLE OF DISTANCES.

1. New York to Boston (a) shore line, via New Haven, New London and Providence, 248 miles; (b) Springfield line, via New Haven, Hartford, Springfield and Worcester, 260 miles; (c) across Long Island, then shore line, 236 miles, plus the sail across the Sound. 2. Connecting lines from the Lower Hudson (a) Yonkers-New Rochelle, 10 miles; (b) Tarrytown-Mamaroneck, 14 miles; (c) Tarrytown-Portchester, 16 miles; (d) Peekskill-Bridgeport, 54 miles; (e) Poughkeepsie-Hartford, 80 miles. 3. Sound Steamer Landing to Boston (a) New London-Boston, 110 miles; (b) Providence-Boston, 45 miles; (c) Fall River-Boston, 50 miles; (d) New Bedford-Boston, 56 miles; (e) Newport-Boston, 65 miles.

———

The AUTOMOBILE MAGAZINE, and particularly the compiler of its tours, will welcome either corrections in work already done or suggestions having in mind better ways and means of accomplishing the same ends. In due time, these trips and their illustrations will be issued in separate pamphlet form for the convenience of subscribers; and not only is absolute accuracy desired, but differences in viewpoint and opinion will help to shape the final result.

The Place of the Mile Record Trial

THERE is no single section in the Metropolitan Riding District better suited for short distance speed contests for automobiles than the eastern shore of Staten Island. It is one stretch of good and level roads practically from St. George to Tottenville, 16 miles or so through the whole length of the island. The towns, though close together, are small—mere specks on any road map. It would be possible to stop an organized run at almost any point en route and pull off an impromptu speed contest. So much better, then, for anticipated new records, when special arrangements have been made with that definite end in view.

Grant City is of itself a small collection of houses about six miles from the ferry landing at St. George, and less than a mile this side of New Dorp, the better known point. To reach it by train, take the Staten Island Rapid Transit direct to Grant City station. To ride there, cross over from South Ferry to St. George, leaving the ferry slip by the left exit, and go straight up to where the way ahead is half blocked by the irregularity of the first cross streets. Bend right just enough to get around this jog in what ought to be a straight road and go ahead a single block, Hyatt street, then turn left. This is Central avenue, which leads downhill for two or three blocks to Tompkinsville. Turn right, up a single block (Arietta street) then left (Griffin street) direct into Bay street, or the Shore road. Follow this through Stapleton and toward Clifton. But just before Clifton, turn right on a splendid macadam road—Vanderbilt avenue—direct to Grant City and New Dorp. It will be necessary to keep a lookout for Vanderbilt avenue for, although the principal thoroughfare on the island, it is unmarked (save for its perfectly macadamized entrance) to this day.

A Sample of American Automobiling
(1902)

THE AUTOMOBILE

MAGAZINE

VOL. IV   APRIL, 1902   No. 4

A Sample of American Automobiling

By Hiram Percy Maxim

AS with everything else, automobiling is more strenuous in Pittsburg than in most other cities. The down-town streets are a little worse and a little more greasy than down-town streets usually are. The hills are considerably steeper and considerably more unexpected in the abruptness with which they arrive at dangerous crossings than is considered strictly conventional. The street cars are a very great deal faster and more reckless.

In the outer districts the streets are extremely narrow as compared with the equivalent in other places. Street car tracks occupy a much greater proportion of the entire street width. Curves are very much more frequent and sharp, and the grades are very much steeper and all-pervading than is usually the case. Ravines, gulches, precipices, cuts, and dead ends abound with the most remarkable frequency.

In the country beyond the suburbs the roads are what would be ordinarily called poor. They are of clay, practically impassable until late spring or early summer, extraordinarily crooked and hilly, but extremely interesting withal.   Coal mines, oil wells, gas wells, clay and limestone quarries, extraordinary railroad crossings, bridges, and river ferries, present themselves on every hand. To the automobilist educated in accordance with conditions existing in the well-regulated East, Pittsburg and vicinity offer more chaos and general strenuousness to the mile than he is at first capable of enjoying.   Where he is inclined toward timidity, one experience is usually all that he indulges in.   Thereafter he confines himself to residential streets where there are no street cars, or the parks, where the precipices are safely walled and the road conditions fairly good.   Where he is inclined toward the adventurous, the pell-mell of it all, the chance and the risk that require a clear eye and a steady nerve, delight him, and he usually adds one more to the feverish Pittsburg street life.

An interesting sample of a Pittsburg automobile drive is found in the short one from the East End residential district to the Westinghouse Works in East Pittsburg, a distance of some ten miles.

The East End of Pittsburg, the main residential district of the city, centers around what is called East Liberty.

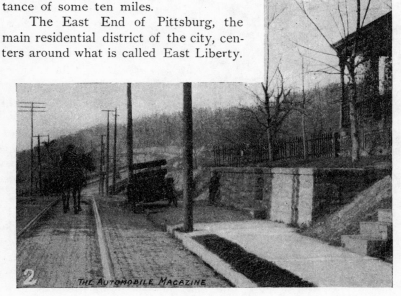

East Liberty is some five miles from the down-town district, or for a more definite spot, the historical old "Point" at the confluence of the two great rivers—Allegheny and Monongahela, where the great Ohio has its birth.   On this historic bit of land the old original block-house yet standing is the starting point from which Pittsburg and vicinity grew.

The larger Westinghouse Works, including the Westinghouse Machine Company, the Westinghouse Electric and Manufacturing Company, and the Westinghouse Air Brake Company, are located due east from Pittsburg, and are in the outermost suburban towns, or boroughs as they are called, of what is generally understood as the Pittsburg district. To reach any of these works from Pittsburg it is necessary to pass through several of the more closely lying towns, such as Wilkinsburg, Swissvale, Braddock, and Bessemer. Each town or borough has its own ideas of what is good enough for a highway, so that be-tween them all, an au-tomobilist has more than plenty of variety. Leaving Pittsburg through East Lib-erty, the only route one can take, leads out the one fairly direct avenue that Pittsburg affords — Penn ave-nue. This avenue was the old turnpike that Geo. Washing-ton survey-ed and laid out as the main road from Wash-ington and the West. Approach-

THE AUTOMOBILE MAGAZINE

ing the city limits from Pittsburg, Penn avenue is a beautiful street, lined with luxurious and handsome residences of the Carnegies, Fricks, Heins, Hornes, Singers, and other wealthy Pittsburg fami-lies, and paved with very poor asphalt in a state of extremely bad repair. The street is occupied principally by two street car tracks, which leave no more than just a safe clearance for a vehicle between the curb and a passing car. In some places this safe clearance is reduced to an unsafe one in consequence of the street taking an abrupt angular turn and the trolley track having to follow it on a curve. The inside of this curve, as a result, approaches within something like thirty inches of the angle where the curb takes its new direction. The combination forms an admirable pocket in which an overtaking car can catch and squeeze an automobile. But such a contingency is, furthermore, not as remote as might be expected, since the cars run very frequently, and between stops at as high a speed as thirty-five miles an hour.

The grades are normal for Pittsburg. This means, however, that there is always a grade one way or the other. They rarely average less than two per cent. For the last mile on Penn avenue leaving the city and approaching the city line, there must be a full mile of a steady two and a half per cent. down grade.

Passing over the city line into Wilkinsburg the street car tracks are left behind and the surface changes from asphalt to a fairly good brick. This lasts for about a quarter of a mile, when one is brought to the Pennsylvania Railroad crossing. This crossing is at grade, and the automobilist has the comfort of knowing

that there are ten tracks to be crossed, almost a continuous passing of trains, some of them express trains going at a very high speed, no gates, and only infrequently a watchman. The track crossings are extremely rough, making it necessary to run slowly over them if one is to avoid chancing a breakdown directly upon the railroad.

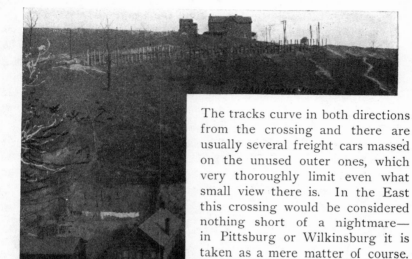

The tracks curve in both directions from the crossing and there are usually several freight cars massed on the unused outer ones, which very thoroughly limit even what small view there is. In the East this crossing would be considered nothing short of a nightmare— in Pittsburg or Wilkinsburg it is taken as a mere matter of course.

Once over this little initiation, the road continues to and through Wilkinsburg center over the vilest brick pavement that the automobile mind can conceive. The street car tracks are again encountered at Wilkinsburg center and remain with one the remainder of the route.

Passing through Wilkinsburg Penn avenue is maintained until

the foot of the hills, which surround the little valley, are encountered, when a sharp turn is made to the right. Penn avenue continues
on, however, and disappears winding a crooked passage over the
hills in the general direction of Baltimore and Washington. Along
the foot of the hills the road runs through what is called Edgewood
and Swissvale. The same succession of narrow streets and double
street car tracks, sharp turns, dangerous pockets, and the everlasting
succession of rushing trolley cars, obtains as elsewhere.

Representative of a very good portion of a part of this road is
photograph No. 2, taken between Swissvale and Braddock. As
will be seen, there is no room for a vehicle between the rail and the

curb. If anything happens to one's automobile, such as a broken
igniter connection, or any other small detail that may require a
stop, the driver must needs make a dive for the curb, mount it, and
get at least half on to the sidewalk ere his engine stops or his vehicle
loses its headway. If a halt is made once short of this position and
the vehicle is a weight beyond a single man's strength to push
over a curbstone, you are certainly in for it. At infrequent places
there are crossroads. They are very rare, from the very nature
of the country each side of the main street. There is usually an
inaccessible hill on one side and a corresponding abrupt slope on
the other, making any form of cross road ordinarily not only
impossible but unnecessary.

In the photograph it will be noticed that the automobile had to be rushed over the curbstone and on to the sidewalk between the thickly planted telegraph and trolley poles. It is also of interest to note the effect of the grades as shown even in this photograph. There is nothing that is level. At the bottom of the dip in the middle foreground of the picture begins a bridge which spans a deep ravine. This bridge not only crosses the ravine at an angle but also has a grade of some three per cent. Also interesting, as is shown by the photograph, is the almost total lack of foliage on the trees. The photograph was taken during the summer season when the foliage should have been at its best. The majority of the trees are dead, due to the continuous smoky and sulphur laden air coming from the many furnaces in the vicinity.

Approaching Braddock more closely, the road winds and twists every few yards. In photograph No. 3 is an interesting example of the disregard of little conventionalities in this respect. The inner rail of the curve runs within six inches of the curb of an already badly abbreviated sidewalk, while the outer rail is guilty of the same offense on the opposite side of the street. The grade approaching this curve is fully four per cent. When two street cars coming in opposite directions and an automobile, and possibly a horse-drawn wagon, simultaneously approach one of these interesting spots, the driver of the automobile usually has a job of prestidigitating on hand, which, even though successfully accomplished, does not always avoid a general mix-up, calling for considerable profanity on the part of both motormen and the driver of the horse-drawn wagon. What would be the result at any one of these points were the street traffic even fairly crowded cannot even be imagined.

Passing the main street, which runs down off the hills into the center of Braddock, the smoky atmosphere becomes more dense, and if the automobilist has not already provided himself with glasses he begins to experience severe difficulties. The atmosphere is actually so saturated with

cinders or specks of dirt that it is almost an impossibility to attempt to drive a motor vehicle of any kind without some protection for the eyes. On foggy mornings, which frequently occur in this locality, this dirt in the air seems to become almost a tangible substance. One will always find, after completing a drive through it, that if there is the slightest crevice in one's wraps through which this air can find its way and impinge upon a piece of white linen, a dark blur will be formed very similar to the dirt blurs we frequently see deposited around ventilating air pipes.

Leaving Braddock, the street approaches Bessemer and the grades become rapidly worse, and the scenery, notwithstanding the general mirkiness and chaos, really imposing. An example of the general effect of things is shown in photograph No. 4. The road from Braddock going east is shown in the right of the picture, with one of the inevitable trolley cars dashing up the grade. On the left is the great Edgar Thompson Steel Mill of the old Carnegie Steel Company, now the United States Steel Corporation. The main line of the Pennsylvania Railroad shows in the middle ground. The usual dense clouds of smoke and cinders is seen pouring from the stacks of the mill and blowing on before the west breeze to add its quota to the general haze.

The Monongahela river lies just beyond these works and can almost be seen in the photograph. Historic old Turtle creek flows into the Monongahela at what is just about the left edge of this picture. The ground is intensely historic, as it was over this precise spot that General Braddock, accompanied by George Washington, met his defeat and rout when marching on Fort Duquesne in 1775. Braddock's army was marched over the ground which is represented by about the center of this picture, and was approaching the hollow shown in the foreground when am-

bushed by the French and Indians from the sides of the ravine, to be described later. The battle and rout took place between what is now the railroad track and the steel mill. It is related by the contractors who built the foundations for the mill, that many interesting relics of the battle were found when making the excavations.

In photograph No. 5 this hollow or ravine is shown more completely. It is the most dangerous place on the whole road for both the trolley car and the automobile. The trolley tracks leading out from Braddock and Pittsburg turn up the hollow a short distance, then cross the bridge just visible at the right of the photo, after which they return on the near side as shown in the foreground. This makes a well outlined "horse-shoe" curve.

.Starting where the trolley car is seen in photographs 4 and 5, the grade is steadily up throughout the entire "horse-shoe," averaging fully five per cent. the entire distance. The immense limestone quarry seen in the background assists in furnishing limestone for the steel mill.

In photograph No. 6 the end of the curve is shown and a car is seen which has just completed the entire "horse-shoe." An idea of the continual grade can be seen from this photo, as also the piling necessary to keep the street from slipping down the hill or any runaway car from going over the hill should it jump the track at the curve. Some day some automobiler will owe his life to these piles.

In photograph No. 7 is shown the bridge, the grade on which it stands and the character of the bottom of the hollow. The houses are occupied by men from the Edgar Thompson Mill.

The character of the roadway is shown by photograph No. 8. The only road is that which lies between the rails of the street car track. It is no easy matter for any heavily laden vehicle to get out of the way of overtaking cars, as is seen in the photo. In the running of cars down these grades extreme care is necessary to avoid disaster. Derailing switches, set normally to derail a car, are provided at the bad curves. When approaching one of these derailing switches, it is necessary that the car come to a dead stand still to enable its conductor to run ahead to the switch, close it and hold it closed until the car has passed over. The switch is fitted with a spring which automatically opens it again afterward.

In photograph No. 9 a car is seen in the act of passing over one of these switches. Should a car get beyond control at this particular switch, it would plunge up the hill shown in the right of photo No. 9 instead of over the bridge and down into the ravine.

Photograph No. 10 shows this piling and the curve as it appears where approaching along the roadway. The steel mills are seen in the distance.

A half mile more and another dangerous curve and hill are encountered, and this time the last one which leads down into East Pittsburg. After turning a corner fully as bad as that shown in photograph No. 10, the road opens up and now shows "Westinghouse Valley." The air as usual is always murky, making the photographs of distant objects impossible to get clear. The works of the Westinghouse Electric and Manufacturing Company are seen in the background, and a train of ore cars on the Carnegie Company's railroad—The Pittsburg, Bessemer & Lake Erie—running along one shelf lower down the face of the hill and incidentally adding its quota to the general smudge.

The road running down the hill is a steady decline of about six per cent. Only that portion between outer rails of the car tracks is it possible to use.

Photograph No. 11 shows the close chances that must be taken. The edge of the hill comes directly to the edge of the outer rail. An automobile driver passing down such a place as this, and being forced to take this outside track in order to pass cars coming up the hill, cannot help thinking of such things as steering connections and steering axles. Any break-downs of any of these parts at such a point would mean either a plunge into the up-coming trolley car or over the hill on to the rocks below.

On several occasions I have heard of front steering wheels seizing on their axles on account of lack of lubrication. Such a thing invariably produces a lunge to the side of the vehicle having the tight box, regardless of any steering maneuvering that can be done. Such an incident on the road in question would be bound to result disastrously.

Piling is also made use of on this hill to hold the roadway from slipping down. This is shown in photograph No. 12, in which also the Westinghouse E. & M. Co. works are more plainly seen.

Finally, at the very foot of the descent, a turn must be made around a corner on a thirteen per cent. grade, the steepest of the entire run. This is an extremely difficult corner for an automobile. Coming down it is all right, as cars can be easily dodged; but going up, when one's engine is at the best struggling hard, with the cars rushing down past this corner at any speed up to thirty miles an hour, it is extremely hazardous; the greatest caution is necessary in taking this corner on the way up. On one occasion the writer avoided a bad smash up only by a few inches, and that only by reversing full power backward down this thirteen per cent. grade.

This completes about as strenuous a ten-mile automobile ride as one can find available in any of our large cities. Taken just before business it serves as an admirable awakening for a busy day and repeated after business gives an exciting finish.

How I Won
the Vanderbilt cup
(1906)

HOW I WON THE VANDERBILT CUP

BY LOUIS WAGNER

EDITED BY WILLIAM GRIFFITH

WHEN a human being travels at the rate of two miles, or even a mile, a minute in competition, depending entirely upon his five senses and a mute companion for guidance, staking his nerve and judgment, his experience or inexperience with the course, against a thousand chances of disaster or worse, he is presumably playing with death. Does he realize or remember it at the time? Never—if he wishes to win.

Since my recent race for the Vanderbilt trophy—certainly the most nerve-wrenching contest in motoring history—my own ideas as to the danger which shadows a driver have undergone a very radical change. They who witness, and not those who race under such extraordinary conditions, are in the path of greatest peril. Which, of course, will hardly be gainsaid, since it is the consensus not only of casual opinion but is unanimously echoed by all my competitors who have expressed themselves on the subject. Since the October tourney an astonishing number of persons have addressed me orally and in writing with respect to international motor racing—the sensations one experiences, the faculties one exercises, the penalties one pays, and so on through the cheerful catechism. Is, in other phrasing, the game worth the candle? This is my reply:

It, of course, would be useless to assert that a driver in a premier motoring event has absolutely no comprehension, not to say apprehension, of danger both to himself and others. He has, speaking from personal experience, far more apprehension than he is credited with or even than those have who are not above hoping vaguely that he will fly the track, so to say. I suppose higher education will lift human nature above this eventually, but the hope is, or appears to be, as fundamentally implanted to-day as is the spirit which inspires an acrobat, a high diver, an intrepid soldier or an automobile driver to dare and defeat disaster in open and honorable competition. At the same time it would be courting destruction in the surest and unsafest way to permit oneself to ponder seriously about it: in fact I hesitate to discuss the subject even retrospectively for fear of some day keenly realizing the danger of the game while it is in progress.

Then there is the element, the fear, of sudden death! Naturally different persons have different ideas and degrees of fear when it comes to swift annihilation. Why, however, is sudden death such a bogie when it was once the contrary in ancient times—the brave days of old, as they have been termed? Why does one sacred litany place it in the van of horrors, beseeching divine deliverance from lightning and tempest, plague, pestilence and famine, from battle and murder and, especially, from sudden death? Perhaps this fear marks a vague dividing line between the present and the past: and some of us are unprogressive enough to favor the past in its attitude toward sudden as compared with any other death.

But great speed—the conquest of space —and danger will ever go hand in hand, in all probability. Under proper conditions, however, which is to say proper precautions, the danger is reduced in contrary proportion to the increase of speed. For example, there are now about one hundred thousand automobiles in use in the United States, and the number of persons who met death in automobiles during the past twelvemonth was proportionately about five times the number of railway wreck victims. On the other hand, during my twelve years as an automobile driver, in races of the first order there have been, so far as my information and experience go, only three fatalities among the expert drivers of the world. Of course the danger is primarily greater to the driver in a big race than under ordinary circumstances, and obviously so, but his training and condition, mental and physical, are such as to reduce tragic possibilities to a very minimum. On the other hand, tires that run true at twenty miles an hour may and do burst at the pressure of sixty or seventy miles. Axles that are rigid at low gears may and do snap like brittle glass when the race is on. Stones or surface impediments that merely jostle the driver in his car going at ordinary speed make a somersaulting automobile when it is doing ninety miles an hour. Ruts that would only stop a machine going slowly upset one going very rapidly. Brakes may fail of performing their duty, a carburetter may explode or one of multiple accidents may happen in the best-regulated machine with disastrous consequence—and to that extent the driver must unquestionably have and hold his life in his hand when mounting his car for a great race.

When I arrived on the Vanderbilt course shortly after dawn on the last and reddest-lettered day in the motoring calendar, I was in absolutely perfect physical condition, so far as went the undertaking before me. Physicians had examined my heart, lungs, eyes and nerves and I had had twelve hours of unbroken sleep. But when I saw the immense multitude massed in and to both sides of the course—conservatively estimated to be a quarter million spectators—I was momentarily panic-stricken. Never in my experience had so many human beings assembled to see a motor race, and the way they brushed aside the course patrol and surged into the road was paralyzing. Would it be possible for eighteen racing cars to negotiate nearly three hundred miles without killing or maiming one, a dozen, a score, a hundred reckless onlook-

ers among those hundreds of thousands? My first thought was to withdraw. My record thus far was absolutely clean—no human lives and not even a serious accident to my account. I looked at Le Blon, at Heath, Tracy, Christie and Shepard who were near by. They appeared nervous, but made no move to withdraw. Then Lancia appeared on the scene—calm, confident, smiling as though the race were already won.

His composure, in fact, made me forget the crowd, forget the danger ahead, forget everything except that my principals had spent a fortune in building a pair of racing cars and sending me three thousand miles to drive one of them to victory or—death, you say? There was no room for death in my thoughts just then—my fixed and sole ambition was to win over Lancia.

Why not from Le Blon or Jenatzy or Tracy or Duray? I was informed that Le Blon, driving a Thomas car, had been promised many thousand dollars if he won, and I fully appreciated and respected the driving ability of Tracy. But something deeper than knowledge and experience, something instinctive, a still small voice amid the vast medley of noises—crashing bands, honking motors and gasoline explosions—was telling me that Lancia was my most formidable opponent, the one barrier between my Darracq car and the coveted honor of winning. There was no animus in the feeling, nothing even approximating hostility, nothing other than a feeling of friendly though intense rivalry. Up to a very few minutes before the Thomas car started on its flight over the two hundred and ninety-seven miles of slippery and sinuous road, my program was chaotic in the extreme. It was not until the second and third cars, followed by the big Fiat with Lancia at the wheel, were bounding down the road in successive flashes that the way to victory became suddenly clear in my mind.

I would win on the turns!

With this plan of campaign decided upon, everything else became of minor importance for the time being. One after another at one minute intervals Lawwell, Shepard, Luttgen and Nazzaro were off. Then came Tracy. At the signal his big car roared as if in a towering rage, leaped forward with a series of volcanic explosions and the splendid American machine was smashing down the course in a highly disquieting fashion. A great wave of pandemonium broke over the crowd, surging and billowing for miles down the course, completely drowning the noise of my machine as, with unhooded engine, we drove up to the starting line. With its small wheels and low-lying body the Darracq was a mere pygmy compared with the huge machines that had gone before, and appeared powerless to win in such company, as the crowd plainly murmured. The murmur, however, gave way to amusing astonishment as the doughty Darracq sped forward with clear, deep-lunged explosions telling of power, ample power to churn the wire driving wheels fast enough to win the trophy over which so many millions have been expended.

Then came five hours that seemed like as many years—five hours of unbroken nightmare.

I had won the two hundred and ninety-eight kilometer over the historic Circuit des Ardennes, the Chateau-Thiery and Gaillon events, had raced successfully at Ostend, Doullens, Scheveningue and Liége and had just recently made the fastest time over the Ardennes course ever made in competition, but I had never known the meaning of terror prior to making the first circuit of this Long Island highway.

Starting in tenth place my time for the first lap, 28:26, enabled me to overtake and pass Nazzaro and Luttgen, then Heath and Le Blon, on the initial circuit, and Shepard at the tape. The score boards, which were admirably arranged and situated around the course, informed me that we, Vivet and myself, were leading Jenatzy, the nearest man, by 1 minute, 35 seconds, while Duray, followed closely by Lancia, was only 16 seconds behind Jenatzy. The leading cars were behaving with wonderful consistency. But the crowd! On rounding the Hairpin Turn for the second time, directly in the road were at least fifty persons as we approached the turn. They swiftly made way, but my car must have brushed at least a dozen coats while taking the turn. I actually shut my eyes and piloted the machine by blind instinct—expecting every moment to mow down several lives. That no one was slain was nothing less than a miracle. For the oil-sodden roadstead, to one traveling faster than a mile a minute, was nothing but a very narrow yellow ribbon fringed at brief intervals with blotches of humanity. As for the eleven sharp bends in the course, it was impossible for me to know from my own vision just when and where they were to be met. For this knowledge I depended entirely upon my companion who directed the way with his hand.

Meanwhile Jenatzy was leading the procession stubbornly pursued by Lancia, the bulletins said. It had been raining, but as we flashed by the grand stand on the fifth round the dark blur of umbrellas and mackintoshes had given way to more brilliant colors as, the rain ceasing, acres of feminine finery were revealed. It was on this round that an amusing incident occurred. As we neared the bulletin board we heard, above the fuss and fume of the car, a mighty cheer sweep over the concourse. Thinking it was for La Belle France, Vivet flaunted his hand to the crowd in recognition of the courtesy. But alas! Poor Vivet, glancing at the bulletin, was chagrined to notice that the crowd was cheering for Tracy who had done the fifth lap in 26 minutes, 20 4-5 seconds, the fastest circuit of the day.

We had dashed into the preceding lap with the throttle wide open and, after trailing Lancia mile after mile for nearly two circuits, had passed him, crossing the line nine seconds in advance. But the scorching pace had burnt the rims from my rear tires and it was necessary to change them, as well as replenish the gasoline and water tanks. This meant delay which, in turn, meant that Lancia gained slightly over four minutes on the Darracq, though it was still leading in point of time by 2 minutes and 8 seconds. Delays are dangerous—as dangerous as foolhardy crowds—under such hairbreadth circumstances, and Vivet, as well as myself, began to realize that the undertaking was not so easy as we had imagined. So with a catch-Lancia-or-die determination we began the second chapter of the swift-moving story. Its dénouement came at the Krug Turn. For ten, twelve, fourteen miles we had been drawing nearer the big Fiat. Thrice we were so close together that a Brobdingnagian blanket might have covered the rival machines, but the narrow course would not permit of our passing. Strategy must succeed where speed had failed.

At last we were face to face with the problem of winning on the turns—or losing.

A mile away was the hazardous Krug Corner—the spot where the race was to be really lost or won, the question of supremacy determined. Fifty yards behind the thundering Fiat came the Darracq. Would Lancia take the turn on the outside? Vivet was watching, measuring every move of the car ahead. Presently the rolling cloud at the core of which was the Italian car, swerved. Vivet waved his hand, my right foot crashed down on the accelerator pedal and the Darracq responded nobly. Between the swerving Fiat and the inner rim of the road was an opening of possibly ten feet. The great crowd swayed backward as the Darracq hurtled into the breach straight ahead. Only the two left wheels were on the ground. A false move and the car would have turned completely over. As, however, the four wheels struck simultaneously, the straining machine straightened out with perfect equilibrium—and the Fiat followed. Over the next ten miles of road we were moving at the rate of a hundred miles an hour and we passed the grand stand at the end of the sixth circuit with Lancia a minute behind.

Three more laps! Could we retain the actual as well as the time lead? Would our armored tire rims survive under the terrific friction? The odor of scorching rubber was in the air, and on the eighth circuit it was necessary to husband the tires, thereby affording Lancia an opportunity to pass by and resume the pacemaking. Otherwise the machine under us was working like a chronometer.

At this stage of the race the most amazing developments were the number of cars that remained in commission. I had never before had such an experience, and several times during the last three or four circuits it would have been easy and practicable for the Darracq to have done fully two minutes better than 27:23, which was registered during the sixth lap, had there been fewer cars in the reckoning. Frequently it was impossible to pass them in the straight-away stretches, necessitating periodical delays between the turns.

Beginning the eighth lap nearly eight minutes in the lead, the mental and physical strain became acute. My brain was in a dizzying whirl and my hunger amounted almost to famine. But the price of satisfying it was prohibitive when every minute counted. The constant crashing and lunging of the car, the vigilance required at the frequent turns, the haunting fear of fatalities and the anxiety regarding tires and mechanism were so exhausting that we lost over two minutes on the eighth round. Hunger, remorseless and fanged, was gnawing, gnawing, gnawing with almost sinister persistency, as it seemed. So began the ninth and next to the final round.

Once again, during this round, the squatty Darracq succeeded in passing Lancia, this time at the Hairpin Turn, and we crossed the tape at the end of this round sixteen and two-fifth seconds in the lead. The sun came out and as we passed the grand stand the visible excitement of the judges and army of spectators became contagious. For the first time during the long, heart-breaking contest we could hear the crowd cheering for France, though victory was still thirty spectral miles ahead. But those scorching tires? Would they last?

The answer to the latter question came with disheartening abruptness. As we swung into the stretch leading to the treacherous Bull's Head Turn, and while going fully eighty miles an hour, one of the rear tires struck a broken glass bottle which had been thrown into the road and collapsed with a terrific detonation. My hopes collapsed with the tire. Victory, so near a minute before, had grown dim and distant in a twinkling.

Some two miles farther on was our emergency station and, without slackening speed, though at the imminent risk of disaster, we got there. If minutes are ever life-long, they were for me then. Every second was a century. The only chance of salvation, so to say, lay in our removable rims. Without realizing what I was doing I took a glass of champagne and two raw eggs, while the emergency crew wrestled in a frenzy with the tires. But if seconds were centuries in the repairing work, the reverse applied to the approaching Italian car. It seemed but the fraction of a moment before a vague speck appeared two miles away on the course. It swiftly became a cloud, then a dreaded outline, and with a sudden rush and roar Lancia thundered by and was gone. Added to this depressing knowledge, an awkward mechanic placed the new rim on wrong, and my brain began whirling. Four hours or more in a vehicle careening at the rate of a mile a minute had destroyed not only my continence but my sense of perspective. I tried to assist in the repairing, but adjudged distances so poorly as to grasp the air many times in trying to catch hold of the tire. The seconds lengthened into one, two, three interminable minutes before the repairing was finished. Then, refreshened by the beverage, with all numbness gone and with still a glimpse of hope beckoning vaguely, we were away again, this time with every ounce of power in play, with care and caution thrown to the winds and with everything hazarded in a genuine death gamble.

There was no more stopping or slackening at turns, no further fear or concern over the reckless crowds that, by this time, were pressing so far on to the course that for many miles there was only a narrow lane open between staring human walls. And the climax?

A mile from the finish it became evident that the dense mass of spectators was beyond control. Dare-deviltry was in the atmosphere. Lancia, of course, had finished. But how long ago? We had started ten minutes after him and hence had that much time to our credit. Had it been overcome by Lancia or had we a fighting chance? Evidently, from the cheering note of the vast throng. As in a trance a bugle sounded and the next moment, with a flash and volley, the Darracq was over the tape—a winner, on the time limit, as the roar of greeting announced plainer than words. Vive la France!

And Vive l'Amerique!

For Tracy performed wonderfully with his American car, considering his discouraging tire troubles. As for the others, I believed I was a full minute faster per circuit than Duray, Lancia, Jenatzy and Clement, and on studying their cars it was evident that none of them was structurally capable of taking the sharp turns as swiftly and safely as the Darracq. In fact, the only turn that bothered me enough to reduce speed was Krug's. My cylinder revolutions were always under perfect control as was shown by the fact that it was only necessary to throttle down three hundred yards on the Hairpin approach to admit of turning there without skidding and of straightening out with a quick double jerk. Lubricating, water cooling, obedience of the magneto were all there and victory was more than half due to the machine. Yes, Lancia, Jenatzy, Clement and Duray are great drivers. Jenatzy, in conclusion, set a terrific pace from the word go, and but for his tire troubles would have finished at least second. Lancia was not quite so fast as was to be expected, but we shall soon meet again at Brescia on his own ground.

And the game? Is it worth the candle? Of course, as it must necessarily be to

. . . "A driving stranger,
Whose hazard is the open road
And the bright eyes of danger."

The Vanderbilt Cup Race (1908)

THE VANDERBILT CUP RACE

SCENES ON THE NEW PARKWAY

Cars of spectators parked at side of grand stand.

The winning Locomobile starting with Robertson at the wheel.

Officials stand. "Car coming."

How "common folk" get home.

W. K. Vanderbilt, Jr., donor of the cup.   Taking in gasoline during the race.

Turning into the Jericho Turnpike.

They came down in an automobile from New York; now they are recovering.

The Isotta mechanic hanging out on the turn to balance car. Note how close Lytle keeps to the inside curb.

Straight stretch on the new Parkway.

The turn from the Old Westbury road into the new Parkway.

Lytle driving the Isotta at the Woodbury turn.

Every time a car passed the crowd swarmed over the course.

Several times water was played through a hose onto the crowd to get them off the track.

Finish of race.   Robertson winning with the Locomobile

Where the Savannah race is run.

The Isotta winning the Savannah race in 1907. Compare this track, clear of spectators and officials, with the Vanderbilt Cup Parkway scene.

Long Island's Century
(1902)

Checking Hill Climbers on Roslyn Hill

THE AUTOMOBILE
MAGAZINE

VOL. IV JUNE, 1902 NO. 6

Long Island's Century

BY FRANCIS P. PRIAL

A WORD or two on the Long Island Hundred Mile Endurance
(?) Run, a bit of streakish description, an ingot or two of
thought, perhaps, a loosely tied sheaf of fact and fancy, an
aftermath of deduction and conclusion. Looking back now, when
the mental and physical dust of that day had been entirely washed
away, it is quite clear that the Long Island Hundred crowns with
laurel primarily the promoting club, and, in another sense, the men
who received the stipulated rewards, these latter deserving more
commendation for holding in check the speed-impulse than perhaps for any other one thing.

For, in this day of motor car development, early though it yet
be, the April 26th Century makes it certain that no very great
merit attaches to any motor car capable of a leisurely hundred
mile run over goodish roads largely devoid of hills and entirely
free from specific ascent or descent calling for that final strain or
that last high burst of speed which search out imperfection and
bring the futile car to final grief. The Run proved beyond perad-
venture that a no-speed one hundred mile automobile amble

through fairly level country is, in these days, no tour de force, but rather a mere parade, an outing, an advertisement of the popularity and pervasiveness of motor-carism, and any self-driven vehicle which (barring of course specious accident) cannot be taken through such a run with highest satisfaction, is fit largely for the scrap-heap, is not for the salesroom, and the offering of such a car to the public were laughable, if it were not criminal; that is, criminality of the shysterian, gold-brick kind.

The run surprised in largeness of entry. The run, despite a

An interested ⦿ lot of A. C. A. Members

bit of petty caviling, reflected several different kinds of credit on the Long Island Automobile Club. It was conceived in enthusiasm and managed with sustained energy. Its projection was a voluntary reaching-forth for a deal of work, criticizable, doubtful, unrequitable work. And once decided upon every available man in the Long Island Automobile Club—an effective, cohereing body of men they are—gave their all to make the event completely successful.

Of the affair itself, so much interest did it excite and so widely and exhaustively has it been photoed and written out that little now remains to be said. It is now generally known that April (26) saw her finish and like one who drowns in drink his sorrow, she went on a high jamboree. That historic Saturday might, nay should have been a tender green day, a day of amethyst skies, and of finely spun sunshine? But no! No! No! The yelping hounds of the weather gods were unleashed all day long and Long Island was cloaked in grievous discomfort. Suffice it to say that it was a dusty, gritty, wind-worn day, one for overcoats, rubbered things and all manner and kind of protective habiliment, aided and abetted at periodic crucial moments by heating and stimulating drafts of fluidities.

There were a few major notable pictures, the start, for instance, the mile ascent of Roslyn Hill, the severely country crowd at Hempstead and, finally, the Babylon of the

At the foot of Roslyn Hill

finish. The heart of the thing was at Pettit's Hotel, in the old town of Jamaica, now legally, but not otherwise, part of New York city, Jamaica, a town of placidity, of solid undisturbable dignity, and seemingly as near the North Pole as to the Tenderloin. The hotel itself is seared and seamed with probably a hundred winters. It was a classic in its day, and many a merry and bibulous crowd foregathered there to discourse on hogs and horses, the amenities of the trotting track, the awards of the country fair and much other gossip of the bucolic life. Even in the earliest day of cycling, Pettit's had not yet lost its halo, and " a run to Pettit's" with a teamster's dinner to boot was a thing to be rolled under the tongue days before and to be rehearsed in the club circle for days afterward. Jamaica and Pettit's, lying only ten miles from New York, exerted and still exerts the charm of a half-agricultural, half-residential country seat. And by-the-by, since land is not sold in Jamaica by the square inch, the glory of Pettit's is not the unspeakable shoddiness enclosed by its four walls, but its obvious indeed, its only excellence is the great straggling yard which flanks it.

At nine in the morning those in interest had gathered at this place, a white and saffron-faced crowd, for the thing meant up and away, at six o'clock, a forbidding hour surely for all city, indeed, for all thinking men. Besides, the morning was darkly cold, and the wet bluster of winds ate into the heart. At that hour a hundred machines and a thousand people were in the hotel yard. Car captains were busy putting on the last final touches of preparation. Scores of helpful men were at their beck and call. Automobile factories seemed to have debouched their practical men, fellows of oil and grime and the horny hand, fellows, real men who know how, each one as familiar with his machine as a Court physician is with the constitution of his King. These, moving hither and thither with much physical and vocal exuberance gave the cars their final grooming. It was amusing, affecting interesting, in a large way. The love of the true mechanic for the inanimate thing made for action—a gun, a yacht, a car and so on—approaches the human.

Hovering, strolling and pushing about were five score scribes open-eyed, ready-eared; also a company of camera men, a regiment of officials and observers, and finally, the fringe of purposeless loiterers, the simply curious, the mob of the open-mouthed. It was, you may be sure, an inspiring sight. The number of machines, the many styles, the tenseness of all concerned—all this spoke a big word for automobiling. As for the competitors, their enthusiasm, their anxiety was simply remarkable. They were as men going into a battle. These were of two classes, the private owner of a pet car, in which he deeply believed and was most anxious to show off, much as a groom puts through the pace a blue-blooded filly, one destined in another summer for a Suburban, for a Derby—the other class, the man of trade, the man with a factory and a ledger, who was staking and quite willing to stake his reputation on the performance of his product in the day's run.

Between nine and ten o'clock the cars had all somehow been gotten into motion, and were well on the way to glory or disgruntlement. Of the start it might be said that there was no uniformity or sequence or style. It was strangely non-military, spasmodic. But these runs are new, complex, biggish, and time and experience will mend, improve and perfect. Later, in events of this kind, there will be more officialism, uniformity and absolutism, and, of course, less of the picturesque. Such was the start.

Through the courtesy of the Long Island Railroad, who provided a special car for the purpose, it was possible to observe the run at two interesting way points, at Roslyn Hill, twenty-two miles out, and at Hempstead, sixty miles away. The hill contest provided no excitement. It developed, in the final analysis, that the rise at Roslyn was no very great shakes, while the 14 per cent. knob at the top of it, which promised a strenuous moment, proved to be but a flea bite and pro-

Nearing the top

vided absolutely no agony. In addition to that there was no visible competition, the final result being a matter of mathematics, and none knew who had won fast time prizes until nightfall.

At Hempstead, one merely saw the proverbial Long Island village. There was the town square, walled in with a shambling hotel, an odd tavern or two, a church and a school, the church, high-spired and immaculately white, a modest house of God. Lining this square were such Hempsteadites as had the leisure of a Saturday afternoon, a hundred or two in number, and the cars sailed through this lane of rustic humans without any very great

First in. Charles D. Cooke and
H. Percy Maxim

claquer or eclat. One after another they quietly came into view, sailed around the turn and passed away. The blood was not aroused.

At the finish, the crowd, official and unofficial, waited for the real work to begin, at four o'clock, or thereabouts. But hours before that time they were aroused from various time-killing devices by the breathless arrival of a car. At first it was thought that a non-competitor was disporting himself; but, as the vehicle rounded in front of the hotel, placard No. 3 appeared on it and the crowd gave it an excited welcome. Shortly after another car came breezing home, the crowd elated, the officials askant. In brief, the vehicles began now to rapidly arrive and it dawned upon the timers and judges that, unwittingly or designedly a dozen entrants had disregarded the "time limit" condition (6 hours 40 minutes for the run, a condition based on the speed laws) and had made a race of it.

A. L. McMurtry's Packard

As soon as this violation of the rules of the contest had been digested the officials stoically ignored all arrivals until the fixed minimum time had elapsed. It was at once bruited about that all cars arriving before the prescribed time would be disqualified, and this was afterward officially done, except that a car violating the rule only ten minutes or less was not cast into outer darkness. The general understanding that the "fast brigade" would surely be disqualified weighed lightly on the crowd and on most of the con-

Elwood Haynes in one of his own make

testants. The former were interested and pleased over what appealed to them as "sport," while any disappointment the disqualified contestants may have felt was swallowed up in the sense of complete satisfaction that their cars had come through in fast time without accident, without development of flaw, or any weakness whatsoever, and they seemed to value that far beyond official blue-ribbonism. In certain private cases there was joy to the full, as, for instance, where A had beaten C on a purely speed basis, the contest being born of boast or claim, or of some other private circumstance. Thus it was a run degenerated, in part, into a race, with a half score of private wagers and comparisons up for settlement.

So, throughout the wasting afternoon, the cars came home, at first proudly and with triumph, later, dolefully halting, and still later, at night-fall and long after, straggling and disgustedly making their way back to the finish. At night there were clinking of glasses, much fluid and solid replenishment and over all compliment, babblement, congratulation, commiseration and explanation, with much truth and a leaven of romance.

Such was the history of the Long Island Hundred—a day of bedevilment, a strenuous drive through dust and gravel, a big collection of handsome and effective cars, an affair managed with courtesy, firmness and justice, a day of import to automobiling, a day proving that a fairly smooth hundred-mile run is meat and drink to the average motor-driven car—this run decided that. And now for more heroic contests, now for still more refinement, efficiency and beauty in manufacture.

LONG ISLAND A. C. ENDURANCE TEST.
April 26, 1901.—(Course 100 miles)
Entries, 82; Starters, 66; Withdrawn or Disqualified, 28; Awards, 37.
BLUE RIBBON—NO STOPS—100 PER CENT.

Vehicle.	Power.	HILL CLIMBS.	
Toledo	Steam	Rochet-Schneider	1.19
Pierce	Gasoline	Locomobile	1.42
Panhard	Gasoline	Winton	1.42
Lane	Gasoline	Peugeot	1.46
White	Steam	Prescott	1.59
White	Steam	Packard	2.03
Packard	Gasoline	Packard	2.06
Century	Gasoline	White	2.06
Elmore	Gasoline	Grout	2.06
Knickerbocker	Gasoline	Century	2.07
Knickerbocker	Gasoline	Panhard	2 08
Haynes-Apperson	Gasoline	White	2 08
Haynes-Apperson	Gasoline	Toledo	2.10
Autocar	Gasoline	White	2.20
Peugeot	Gasoline	Autocar	2.30
Oldsmobile	Gasoline	Haynes-Apperson	2.33
Toledo	Steam	Lane	2.34
Packard	Gasoline	Prescott	2.40
Winton	Gasoline	Winton	2.59
Winton	Gasoline	Gasmobile	3.05
Rochet-Schneider	Gasoline	Knickerbocker	3.35

LONG ISLAND A. C. ENDURANCE. TEST— *Continued.*

RED RIBBON—98 PER CENT. AND OVER.

Vehicle.	Power.	P. C.
Prescott	Steam	99
Peerless	Gasoline	99
Panhard	Gasoline	98
White	Steam	99
Gasmobile	Gasoline	96

HILL CLIMBS.

Long Distance	3.38
Gasmobile	3 42
Elmore	3.57
Peerless	4.04
Wheel Within Wheel	4.14
Olds	4.16
Haynes-Apperson	4.19
Haynes-Apperson	4.45
Peerless	4 53
Knickerbocker	5.02
Knickerbocker	5.36
Pierce	6 42
Gasmobile	6.46
Panhard	7.22
Torbensen Gear, Ltd	10.42
Toledo	11.46

YELLOW RIBBON—95 PER CENT. AND OVER.

Gasmobile	Gasoline	95
Gasmobile	Gasoline	96
Torbensen	Gasoline	97
Peerless	Gasoline	97
Knickerbocker	Gasoline	97
Locomobile	Steam	96

WHITE RIBBON—91 PER CENT. AND OVER.

Vehicle.	Power.	P. C.
Haynes-Apperson	Gasoline	93
U. S. Long Dist	Gasoline	91

VERY HIGHLY COMMENDED—86 PER CENT. AND OVER.

Vehicle.	Power.	P. C.
Grout	Gasoline	87
Gasmobile	Gasoline	86

HIGHLY COMMENDED—80 PER CENT. AND OVER.

Vehicle.	Power.	P. C.
Prescott	Steam	83

GASOLINE CONSUMPTION FOR THE 100 MILES.

Vehicle.	H. P.	Weight.	Passengers.	Gals. gas used.
Grout	4	900	2	12
Toledo	7½	1.500	2	12 15-18
Toledo	7½	1.400	2	13 7-9
Lane	9	1,350	4	17
Olds	4	800	2	3 1-6
Torbensen	5	800	2	4 5-9
Knickerbocker	6½	990	2	5
Knickerbocker	5	1.010	2	4 2-9
Knickerbocker	5	1.050	4	4 5-18
Autocar	..	1,000	2	5½
Winton	8	1 800	2	5 5-9
Peugeot	11	1,920	2	5 5 9
Elmore	5	1,000	2	5 7-9
Peerless	16	1,600	2	6
Panhard	16	2,600	4	13

Awards hill climbing test. For steam vehicles, all weights and powers. J. M. Page (Locomobile) time 1.42. Gasolene machines, under 1,000 poounds. W. J. Stewart (Autocar) time 2.30. Gasolene machines between 1,000 and 2,000 pounds. Percy Owen (Winton) time 1.42. Gasolene machines, over 2,000 pounds, and open class. Oliver Jones (Rochet-Schneider) time 1.19.

The Lesson of the Show
(1902)

The Lesson of the Show

By S. Wallis Merrihew

PERHAPS the best judgment to pronounce on the automobile
show at Chicago which came to an end on March 8 is to
say that it fittingly typified the art and industry at this
time. Caution might suggest the addition of the words "in the
West," but this is too great a qualification. The error, if error
there be, is less in the first statement.

It would not be easy to imagine a greater change than a year
made in the two Chicago shows. The first was disappointly in-
adequate, falling short of utter failure by a very narrow margin.
It is possible that even there the parallel holds, and that western
automobilism of that day was also very callow and immature.

At any rate, a great, a wonderful, improvement took place in
the year which elapsed. The strides that the industry made in
that period were matched by a similar advance in its western show
function. Whatever doubt may have existed then regarding the
permanence and extent of the motor vehicle movement has by
this time vanished. There is nothing illusory, nothing evanescent,
in an industry which could make such a showing as met the eye
at Chicago.

The exhibits were fittingly housed. The Coliseum, which was
built to contain Libby Prison, the celebrated edifice having been
transported, brick by brick, from the banks of the James to the
shores of Lake Michigan, is spacious and of dignified architectural
design. Exteriorly it falls much behind Madison Square Garden.
But its interior does not suffer by comparison. Indeed, there is
considerable similarity in the two structures. The chief difference
is found in the absence of the series of galleries which mark the
New York building, the Coliseum having but one adjunct of the
sort.

Spacious as was the building, it was fairly well filled. A few
vacant spaces were to be seen, but they did not number a half
dozen all told, and, as if to make up for this, a few of the exhibitors
were somewhat cramped for room.

Despite the act that the absentees included a number of very
well known makers, principally in the East, and that no foreign
vehicles were shown, the exhibition was a representative one.

Every type of vehicle now on the American market was there. Every maker who felt that he had something that appealed with force to the public of the great Middle West made his bid for recognition and favor. Consequently there were new vehicles in plenty and some modifications of old ones. Only a little over three months had elapsed since the holding of the New York show, but in that time much work had been done and many changes made.

The improvement of the motor vehicle, its advance toward approximate perfection, is the task which makers have set themselves to perform, and users are almost equally interested in seeing it realized. Consequently, the first question to be asked is, has material progress in this direction been made?

As far as the show under consideration is concerned, no better reply can be made than is contained in the comments of two visitors to Chicago, one a tradesman, the other an automobilist entirely free from trade alliances. Starting from the same point, and bringing to their task equally keen observation, they arrived at conclusions diametrically opposed.

"The show is more interesting than that at New York," said the amateur. "There is more that is really new, more that is an advancement, than there was any reason to expect. I turn from an examination of the most novel vehicles firm in the belief that we are on the right track."

"It is useless to conceal the fact that the showing is a distinctly disappointing one," was the summing up of the tradesman. "There are many new vehicles, but few novelties in construction, little of the real improvements that I looked for. The progress, although it is there, is slower than I supposed it would be."

Two things stood out from the ruck, one of them with the distinctness of a mountain peak set in a great plain.

The first was the signs—for it was only an indication—of forthcoming changes in the design of steam vehicles. Its mate—the prominence referred to—was the wonderful growth of the popular priced gasolene runabout, so called.

Taking up the latter first, it may be fittingly likened to a prairie fire. It is of, for and by the West. The effete East may view it with indifference, turn to it the cold shoulder; it makes no difference to the sturdy westerner. The movement has his approval, and in his thoroughly characteristic way he has passed it on as a good thing; and it has gathered force as it progressed until now nothing can stop it.

There is nothing surprising in all this. The Middle West partakes of its pleasures sparingly, mingling them frequently with business. The horse and buggy is its sign manual. What the bow and arrow or the tomahawk was to the aborigines of this continent, the musket to its first white settlers, the horse and

buggy is to the denizens—urban as well as suburban—of the Middle West. It is the means of transportation between town and country, village and city.

Therefore, the popular automobile, the vehicle of the masses, could be nothing but a horseless and a shaftless buggy.

Price foreordained this; the fitness of things re-enforced and clinched the matter. Both a disinclination and an inability to pay fancy prices existed. Yet progress demanded that the newest development of the day should have attention, that such an improvement as the automobile was admitted to be should not have turned to it the cold shoulder.

Out of this feeling grew the desire for a horseless buggy, to be sold at a price that the West deemed reasonable. As whenever a sufficiently strong demand for a thing exists, some one arises to supply it, so the Olds vehicle was designed, assumed form and almost immediately acquired wide popularity.

Until this came the West, outside of a few of the larger cities, regarded the automobile with a languid interest. With it, and its followers of the same type, came the awakening. That awakening, or its extent, became apparent only at the show under notice. There were exhibited for the first time well nigh a dozen vehicles of the type referred to. Then the country dealers and users poured forth to examine, to criticise and to buy. The design did not matter so much as did the price, although, for the matter of that, there was no very great variation in either.

As regards the latter, the extreme figures were $500 and $800. Nothing under the former was offered, scarcely anything over the latter could get a hearing. Rightly or wrongly, there existed a strong feeling that no maker was justified in asking a greater price than the one mentioned.

It need scarcely be said that the popular vehicle is one using a gasolene engine for its propelling mechanism. Its size, weight and price would, across the water, cause it to come under the head of a voiturette; but, again it is almost unnecessary to add, it is radically different from the voiturette. Its lines and design are purely—even aggressively—American. The engine has a single cylinder, is placed horizontally in the rear of the vehicle—usually under the seat. The simplest form of transmission is used—chain to a live rear axle, with differential. Two speeds forward and reverse are alone provided.

The vehicle itself is in keeping with this simple motor equipment. Wire wheels and tubular running gear, a buggy-like body carrying two passengers, long leaf springs running longitudinally—these are the distinguishing features. Sometimes, although rarely, elliptical springs are fitted, and a few other minor changes made, but they are not of a nature to require any transference of the vehicle to another class.

Such is the automobile which was clearly the popular type at the Chicago show. Its sales are certain to be limited only by the ability of its makers to produce it. And the production will be enormous. Such a vehicle lends itself readily to rapid building, and it is doubtful whether even the steam vehicle manufacturers will be able to produce with greater facility.

Genuine novelty in the gasolene type of automobiles, however, was reserved for two vehicles also shown at Chicago for the first time.

The first was the Friedman vehicle, in which a friction drive or transmission is employed. A small friction wheel is forced against the face of the engine fly wheel, and the power thus obtained is communicated to the rear axle by means of chains and sprocket wheels. This method is not entirely new, being a mod-

A String of Darracqs.

ification of transmission devices employed abroad; and it is not, of course, to be condemned without trial. Only successful use, however, can remove the doubts one instinctively entertains regarding its efficiency under the stress of all around road riding.

The second vehicle embodies a radical departure in the design of gas engines. It is fitted with what is termed the Caloric or hot air engine. The claim is made that the heat which in explosive engines is gotten rid of by means of water jacketing and other devices, is here retained and utilized to the fullest possible extent, being really converted into power. The heat is applied to the bottom of the cylinders; air is then taken in and compressed in the cool upper end of the cylinders and transferred to the heated end, where it expands and forces the piston outward. The hot air is then expelled from the heated end at the same time another cold charge is taken in. In operation, the vehicle handled well and did much to bear out the claims made for it.

The other forms of gasolene automobiles are too well known to require extended mention. The showing was a complete one, the range of vehicles being the widest possible. Notable was the new three cylinder car of the International Motor Car Co., which was striking in design and finish, the new Fournier-Searchmonts, and the big Packard surrey.

The trend in the direction of the foreign type of vehicle was not as marked as it was at the New York show. This is true even if allowance be made for the unusual number of popular priced vehicles already touched on at length.

Yet the movement is certain to be carried to its logical conclusion unless the user steps in and interposes a veto. In a nutshell it is the conflict of the carriage and the road locomotive. The latter is the newer, as well as the more costly and fascinating, and at present it is decidedly the more talked about. But it remains to be seen whether this popularity is of the transient or the enduring kind. The public, in common with the trade, is unable to speak as a unit. A large portion of both is engaged in the task of coming to a decision; the pros and cons are being weighed, and in due course the verdict will be rendered, without the pro-carriage and the pro-locomotive advocates having much to say in the matter.

Returning to the consideration of the other epoch-marking feature of the show, the evidence—or should it be called merely a hint?—of forthcoming changes in steam vehicles.

Save in the matter of an increase in weight and size, steam vehicle designs have remained almost stationary since their introduction. They were then and ever since emphatically horseless carriages. The rising tide which has swept such a large proportion of the gasolene manufacturers over to an endorsement of the foreign model, has, until very recently, left the steam vehicles almost untouched. Carriages they were at the beginning, and carriages they appeared destined to remain until the end of the chapter.

So it looked at the New York show. In the brief interval

much took place. If credence be given to the stories afloat, and they be added to what is really known, there is plenty of change coming.

At Chicago, however, the impending movement had but three vehicles as heralds. They were those of the International, Foster and Milwaukee concerns, and in that order they should be ranked, as regards departures from accepted standards, the last named being the most distinctly foreign appearing of all. By this is meant that they suggest the bonneted vehicle, gasolene by preference and as a rule, but seemingly not destined to continue to mark that

Taken While a White was Waiting.

type exclusively. Such design is a departure from the conventional carriage form; and as there is in some quarters a very decided tendency to get away from this form, its popularity grows apace.

It is the vehicle design almost solely that steam automobile builders seek new fields. The engine, boiler, etc., are left untouched. They appear to be subjected to no innovating attacks, but, on the contrary, to have established quite beyond cavil their right to exist practically unchanged.

Users have long ceased to look for startling innovations in electric vehicle designs.

Here, even more than is the case with the steam class, carriage ideas prevail. Some changes are necessary when the horse is displaced by a battery and a motor, but they fall far short of those called for when steam or gasolene engines are coupled with road vehicles. And the electric vehicle, largely by reason of its field being more circumscribed than is that of its sister vehicles, has always been produced in a larger variety of patterns.

Consequently detailed changes merely were seen in this section. They were in the direction of an increased radius, in many cases of slightly greater speed, more economical transmission of power and greater battery efficiency. Not a few new vehicle designs made their appearance also, notwithstanding the fact that in this respect they have always led.

These and other observations will come to the experienced automobilist who critically examines the vehicles at such a show as that held at Chicago. Of attention—commanding departures from accepted standards there was little—almost nothing. He who expected or looked for such was doomed to disappointment. The art has reached too advanced a stage to warrant one to look for anything of the kind. Toward the goal which users and makers alike so ardently desire to reach, the progress must necessarily be slow. The day for advancement by leaps and bounds has gone by.

If, on the other hand, the user looks for a widening range of choice—prices, different standards of excellence, variety of design, all these being had in mind—he will not be disappointed. On every hand he will find what he wants embodied in the different types.

Reliability remains the chief desideratum. Not even speed, highly as it is valued, takes precedence over the former.

To this end improvements in details are constantly going on. Where a year ago ground for complaint existed, the causes have been removed as far as can be done in advance of the riding season. New ones will, of course, arise under the stress and strain of severe usage. But unless all signs fail, they will be fewer in number and of a less serious nature.

Notwithstanding considerable progress has been made in the direction of uniformity of design—the difference between the New

York and the Chicago shows even being noticeable, no user need look in vain for any particular departure from standards as far as they may be said to be established. Both in vehicle and engine design he may obtain what he wants if he looks closely for it. There is scarcely a disputed point—engine position, number of cylinders, transmission, ignition, steering, wheels, reaches—that the doctors do not disagree upon. The result is that the purchaser has it in his power to select almost 'at will.

Some Chicago Show Observations

By W. J. Morgan

A THICK set, bearded, broad-shouldered man visited the Chicago show when it was but half over. His face seemed familiar to an Automobile Magazine representative who finally recognized in him the great French manufacturer, M. Clement, President of the Panhard-Lavassor Company, of Paris. M. Clement seemed to be doing the show incog., and his two friends were equally mysterious and reticent. The writer last saw Mr. Clement at Malden, Mass., where he and I sat on a wagon together at the finish of the 1896 Linscott Bicycle Road race. This particular Frenchman is one of the greatest in a mechanical way that France has produced, and he was the pioneer maker of bicycles there, the Clement being the first "modern" bicycle, which is a son of the old velocipede and father of the still more modern ordinary bicycle which in turn was a sort of step-father to the present safety. I rode a Clement twenty-three years ago in England, only deserting it when the English manufacturer had run away from the French builder in the way of improvement.

History repeats itself, and once again the Frenchman is leading and it cannot be denied that both the English and American manufacturer has the French model in view when drawing his designs of his automobile. In some cases the Chicago Show looked very Frenchified, and the Frenchmen smiled when they saw American efforts in that direction. Mr. Clement said he was glad to see the Americans copy a good thing, and they would be given ample opportunity to copy some more before the French maker had completed his improvements. One of Mr. Clement's companions bluntly stated that the American builder was about five years behind the French one, and there was much to be learned by the Yankee before he would make an automobile that would pass muster in France.

The various forms of power in a motive way seen at the show interested many people, and each form had its advocates. Steam held its own very nicely, and much of the revival of steam carriage interest can be traced to the White Sewing Machine Co.'s very satisfactory vehicle. Some of the older companies should feel thankful for this since it cannot be denied that many boilers have been more or less faulty and things of dissatisfaction to the unfortunate possessors of steam carriages. Under the guidance of the White success there seems to be an improvement all along the line in the way of boilers, all of which gives promise of a lengthened life for the use of steam as a vehicle power.

There was a decided improvement in the display of electric carriages. The electric power machine is certainly coming to the front and the improved battery is responsible for its doing so. The improvement in charging facilities has also much to do with this since when the owner of an electric carriage can have his own individual charging plant or when he will be able to take power from the street by slipping a coin into a convenient slot machine, then will the high noon of the electric automobile arrive.

Nothing much need be said of gasolene except that the explosive engine was there in force and various forms. Simplicity in construction seems to be the very wise endeavor of the manufacturer of gasolene engines. Absence of odor and elimination of noise are two much to be desired improvements which Yankee ingenuity is gradually giving to the explosive engine.

Some of the women who affect motoring are passing fair and some others are past.

The difference between pride and vanity in motoring is that we have one and the other fellows have the other.

The poetry of automobilic motion is synonymous with the motion of automobilic poetry when the editor tosses it into the waste basket.

Alcohol for Automobiles
(1902)

Alcohol for Automobiles

By R. F. Collins

IF the automobile has undergone such astonishing headway the last few years it is because the new vehicle is now universally regarded as one of the greatest and most direct factors in the world's economy. As a sport and a pastime it will always, of course, grow in favor and will attract a constantly widening circle of supporters who enjoy the new sensation of being master of their own transportation while profiting from an economy of time, but were it not for economy in other directions it is doubtful whether the motor vehicle would ever have become so popular as it is at the present moment.

If the motor vehicle is to become something more than a toy and expensive plaything, it must have other advantages over the horse-drawn vehicle besides mere endurance and speed. The owner of an automobile must find that it is a good investment and see, after calculating his year's expenses, that he has got more out of the motor propelled vehicle than he previously did from his horse-drawn one, and that, moreover, it has cost him less. When this fact is recognized by the world the automobile will become universal.

Doctors and other professional men will not employ horse-drawn carriages when they can get about so much more cheaply and quickly with automobiles. The tradesman will see his profits steadily increase when he employs motor delivery which will carry his goods to their several destinations in half the time and do the work of six horses; the farmer will get rid of his prejudice against automobiles when he employs motor wagons for all the purposes of transport and sees that the power used in the wagons can be utilized in the place of motors and traction engines for driving his machinery.

But personal interest is not alone in giving such a universal character to the automobile. The motor vehicle needs fuel, and this must be obtained as cheaply as possible. On the European

Continent the importance of supplying this fuel is attracting a good deal of attention from agriculturists and the different governments. In time the demands will be so enormous that the industry which undertakes to supply the fuel will be in an extremely prosperous condition, and the question which is just now such a burning one in France, Belgium and Germany is whether the future supplies are to be provided by foreign petroleum producers or by home agriculturists.

Already many millions of dollars are spent every year upon the purchase of foreign petroleum, and if this money can be put into the pockets of native producers it will mean, they say, a permanent and marvelous revival of the agricultural industry. Besides, can the present production of gasoline possibly keep pace with the requirements of automobilism? The advocates of alcohol say that it cannot, but after all it matters little, for so long as they are favored by sufficiently high import duties they hope to force the use of alcohol on automobilists by supplying it at a lower figure than any of the petroleum products can be marketed for against a tariff.

Illustrated Trade Note

Following Out His Ideas of a Perfect Automobile

For some years past this alcohol propaganda has been carried on in France, but it was only in the fall of last year that any real attempt was made to create a general interest in the question by the tests made in Paris under the direction of the Minister of Agriculture. Until these official tests former experiments had given only doubtful results, for not only has the consumption of alcohol been higher than that of gasolene but the former caused considerable trouble by corroding the valves of the motor which had to be ground regularly every day, and if the motor were left alone for any time there was a hard deposit in the cylinder which could only be removed by a chisel.

These drawbacks have been almost entirely eliminated, and it is even claimed entirely removed, by carburetting alcohol with fifty per cent. of benzine, which at the same time greatly increases its efficiency. It is only in this form that alcohol is now used. The consumption has also been reduced in certain types of motors until now it is scarcely more than that of gasolene. In some cases even where excise duties have been suppressed on alcohol, there is already a decided advantage in alcohol's economy over gasolene. The new spirit has therefore made considerable progress, but not sufficient to warrant the hope that it can yet enter into successful competition with the petroleum product.

Some more light is to be thrown on this question by the fresh series of tests to be carried out by the French Minister of Agriculture, who is organizing a big run of alcohol vehicles through the beet root districts of the north of France. This will be followed by an international exhibition of alcohol motors and vehicles. In all the tests being held, moreover, special attention is given to alcohol, and the comparison is very interesting as showing that the spirit is getting near to the efficiency of gasolene. If permission can be obtained at all to run off the annual Paris-Bordeaux race all the competitors will have to use alcohol in their motors.

In Germany the utilization of alcohol seems to be making remarkable headway if we are to judge from the number of vehicles running there with this spirit and the alcohol shows that are being held in different parts of that country. One of the biggest of these alcohol motor exhibitions has just been held in Berlin, where the automobile firms using alcohol motors claim to have secured astonishing results in the way of economy, though nothing seems to have been done in getting accurate results by official tests. All the makers, however, confess that they are obliged to start the motors with gasolene, as alcohol will not volatilize properly unless the engine is warm.

It is impossible yet to say whether this stupendous effort to popularize alcohol for automobiles will result in the universal employment of the carburetted spirit, for everything turns upon the question of cost, and while no doubt the price will be reduced, it is clear that it must have a fairly large margin of economy if it is to take the place of gasolene.

The whole question is, indeed, an extremely open one, and unless the import duties on petroleum are heavily increased the manufacturers of gasolene would have very little difficulty in lowering their prices to compete with alcohol, though the government is said to have some remedy up its sleeve against any such contingency, notably in taking over the petroleum refineries and making them governmental establishments.

For the moment the question is interesting because it is giving to the automobile a vast importance as a factor in the industrial prosperity of the country. The motor vehicle is no longer regarded as an instrument of pleasure for the rich, but as a means of contributing enormously to the national resources, and not the least merit of the alcohol propaganda is that it has induced the European farmer to look upon the automobile as a source of profit to himself and has thus created a practical interest which will result in the growing employment of industrial vehicles.

Paris, March 15.

Newspaper Heading Illustrated

" Notes and Comments "

Touring in Automobiles
(1901)

TOURING IN AUTOMOBILES

By Henry R. Ṣutphen

SEVERAL years ago the bicycle suddenly made a prodigious leap into public favor, a result largely due to the fact that it provided people of moderate means with an entirely new and fascinating amusement—the exploring of the particular locality in which they lived, but about which they had usually known little or nothing.

For the natural man, only one means of locomotion is available—his legs, and their radius of action is necessarily limited. Given the use of the four legs of a horse and we can of course go much farther afield, but the cost is at once tremendously increased, thereby placing this mode of locomotion out of the reach of the average citizen. But the bicycle rider can easily compete with the horse in the matter of distance covered and the only expenditure is that of his own strength and energy.

And so everybody took up bicycle riding and enjoyed the novel sensation of becoming acquainted with the outlying country

GASOLINE TOURING VEHICLE.
EQUIPPED WITH THREE-CYLINDER ENGINE AND WOODEN WHEELS.

about his home. In short, it is the touring capabilities of the bicycle which account for its popularity.

Touring in itself is a pastime of which one may never tire, provided only that we do not have to work so hard to obtain the pleasure as to be unable to enjoy it. And to be popular, the cost must be moderate.

The automobile of to-day offers itself as a factor in touring. It cannot be said that the ideal has been evolved, but the manufacturers have at least put practicable machines upon the market and each new model shows an improvement upon its predecessor. It is the history of the bicycle repeated, even in the matter of high prices

GASOLINE RUNABOUT.
FUEL CAPACITY FOR 100 MILES.

and slow deliveries. But the manufacturers have learned something by their experience in the bicycle trade, and the development of the automobile should be proportionately hastened.

France and Germany have given most of their attention to the development of the gas engine or hydro-carbon form of power, while inventors in England and in the United States have worked more particularly upon the steam and electric types. Then there are the imperfectly developed alcohol and liquid air motors and half a dozen other forms of power that are still in the "blue-print" stage. For all practical purposes, our choice of a touring automobile must be made between the gasoline and the steam carriage.

Electricity is manifestly out of the question for touring purposes, its radius of action being absolutely limited, and its cost of operation comparatively high. The same objection applies to all similar systems, such as the widely exploited liquid air motor. The successful touring machine must be a prime mover, or one that develops its own energy from the raw fuel.

Gas and steam then are the alternatives, and how shall we decide between them?

Casting up their respective merits and demerits, we find that in the matter of first cost, the steam automobile has a decided advantage. But, on the other hand, the hydro-carbon vehicles are much less expensive to maintain and operate, and are therefore cheaper in the long run. In this connection, it may be remarked that the figures put forth by the manufacturers, as to the cost of operation, are apt to vary widely from those obtained by users in actual practice. Furthermore, one operator may get better and more economical results from a given machine than can another, presumably of equal intelligence. The personal equation enters here.

Safety is of course a paramount consideration. Both the steam and hydro-carbon systems use the highly inflammable gasoline or naphtha as a source of power supply but the method of application is different. The steam automobile employs a gasoline flame to turn the water in the boiler into steam. This gasoline or naphtha is carried under pressure in the fuel tank, and any leak or overflow is liable to start a fire which may do great damage to the vehicle, and result in serious injury to its occupants. In the popular view, it is the boiler that is the dangerous part of the steam-driven vehicle, but this is erroneous. A tube boiler, made by any reputable firm, cannot possibly burst, like a shell boiler. The most it can do is to blow or burn out a tube and a slight leakage of steam is the only visible result.

The hydro-carbon system, too, uses gas which is generated from gasoline within what is called a carburetor. After being mixed with air it is drawn into the engine cylinder, compressed and exploded by an electric spark. The principle of expansion of gas to move a piston is the same as in the steam engine. But the gas engine dispenses with the boiler, or rather combines boiler and cylinder in one piece. It is therefore a one unit motor as opposed to the two units, boiler and engine of the steam carriage. No flame of fire comes near the gasoline itself, but great care must still be used in filling the fuel tanks. No system that employs gasoline as a fuel or motive power can ever be absolutely safe. The gas engine with electric ignition reduces the danger to a minimum, but it is still there.

The manufacturers realize this defect and inventors are constantly at work trying to overcome it. What is particularly wanted is a successful kerosene oil burner for the steam automobile and the corresponding development of an internal combustion motor, using kerosene oil gas as its motive power.

In order to determine the best forms of power for long distance touring in England, the Automobile Club of Great Britain arranged last year for a thousand mile endurance run. During this test the hydro-carbon system made the best showing on the three points of reliability, speed and low cost of operation. Following this example the Automobile Club of America intends to arrange for a five hundred mile endurance test run between New York and Buffalo, some time during the coming season. This test will be open to all vehicles seating two people side by side, awards being made upon the following basis: Fewest stops, greatest carrying capacity in proportion to weight, and least cost for repairs. An average speed of twelve to fifteen miles an hour must be maintained during the entire run. This is the sort of experimenting that is certain to yield profitable results, both to the manufacturer and to the user of motor vehicles, and such a test is assuredly of more value than a dozen so-called road races. If the data for the New York-Buffalo test were at hand to-day, the tabulated results would materially assist the intending purchaser in determining which form of automobile is most likely to answer his purpose for touring on the average American roadways. In the absence of such data we can only draw our conclusions from private experience and theoretical knowledge.

With American roads as they are the question of construction becomes important. The prevailing type of steam vehicles is too light to stand hard usage. The makers of gasoline machines have more generally realized the futility of attempting to put heavy motors on bicycle running gear and the present type of hydro-carbon vehicles is consequently more practical for touring use. But there is no reason why the steam automobiles should not be built to fulfil every requirement.

In the matter of repairs, the liability to breakdowns, and general efficiency, there is something to be said for both types.

Both the steam engine and the hydrocarbon motors need careful and intelligent attention, if they are to give the best, or even satisfactory results. They are each liable to unexpected and annoying breakdowns, but it is certainly easier to locate the source of trouble in a steam engine than it is in a gas motor. In the first place, the steam engine is more familiar to us, both in theory and practice; and secondly, the gas engine is complicated by its electrical sparking apparatus, and electricity is a notoriously elusive fluid. The man who really and thoroughly understands the working of the petroleum gas engine must be a well-

what *is* the matter with a gas engine, let alone repairing it, with no tools at hand but a rusty spanner and a bicycle screwdriver.

In general efficiency, the steam vehicle has the advantage in ease of control and possesses decidedly greater flexibility of operation. The reversing process is perfect, since the locomotive link motion is used, and the engine can be started by simply letting steam into the cylinders. The gas engine cannot be reversed, and back motion can only be obtained by means of gearing. Moreover, the internal combustion motor will not start itself from a state of rest.

TOURING IN FRANCE.

equipped mechanical engineer and something of an electrician as well. The old dictum that "knowledge is power" was never better exemplified than in the handling of a hydrocarbon motor. On the whole, when a breakdown occurs, the owner of the steam carriage has the better chance of reaching home under his own power. Locomotion is possible even with smashed water gauges and leaky tubes, but the gas engine will not run at all if there is anything radically wrong with its essential functions. And it is often a labor of hours to find out just

The initial impulse must be given by hand or through some auxiliary mechanical device. The steam engine's speed can be governed with perfect certainty, either by throttling or by the cut-off, while the gas motor generally works best at a certain high normal rate, which must be reduced by gearing. Against this, the internal combustion motor is much less delicate in its fundamental working parts, it works on a one unit system as opposed to the two units of steam or electricity, and, generally speaking, it can do rougher and harder work than the steam engine. Moreover, it needs but one fuel, gasoline, as against both water and gasoline which must be supplied to the steam engine. It is true that water is used for cooling purposes on all large gasoline motors, but the quantity is comparatively small, and its chemical purity is not so important as though it were to be used inside a boiler.

Of course the great difficulty confronting the manufacturer is not to make a machine that will run, but a machine that anyone can run. So far as possible, it must be automatic in operation and above all it must be virtually fool-proof. There lies the rub. The makers of the steam carriages have been especially ingenious in providing automatic governors for their machinery. If everything works perfectly, the water level, the steam pressure, and the fire are all looked after automatically, and the operator has only to manage his levers and enjoy the scenery. But it is not possible to wholly dispense with human intelligence and attention, nor even to substitute for it beyond a certain fixed point. The sooner that the owner of an automobile gets rid of the idea that machinery can be built and run on the "you press the button" principle, the quicker he is likely to arrive at his destination. To the ordinary observer, the familiar type of steam automobiles that go flying so swiftly and gracefully around our streets, appear like very simple machines. A sprocket chain and a couple of levers is about all that he can see and he vaguely concludes that the rest of it is in the box. But let him open that box and look within and he will see what is virtually a locomotive engine in miniature, with cylinders, valves, link motion and all complete. Would he feel himself competent, after reading a dozen-paged manual of instruction, to mount the foot plate of "No. 999" and take the "Empire State" through to Albany? And a locomotive does not have to be steered.

A machine is a machine, whether it is employed to peel apples or to supply the motive power to a World's Exposition, and the best results can only be obtained by a thorough knowledge of its powers and an intelligent direction of them. To be a successful *chauffeur* one should be able to take his machine apart, clean, inspect and assemble it again. The famous French automobilists pride themselves upon being prac-tical machinists and the little knowledge that may come in so usefully on the occasion of a turn in the park is simply price-less when one is really touring. It is folly to start away from home unless you thoroughly know your steed. Look at a loco-motive engine just after it has hooked on to its train and is about to start on a long run and you are pretty sure to see a man in overalls walking around the big machine with an oil can in his hand. One would naturally suppose him to be the fireman, such a prosaic job as oiling should be beneath the dignity of the engineer. But not so; it is the engineer himself and the regulations especially require that he shall perform this final grooming of his iron steed in person. And the reason is that he may at the same time thoroughly inspect the all-important running gear of the machine. The oil cups are not always placed in positions of the greatest convenience for the oiler's back; in fact, they are often quite inconveniently situated, the idea being to make sure that certain important working parts shall come under the eye of the engineer.

There is certainly a happy medium between the practice of the French engineers, who build their automobiles with as much machinery as possible in sight, and that of the American manufacturer, who tries to put all the working parts into the box. It is absurd to pretend that the motor vehicle is nothing more than a horseless carriage, even to its incongruous and useless dash-board, and consequently to ignore the fact that it is a real machine. It is equally ridiculous to unnecessarily expose delicate working parts to the deteriorating effects of dust and weather. The ideal touring automobile should be neither a park trap nor a road locomotive.

It is impossible in a general article, to give more than the barest outline of what the amateur automobilist ought to know before he has earned the right to call himself a *chauffeur*. Accordingly no attempt has been made to discuss matters purely technical, such as the respective merits of two or four cycle gas engines, the mysteries of the "jump" and "wipe" spark, differentials, "flash" boilers and the like. These things the layman must learn from practical and sometimes bitter experience. But some essential points in practice may be briefly noted. Brakes are a part of the

ELECTRIC RUNABOUT.
25 MILES RADIUS OF ACTION.

GASOLINE TOURING VEHICLE.
EQUIPPED WITH SINGLE CYLINDER ENGINE
AND WIRE WHEELS.

construction that should be carefully looked after. The French law requires that every motor car must be fitted with at least two brakes, one of which must work directly upon the rim of the wheel. Of course, the latter would only be used in emergencies, as it is apt to injure the tire or even to strip it entirely from the wheel. But a shoe-brake upon the circumference of the drive wheels is the most powerful brake that can be devised and it is better to lose a set of tires than to be smashed up altogether. Speaking of wheels, brings up the question of wood versus wire. The later practice seems to be in favor of the wood wheel for medium and heavy-weight carriages. Its strength and elasticity are greater, it is not so liable to deterioration, and it is easier to keep clean. The tubular steel wheel is still a third type, but it is not in general use as yet. In a touring automobile, it is an obvious advantage to have all four wheels of the same size, as then the one extra tire carried will fit in any place.

Three or four wheels? The advocates of the three wheeler claim lighter draught, easier steering and greater flexibility in withstanding severe strains. On the other hand, the four wheels afford much greater stability and the general verdict is decidedly in their favor. In this connection it may be said that a low center of gravity is essential in any automobile intended for work over rough roads. The absurdly high electric stanhopes, for example, are only fitted for park use and are none too safe there. A high carriage is absolutely unsuited for touring, for remember that you no longer have the weight and mobility of the horse to balance the imperfectly adjusted load.

In the use of the steam carriage it is important to keep the gasoline burner clean. The gasoline itself should be strained before being run into the fuel tank as any foreign matter will quickly clog the fire-holes. The manufacturers all advise the use of "soft" water in the boiler. Otherwise chemical action is set up that quickly shortens the boiler's life. Still better results will be obtained by using only distilled water, but this is naturally impracticable when on a tour. But every farmer's wife knows the difference between "soft" and "hard" water. The water-glass is of course the chief object of solicitude on the part of the steam carriage operator. The tell-tale however, is not always accurate, and it will not do to place implicit faith in its reading. The gasoline level in the fuel tank should be looked after with equal care and the spanner and oil-can should always be at hand to minister to loosened nuts and squeaky bearings. Extra large fuel and water tanks are obviously a part of any long distance equipment; also a well equipped tool box and plenty of extra parts.

On the question of pneumatic versus solid tires, the experience of the French automobilists should be helpful. To-day ninety-eight per cent. of French motor vehicles are fitted with pneumatics, and the solid type has virtually disappeared. It has been found by experiment that (in France) the pneumatic tires cost ten francs less than the solid, and wore four months longer. Moreover, the life of the motive machinery was noticeably prolonged, particularly in the case of electric batteries. It was shown by experiment that twenty-five miles an hour was about the limit of safety for a car fitted with solid tires and running over a perfect road. At higher speeds, the vibration was so great that the motor was in imminent danger of wrecking itself. The same machine with pneumatic tires could be speeded up to sixty and seventy miles an hour with entire safety. It may be added that only the double tube pneumatic is used abroad, the American single tube being entirely tabooed.

The steering mechanism should be carefully designed, for upon its efficiency depends the comfort and the safety of the driver. A perfect steering device should call for a small expenditure of force on the part of the operator, and there should be adequate provision for taking off and distributing shocks due to sudden jars or obstructions in the course of the wheels. Moreover, it must act quickly so that, if necessary, the carriage may be turned within its own length. All of these requirements are mechanically possible and should be met by any good manufacturer. In this country the lever is generally used, while the continental manufacturers prefer the steering wheel. For high speeds, the wheel is undoubtedly preferable, and the later American models show that it is coming into favor over here for general use.

The sparking of gasoline motors is one of the minor perplexing problems and there are two general systems—dry batteries and the magneto or mechanical generation of the current. In the use of batteries there are frequent difficulties with the insulation, owing to careless wiring and as there is no way of ascertaining the present degree of battery efficiency to guard against a sudden giving out, it is necessary to carry along an extra set. The magneto system has been adopted lately by one of the oldest and best known American automobile manufacturers and as the result of years of experimenting with both types.

In the transmission of the power from motor to wheels, gears or belts may be employed. Each system has its good and weak points, but the solid gears in mesh are most in favor with explosive motor builders. With a motor, such as the steam engine, that can be effectually throttled, the difficulty of speed reduction virtually disappears.

In cold weather, freezing up is an unpleasant contingency, and in this respect the gasoline motor has the advantage over the steam carriage. With the latter, the water should be drawn off whenever the carriage is out of commission in the stable, and not infrequently during an unusually long wait while on the road. With the gasoline carriage, there is only the freezing of the water in the water-jacket to guard against, and this may be done by the addition of chemical compounds. Calcium chloride is said to yield exceptionally favorable results.

The ideal engine for automobile, and indeed any form of power work, would be the rotary, but the successful motor of that type has yet to appear. Parsons has succeeded in making his steam turbine motors applicable to certain types of marine construction, but the reciprocating engine still holds its own elsewhere. Innumerable patents have been taken out for rotary engines, but not one has proven itself commercially available. As compared to reciprocating motors, the rotary is either too heavy or it is less durable, or less economical, and the test of actual practice is the only one worth considering.

It is fortunate that in this country the popular interest is rather in the line of touring than of racing. The latter is not an avocation or a recreation, but a pure game, and a mighty expensive one at that. It is the twentieth century sport of kings and just as much beyond the poor man's purse as is a modern cup defender. Some of the successful French racing machines command enormous prices, simply on account of their triumphs on the road, precisely as with a winning race horse. But touring is for all, and with the betterment of the public highways, it may be pursued at a very moderate cost. Already the idea has been broached of a national highway from ocean to ocean, with subsidiary branches in other directions. Just the other day the various automobile clubs in the East decided to undertake the work of putting up sign-boards along the common roads of New York and the neighboring States, and in general, the automobilists are taking up and carrying on the good work started and continued by the bicycle riders, for the improvement of public highways.

Automobile Development
(1900)

AUTOMOBILE DEVELOPMENT

By M. C. Krarup

THREE "cycles of Cathay" have been concentrated in the few years which separate the opening of the twentieth century from the first practical application of the electric storage battery and the first mounting of a gasoline engine on a mechanical vehicle.

Automobilism rests squarely on these and the steam-engine; the three physical pillars of modern civilization. It would be impossible except on this foundation. It stands as the most important attack upon our

ing into a brief notoriety, only to vanish by reason of their inherent defects.

With perhaps 50,000 mechanical vehicles in use all over the world, it seems preposterous even to think of the possibility that further experience might condemn them to disuse. They are regularly used for carrying mail and provisions to military forts through a wild, roadless country in French Soudan; they have proved of high value in solving the transportation problems in the war against the Boer republics; they form a

THE ROBINSON HEAVY GASOLINE
MOTOR CARRIAGE.

"PEERLESS VOITURETTE," CONVERTIBLE
FRONT SEAT.   GASOLINE MOTOR.

wonted mode of living, which, without yet being brought to a successful close, seems destined to succeed completely because it involves no really new problems, but only painstaking application of knowledge which the world has already made its own. There is hardly room for the assumption that automobilism may be a huge fallacy, and that the thousands of motor vehicles now existing may disappear as completely under the horizon of a few years hence as did the steam road-wagons, which, since 1784, have appeared and reappeared on the scene at intervals of about thirty years; in each instance spring-

much-illustrated feature in French and German army maneuvers; physicians are employing them for professional calls, and in all the centers of civilization they are being more and more widely used for pleasure-driving, and for short hauls of freight, for trucking and merchandise delivery.

Nevertheless the question is asked: Are they being used on their merits, or for the sake of a theory in their favor, or perhaps for advertising, or in order to satisfy personal vanity?

It has been alleged that in a society where financial disparity did not exist, automobile pleasure-carriages could not be sold; that they are made and used only because there are persons to whom cost is a subordinate question. And it is reasoned that, this being the case, the present use of automobile pleasure-carriages decides nothing as to their real merits compared with older methods, and furnishes no decisive argument for their continued use, which must eventually be determined on the point of merit alone.

Perhaps, it is also said, the automobile movement, with its hopes and its disappointments, will prove such a fillip to the energy of horse-breeders, that soon the horse and its animal mechanism will become the subject of close and intelligent study, on entirely new lines, with the result of largely increasing its usefulness and decreasing the cost of its keep, even as we know that many half-

ducing them in earnest, for all classes of work, be overcome ? considering that no automobile will show its full value before a large portion of the road system has been improved.

body undertakes to answer these questions, or other expressions of doubt in regard to the future of the automobile. They must be answered by facts accomplished. It is realized by those best informed that a good deal of faith is required to be a stanch automobilist, and while many are strong believers on the basis of very poor reasoning, there seems to be no shorter road to the true faith than through a thorough study of automobiles in their practical workings, following upon a very complete technological education.

THE HYDRO-CAR.

THE ST. LOUIS "OVERLAND" GASOLINE CARRIAGE.

civilized tribes get much more and better work out of their horses than we do.

The warmest friends of automobilism themselves feed the pessimism of the doubters when they point to the great benefit which will be derived from automobilism through the road improvements that must go hand in hand with it. At the rate of $4,000 per mile only a small percentage of the road mileage in the United States could be radically improved for one thousand millions of dollars; and if road improvement on this extensive scale is really required to assure the successful operation of another one thousand million dollars' worth of automobiles, how shall the initial difficulty of intro-

It is in this respect rather characteristic that the greatest enthusiasm for automobilism is found among those who prefer the explosion motor vehicle, which at present is much cruder in the quality of its performance than either the electric or the steam vehicle; and it is also notable that some of the best explosion motor vehicles are designed by electrical engineers, some of the best steam vehicles by photographers, and some of the best electric carriages by bicycle manufacturers. Automobile progress depends to such an extent on all of the principal discoveries of the past century, that it is hard to find men in the orthodox M. E. profession who are masters in all the questions

RICHARD DUDGEON'S STEAM CHAR-A-BANC,
MADE 1860.

THE BAKER ELECTRIC RUNABOUT.
WEIGHT ABOUT 500 LBS.

THE DAIMLER HEAVY DELIVERY
WAGON (GASOLINE).

involved in automobile construction. Automobilism draws its designers from many
vocations. They fumble and grope in the
beginning, but learn as they proceed; and
when the results accomplished by all of them
are exhibited, as they were recently on two
successive occasions in New York, the public at large is induced to believe that it may
form an approximate idea of the automobile
development that has been reached; but,
unfortunately, an indoor "show" fails to
reveal much that is of the highest interest
for judging of the real fitness of the various
carriages, under working conditions; and
again the public must fall back on what
faith they can muster, and such evidence
of faith on the part of manufacturers as one
may be disposed to find in a gorgeous display, elaborate workmanship, and expensive
finish.

A really competent opinion can only be
formed by those who are, or might be, automobile engineers themselves, and this qualification can at present only by courtesy be
admitted as properly belonging to any one
person; automobile engineering not being a
small, special branch of mechanical engineering, but, on the contrary, one that comprises
all the requirements of all branches of engineering, in their most exacting form; with
the additional requirement of experience
in the art of carriage building and familiarity with all the changing conditions under
which vehicles must be used. Practically,
automobile engineers do not exist, but the
best automobile results are obtained by
co-operation between persons qualified, each
in one of the branches of knowledge entering into the construction.

This is the situation especially for the
gasoline motor vehicle, less so for the steam
vehicle, and in a still smaller degree for the
electric carriage. The three types are therefore reaching toward perfection in the reverse of the order named; but on the other
hand, the electric vehicle and the steam
phaeton or surrey have limitations that
seem unavoidable, while the explosion motor
vehicle, once perfected, seems to be adaptable to all kinds of work for which horses
and wagons have heretofore been employed.

The electric and steam carriages as known
at present are to all intents and purposes
new commodities, highly useful in their way,
but their value is to be judged from a personal standpoint in each case without any reference to what previously has been done by

horses. They are adapted for certain kinds of work in the hands of certain classes of people, and, to paraphrase Lincoln's well-known remark, "if the kind of service they are adapted for is the kind of service a person wants, then such a person is just the kind of person who should buy that kind of a vehicle." The gasoline motor vehicle is more like an unbroken horse; it will not do any work quite satisfactorily, but nothing that we are accustomed to look upon as vehicular work is beyond its scope and possibilities.

As the limitations of the steam carriage are very largely conditioned by the high degree of skill, care, and watchfulness which they exact, and the great bulk of the boilers and tanks; it seems to the writer that the future of the steam system for automobiles would be brighter, and its field larger, if more ingenuity were expended on devising a suitable form of steam horse entirely dissociated from the carriage proper, so as to leave the latter free from the encumbrance of machinery, and frankly acknowledge the motor portion as the delicate engine which it is, wherever it is placed. But nothing has been done in this respect, and nothing will probably be done, unless the need arises for steam vehicles to be used for other than purely pleasure purposes.

What is the present status of automobilism? The question cannot be decided on technical grounds, because nobody's competency to give the decision is admitted. Each constructor is entitled to his opinion. The public can have none, except as it may judge from what the various vehicles prove themselves in practice. The exhibitions give only clues in this respect, but leave a multitude of questions unanswered. They show styles, and workmanship, but fitness only in the meagerest fashion. Still, a few data are beyond controversy, mainly the favorable ones.

Electric carriages of the larger sizes are practically where they were a year ago. The latest development tends toward diminutive electric piano-box runabouts, so small and light that two storage cells, weighing less than two hundred pounds, will propel them as far as three-thousand-pound batteries will propel a five-thousand-pound electric cab. These light electric vehicles are not subject to those troubles with the air tires that form one of the most formidable items of expense in the maintenance of the full-sized electric carriages.

THE WALTHAM "VICTORIETTE."

THE "KNOX" SINGLE CYLINDER, 5-HORSE-POWER MOTOR—AIR COOLED.

THE "CANDA" GASOLINE VOITURETTE.

ENGINE AND CONTROLLING APPARATUS
OF " VICTOR " STEAM RUNABOUT.

THE " AUTO-BI,"
RECENT TYPE OF MOTOR BICYCLE.

Two of the largest producers of electric carriages, the American Bicycle Company and the Electric Vehicle Company, have this year supplemented their stock with gasoline vehicles of very substantial design, and containing original features in construction. These are both illustrated herewith, and it is perhaps worthy of special notice that the Electric Vehicle Company's gasoline carriage supports the engine, and driving mechanism, entirely on the running gear, leaving the carriage box free for other purposes. The spark shifter is automatically regulated according to the engine speed, by means of a governor, a provision which removes one of the features in the management of gasoline vehicles which troubles beginners most.

It is one of the most decided advancements of the year, that speed regulation, by throttling of the explosive mixture, has been perfected—as in this carriage and several others—so that now all voluntary speed changes of the vehicle may be effected as easily as with a steam-engine, while the variable gears need only be used when the speed of the engine is insufficient to produce the desired speed of the vehicle, or the power insufficient to overcome the resistance from road and wind with the normal gear. Indirectly the throttling system, which is more specially American than any other feature of the gasoline-engine vehicles, contributes to reduction of noise, reduction of the amount of cooling water to be carried, and reduction of the disagreeable shaking of the carriage—three shortcomings which have militated strongly against gasoline vehicles in the past. The value of the throttling system depends principally on the fact that, for nine tenths of the work of a vehicle, the full-sized explosion that may be produced in the cylinders develops much more power than can be utilized, and much more heat, and vibration, than desirable. The most original and effective throttling system is perhaps exemplified in a radically new motor, which at the Madison Square Garden show was exhibited in a little three-wheeled vehicle. Although capable of as high as five-horse-power, the single cylinder motor of this little carriage worked with perfect regularity at a power development not

DOUBLE CYLINDER GASOLINE ENGINE
OF THE " AUTOCAR."

MARSH MOTOR CYCLE.

DE DION "MOTORETTE."
NEW YORK TYPE.

THE "GASMOBILE."

exceeding three fourths of one-horse-power, and seemed better adapted for light work than any of the other air-cooled motors, mostly of French design, usually employed in motor cycles and very light carriages, in which the power application is regulated chiefly by the spark shifter. In the new American motor referred to, the compression of the explosive charge is variable, but its composition constant, and the spark, while not automatically regulated, except for starting the motor, is fired in the middle of the combustion chamber, in order to reduce the time for flame propagation, but is not retarded or advanced according to the engine speed.

In variable-gear-devices no radical improvements are recorded, and sparkers and vaporizers still leave much to be desired in the majority of vehicles.

The prominence of the water coils, in which the cooling water is exposed to radiation of heat, constitutes one of the esthetic drawbacks to the larger sizes of gasoline vehicles, from which no relief is in sight, but otherwise, it seems to be generally admitted that there is freer scope for artistic, and striking design in this type than in either steam or electric vehicles. It would probably be more correct to say that the necessity for new design in the gasoline vehicle is more pronounced, and that the necessity has caused the radical departures from ordinary carriage lines by which the gasoline vehicle distinguishes itself, sometimes offensively, but oftener in a manner pleasing to the eye and grateful to the natural demand for new contours in new things. Among the illustrations will be noticed one representing a carriage made by the Auto-

THE "CENTURY" ELECTRIC VEHICLE
ASCENDING STEEP BRIDGE APPROACH
(SYRACUSE, N. Y.).

ROADS OVER WHICH THE REMINGTON
AUTOMOBILES ARE TESTED.

mobile Company of America, in which this happy boldness of design is well merged in a harmonious *ensemble*.

In the massive Daimler freight wagon is shown one of the first American applications of the explosion motor system to heavy work, but the pattern is almost if not quite identical with Daimler wagons built in Europe for the same class of work.

A number of heavy gasoline touring carriages have been developed, of which the Robinson carriage is a good example. They represent a school of automobile engineering which studiously avoids everything flimsy and untried, in favor of the safety against breakage that may be obtained by the use of heavy material and painstaking workmanship, and it seems to be well established that these heavy carriages can actually travel over bad roads at high speed; but those who look to automobilism for all-round usefulness, find it difficult to discover the germ of further progress in a system of construction by which two to three thousand pounds of material are required for the transportation of two or four persons. Still the ratio of weight to pay-load is said to be smaller than that between the weight of a Pullman sleeping-coach and its full complement of passengers.

In steam-vehicle construction there is a similar divergence of opinions in the matter of weight. The extremely light steam phaetons of a year ago have practically been discarded. Even those manufacturers who prefer light construction have increased the weight from five hundred to seven hundred and fifty pounds, and the opposite faction, which is more numerous, produces carriages which average about fifteen hundred pounds. The addition of material is partly in the carriage portion, but also largely in the boiler and engine. Boilers and water-tanks are made larger than formerly, and in racing vehicles attain a special size with a view to sustaining high speed for a long time. Engine construction, with all its minor variations, is kept well within the experience of time-honored steam-engine practice, and nothing radically new has cropped out. In fact, there is a marked reaction from the

preference for automatic regulation of the operative functions of the engine, which was incorporated in the first successful American steam automobiles. Most builders now lean to the opinion that automatic devices lull the operator's watchfulness unduly, and become a source of danger to the integrity of the engine through failure to operate reliably. By dispensing with the automatic devices, they simplify the mechanism, and throw the burden of correct operation upon the skill and care of the driver. Several builders go so far as to warn prospective customers from purchasing, unless they are willing to take upon themselves all the responsibilities of a locomotive engineer. A notable exception, in this respect, is the Overman Automobile Company, which makes the Victor steam carriages. In this vehicle the principle of automatic regulation is carried out consistently; to such a point of completeness that an entirely unskilled person may operate it after a few minutes of instruction; but the automatic devices are supplemented by others, that permit the operator to throw them out of action, and regulate the functions of the engine by hand. The carriage body is entirely of metal, and the steam exhaust is made invisible by fine comminution through sixty small apertures in the exhaust tubes.

In all of the steam pleasure-carriages, so far produced, the entire carriage body is filled with machinery, and no space is available for baggage; but a makeshift arrangement is made in some instances, permitting a trunk to be strapped to a shelf bracketed behind the seat. Lately, steam delivery-wagons have been placed in the market, in which the carrying space is obtained by means of an inclosed superstructure over the rear portion, and the chimney is boxed in and extended through the ceiling of this superstructure. Many different patterns of chimney hoods have been tried during the past year, with a view to preventing the wind from blowing into the gasoline burner and interfering with the regularity of the flame and the steam generation. Most troubles in this respect are said to have been overcome.

The Care
of the Automobile
(1901)

THE CARE OF THE AUTOMOBILE

By J. A. Kingman

THE automobile is an inanimate object. Man invented it and only man can make it run. The perfect performances of an automobile reflect the skill and judgment of the man who is operating and caring for it. On the other hand, the ingenuity of the inventor and the skill of the manufacturer will be thrown away if the automobile gets into the hands of a man who either can not, or will not, operate it properly. It is evident that the automobile must be operated judiciously and maintained carefully if good results are to be obtained. Whatever machine you buy, study its mechanism thoroughly, and do not be in too much of a hurry to get out on the road. When you do, take things easily, and be content with moderate speed.

The purchaser of an automobile should not attempt to run the carriage until he understands its mechanism. He should know what each part is, and what function it performs. He should find out which parts require the most attention and what attention to give them. This is certainly the proper way to begin. The actual operation is a simple matter; it is easy to learn how to operate a few levers. Anyone can run an automobile, but one should know, not only what to do, but why to do it. One mistake beginners make is to run the automobile too far when first learning. The novice should be content with a few miles on the first day, increasing the distance each day very slightly. He will learn something about the machine every day, and by taking it easily, will avoid trouble through inexperience. Any new machine should be run carefully and slowly at first, in order to limber it up properly. A new automobile is not ready for a long run. There is another reason why a beginner should take it easily. If he makes a bad blunder he is apt to lose confidence in himself. This is not true in all cases, but it is in a great many. Most men do not realize what a powerful instrument an automobile is until they operate one and make some mistake. Then they have an exhibition of the pent-up energy stored in the carriage box, and if that power is improperly applied, damage will result.

Another great trouble with novices is that they try to make too much speed. This is most dangerous. When an inexpert operator is speeding his machine, he is apt to become excited, and thus lose control of it. It is very exhilarating to travel at a high rate of speed, and the temptation to do so is great. A beginner may appreciate the danger, and have vowed never to make more than ten or twelve miles an hour; yet, in a week, he will probably be disappointed if he cannot beat every automobile or trolley car in his neighborhood. Even the expert chauffeur should not use his automobile for racing if it was not built for it. A racing automobile is designed for racing; an ordinary automobile is not. If a man has an ordinary automobile and races in it, he is abusing its powers. He is expecting it to do work for which it was not intended. And if he has trouble, it is his own fault. An automobile capable of running at a high rate of speed is valuable in case of an emergency; but it does not follow that because it is fast that it should always be run up to its limit. And it is a mistake to do it. Never turn corners swiftly. There is danger in it. The centrifugal force may cause an upset. Even if it does not, it is also bad for the machinery. Never attempt great speed in climbing hills. It may be gratifying to own a machine which is a swift and sure hill climber, but you should not force the automobile. Steam and electric machines are propelled up hills by simply giving the motor more steam or electric current. Gasoline carriages are operated differently. A low, or hill climbing gear is thrown into play, which reduces the speed of the vehicle but increases its driving power. This caution against speed in hill climbing applies particularly to electric and steam vehicles. A storage battery is sensitive, and the electric vehicle should be taken up a hill at the rate of speed which is best for its particular battery. Steam carriages are notable hill climbers; but this is no reason why they should be abused every time a hill is attempted.

The life of an electric vehicle is in the storage battery. The most unskilled person can operate an electric carriage with very little instruction; but the care of the battery is highly important. The manufacturers of electric vehicles buy their storage batteries instead of making them. The manufacturer of the batteries sends out with each a set of instructions for charging and taking care of it. These instructions should be carefully followed. For instance, a battery may require charging up to a certain voltage. The limit indicated must not be exceeded. When the carriage is operated the battery is discharged, and if it is not operated properly, the battery will be affected. No battery can be charged up to its full limit and discharged to its lower limit if it is expected to last any time. A storage battery of, say, thirty - six cells, is divided into four parts, the voltage of nine cells being one-quarter of the voltage of the battery. When the carriage is started it should be started on the first speed, that is, nine of the cells should be put into operation first, and the remainder later. If it is started on the fourth speed, the entire voltage is used. This means the entire strength of the current is turned into the motor, with the very probable result that some of the connections will be burned out. Therefore always start slowly. An electric vehicle should be operated occasionally if not in regular use, for if it is left standing the battery is sure to depreciate.

The operation of the electric vehicle is an easy matter, and the machine is free from objectionable features. That is there is nothing to watch or attend to beyond the handling of the levers. Yet the battery must be carefully maintained if it be expected to give its full mileage and last well. The renewing of the acid is not a pleasant task. Neither is the cleaning of the plates. Both must be attended to, however, if satisfactory results are to be obtained. Storage batteries differ materially in construction and in the method of operation. Read the instructions accompanying the battery, and see to it that they are regularly and carefully followed. The electric wiring and connections should be frequently inspected. See also that the binding posts are tight and that the insulation is perfect. The motor requires regular inspection and proper lubrication.

The gasoline carriage depends for its power on the explosion of a minute charge of mixed air and gasoline vapor in a cylinder. The explosion is produced by an electric spark. This is obtained from an induction coil, the electric current being provided by a battery of small cells. The principal trouble with a gasoline carriage is the sparking device. Some have one cylinder, others having two or more cylinders are of the multi-cylinder type. Each cylinder has its spark in order to explode the gasoline in it. An insulated sparking plug is screwed into the closed end of each cylinder. A device called a "trembler," or "vibrator," automatically makes or breaks contact so that the spark is produced

A TYPICAL AUTOMOBILE STATION
WHERE VEHICLES ARE STORED, CLEANED AND MADE READY FOR THE ROAD.

at the proper time. The contact is made by a fine platinum point or points. These should be kept clean. If they are foul the dirt will act as an insulator and no spark will be produced. If there is no spark there can be no explosion, and the motor will not run. The sparking plug, which is screwed into the head of the cylinder, should be kept properly insulated, otherwise the spark cannot be produced. The motor of a gasoline carriage is started free from the carriage and thrown into gear later. In starting a motor it is advisable to close the compression or relief cock to make sure that the compression is good. Then the compression cock is opened and the crank is turned. This turns the fly-wheel and sets the motor running. The carriage is started by throwing in the low gear by a clutch. The low gear is used in order to give enough power to start the vehicle. Once it is under way not as much power is needed to propel it. The clutches which are used to throw the different speed gears in and out of operation should be kept properly tight. The gears themselves must mesh properly, and be kept well lubricated. If they are enclosed in a gear case, change the oil when necessary. The motor runs in oil, and thus does not require attention except to renew the oil occasionally. Some operators make the mistake of putting too much oil in the crank case. This may cause the cylinder to be flooded with oil, which will give a blue smoke in the exhaust, and also foul the sparking points.

The gas for the explosion is made in a device called a carburettor. When it is produced the charge is drawn into the cylinder through an inlet valve, the piston moving away from the head of the cylinder. On its return stroke the piston compresses the charge and the spark explodes it. The piston is driven to the other end of the cylinder, and again returning, exhausts the product of combustion through an exhaust valve. Carburettors are of many kinds. They should be kept clean, so that no carbon may enter the cylinder and be deposited on the sparking points. It will be seen that the spark is the life of the carriage. If the motor will not run, examine the sparking device. Turn the crank first. If the buzzing of the induction coil is heard, then the electrical connections are perfect. The trouble is then probably with the contact points or sparking points.

In gasoline carriages the power transmission devices are so arranged that the motor has to be thrown out of gear before the speed gears can be changed. If this is the case never fail to throw the engine out of gear first. You may have a set of badly broken gears if you do not. If you have a single cylinder motor always put the engine on a center after returning to the stable. This closes the valves and prevents oil from running into the cylinder. Also close the gasoline valve so that the carburettor will not be flooded. All gasoline carriages of any size have a water jacket to keep the cylinder cool. The water must be changed occasionally, for if the motor becomes overheated it will not run. The water is kept in circulation, sometimes by gravity feed, but more often by a centrifugal pump. This pump must be kept running properly else the motor will quickly become overheated. Use good gasoline and strain it carefully before filling the tank.

I will now pass on to the steam carriage. In getting up steam, which usually takes from eight to ten minutes, see that the boiler is about three-quarters full of water, and that the gasoline tank is full and under the desired air pressure. Heat the torch thoroughly and use care in inserting it. Where most operators get into trouble is that they either do not heat the torch sufficiently well, or turn on the gasoline too quickly. Open the safety valve when getting up steam, otherwise the steam gauge may show a false register. While the boiler is making steam see that the water tank is filled, and that the valve leading from the tank to the pump is opened. Oil the machinery thoroughly, and see that all bolts and screws and the driving chain are tight. In starting, open the throttle very slowly. This gives the water which may have accumulated in the cylinders and steam chest, time to escape through the exhaust. If you start up suddenly the chain may be broken or damage done to the engine. Some steam carriages are provided with cylinder relief cocks which are opened when the carriage is started. These are not necessary, however, if it is always started slowly. The principal matter to attend to on the road is the water supply. The water is pumped from the tank into the boiler by a pump connected to the crosshead of the engine. The pump is working all the time when the carriage is running, and pumps water into the boiler when the by-pass valve is closed. When this valve is open the water forms a circuit returning to the water tank. It is important that the pump be kept in good condition, for no boiler can make steam without water. The pump check valves need occasional cleaning, as dirt or grease affect their proper action. If the pump gets "air-bound," open the by-pass valve. This allows the air to escape from the pump into the water tank. The operator should watch the water gauge, because if the boiler become empty it will be "scorched" or "burned out." This is not dangerous, as the escaping steam puts out the fire, and it is not serious, as a scorched boiler can be repaired easily. However, it is something to be avoided. It is always the result of carelessness. The boiler should be blown off occasionally. About every forty or fifty miles that the carriage is run, if the water be very bad. Blowing off the boiler cleanses it, and prevents scale from forming on the tubes. The boiler requires no care beyond keeping it supplied with water and blowing it off as indicated. Always turn out the fire before blowing off the boiler.

The burner requires regular cleaning as the small openings are apt to become clogged with soot. If the boiler does not steam well it is probably due to the burner. This can be cleaned without removing from the carriage. Brush the top plate of the burner thoroughly with a small stiff brush, inserted through the door leading into the firebox. Blow out the fine particles of soot with an air pump. If the atomizing nozzle leading to the burner is stopped up, this can be cleaned out with a piece of fine wire. The fire may also burn poorly through an insufficiency of air pressure, or because of some stoppage in the gasoline piping leading from the gasoline tank to the burner.

The engine is very generally of the marine type, set vertically. Two simple pressure cylinders are used with the ordinary link reversing gear. The bearings are not oiled by splash-about lubrication, and should be carefully attended to. Oil the wearing parts at least every time that the carriage is used, and whenever the engine does not run easily. The cylinders and crossheads need frequent oiling. The chain which does the driving is capable of easy adjustment, and should be kept at the proper tightness. It should be kept clean and well lubricated.

If the steam carriage is to be left standing, under steam, it is advisable to turn out the fire completely. On returning, be careful, in lighting the fire, to let out the crude gasoline, and wait until the vapor appears. If the steam gauge shows thirty or forty pounds

pressure, the fire can be lighted with a match. When leaving the vehicle without attention shut the safety lock, so that no one can start the carriage by tampering with the throttle. This also applies to the safety lock on electric carriages. Use good store gasoline, about seventy-four test, and when possible, strain it carefully before filling the supply tank.

The problem of tires ceases to be an important one if they are cared for in the proper manner. The most important point is to keep them well inflated. They should be pumped up hard at all times. The manufacturers recommend that a pump be used to which is fitted a pressure gauge. Thus the desired air pressure can be obtained. This is usually about sixty or seventy pounds to the inch. Not such high inflation is required in very warm weather as the heat increases the pressure in the tire. This is the most important feature. If a tire is run soft the rubber is apt to be cut where it touches the rim of the wheel. Moreover, the tire is designed to run at a certain inflation, and will not wear well unless it is properly pumped up.

Careless operation is responsible for a good deal of trouble. The carriage should be run slowly over car tracks and over bad stretches of road. If an operator uses common sense he will have no trouble with his tires. Keep gasoline and oil off the tires. The former is a very powerful solvent and destroys rubber rapidly. Do not pump up the tires with a dirty or greasy pump. If a tire proves defective, the manufacturer will replace it. When one is punctured, have it repaired as soon as possible. If a temporary patch can be effected, so much the better, for it will be ruined in a short time if it is run while entirely deflated. Wheels should be kept true and the bearings well lubricated and properly adjusted. The automobile is a carriage and should receive the same treatment as any horse-drawn vehicle. After a long run it should be thoroughly cleaned and inspected. If any parts need adjustment or repairs, have them attended to at once, so that it will be ready to run at a moment's notice.

The automobile has come to stay; it is no fad. It is too useful and practical for that. The betterment of the roads will help automobiling greatly. But what will help more will be the chauffeurs who operate in a careful and judicious manner, and give to their machines the inspection and care which their use requires.

The Meaning of the Vanderbilt Cup Race (1906)

Why this event will probably be abandoned on public roads; the spectators who will not "keep back."

THE MEANING OF THE VANDER-
BILT CUP RACE

BY JAMES E. HOMANS

THE automobile is still an adolescent thing. Its play days are not yet past. It has until now proved little more than a source of amusement to its proud possessor. As to what it will be in the future, as to what its possibilities of usefulness in the world, as to what its influence on mankind and affairs, we who prophesy and anticipate are only like the fond relatives of a promising child. We expect much—not too much; we hope for more, and are confident; we are assured of enough to warrant enthusiasm.

The great race of October 6th proved all this. It was both encouraging and discouraging. It was discouraging because it showed beyond question that there is still hard and persistent work ahead before the motor wagon is all that it must become; that we are still far from finalities. It was encouraging because it is certain that the near future will look back and marvel at the records achieved with "present crudities," just as we of to-day remember with amazement the motor carriage records of seventy and eighty years ago.

This year's Vanderbilt Cup Race, like its predecessors of 1904 and 1905, was a race between cars purposely built for speeding, and intended for no other use whatsoever. Only two of the competitors, the Christie and the Haynes cars, were of stock models, such as are offered to the buying public. The former of these two was in the race by an accident, wholly unforeseen and very much deplored; the latter, by virtue of that heroic quality well named "cussedness." Haynes "held her nozzle agin' the bank" until he was last in the race, and two and one-half laps, seventy-five miles at least, behind the winner. So much for the chances of the common-service motor in such a test.

Haynes was right, however. He was true to precedent and tradition, orthodox to the very spine of him; no friend of innovations. The original automobile endurance tests in France were planned solely, as he knew well, for common-service cars. So strenuous on this point were the projectors of these contests that, in the second Paris-Bordeaux race of 1895, the two leaders, a Panhard and a Peugeot, were ruled *hors de concours*, because they carried only two passengers, instead of the stipu-lated four. In those old days folk learned the real merits, the speed capacities and the staying powers, of the machines offered them for sale. Now they hear only that a man named Darracq, who also builds touring cars, has produced a speeding engine, which, with the help of the "man behind the wheel," has outrun the speeding engines of some half dozen of his competitors. As to how his touring cars compare with theirs, they have only rumor and advertisement for information. Darracq has gained some valuable publicity, and Wagner is reckoned among the heroes.

While making these observations, we must not forget conditions. In 1895 any kind of motor was a novelty, a thing to draw a crowd. Popular interest was keen regarding all its doings. At the present day there would be nearly as small a sporting interest in a prospective speed contest of family touring cars, as in a street race between a milk wagon and a doctor's buggy. The malodorous scent of commercialism would be so pronounced as to stifle large enthusiasm. We want something out of the ordinary. That is the reason why we get it.

It is the patronage of the wealthy class that has made the automobile what it is; that has furnished the incentive for its rapid development, rendering possible approximations, perhaps otherwise delayed. So far, this is fortunate. One step more, and it seems unfortunate. The designing engineer has never had exclusive control of the machine. His patrons, upon whom his living depends, have not only demanded a contrivance that shall be capable of certain performances, but also one built on certain lines and embodying certain acceptable traditions of design. These traditions of design have often been otherwise than logical and scientific. Thus it is that there is a radical revolution ahead, when we shall learn some things now unrecognized.

We have already begun to learn new things with the advent of the commercial automobile. We have found out that designs, perfectly tolerable for touring cars, are absurd for burden-bearers or trucking vehicles. That is the first forward step. The engineer has gained a free hand at last, and has begun to do things.

Car coming!!

Jenatzy (Mercedes—3rd place) rounding the turn near Roslyn.

Another forward step is ahead. We shall learn that a machine that can "stand up" under excessive speed conditions—and the near future will demand such a machine—must differ in many essential particulars from presently familiar models of either touring cars or freight wagons. Here again the free hand must be given.

In this digression we would fain argue for the kind of speed contest that would primarily interest the automobile engineer, really instruct the public, and contribute to the evolution of the perfect car.

Let it be understood that a car is wanted that could run beside the limited express from New York to Chicago, we may say, without requiring stops every now and again to repair some ridiculous cacopragia in a mechanism supposedly competent for service. Then, let the boss designers wheel out their freaks and fancies, and let the rest of us watch for the survival of the fittest. The Cup won in such a contest would entail a clear title to enduring fame. Furthermore, the victorious nation, or the victorious engineer, would have achieved a distinction that is also distinctive. Such a race would be a real trying-out for speed, just as the Glidden tour is a trying-out for endurance.

In the recent cup race, a French designer won the trophy, for 297 miles in 4 hrs., 50 mins., 10⅖ secs., thanks to his excellent machine and the stoutness of his German-French driver. An Italian was second, completing the ten rounds in 4 hrs., 53 mins., 28⅖ secs. Two more Frenchmen followed him, and a German came fifth. And these five completed the whole ten rounds. Two Italian cars and one American ended with the ninth round. The remainder were hopelessly in the rear.

These facts in no sense argue the eternal superiority of French cars, nor yet even the temporary discounting of the Italians, Germans and Americans. They are comparable to the victory of a team of English athletes over Americans, which proves to no one the muscular superiority of all Britons; or to the long-deferred recent naval victory of Harvard over Yale, which can scarcely be expected to result in desolating New Haven class-rooms. There are some demonstrations that do not demonstrate excessively.

There is another thing about which we may justly wonder, and that is why America, the supposed premier nation in mechanics—whose locomotives run in almost every land, and whose harvesters go everywhere but to New Zealand—has never, but once, gained first place in an international automobile contest. That once was ten years ago, almost to the day, on October 14th, 1896, when an American runabout, designed and built by Charles E. Duryea, won the "Liberty Day" run from London to Brighton, England, and, in perfectly fair contest, out-distanced the Panhard-Levassor, victor of the previous June's Paris-Marseilles race. Duryea is still America's champion, just as he was for long her sole motor representative in European countries.

Something over seven months after Duryea's victory, on May 30th, 1897, Alexander Winton achieved what was to that date the world's mile record, 1 min., 46 secs., on a prepared track at Cleveland. What he could have done in a set contest may be problematical. What Americans could have done with distinctively American models is also problematical. Most of them have adopted French precedents, and are still outclassed by the French.

The nearest American record achieved

the daring men raced their cars without slowing.

in recent years, was third place won by Tracy (Locomobile) in the 1905 Vanderbilt race. He was the only American completing the ten rounds in that year. He is the only American who ever completed the full number of rounds in an international motor contest. This may argue that the trouble lies almost entirely with American drivers, and that there is something stale about machines America offers in such contests. This does not involve the inferiority of American touring cars, as we have already agreed. But, if a speed contest—even a purely sporting event—can show anything at all, it will show up flaws in material and bungles in workmanship. If these things are habitual failings with the Americans, Heaven help the Americans. People will think they never turn out decent work.

We may doubt the superiority of foreign-built machines until we find them used in increasing numbers by people whose choice is not determined solely by the *eclat* of a high-sounding name. Yet we find that, in spite of the preposterous import duty, the foreign car is the rule rather than the exception with wealthy motorists. Such people will explain this apparent fact by alleging that the American machine will not "stand up" like its European rival; that the material is not as good; that the workmanship is not as reliable. While several wealthy motorists conspicuously use only American cars, the majority of them consider such a course a sure indication that one "cannot afford to do otherwise," or else knows sadly little of automobiles.

The popular preference for the foreign car may be called a "fad" and a "pretense," if one inclines to use these terms. The builder, however, can be accused of no such weakness. His interest lies solely in the direction of enhancing his own reputation. Yet, what do we find? The importation of automobile parts by the foremost American automobile manufacturers is very extensive—let us refrain from figures. Nor is this importation concerned solely with minor accessories, nor with finishings. The essential and delicate parts are principally concerned. Thus, the cylinders of several, at least, of our foremost cars are cast in France. Nor is the fact advertised. One builder, acknowledging this practice, explained it with a laconic "because French castings are better." Another, more communicative, stated that, "French castings are preferable, because the French founders are metallurgists as well, men who can make their own mixtures and achieve dependable results, as is not the case in this country. Their castings are cleaner, and blow-holes are less common." He alleged further that only about two per cent. of the work is discarded. Another builder, hearing these allegations on the superiority of French castings, pooh-poohed the notion. "Why," said he, "I have my cylinders cast right here in the city. They are plenty good enough for anyone." "What is your percentage of discards?" he was asked. "Oh, something less than fifteen per cent."

It may be that the American workingman is getting the blame for our rotten armor plate, and that prudent manufacturers hesitate to trust him with so important a product as an engine cylinder. One may conclude what he thinks best. We have French workmanship on three or four of our best-known cars, so why look abroad?

A certain American motor car builder, equally prominent as a designer and a

Why so many tires were worn out.

sportsman, asserted: "I unhesitatingly claim that I have the best and most reliable car on the American market. It is carefully designed throughout, and heavy enough and strong enough to withstand any kind of usage. I got one of the best French cars and took it apart, piece by piece, noting how each part was formed and assembled. Then I made as close a copy as I could of its best points. My car cannot be beaten." Another one!

All this may seem very much like "ill-natured criticism," and to have very little to do with our subject-matter. It must be remarked, however, that the lay public does not understand the full significance of speed contests. Seeing American machines habitually worsted, it concludes with unintentional injustice, that they are all mere flimsy structures, carelessly put together, made only to sell at a big profit, and quite unsuitable for people who do not delight in breakdowns, disablements and repairs. There is positively no reason why an American machine cannot attain and maintain as high a speed as any Frenchman's. National pride demands that one of them should make at least as good a showing. Furthermore, it is a mere matter of sound business policy that the attempt be made.

There is a good modicum of truth in the theory that the best efforts should be expended on common-service cars, and that the high-speeders should be left to amuse those who can afford them. There is another side, however. The high-speed car exists solely for test conditions. What it can do is an indication of what can be done. What it cannot do marks a limitation that calls for serious attention. The motor car at high speed is like some other objects under the lens. Speed magnifies their good points, and makes their weaknesses conspicuous. It is like the high-pressure water test for a steam boiler, or any one of the numerous severe tests for structural steel. It is strenuous. If there be a flaw anywhere, a rupture is sure to follow, and the seat of a dangerous weakness is discovered. The speed race, therefore, cannot fail to shed new light on some doubtful points. It is an excellent method for learning "how not to do it." It is a test for the automobile itself, not for any particular make or model.

In making all these observations we must not overlook the fact that the automobile is a thing of singular complexity. This does not mean that it is mechanically more complicated than a calendar clock or a typesetting machine. It indicates merely that the involved operative conditions represent nearly the supremest degree of difficulty. In dealing with a vehicle of any order, it is assumed to con-

Wagner takes turn at full speed.

stitute one element of a machine, the other element being the road upon which it travels. Thus, the railroad locomotive and its track constitute a mechanical working unit. High speeds and great work are possible, because the interaction of the two elements is as easy and complete as human skill can make them. The smooth and even rails allow high speeds with small vibration. The horse wagon runs upon a roadway by no means smooth or even, but its movement is easy, because only relatively moderate speeds are attempted. The automobile, however, is, in our expressive slang, "up against the real thing." It is the active element of still another machine for annihilating distance, but it must achieve high speeds upon a surface that renders them both difficult and destructive. The ideal automobile is the self-mover, which can endure as well as move; many automobiles thus far constructed have been merely self-destroyers, suicide-machines, and ingenuity has been taxed to the limit to postpone the sad consummation. The gravest problem is to smooth the roadway, and when that is fairly accomplished the determination of other questions will be simplified.

That this knotty problem is already well in hand is evidenced by the great decrease of roadside accidents and breakdowns within the last two years. We are gradu-

ally and surely working toward the completely satisfactory common-service vehicle, be it for touring or for haulage.

On October 6th we learned again, however, the same old tedious lessons of the presently existing limitations of the automobile. So far as concerns structure and endurance the flying motor wagon is a present reality; only its flights are discouragingly short and disgustingly full of stops and disablements. We have motor wagons that can make a speed of sixty miles and more per hour, but, safe it is to say, few indeed that may be depended on to run sixty miles and more in any one hour. Nor is this the fault of the machines themselves. They are like the man who boasted that he could outrun anybody, if only his "wind would not give out." It is the familiar old story of the "tire that tires"; the "inflated wind bag," which, like its human prototype, "fizzles out," when called on for real work; the ubiquitous air cushion that marks every motor car a dependent invalid.

The Vanderbilt Cup Race was a veritable massacre of pneumatic tires. The wake of the devil wagons was strewn as thick with bursted shoes and air tubes as the range of a Gatling gun with the fragments of departed enemies. Nearly every other car passing the grand stand pounded along over frayed ribbons of rapidly deteriorat-

Tracy—who made the fastest single lap of the race—passing the grand stand in his Locomobile.

Lancia—(Fiat) winner of 2d place—at "hair-pin" turn.

ing case tubes. One was reminded of a beggar running from a watch-dog, when he had hoped to see only the triumphal progress of a king of the winds.

Here are some of the tire casualties, as announced occasionally from the press stand:

Cagno stops at East Norwich: tire trouble.

Le Blon replaces three tires just after leaving Albertsons.

Le Blon bursts a rear tire.

Lawwell bursts two tires.

Wagner has tire troubles.

These are only a few of the troubles. Tracy smashed eight tires, and the delay entailed, more than any other evident difficulty, contributed to his loss of the race, despite his record lap of 26 mins., 21 secs., for the 29.7 miles, an equivalent of 67.63 miles per hour.

They tell us that the pneumatic tire has

The photographers were worked to a standstill.

Christie has tire trouble at Jericho.

Le Blon loses one tire at Hempstead turnpike.

Lawwell changes two tires at Jericho: loses fifteen minutes.

Tracy punctures a tire at Jericho.

Tracy has tire trouble near Bull's Head Hotel.

made the automobile possible. Would to Heaven that inventive genius had been set the task of making the automobile possible by some other means. We might already have seen glimmerings of the consummation we must inevitably begin striving for at no distant day.

The pneumatic tire was first devised to

Risking death at every corner.

impart a necessary spring effect of the springless bicycle—to render the "safety bicycle" safe. It was adopted into automobile construction, along with those other bicycle traditions, the tubular under-frame and the suspended wire wheel, both happily extinct. Combined with springs borrowed from a horse wagon, it made the automobile a sort of mechanical Frankenstein, affording more room for complaints than for passengers.

The pneumatic is of great use is giving the wheel a grip on the road surface, thus greatly increasing tractive efficiency. It also "swallows up" small obstacles, such as pebbles, absorbing numerous minor jolts. Furthermore, it renders riding easier.

The fatal deficiencies of the pneumatic tire lie in its inability to resist large stresses which tend to deform it sidewise and rend its walls, also its liability to cutting and puncture. In order to perform its functions properly, it must be made in generous proportions. The same thing, then, that renders effective its resiliency and tractive power, exposes it to quick de-

Christie's freak car.

461

Duray—(Lorraine-Dietrich) winner of 4th place—"skidding" at the "hair-pin" turn.

Wagner (Darracq) crossing the finish line and winning the race.

struction, especially at high speeds. It is not the nail in the road that punctures it, but the awful racking from one side and then from the other, as the moving car sways continually on its flexible supports. Beyond a certain point of speed, therefore, the pneumatic tires become an unmitigated nuisance, the greatest imaginable obstacle to motor car development.

There may be readier solutions, partial ones, at least, for the trouble than might be suspected. The traditional small wheel, so pretty to see and so readily driven, demands a heavy tire. A higher wheel, could prejudice be overcome, would reduce the trouble, because it would reduce the size of the tire for a good resilient effect. A moment's reflection shows this. No one heard of pneumatics in the days of the high wheel bicycle. They were not needed. For an automobile, however, the larger wheel must needs be more than proportionally stronger and heavier, to resist side stresses. It would also require a larger engine torque to drive it. Some have suggested that a broader wheel tread would contribute to the same end. There is also a large prospect of alleviation, when automobilists have turned their attention to the designing of springs especially suited to motor carriage requirements. The familiar shock-absorbers in some measure approximate this end by

restraining the springs from pounding the tires to shreds, as we may say. Experiment has shown that they actually contribute to the life of tires, under ordinary conditions, but they are of small use at high speeds, because the destroying stresses are then mostly lateral.

The accidents were fewer at the last Vanderbilt Race than at any previous contest of the kind. That is encouraging to say the least. It shows that our designers have profited by former mishaps. Every break that occurs in such a test is of genuine service to the world, even if the driver also breaks a few bones. It reveals the fact, that still further study is required on the suffering part. It is not only in the engine and transmission that we must look for flaws, but also in those vital parts, on which depends the safety of the passengers —the brakes and steering gear.

There have been several sad accidents of late with steering gears. In the Cup Race, Dr. Weilschott's steering gear gave way, and he was "almost persuaded" to forego steering for good and all.

The other accidents are among the inevitables as seen in our present stage of knowledge. A skidding car is merely one acting in obedience to law involved in the nature of motion. We can guard against the injury liable to follow; we cannot eliminate the tendency.

The profile course on grand-stand by which the relative positions of the racers were shown.

The Automobile Races at Newport (1900)

Mr. A. L. Ritter,   Mr. Spencer Crane,   Mr. De Forrest,
In the Newport Races.

Mr. W. K. Vanderbilt, Jr., in his French Racing Machine, Going at the Rate of 35 Miles an Hour.

Society's Enclosure, Aquidneck Park, Newport.

The Automobile Races at Newport.

Twentieth Annual Championship of the United States National Lawn Tennis Ass'n.—Newport Casino, Aug. 14-21, 1900.

Column headings: Preliminary Round. | First Round. | Second Round. | Third Round. | Fourth Round. | Final. | Winner of All Comers.

Preliminary Round:

R. C. Thomas
K. Horton
J. P. Paret
Kreigh Collins
L. E. Ware
I. Wright
H. Foster
B. C. Wright
G. L. Keyes
G. W. Lee
C. B. Schley
F. B. Alexander
M. G. Chace
A. Codman
L. H. Waidner
E. P. Fischer
Samuel Hardy
H. H. Hunnewell, Jr.
W. H. Warnock
S. H. Williams
W. A. Larned
James D. Pell
J. C. Davidson
H. C. Clews, Jr
Richard Peters
H. M. Ashe
A. W. Gore
H. N. Rawlins
Holcombe Ward
Clarence Angier
W. J. Clothier
C. R. Budlong
Edward A. Taft, Jr.
A. F. Fuller
E. Stillé
E. D. Black
Henry Thornton
Sumner Hardy
W. E. Putnam, Jr.
H. A. Plummer, Jr.
H. H. Hackett
G. L. Wrenn, Jr.
V. H. Friedman
E. P. Kirkland
J. A. Ryerson

First Round:

D. F. Davis
H. E. Avery
J. Appleton Allen
L. D. T. Quimby
Horton
Collins, 2-6, 9-7, 8-6, 6-4
Ware, 5-7, 6-1, 7-5, 7-5
Ware, 6-2, 6-4, 6-2.
Wright, 6-1, 6-1, 6-2
Lee, 3-6, 6-2, 4-6, 7-5, 6-3
Alexander, 6-3, 6-1, 6-2
Chace
Fischer, 6-0, 6-1, 0-6, 6-2
Fischer, 2-6, 7-5, 6-4, 6-3
Hardy, by default.
Williams, by default
Larned, 6-0, 6-0, 6-2
Pell, by default
Clews, by default
Gore, by default
Ward, by default
Clothier, by default
Budlong, 6-0, 6-0, 6-2
Fuller, by default
Black, by default
Hardy, 6-2, 7-5, 6-2.
Hackett, 6-4, 6-0, 6-4
Wrenn, by default
Ryerson, 6-1, 6-2, 6-3
R. D. Little
Deane Miller
R. Stevens
R. D. Wrenn
J. R. Carpenter, Jr.

Second Round:

Davis, 6-0, 6-3, 6-1.
Allen, by default.
Collins, 6-2, 6-4, 6-0
Wright, 6-3, 6-2, 6-4
Alexander, 6-3, 6-4
Chace, 3-6, 6-2, 6-3, 4-6, 6-4
Hardy, by default.
Larned, 6-0, 6-1, 6-0
Gore, 6-0, 6-0, 6-0
Ward, 6-4, 6-3, 7-5..
Budlong, 6-1, 6-2, 6-1
Black, 6-2, 3-6, 3-6, 6-2
Wrenn, 6-1, 4-6, 9-7, 6-4
Little, 6-0, 6-1, 3-6, 6-2
Stevens, by default
Wrenn, 6-3, 6-0, 6-1.

Third Round:

Davis, 6-4, 0-6, 4-6, 7-5, 6-2
Wright, 6-3, 1-6, 4-6, 6-3, 6-4
Chace, 6-2, 6-3, 6-2
Larned, 6-1, 6-1, 6-3
Gore, 6-1, 2-6, 3-6, 7-5, 6-3
Black, 8-6, 2-6, 6-4, 9-11, 6-4
G. L. Wrenn, 1-6, 6-2, 6-0, 6-2
R. D. Wrenn, 6-0, 6-1, 7-5

Fourth Round:

Wright, 4-6, 4-6, 8-6, 6-3, 6-2
Larned, 6-1, 6-1, 4-6, 6-0
Gore, 6-0, 7-5, 6-0.
G. L. Wrenn, 6-4, 6-1, 6-4

Final.:

Larned, 11-9, 8-6, 1-6, 6-4
Wrenn, 9-7, 1-6, 0-6, 6-2, 6-2

Winner of All Comers.:

Larned, 6-3, 6-2, 6-2

M. D. Whitman, Champion 1899.

Whitman, 5-4, 1-6, 6-2, 6-2. Champion 1900.

What it Costs to Run an Automobile (1910)

WHAT IT COSTS TO RUN AN AUTOMOBILE

By JOHN EARL

Some Live Facts Which Show that Motoring Is Not Exclusively a Rich Man's Game

IN HIS thirty years as country doctor at West Clarendon, Massachusetts, Thomas Sawyer had gleaned whatever profit there lies in a wide experience of horses. He felt that he knew the equine race from tail to muzzle. He had lived with it by day and dozed behind it on lonely rides at night; he had bought, sold, and even—but only once—raised horses. It was because of his long acquaintance with the animals that a friend called to ask him how much it cost to keep one.

"Why, that depends," replied the worthy physician. "At the present price of feed, not far from four dollars a week."

"Counting interest on the investment?" asked the inquirer.

"Of course not. Nobody ever counts the interest on a horse investment."

"But the depreciation—of course you count that?"

"What are you talking about, man? There isn't—well, perhaps there is depreciation in a horse, now you speak of it, but I never heard of any one figuring on that when he bought one."

"Then there's the time and labor expended on caring for a horse," the other continued. "That ought to be counted in. And the vets' bills, repairs on carriage and harness, interest and depreciation on carriage and harness, stabling, not to speak of——"

But the physician, becoming restive, interrupted.

"Back up," he exclaimed unprofessionally. "The man you want to talk with is a life insurance actuary. I know that it costs me not far from four dollars a week to feed and shoe my horse. What's on your mind, anyway—are you going to buy one?"

"Perhaps I would if I had any use for a horse," his visitor remarked. "But I haven't. I was only wondering why you don't get an automobile instead."

"Get an automobile!" repeated Dr. Sawyer in amazement. "You must think this country practice of mine is a gold mine."

The very next week the physician's horse, which in the two years it had helped minister to the sick of West Clarendon, had shown a peculiarly equable, placid temperament, took fright at a trolley car on the new line which has penetrated that country, ran away, broke its leg, and had to be shot. Whereupon Dr. Sawyer, with many a sigh over the loss he had sustained, bought—another horse.

The nub of this otherwise aimless and rambling anecdote is that Dr. Sawyer, although he believed he knew all about horses, was actually ignorant of what it was costing him to keep one, and, although he pretended to no knowledge of any definite sort about automobiles, held a firm conviction that no country physician could afford a machine. And this state of affairs presents sharply two situations which, like the rat hole in Abraham Lincoln's law office, "will bear looking into."

How much does it cost to keep an automobile? What are your expenditures on your machine, including everything, and how much would I be out of pocket at the end of the year if I purchased one? These are questions with a direct appeal to the two great divisions of the civilized human race, those who own machines and the others who would like to.

Possessors and would-be owners fall, by a generous method of classification, into three groupings. In the first, immensely the largest numerically, are the people of moderate income who feel justified in keeping a car for pleasure purposes, whose consciences nevertheless demand that they incur a minimum of expense in gratifying the desire. Among them are found both the wage-earners who clean, adjust, and drive their own machines, and the more prosperous individuals who can afford to keep a chauffeur, yet no less than the others must make every penny count.

The second class, a rapidly growing one, includes men, and many women, who buy a car for business ends. There are all kinds among them—physicians, collectors, contractors, letter carriers on rural routes, army paymasters, salesmen, and others "too numerous to mention." To them the machine becomes an asset in their inventory of efficiency, and beyond either of the other classes they are able to tell how much their automobile is costing them.

In the third grouping you find those fortunate ones who have neither the taste nor the compulsion to count expense. They may have one car or several; it is said that John Jacob Astor's garage at Newport has sheltered as many as seventeen during the season. If they are in society the smallest number they can readily get along with will probably be three—an electric victoria for town use, a runabout, and a touring car. If they were to be told exactly what it costs them to ride a mile in an automobile they would probably be a little surprised, but only mildly interested. Expense is not a consideration.

It hardly needs to be pointed out that the question of the cost of keeping an automobile is one to be approached thoughtfully and answered with many reservations. It presents so difficult a problem, indeed, that experienced salesmen seek to evade it altogether when talking with prospects, while some journals devoted to the trade have adopted a policy of excluding anything on cost

of operation. It is the subject least frequently touched upon in the great volume of automobile news and treatises which daily finds its way into the public prints.

Nevertheless there are data which throw light into the dark corners of the problem. There are, on one side, records of manufacturers' tests, some of which have been of great interest. They have been honestly conducted and have demonstrated facts of immense importance to automobilists, but in studying them it is well to remember that the cars were handled by operators of the highest skill and adjustments were perfect.

Here, for instance, are the results of a test made for the purpose of comparing the cost of driving a horse and buggy and a light runabout. It was conducted under the supervision of the contest board of the American Automobile Association. A road buggy and the runabout were driven for six days of six hours each over a predetermined route in New York City and vicinity. The needs of each vehicle were supplied at roadside stores at current market prices, account being kept of every item of expense entailed. The horse with two passengers in the buggy traveled 197 miles with the following expenses:

Hay	$1.20
Oats	4.50
Straw	.30
Shoeing	.498
Grease	.0012
Depreciation	3.349
Total	$9.8482

The cost per mile for two passengers in the horse-drawn vehicle thus reduces to five cents a mile, and the average daily distance covered was nearly thirty-three miles.

The automobile in its week of thirty-six running hours covered 457 miles at the following cost:

Gasoline	$ 5.60
Oil	.60
Grease	.13
Depreciation on car	3.66
Depreciation in tires	6.85
Total	$16.84

The cost for two passengers per mile was three and seven-tenths cents and the average daily distance covered 76 3-10 miles.

Various comment is possible on this test. Horse feed would not run to so high a figure if the animal were kept in one's home stable, especially if that stable chanced to be in a small city or a village. Yet neither would any except a very good horse be able to travel thirty-three miles a day for a week over the paving stones, asphalt, and macadam of metropolitan streets, and even a good one could not hold the pace for many weeks in succession.

A Message from St. Louis

Outside of factory tests few, if any, automobilists have been able to operate even runabouts at so low a cost as one and eight-tenths cents per passenger mile. Yet it appears that the careful ones among the laymen have not found the cost of automobiling prohibitive. An especially interesting account book is that of a St. Louis suburbanite for the reason that his expenditures in the second and third years of ownership of a four-cylinder, sixteen horsepower runabout are available. This is the period when repair expenses are popularly supposed to pile up. In the first year, accidents excepted, a machine ought never to be in the shop.

The St. Louis suburbanite had his car thoroughly overhauled on the 1st of November at a cost of $52. Up to the following 30th of October his actual expenditures had been as follows:

Repainting and improvements, $42; gasoline, $24.55; lubricants, $4.80; tires and repairs, $41.75; repairs at shop, $16.60; replacement of worn parts, $9.65; batteries and recharging, $4.20; new accessories and tools, $7.95; insurance, $10; license, $5; taxes, $7; miscellaneous, $9; total, $234.50, or $19.54 a month. In the year these figures cover the car ran 3,550 miles, at a cost of six and two-thirds cents a mile for two passengers.

In the St. Louis man's account, it will be noted, no allowance is made for depreciation, but he asserts that at the end of the third year the car looks as well and runs better than when it was new. It

has had good, intelligent care—the sort of care any man would give a horse. Its owner devotes a half to three-quarters of an hour to cleaning it after every ride of more than twenty-five or fifty miles, and has found the time profitably spent. He notes that to keep a single horse and surrey in the suburb where he lives costs from $25 to $30 a month, an annual total considerably in excess of his automobile expenditure, quite apart from the consideration of greater possibilities with the machine.

The figures thus far given deal with runabouts—the lightest and cheapest type of automobile. Some runabouts may be fitted with rumble seats, thus transforming them into carriages for four, and between the runabout and the touring car there is a class known as tourabouts, capable of carrying four economically.

It is the touring car proper, however, that exerts the most general appeal for pleasure purposes, since it can accommodate the entire family, or the owner, his wife and friends, off for a day's jaunt. The experience of an Ohio man with a small touring car of 1909 model will therefore prove of interest. It is general knowledge that the day of the touring car as big as a Pullman, capacious, expensive and of enormous power, is past except on special order. The popular touring car of to-day seats five comfortably, and with a couple of emergency seats will take care of seven.

The Ohio man's machine was of an inexpensive make adapted to five passengers. It cost him $2,100, and at the end of the first year he estimated its cash value at $800. A depreciation so enormous, as is well understood, is estimated on a motor's stability alone, and bears no relation to the question of service. It is the result of faddism, the desire to own each year the newest wrinkles. Now that the automobile and its equipment are fairly standardized, novelties consist mainly of such details as concealment of side door hinges or a detachable tire carrier at the rear instead of on the running board, and the result seems certain to be that in the near future there will exist no such differences between purchase price and possible selling price at the end of a year's use as has forced owners to charge up big losses against their cars hitherto.

In eight months' operation, covering 6,588.8 miles, the Ohio man's touring car cost him: Tires, $255; repairs, $72; gasoline, $60; insurance and supplies, $75, a total of $362. In the following summer he had the car overhauled for $88.55, and painted for $55; his other expenses except insurance amounting to $134.48, a total of $258.03 for 2,740.4 miles.

In considering the question of how much it costs to own an automobile one instinctively institutes comparisons between the motor and the horse. Nor is the comparison an unfair one when drawn on a mileage basis. The principal difficulty is that few horse owners have any idea of how much it costs them to drive a mile. Many of them, like the Doctor, have been content with the knowledge that feed and shoeing amount to a certain sum which is not more than they can afford, without dipping into the more complex calculations which depreciation and other charges involve, while they are firmly convinced that any sort of motor car would drag them by main force into the realm of high finance.

To begin at the beginning of the parallel, both automobile owners and horsemen are controlled by the desire to promote either their business or their pleasure. In each case the question of expense should be carefully considered. The man who buys a machine ought not to be moved wholly by the favorable test results manufacturers lay before him, but the purchaser of a horse is very likely to decide his problem on the ground that his father or his neighbor, neither more prosperous than himself, was able to keep a horse and that he is justified in pursuing the same policy.

Here are some data on horse cost which should prove of interest to every owner and possible purchaser. They are obtained from a sales agent for a big bakery, who finds a horse and buggy a necessary part of his business equipment in the suburban towns near New York City. Outfits of the same type are utilized by physicians, collectors, etc., and are equally well adapted to pleasure purposes.

This salesman notes at the outset that at the present time horses are at top-notch prices. He selects his animals on the basis of their road qualities. They must be sound and kind and from six to eight years old. At present prices such horses bring an average price of $250. He uses a steel tired buggy, built for service rather than looks, at a price of about $150. Harness of the heavy buggy type, single strap, made by a well-known firm, costs $40, and other equipment totals the whole outfit to $500. He finds $22 a month reasonable board, and $20 a year covers medical attendance, hire of a livery horse in case of lameness, and clipping. Every year the buggy demands a new set of steel tires and painting, and after the first few years trips to the repair shop begin, the cost of repairs in this salesman's experience averaging $35 a year. Another $10 goes to mending harness and equipment.

Wear and Tear of Horses

Pounding over hard roads develops some blemish in a horse after about four years, at the expiration of which it is more profitable to sell the animal than try to use it any longer. It brings then about $125. The vehicle after that length of service commands only $35 to $40, while the depreciation in harness and other equipment amounts to about $15 a year. Here are the figures on the horse:

Original cost	$250
Cost of buggy	150
Cost of harness	40
Cost of other equipment	60
Board at $22	264
Shoeing at $2 a set	24
Doctor, clipping and hiring extra horse	20
Interest on $500 at 6 per cent	30
Depreciation in value of outfit	70
Repairs	45

From these figures is derived a total annual expense of keeping such an outfit as described of $453, exclusive of original cost. The salesman who supplies them finds that fifteen miles a day six days in the week is a good traveling road average and that when he has driven twenty miles a day for a couple of weeks the horse invariably requires a period of rest. The horse therefore yields 4,500 miles in 300 working days, or ten cents a mile, which is probably rather more than Dr. Sawyer and other horse owners imagine.

Obviously the record of such a horse outfit as described should be set against that of the runabout, since each is adapted only for two passengers. Touring cars may be set against two-seated carriages, which for much service require two horses.

Among men who employ automobiles in their business physicians are best able to give an account of cost. Their favorite machine is naturally the light runabout, easily handled and not severe on tires and gasoline. Some of them prefer solid tires because of the slightly greater certainty they offer of reaching an appointment on time, and there are scores, possibly hundreds, of country doctors who endure whatever disadvantages pertain to the solid tired, high wheel vehicle because their travels take them over rutty country roads where there is constant danger of scraping an engine swung from artillery wheels.

One country physician who speaks from the depths of eight years' experience with gasoline cars, in which time he has owned three successively, found at the outset that the cost was greater than that of one horse, and, although he reduced his cost per mile to eight cents, "estimates" that his last machine, which gave him 24,600 miles at an average of eight cents, costs four times as much as a horse and a buggy for the same amount of service. His first car charged him in the first year of ownership with 25 per cent of its original cost in maintenance and repairs; in the second year with 35 per cent, and in the third, when it was little used, with 20 per cent. Then it was sold for 20 per cent of its first cost. His mileage cost with this early machine boiled down to 15 cents.

His next motor, which he ran 28,900 miles in three years, cost 20, 25 and 30 per cent annually for repairs and maintenance, and was sold for 20 per cent of its cost. His third car is in its third year. It cost him the first year 10 per cent of its cost; in the second 25, and

now is running well and would bring 30 per cent of its purchase price. This car has cost him about eight cents a mile for 24,600 miles.

This physician is certainly not an optimist on the automobile question, and, inasmuch as he speaks with the authority of eight years' acquaintance, his comments are worth a moment's consideration. He spends about an hour a day working on his car. Engaged in rural practice as he is, he finds that the motor saves him about one-quarter of a working day, besides enabling him to make more money by covering a wider range of country. He believes his radius of employment has been enlarged one-half. But since, in his opinion, the total cost, including interest on the investment, depreciation and repairs, with running expenses all considered, is about four times as much as horses and buggy for the same amount of work, he arrives at the deduction that "if in a man's business the time actually saved is worth the cost and expense, then a car is a necessity to him, but to others it is a delusion and a snare."

Automobile vs. Train

An interesting factory test of the cost of automobile operation was that in which a comparison was drawn between a runabout for a salesman's use and a train. It lasted six days, on three of which there was heavy rain, and took two men over the country roads of New Hampshire, Vermont, and Massachusetts, a total distance of 787 miles. The cost for the two men by automobile, figuring in the salary of the driver at $12 a week, his hotel bills, and depreciation of machine and tires, but not interest on the investment, was $115.67, less than a cost of one per cent per mile per passenger.

The estimate of the same trip by rail —which it was judged would consume three weeks instead of six days—included only one man's hotel bills and salary, but an item of $22.50 for handling a trunk for three weeks, and totalled $202.24, a balance of $86.57 in the machine's favor.

With such a mass of conflicting evidence relative to the cost of an automobile, what standards is the earnest seeker after light at liberty to accept? Is there any solid ground of certainty on which he may plant his feet? Has he assurance in buying a car that he is not mortgaging his financial future?

To all such interrogations qualified answers must be given. But the qualifications need not be more formidable than if a horse, or even a sailboat, were involved. In one case or the other the deciding factor is the human element. The car purchased may be a good or a poor one, and human judgment is fallible. Having obtained possession of a good machine, a good horse, or a good boat, it becomes a question of the man's brain which manages these pieces of property. It is as possible to run a horse off its feet and wreck him for life in six months as it is to knock half the value out of a car or send a catboat to ruin in the same time.

Assuming that the automobile purchaser is a man of sense, content with moderate driving, cleaning and adjusting his car when necessary, or having such work done for him, he may rest easy that he will get good service at a fairly definable cost. He may know in advance what his storage bills will be. He can count on a certain number of miles from each gallon of gasoline, and the price of fuel will fluctuate between fourteen and twenty cents. Lubricating oil and grease may be estimated with reasonable accuracy. Even as to tires there is no great uncertainty, for several good kinds are manufactured to-day and sold with a system of adjustments, so that a man may purchase a set guaranteed for 5,000 miles with an agreement that if they give out before they have run that distance he may buy a new set for the proportionate difference in cost between the mileage they have rendered and what they were guaranteed to give.

If there exists apprehension as to the amount of depreciation, the owner's mind may be set at rest even on that point. The truth is that, while the active life of a well made automobile is not definitely known, it is very great when adjustments, replacements, and repairs are promptly made. One experienced automobilist says that, given a horse at six years old, the beginning of its prime, and a car, he will drive the car thousands of miles to the horse's hundreds and still be using it after the horse is dead. It is probable he is not overstating the case if he is careful to see that the car receives as considerate attention as the horse. And there again the human element enters—how nearly ideal treatment can you render your machine? To this residuum all speculations on automobile cost reduce themselves in the end.

The third class of owners to which reference has been made in this article demand brief notice, for there is almost no limit to the amount of money which may be spent in cars. Brewster's millions might have been readily absorbed in the game. In addition to a garage charge of $40 a month and chauffeurs' salaries at $150, there are the commissions the canny driver exacts from everyone who caters to his master's needs. These may fairly average fifteen per cent on everything, and that amount is tacked of course to the selling price. There are tires to be changed frequently in order that the servant may both sell the old ones and reap a commission on the purchase of new ones. There are owner's tips to everyone who renders him a service either in the garage or on the road, and greater than all, perhaps, there is the entertaining, which might have been indulged in had the owner not been a motorist, but would certainly have cost him less money. Happy the man who need not concern himself as to the cost of keeping a machine.

But the man who does have to figure closely should not leave out of his calculations the item of possible profit. Can you use it in your business? Will it improve the health, as well as enhance the pleasure, of yourself and your family? Will it enable you again to get into touch with phases of life which have been denied you? Set down the pro and contra on a piece of paper, first having obtained all possible data as to expense of maintenance, and if you can exercise cool judgment on the sum of your columns you need not fear going far astray.

DATE DUE